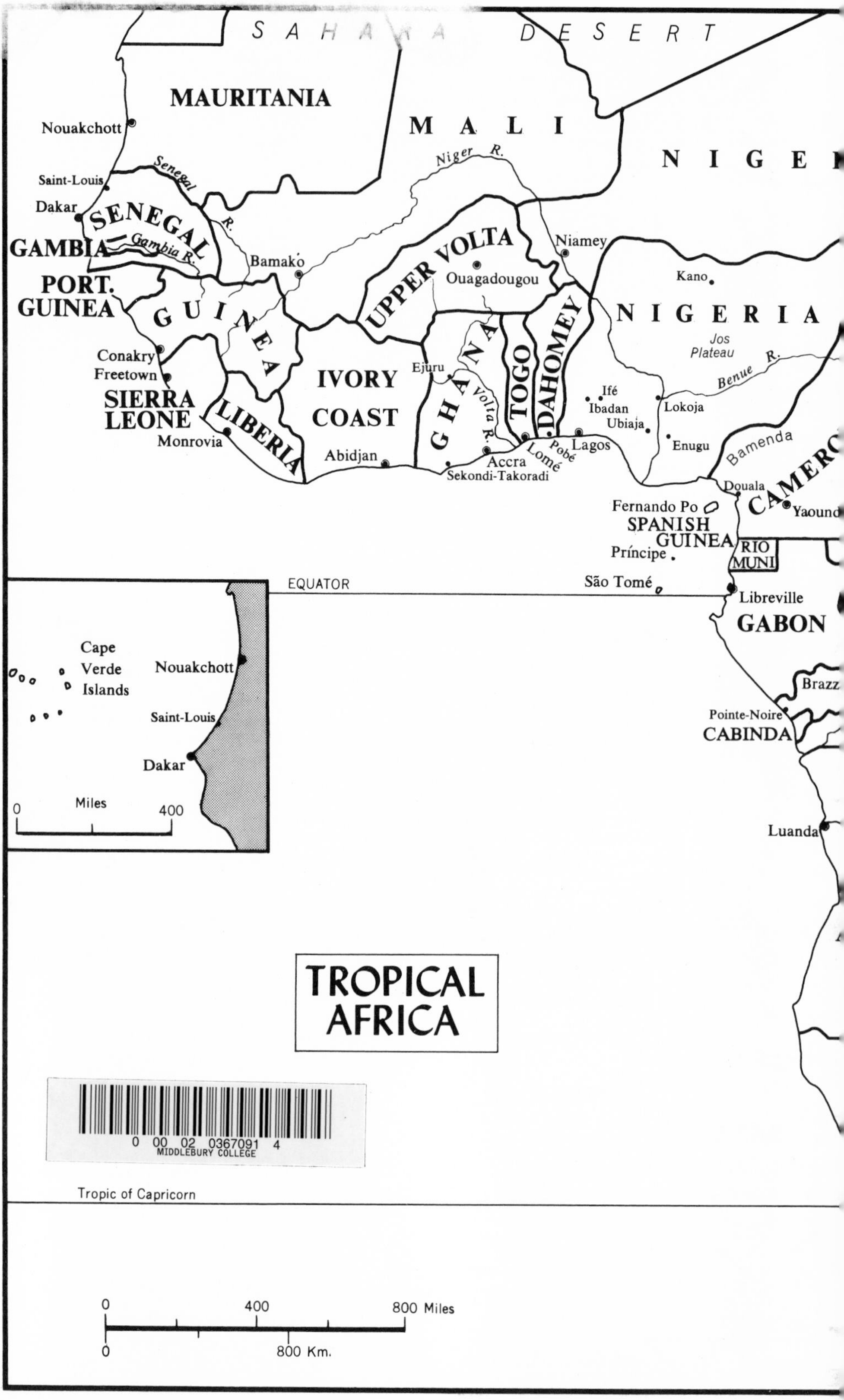
TROPICAL AFRICA
SAHARA DESERT
MAURITANIA
MALI
NIGER
Nouakchott
Senegal R.
Saint-Louis
Dakar
SENEGAL
GAMBIA
Gambia R.
PORT. GUINEA
GUINEA
Bamako
Niger R.
UPPER VOLTA
Ouagadougou
Niamey
Kano
NIGERIA
Jos Plateau
Benue R.
Conakry
Freetown
SIERRA LEONE
LIBERIA
Monrovia
IVORY COAST
Abidjan
Ejuru
GHANA
Volta R.
TOGO
DAHOMEY
Accra
Sekondi-Takoradi
Lomé
Pobé
Lagos
Ifé
Ibadan
Ubiaja
Lokoja
Enugu
Bamenda
Douala
Yaound
Fernando Po
SPANISH GUINEA
RIO MUNI
Príncipe
São Tomé
EQUATOR
Libreville
GABON
Brazz
Pointe-Noire
CABINDA
Luanda
Cape Verde Islands
Nouakchott
Saint-Louis
Dakar
0 Miles 400
Tropic of Capricorn
0 400 800 Miles
0 800 Km.

ESSAYS ON THE THEORY OF JOINT PRODUCTION

edited by

Luigi L. Pasinetti

New York Columbia University Press 1980

First published as *Contributi alla teoria della produzione congiunta*

Library of Congress Cataloging in Publication Data
Main entry under title:

Essays on the theory of joint production.

Translation of Contributi alla teoria della produzione congiunta.
Includes bibliographical references and index.
1. Production (Economic theory)—Addresses, essays, lectures. I. Pasinetti, Luigi L. II. Title: Joint production.
HB241.C6613 1979 338′.001 79–20620
ISBN 0–231–04988–9

Printed in Great Britain

Contents

Preface

The present work appeared first in Italian as *Contributi alla teoria della produzione congiunta* (Bologna: Il Mulino, 1977). The essays here collected – with the exception of those, by Schefold, Steedman and Pasinetti, on vertical integration, which were written in English to begin with – have been translated into English for the present edition by Richard Dury, with revisions by the authors. Financial support from the CNR, Rome (CT 78.01826.10) is gratefully acknowledged.

Milan
January 1979 L.L.P.

Notes on the Contributors

Salvatore Baldone
Professor of Economic Analysis, Faculty of Political Sciences, Università degli Studi, Bologna, Italy

Carlo Felice Manara
Professor of Geometry, Faculty of Mathematics, Physics and Natural Sciences, Università degli Studi, Milan, Italy

Luigi L. Pasinetti
Professor of Econometrics, Faculty of Economics and Commerce, Università Cattolica del Sacro Cuore, Milan, Italy

Alberto Quadrio-Curzio
Professor of Political Economy, Faculty of Political Sciences, Università Cattolica del Sacro Cuore, Milan, Italy

Bertram Schefold
Professor of Economics, Institut für Markt und Plan, Johann Wolfgang Goethe-Universität, Frankfurt-am-Main, W. Germany

Ian Steedman
Professor of Economics, Department of Economics, University of Manchester, Manchester, England

Paolo Varri
Professor of Economic Analysis, Istituto Universitario, Bergamo, Italy

Introductory Note: Joint Production

LUIGI L. PASINETTI

1 Joint production as a general scheme

Joint products, i.e. those goods that cannot be produced separately from each other – such as wool and mutton, iron and coke, and so on – were for a long time a subject of only secondary interest in economic theory, although they cropped up regularly, in the economic treatises, in sections devoted to 'complications'. Indeed, if the importance of processes of joint production were limited to such cases, which we may call cases of joint production proper, it would be possible to deal with them as of secondary importance.

However, it has recently been realised that the model of joint production is of much more general application than was thought. To be more precise, it has been realised that this model is the one most suitable for the analysis of processes of production with fixed capital. This being the case, it would clearly be wrong to carry on talking of it as a secondary subject, since fixed-capital production processes, i.e. processes with capital goods that last several years, are the norm in the industrial world.

Sraffa himself uses precisely this argument in justifying the chapters of his book devoted to joint production: 'The interest of Joint Products does not lie so much in the familiar examples of wool and mutton, or wheat and straw, as in its being the genus of which Fixed Capital is the leading species. And it is mainly as an introduction to the subject of fixed capital that the . . . chapters devoted to the intricacies of joint products find their place.'[1]

2 Difficulty of treating fixed capital as a 'stock' and possibility of treating it as a 'flow'

In the traditional theory (marginal theory) that has dominated our university teaching since the 1870s, problems of fixed capital are approached in a very different way. The tendency to consider capital as a 'factor of production', on the same footing as land and labour, has led to the

[1] P. Sraffa, *Production of Commodities by Means of Commodities* (Cambridge: Cambridge University Press, 1960) p. 63.

conception of capital as a stock that, together with the other 'factors of production', produces an annual flow of final goods: the net national income or net product.

This opposition between stocks and flows, however, has been the source of many difficulties. Unlike land and labour, 'capital' is not something that can be taken as an external element but is something that itself derives from the production process. A part of the capital itself ('circulating capital') consists of goods that, after they have been produced, are entirely absorbed by the production process. They therefore have all the characteristics of a 'flow'. In addition, even that part of capital that lasts for several production periods ('fixed capital') is consumed year by year and is periodically reintegrated by a new flow: the flow of replacements, to which is added (though the two cannot always be distinguished clearly) the flow of new investments.

We therefore find ourselves in the presence of something of a hybrid – a stock which is not entirely a stock and which, even in the part that seems to look like a stock, is nevertheless something that by the end of each year has changed from what it was at the beginning.

In these conditions, what is the meaning of 'replacing' exhausted capital goods with other goods that normally are physically and qualitatively different? What is the meaning of 'maintaining capital intact'? What is the meaning of talking of a stock called 'capital'? These are questions to which it is difficult to give a satisfactory answer. And every attempt to give an answer clashes with a series of insurmountable difficulties and with problems that have been proved to be insoluble, except with recourse to drastic assumptions and to models of such a high degree of abstraction (one-commodity models) as to lose every connection with the reality of an industrial world.

Faced with these intricacies, the discovery (or rather, as we shall shortly see, the rediscovery) of the method of joint production, adapted to the study of problems involving fixed capital, has had a liberating effect. In a scheme of joint production, all the elements of the analysis are reduced to 'flows'. And capital goods, of whatever nature, can be considered as inputs into the production process at the beginning of the year and as outputs at the end. Naturally, not all capital goods are always found at both ends (as input and as output) of the production process. Some of them enter never to emerge again. But those that outlast the yearly period of the production process, to be reused in successive years, are considered as products jointly produced with the final goods. In this way, capital goods become a part of the total gross product that annually comes out of the production process.

In this scheme of production, the notion of 'stock', which was the main source of the hybrids and confusion, disappears entirely. All the elements of the analytical scheme are reduced to flows. Or, if preferred, a single and homogeneous conceptual category – that of flow – is used as a foundation for the whole analysis: there are input flows at the beginning of the year and output flows at the end. The whole scheme becomes simpler and more elegant, more flexible and fruitful.

3 A general scheme of flows

It is not only because of simplicity and analytic elegance that this method of analysis, so different from that of traditional marginal theory, has emerged. As is always the case with matters central to economic theory, a radical change of method is inevitably associated with profound theoretic reasons.

I have elsewhere already given an interpretation of the historical development of marginal theory as a return to the pre-classical concept of national wealth understood as a 'stock', to be accepted as exogenously given.[2] If this is so, then it seems quite logical that marginal theory should deal with capital in the way most consistent with that conception, i.e. as a stock.

But the classical economists proceeded in a quite different manner. As has been pointed out,[3] one of the most interesting innovations of the classical theories (following on physiocratic lines) was precisely the break they made with the traditional concept of the nation's wealth as a stock and the adoption of a concept of wealth linked with the annual product of the economic system as a whole (national wealth considered as an annual flow of goods).

If this interpretation is correct, then the method of considering fixed capital at the end of each year as part of the flow of production, jointly with all the other products, is a method which – besides being analytically the simplest one – appears as the one which is best suited to the characteristics of classical theory. Sraffa seems to be thinking along these lines when he remarks that the method 'fits easily into the classical picture of an agricultural system where the annual product, in Adam Smith's words, naturally divides itself into two parts, one destined for replacing a capital, the other for constituting a revenue'.[4]

But the most interesting confirmation of this interpretation is the fact that, after Smith, the classical economists did actually come to employ this method. Torrens was the first to make use of it, in a critical work on Ricardo's theory of value; and Ricardo himself, while rejecting Torrens's

[2] L. L. Pasinetti, *Lectures on the Theory of Production* (London: Macmillan; and New York: Columbia University Press, 1977) pp. 2–4, 24–6.

[3] Ibid., pp. 2–3.

[4] Sraffa, *Production of Commodities*, p. 94.

criticisms, accepted the method (in the third edition of his *Principles*). So did Malthus and, later, Marx.[5]

We should not be surprised, therefore, that, with the emergence of marginal economic theory, this method was abandoned; nor should we be surprised that, with the recent revival of the themes and methods of the classical economists, the consideration of fixed capital as part of the total gross product has been punctually rediscovered.

The logical process of generalisation has, perhaps, gone ahead even too rapidly. Those that in the traditional theory were the factors of production – capital, labour and land – have each found a particular place. Production with fixed capital has become a special case (though the most important one) in the general scheme of joint production. Labour has found its natural place as an annual flow of labour services. (Von Neumann has even gone so far as to consider it in no different way from any other good, as if it was only necessary to input goods for it to give an output of labour services.) And production processes using natural resources, i.e. non-reproducible means of production, such as land and mineral deposits, have been framed as something of an 'inverse' with respect to the processes involving joint products. In other words, on the analogy of the single-production process producing many joint products, the case has been introduced of the many production processes (each with 'land' of different fertility) which produce a single product. A single theoretical scheme of joint production, embracing joint processes as well as joint products, has thus become a general model for the analysis of all the processes of production.

4 Origins of the present work

However we interpret past events, the fact remains that the method of considering joint production as the general framework into which all types of production processes are inserted has by now asserted itself and is widely spreading. Indeed, as previously mentioned, the logical process of generalisation may even have proceeded too quickly. On one hand, it has at last, quite naturally, been felt necessary to devote to the analysis of joint production the energy and attention that in the past, when the subject was considered of secondary importance, tended to be withheld from it, owing to its analytic complexity. On the other hand, on the wave of enthusiasm and mathematical elegance, there has been a tendency to concentrate efforts on the most general possible case of joint production. Unfortunately, this case is so general as to allow too many possibilities, and these have indeed led to many negative conclusions and to very few positive ones.

[5] Cf. Sraffa's careful references, ibid., pp. 94–5.

It would seem, therefore, that the time has come to pursue not only general but also specific research. In other words, it appears that the time has come for in-depth analysis and specificity, within the general scheme – provided, of course, that the specificity concerns cases which, although particular, are relevant. And this seems to be precisely the case of fixed capital and non-reproducible means of production.

The essays collected in this volume aim to make a contribution in this direction. They started from a series of discussions, over several years, that I sought to encourage at the Economics Institute of the Università Cattolica of Milan and at the University of Cambridge.

Chapter 1, by Carlo Felice Manara, is an article that had already been published in Italian, and has become well known. It represents the first attempt to translate Sraffa's treatment of joint production into the language of matrix algebra.

Chapter 2, by myself, is an essay on vertically integrated sectors which proposes a tool of analysis (the vertically integrated sectors) that emerged from an earlier work of mine on non-proportional economic growth.[6] Here it is introduced into the general scheme of joint production. This analytic tool is given a series of applications relative to the theory of value, the theory of economic growth (with and without technical progress), and the problem of the reduction of prices to weighted quantities of labour. A further application is given immediately afterwards in an essay by Ian Steedman (Chapter 3), who, in discussing Sraffa's distinction between basic and non-basic commodities, uses Manara's formulation but does so with reference to the matrix of the vertically integrated units of productive capacity that appears in Chapter 2. This discussion by Steedman has in fact stimulated me to add a further note on the same subject (Chapter 4).

After these chapters on joint production in general, there comes a group of three essays – by Paolo Varri, Salvatore Baldone and Bertram Schefold – concerned specifically with the problems of production with fixed capital. The essays by Varri and Baldone (Chapters 5 and 6) are complementary and complete each other. In fact, they were conceived and worked out with close collaboration between the two authors. The essay by Schefold (Chapter 7) is of much wider scope and was produced quite independently, as a development of his remarkable earlier work on joint production in general[7] (a work of which I saw the beginning, as his supervisor at the University of Cambridge). It is quite natural that scholars working in different places on the same subject should occasionally come

[6] L. L. Pasinetti, 'A New Theoretical Approach to the Problems of Economic Growth', in *Pontificiae academiae scientiarum scripta varia*, no. 28 (1965) 571–696; repr. in *The Econometric Approach to Development Planning* (Amsterdam: North Holland, 1965).

[7] B. Schefold, *Theorie der Kuppelproduktion* (*Mr. Sraffa on Joint Production*) (Basel: printed privately, 1971).

up with similar results. This has happened here with Baldone and Varri on one hand and Schefold on the other. Presenting their work, however, I have decided not to ask the authors to eliminate possible duplications, which, anyway, are few. Moreover, the authors' results, even when they coincide, have been reached after starting with different approaches and using different procedures. I thought, therefore, that this itself would be of interest and constitute a stimulus for further research.

Chapter 8, the final essay in the collection, is by Alberto Quadrio-Curzio, who explores the meaning and consequences of introducing non-produced means of production into the model. Quadrio-Curzio is specially concerned with the problem of price formation and the role of rent in the distribution of income. This essay is parallel to those of Varri and Baldone. The latter start from a simple scheme of single production and then introduce production processes which use machines lasting several years (fixed capital), while Quadrio-Curzio starts from the same simple scheme of single production and then introduces production processes which use non-produced means of production, such as land and natural resources.

All the authors who have contributed to this collection are far from believing that their task is complete. The problems waiting to be explored are numerous. Think, for example, of the case of production with fixed capital and with non-produced means of production and/or with machines that are obsolete but are still productive – a case that is halfway between that of production processes with machines incorporating the latest techniques and that of production processes using natural resources.

The authors hope to receive encouragement to continue and at the same time to spread interest in the subject, so that other scholars may be stimulated to undertake further research.

5 Acknowledgements

On behalf of all the contributors, I thank the Consiglio Nazionale delle Ricerche, Rome, for financing the research project 'Fixed Capital and Natural Resources in Linear Models of Production' (CT 73. 00412. 10 and CT 78. 01826. 10), of which the present publication is one of the outcomes.

In addition, I should also like to thank the editors of the journals *L'industria*, *Studi economici* and *Metroeconomica* for kindly allowing republication of articles by Manara (Chapter 1), Varri and Baldone (Chapters 5 and 6), and myself (Chapter 2), respectively. The other essays, in their present form, are published here for the first time.

Milan
October 1976

L.L.P.

CHAPTER ONE

Sraffa's Model for the Joint Production of Commodities by Means of Commodities[1]

CARLO FELICE MANARA

1 Aim of this essay

The present essay aims to analyse the model presented by Piero Sraffa in the second part of his book *Production of Commodities by Means of Commodities* (1960). There already exist analyses of the first part of the book, dealing with single-product industries and circulating capital: for example, the analyses by P. Newman (1962) and V. Dominedò (1962). But to my knowledge there has been no mathematical analysis of the second part of the book, 'Multiple-Product Industries and Fixed Capital'. It is hoped, therefore, that the present analysis may prove useful, and that not solely for the aim, shrewdly identified by Newman (1962), of '*translat*[*ing*] Sraffa's work into the more widely used Walrasian dialect of mathematical economics'. My aim is above all to analyse the logical foundations of Sraffa's treatment and to attempt to enunciate hypotheses that make his model viable. Such hypotheses are not always stated clearly and explicitly by Sraffa, perhaps because he makes very limited use of the mathematical language and so considers it unnecessary to specify the precise conditions under which the relationships of which he writes are capable of having sense.

But one of the advantages of translating arguments expressed in ordinary language into the mathematical 'dialect' is that it enforces a rigorous analysis of assumptions and does not allow one to leave anything to 'intuition' or to 'evidence'. One may risk being led astray if such evidence is uncertain or deceptively convincing. It goes without saying that, since the

[1] Originally published as 'Il modello di Sraffa per la produzione congiunta di merci a mezzo di merci', *L'industria*, no. 1, 1968, pp. 3–18.

present treatment aims to be mainly mathematical, references to economic content are merely occasional. Where hypotheses are formulated, it is on the explicit understanding that it is left to economists to judge whether they are acceptable or not.

2 Notation

For notational convenience, we shall slightly alter Sraffa's symbols according to certain conventions.

We follow Sraffa in using k to refer to the number (obviously an integer) of commodities and of industries in the economic system under examination.

The formulation of the model we are interested in here is based on the consideration of $2k^2$ quantities of commodities, which can be conveniently indicated as the elements of two square matrices of order k.

We shall call **A** and **B** these square matrices, their elements being, respectively, a_{ij} and b_{ij} $(i, j = 1, 2, \ldots k)$. In a similar way to Sraffa (1960, section 51), a_{ij} indicates the quantity of the ith commodity that enters as means of production into the jth industry, and b_{ij} indicates the quantity of ith commodity produced by the jth industry. Hence, the rows of matrices **A** and **B** correspond to the commodities (understood respectively as means of production and as products) and the columns correspond to the industries of the economic system.

We shall indicate by

$$\mathbf{p} = [p_1, p_2, \ldots p_k]$$

the vector the components of which are the prices of individual commodities; therefore the first, second, third, kth component of the vector $\mathbf{p}$ is the price of, respectively, the first, second, third, kth commodity. We shall then indicate by

$$\mathbf{q} = [q_1, q_2, \ldots q_k] \tag{1.1}$$

the vector the components of which are the quantities of labour used by the industries. Finally, we call the rate of profit r (cf. Sraffa, 1960, section 4) and the general wage rate w.

We shall adopt the conventions of matrix algebra as generally used nowadays (cf. Manara–Nicola, 1967, Appendix II): in particular, when we indicate a vector $\mathbf{x}$ we shall consider it every time as a row vector, i. e. as a matrix of the special order $1 \times k$; the column vector having the components of the vector $\mathbf{x}$ will be indicated by the symbol $\mathbf{x}_T$, i. e. as a matrix of order $k \times 1$ obtained from a row vector, i.e. from a matrix of order $1 \times k$, by means of transposition.

In particular, we point out that, having for example indicated a matrix as **A** and a vector as **x**, by the notation

$$\mathbf{A} > \mathbf{0}, \qquad \mathbf{x} > \mathbf{0} \tag{1.2}$$

we mean to indicate that all the elements of the matrix (and the components of the vector) are positive numbers. By the notation

$$\mathbf{A} \geq \mathbf{0} \text{ and respectively } \mathbf{x} \geq \mathbf{0} \tag{1.3}$$

we mean to indicate that all the elements of the matrix (and the components of the vector) are non-negative numbers, and that at least one element (or one component) is a positive number.

Finally, with the notation

$$\mathbf{A} \geqq \mathbf{0} \text{ and respectively } \mathbf{x} \geqq \mathbf{0} \tag{1.4}$$

we mean to indicate that all the elements of the matrix (or, respectively, the components of the vector) are non-negative numbers, not excluding the possibility that they may all be equal to zero.

With the conventions that we have decided to adopt, the fundamental system of equations of Sraffa's model (cf. Sraffa, 1960, Section 51) is written in the single equation

$$\mathbf{pA}(1+r)+w\mathbf{q} = \mathbf{pB} \tag{1.5}$$

Clearly, every component of the vector which is on the left-hand side of (1.5) represents the production cost of a single industry (a cost including the cost of acquiring commodities used as means of production, the reward of capital and wages for labour). The corresponding component of the vector on the right-hand side of (1.5) represents the revenue of the above-mentioned industry.

From the economic meaning of equation (1.5) and of its symbols we can immediately obtain that, for the matrices, the vectors and the constants r and w, the following relationships must be valid:

$$\mathbf{A} \geq \mathbf{0}, \qquad \mathbf{B} \geq \mathbf{0} \tag{1.6}$$

$$\mathbf{p} \geq \mathbf{0}, \qquad \mathbf{q} \geq \mathbf{0} \tag{1.7}$$

$$r \geq 0, \qquad w \geq 0 \tag{1.8}$$

An observation of which we shall later need to make use is that it is possible arbitrarily to reorder the columns of the matrices **A** and **B**, making any interchange, as long as the same interchange is carried out on the components of the vector **q**. Similarly, it is possible arbitrarily to reorder the rows of matrices **A** and **B**, making any interchange (even an interchange that is different from the interchange that may have been carried out in the columns), as long as the same interchange is carried out on the elements of the vector **p**.

Since the interchange of the columns of a matrix is obtained by right-hand side multiplication of the matrix by a matrix **S**, which is the product of suitable exchange matrices (see, for example, Manara–Nicola, 1967, Appendix VI), and since the interchange of the rows of a matrix is obtained by left-hand side multiplication of the matrix by a suitable matrix $\mathbf{Z}^{-1}$, which is the product of suitable exchange matrices, equation (1.5) is equivalent to an analogous equation written in the form

$$\mathbf{p}^*\mathbf{A}^*(1+r)+w\mathbf{q}^* = \mathbf{p}^*\mathbf{B}^* \tag{1.5a}$$

where we have defined:

$$\mathbf{p}^* = \mathbf{pZ}, \qquad \mathbf{q}^* = \mathbf{qS}, \quad \mathbf{A}^* = \mathbf{Z}^{-1}\mathbf{AS} \qquad \mathbf{B}^* = \mathbf{Z}^{-1}\mathbf{BS} \tag{1.9}$$

It is worthwhile pointing out explicitly that the situation we are referring to here does not occur in the case of single-product industries, considered in the first part of Sraffa's book. Indeed, in the matrix considered there, it is not possible to reorder the rows and columns with interchanges which are different from one another, owing to the different meaning that the elements of the matrices have in that case.

3 Conditions of viability of the price system

We now propose to examine the conditions under which the fundamental equation (1.5) – the equation which, as we have pointed out, establishes the balance between revenues and expenditures of the various industries of the economic system under consideration – is viable. In fact, it appears from Sraffa's analysis that the purpose of the vector equation (1.5) (or of the system of equivalent equations given in Sraffa, 1960, section 51) is to determine the commodity prices when the other elements of the equation are fixed. It is quite obvious that such prices must constitute the components of a positive vector, i.e. of a vector satisfying (1.7). Let us suppose for the sake of simplicity that all the commodities under consideration are basic commodities (we shall come back later to the distinction between basic and non-basic commodities). The simplifying hypothesis that we propose here yields the consequence that equation (1.5) should be sufficient to determine the price vector – of course, when certain conditions are fulfilled. These conditions are not enunciated in Sraffa's work, and it is upon them that we shall dwell at this point.

With this in mind, let us write the fundamental equation (1.5) in the following form:

$$w\mathbf{q} = \mathbf{p}[\mathbf{B}-\mathbf{A}(1+r)] \tag{1.10}$$

The analysis that we intend to make has the aim of investigating the conditions that must be fulfilled by matrix $[\mathbf{B}-\mathbf{A}]$, or, more generally, by matrix $[\mathbf{B}-\mathbf{A}(1+r)]$ with

$$r \geq 0 \tag{1.11}$$

so that the vector equation (1.10) is solvable and gives a positive price vector as a result.

The necessity of precisely indicating the conditions under which this situation can come about leads us to the enunciation of certain basic hypotheses (which we shall label UA – 'unstated assumption' – 1, 2, etc.) chosen from among the many possible. As concerns their economic significance, it has already been mentioned that we intend to accept the opinion of economists, who are better able to evaluate the soundness of the hypotheses themselves and of their economic implications. We shall limit ourselves to pointing out that without these hypotheses (or equivalents) the model represented by (1.10) would not be 'viable'.

UA 1. The overall quantity of every commodity used as a means of production is less than the total quantity of the same commodity produced in the whole economic system.

In the vector notation we are adopting, defining

$$\mathbf{s} = [1, 1, \ldots 1] \tag{1.12}$$

hypothesis UA 1 may be expressed by the following relation:

$$[\mathbf{B}-\mathbf{A}]\,\mathbf{s}_T > \mathbf{0}_T \tag{1.13}$$

UA 2. There exists at least one positive vector of prices, $\hat{\mathbf{p}}$, such that the value of the commodities used as means of production by every individual industry, evaluated at those prices, is smaller than the value of the products, also evaluated at those same prices.

This hypothesis may be translated into the following formula:

$$\exists\hat{\mathbf{p}}\{\hat{\mathbf{p}} > \mathbf{0} \wedge \hat{\mathbf{p}}[\mathbf{B}-\mathbf{A}] > \mathbf{0}\} \tag{1.14}$$

This hypothesis is analogous to that implicitly offered by Leontief (1951) for the 'viability' of his model.

We shall now indicate with X the set of column vectors with non-negative components, i.e. define

$$X = \{\mathbf{x}_T \,|\, \mathbf{x}_T \geqq \mathbf{0}_T\} \tag{1.15}$$

Let us then denote with $U(r)$ the set of column vectors belonging to X and such that, for every vector $\mathbf{x}_T$ of $U(r)$, the following relation holds:

$$[\mathbf{B}-\mathbf{A}(1+r)]\mathbf{x}_T \geq \mathbf{0}_T \tag{1.16}$$

In other words, we define

$$U(r) = \{\mathbf{x}_T | \mathbf{x}_T \in X \wedge [\mathbf{B} - \mathbf{A}(1+r)]\,\mathbf{x}_T \geq \mathbf{0}_T\} \tag{1.17}$$

It is easy to prove that the set $U(r)$ is a convex polyhedral cone. Since clearly

$$\mathbf{s} \in X \tag{1.18}$$

it follows immediately from hypothesis (1.14) that there exists a value of r (to be exact, the value $r = 0$) at which the set $U(r)$ is not empty.

Since the vector function of the real variable r given by the expression

$$[\mathbf{B} - \mathbf{A}(1+r)]\,\mathbf{x}_T \tag{1.19}$$

is clearly continuous, we can easily deduce from what has been said so far that the set of values of r (belonging to the half-line defined by relation (1.11) in correspondence to which the set $U(r)$ is not empty) is an interval closed on the left-hand side and not empty. Similarly, let us denote with P the set of vectors having non-negative components; i.e. let us define

$$P = \{\mathbf{y} | \mathbf{y} \geqq 0\} \tag{1.20}$$

We shall call $V(r)$ the set of non-negative vectors such that, for every vector $\mathbf{y}$ of $V(r)$, the following relation holds:

$$\mathbf{y}[\mathbf{B} - \mathbf{A}(1+r)] \geq \mathbf{0} \tag{1.21}$$

In other words, we define

$$V(r) = \{\mathbf{y} | \mathbf{y} \in P \wedge \mathbf{y}[\mathbf{B} - \mathbf{A}(1+r)] \geq \mathbf{0}\} \tag{1.22}$$

It is easy to demonstrate that set $V(r)$ is also a convex polyhedral cone.

From hypothesis (1.14) it follows that

$$\hat{\mathbf{p}} \in P \tag{1.23}$$

Consequently, it follows from hypothesis (1.13) that, at least for one value of r (to be exact, for $r = 0$), the set $V(r)$ is not empty. Since the vector function of the real variable r given by the expression

$$\mathbf{y}[\mathbf{B} - \mathbf{A}(1+r)] \tag{1.24}$$

is clearly continuous, it then follows, from what has been said so far, that the set of values of r (belonging to the half-line defined by the relation (1.11) in correspondence to which the set $V(r)$ is not empty) is an interval closed on the left-hand side.

Let us now make the following hypothesis:

UA 3. $$\det[\mathbf{B} - \mathbf{A}] \neq 0 \tag{1.25}$$

This ensures that, for at least one value of r (the value $r = 0$), the vectors forming the rows of the matrix $[\mathbf{B} - \mathbf{A}(1+r)]$ are linearly independent.

Since the real function $f(r)$ of the variable r defined by

$$f(r) = \det[\mathbf{B} - \mathbf{A}(1+r)] \tag{1.26}$$

is clearly continuous, the set of values of r belonging to the half-line defined by relation (1.11) and such that

$$\det[\mathbf{B} - \mathbf{A}(1+r)] \neq 0 \tag{1.27}$$

is an interval closed on the left-hand side, and having $r = 0$ as its minimum.

Let us consider the values of r belonging to the half-line defined by relation (1.11) for which both sets $U(r)$ and $V(r)$ are not empty and for which (1.27) holds. From now on we shall, for convenience, use $\mathscr{I}$ to refer to this interval.

4 A further condition for the viability of the price system

Hypotheses UA 1, UA 2 and UA 3, explicitly stated in section 3, are necessary if the model under consideration is to have solutions with economic meaning. However, they are not yet sufficient. Indeed, if we consider the fundamental equation of the model, which for the convenience of the reader we shall write again in the form of (1.10),

$$w\mathbf{q} = \mathbf{p}[\mathbf{B} - \mathbf{A}(1+r)]$$

it is evident that the equation itself does not possess as a solution a price vector which is positive for *any* vector $\mathbf{q}$ of the quantity of labour absorbed by the industries of the system.

The validity of this is proved by the following example. Assume that

$$k = 3 \tag{1.28}$$

and consider the matrices $\mathbf{A}$ and $\mathbf{B}$ given in the following manner:

$$\mathbf{A} = \begin{bmatrix} 1 & 2 & 1 \\ 2 & 1 & 3 \\ 1 & 2 & 2 \end{bmatrix} \tag{1.29}$$

$$\mathbf{B} = \begin{bmatrix} 2{\cdot}9 & 1{\cdot}2 & 1{\cdot}9 \\ 1{\cdot}2 & 2{\cdot}9 & 3{\cdot}9 \\ 0{\cdot}1 & 1{\cdot}2 & 3{\cdot}9 \end{bmatrix} \tag{1.30}$$

These two matrices satisfy hypotheses UA 1 and UA 2, the latter being clearly satisfied when we assume a vector $\hat{\mathbf{p}}$ given by

$$\hat{\mathbf{p}} = [1, 1, 1] \tag{1.31}$$

It is easy to verify that hypothesis UA 3 is also satisfied.

It is also possible to verify that all the commodities considered in the model under examination are basic commodities: the reader may check this (we ask him to accept it for the time being) after examining our treatment, in section 6, of the problem of basic commodities. He will then, by the criteria advanced there, also be able to judge whether a particular model, with matrices such as **A** and **B**, also admits the existence of commodities that are non-basic, in accordance with the terminology and definition given by Sraffa (1960, section 58).

On the other hand, we can verify that with

$$r = 0, \qquad w = 1 \tag{1.32}$$

the vector of the quantities of labour given by

$$\mathbf{q} = [1{\cdot}73,\ 1{\cdot}66,\ 0{\cdot}47] \tag{1.33}$$

yields the following price vector:

$$\mathbf{p} = [11,\ 1,\ -0{\cdot}7] \tag{1.34}$$

– that is, a vector of prices which are not all positive.

From the example just examined we can infer that, for the model to be 'viable', we must state some further hypothesis which will provide the conditions under which, in equation (1.10), given the values of r and w, a vector $\mathbf{q}$ of quantities of labour yields a positive vector of prices, at least under the restrictive hypothesis we have accepted, i.e. the hypothesis that all commodities under consideration are basic commodities.

In order to state such a hypothesis, consider a matrix $[\mathbf{B}-\mathbf{A}(1+r)]$, corresponding to a value of r belonging to the interval defined at the end of section 3. Let us call $V'(r)$ the set of vectors $\mathbf{z}$ given by the formula

$$\mathbf{z} = \mathbf{p}[\mathbf{B}-\mathbf{A}(1+r)] \tag{1.35}$$

when $\mathbf{p}$ belongs to the set $V(r)$. The set $V'(r)$ could be called the 'image' of $V(r)$ by the linear application given by the square matrix $[\mathbf{B}-\mathbf{A}(1+r)]$; it is defined by the formula

$$V'(r) = \{\mathbf{z} \mid \mathbf{z} = \mathbf{p}[\mathbf{B}-\mathbf{A}(1+r)] \wedge \mathbf{p} \in V(r)\} \tag{1.36}$$

From the definition that we have given of $V'(r)$ it follows immediately that

$$\mathbf{q} \in V'(r) \rightarrow \mathbf{p} = \mathbf{q}[\mathbf{A}-\mathbf{B}(1+r)]^{-1} > \mathbf{0} \tag{1.37}$$

Hence we may state the hypothesis we have in mind in the following way.

UA 4. For any given value of r belonging to the interval $\mathscr{I}$, the vector $\mathbf{q}$ belongs to the set $V'(r)$. In mathematical terms:

$$r \in \mathscr{I} \rightarrow \mathbf{q} \in V'(r) \tag{1.38}$$

5 A case of non-existence of the 'standard system'

The importance of the standard product in Sraffa's system is well known: in the case of single-product industries (dealt with in the first half of his book) it serves as standard for measuring the value of overall product and for measuring the wage rate and prices. The standard product seems to have a similar importance in the case of joint production. In this second case, however, it seems that also Sraffa realises the potential complications in the definition of the standard product. At least we can interpret in this sense Sraffa's assertion (Sraffa, 1960, p. 47) that for the construction of the standard product negative multipliers must also be considered.

Nevertheless, it does not appear that Sraffa has experienced the slightest doubt concerning the possibility of imagining the existence of a standard product, even though this possibility is not generally verified, but must be postulated by means of a suitable hypothesis on the matrices which we have called **A** and **B**.

Further to clarify this statement, we point out that the set of multipliers which give rise to the standard product is defined by the equation

$$(1+R)\mathbf{A}\mathbf{x}_T = \mathbf{B}\mathbf{x}_T \tag{1.39}$$

This vector equation is obtained from (1.5) by setting

$$r = R, \qquad w = 0 \tag{1.40}$$

The components of the vector $\mathbf{x}_T$ (defined but for a common multiplicative factor) are coefficients of the linear combination of industries which give rise to the standard product. The equation (1.39) is a translation of the system given by Sraffa (1960, section 63). Here we assume that all the commodities considered are basic commodities. It will be explained why this hypothesis is not restrictive, and the reader will be able to translate our equation, after the existence of non-basic products has been discussed (section 6 below).

Equation (1.39) may also be written in the following form:

$$[\mathbf{B} - \mathbf{A}(1+R)]\mathbf{x}_T = \mathbf{0}_T \tag{1.41}$$

In accordance with classical theorems of algebra for systems of linear equations, this equation may be satisfied by a vector $\mathbf{x}_T$, other than the null vector, only if

$$\det[\mathbf{B} - \mathbf{A}(1+R)] = 0 \tag{1.42}$$

In addition, the economic meaning that Sraffa attributes to the standard product makes sense if, and only if, the vector $\mathbf{x}_T$, associated with a value R that satisfies (1.42), is defined as unique but for a multiplicative factor. This occurs if the value

$$r = R \tag{1.43}$$

is a simple root of the algebraic equation

$$\det[\mathbf{B}-\mathbf{A}(1+r)]=0 \tag{1.44}$$

All these conditions are verified for Sraffa's model in the case of single-product industries, on the basis of well known theorems of Perron and Frobenius. But, in the case of the model that we are interested in here, these conditions may not be fulfilled. This is shown in the following example, where it is not even possible to construct the standard product – at least, if we remain in the field of real numbers.

Consider a model in which

$$k=2 \tag{1.45}$$

and in which we have

$$\mathbf{A}=\begin{bmatrix}1 & 1{\cdot}1\\ 1{\cdot}1 & 1\end{bmatrix} \tag{1.46}$$

$$\mathbf{B}=\begin{bmatrix}1{\cdot}09 & 1{\cdot}144\\ 1{\cdot}144 & 0{\cdot}99\end{bmatrix} \tag{1.47}$$

If we define

$$1+r=t \tag{1.48}$$

then we can easily see that the equation

$$\det[\mathbf{B}-\mathbf{A}t]=0 \tag{1.49}$$

becomes, in this case,

$$0{\cdot}21\,t^2-0{\cdot}4368\,t+0{\cdot}229636=0 \tag{1.50}$$

which does not have any real root.[2]

On the other hand, it is easy to verify that the matrices **A** and **B**, given respectively by (1.46) and (1.47), satisfy hypotheses UA 1, UA 2 and UA 3.

Consequently, for Sraffa's propositions to hold, it is necessary to add the following hypothesis.

UA 5. The algebraic equation, in the unknown r,

$$\det[\mathbf{B}-\mathbf{A}(1+r)]=0 \tag{1.51}$$

has at least one real and positive root. This root (or the smallest of the real

[2] The terms 'real number' and 'real solution' are used here in the precise technical sense of mathematics and not in the rather vague sense adopted by Sraffa (1960, section 50). In this section, indeed, so far as I can understand, Sraffa uses the expression 'real solutions' to mean, perhaps, 'solutions that have economic meaning' or 'solutions that have a correspondence in reality'.

and positive roots, if there is more than one) is a simple root of the algebraic equation (1.51).

The final clause, which postulates that the root, or the smallest root, must be a simple root of equation (1.51), is based on the following considerations. From what is said by Sraffa (1960, section 64) it appears that, for reasons inherent to the economic meaning of the standard product, he wishes to adopt the convention that, if there is more than one positive root, then the smallest one, which we may call ρ, is to be taken as the root of equation (1.51) for the construction of the standard product. However, if the construction of the standard product is to have sense, it is necessary that the corresponding equation (1.41) have only one solution vector, defined but for a multiplicative constant. Indeed, the circumstance that would result if (1.41) had at least two linearly independent vectors as solutions would be contrary to Sraffa's intentions. But this could only occur if the root ρ is not a simple root for equation (1.51).

6 The distinction between basic and non-basic commodities

As is well known, the distinction between basic and non-basic commodities is essential to Sraffa's analysis; this is because, among other reasons, according to his point of view, it is the former that determine the vector of prices that satisfies the fundamental equation of his model.

The distinction between basic and non-basic commodities is given in Sraffa (1960, sections 58 ff.) and will be translated into the mathematical notation adopted here. To this end, let us suppose that certain m commodities of our economic system are non-basic. Clearly,

$$m < k \tag{1.52}$$

and for convenience we may assume that

$$k = j + m \qquad (j > 0) \tag{1.53}$$

Making use of the remark stated in section 2, we can imagine that we have reordered the rows of matrices **A** and **B** (and consequently also the elements of the vector **p**) so that the commodities we are interested in correspond to the last m rows of the matrices themselves.

To make things clearer, after this reordering, we can consider each of the matrices **A** and **B** as partitioned into two other matrices: we shall call these $\mathbf{A}'$, $\mathbf{A}''$ and $\mathbf{B}'$, $\mathbf{B}''$ respectively. $\mathbf{A}'$ and $\mathbf{B}'$ are rectangular matrices of order $j \times k$, while matrices $\mathbf{A}''$ and $\mathbf{B}''$ are also rectangular but of order $m \times k$. We therefore write

$$\mathbf{A} = \left[\frac{\mathbf{A}'}{\mathbf{A}''}\right], \qquad \mathbf{B} = \left[\frac{\mathbf{B}'}{\mathbf{B}''}\right] \tag{1.54}$$

By means of matrices $\mathbf{A}''$ and $\mathbf{B}''$ we now construct a $2m \times k$ matrix $\mathbf{D}$, as follows:

$$\mathbf{D} = \left[\begin{array}{c} \mathbf{A}'' \\ \hline \mathbf{B}'' \end{array}\right] \tag{1.55}$$

According to the ideas put forward by Sraffa, if the m commodities corresponding to the rows forming matrices $\mathbf{A}''$ and $\mathbf{B}''$ are non-basic, then matrix $\mathbf{D}$ is of rank m.

In other words, of the columns of matrix $\mathbf{D}$, only m columns are linearly independent, and therefore all the others can be obtained by a linear combination of these.

Making use once more of the remark stated in section 2, we can think in terms of having reordered the columns of matrix $\mathbf{A}$ and matrix $\mathbf{B}$ (and therefore also the elements of vector $\mathbf{q}$), in such a way that the m columns that form a base for the columns of matrix $\mathbf{D}$ are the last columns of such matrices.

Assuming that this reordering has been carried out, the condition stated by Sraffa for the m commodities corresponding to the last m rows of matrices $\mathbf{A}$ and $\mathbf{B}$ to be non-basic can be translated in the following way.

Let us imagine that each of the matrices $\mathbf{A}$ and $\mathbf{B}$ is partitioned into four sub-matrices, $\mathbf{A}_{11}$, $\mathbf{A}_{12}$, $\mathbf{A}_{21}$, $\mathbf{A}_{22}$ and $\mathbf{B}_{11}$, $\mathbf{B}_{12}$, $\mathbf{B}_{21}$, $\mathbf{B}_{22}$, respectively. Matrices $\mathbf{A}_{11}$, $\mathbf{B}_{11}$ are square of order j; matrices $\mathbf{A}_{22}$, $\mathbf{B}_{22}$ are also square of order m. We have, therefore,

$$\mathbf{A} = \left[\begin{array}{c|c} \mathbf{A}_{11} & \mathbf{A}_{12} \\ \hline \mathbf{A}_{21} & \mathbf{A}_{22} \end{array}\right], \qquad \mathbf{B} = \left[\begin{array}{c|c} \mathbf{B}_{11} & \mathbf{B}_{12} \\ \hline \mathbf{B}_{21} & \mathbf{B}_{22} \end{array}\right] \tag{1.56}$$

The commodities corresponding to the last m rows of the two matrices $\mathbf{A}$ and $\mathbf{B}$ are non-basic, according to Sraffa's definition, if there exists a matrix $\mathbf{T}$ of order $m \times j$ such that

$$\mathbf{A}_{21} = \mathbf{A}_{22}\mathbf{T}, \qquad \mathbf{B}_{21} = \mathbf{B}_{22}\mathbf{T} \tag{1.57}$$

Matrix $\mathbf{T}$ is a matrix obtained from the coefficients of the linear combination by means of which the first j columns of matrices $\mathbf{A}''$ and $\mathbf{B}''$ (obviously after the reordering we have referred to) are expressed by means of the last m columns.

We may therefore construct the matrix $\mathbf{M}$, square and of order k, in the following way:

$$\mathbf{M} = \left[\begin{array}{c|c} \mathbf{I}_j & \mathbf{0} \\ \hline -\mathbf{T} & \mathbf{I}_m \end{array}\right] \tag{1.58}$$

where $\mathbf{I}_j$ and $\mathbf{I}_m$ are the identity matrices, of orders j and m respectively.

On the basis of (1.57) we easily see that the matrices

$$\overline{\mathbf{A}} = \mathbf{A}\,\mathbf{M}, \qquad \overline{\mathbf{B}} = \mathbf{B}\,\mathbf{M} \tag{1.59}$$

have the following form:

$$\overline{\mathbf{A}} = \left[\begin{array}{c|c} \overline{\mathbf{A}}_{11} & \mathbf{A}_{12} \\ \hline \mathbf{0} & \mathbf{A}_{22} \end{array}\right], \qquad \overline{\mathbf{B}} = \left[\begin{array}{c|c} \overline{\mathbf{B}}_{11} & \mathbf{B}_{12} \\ \hline \mathbf{0} & \mathbf{B}_{22} \end{array}\right] \tag{1.60}$$

where, in particular,

$$\overline{\mathbf{A}}_{11} = \mathbf{A}_{11} - \mathbf{A}_{12}\,\mathbf{T}, \qquad \overline{\mathbf{B}}_{11} = \mathbf{B}_{11} - \mathbf{B}_{12}\,\mathbf{T} \tag{1.61}$$

We may now separate in vector $\mathbf{q}$ the first j components from the last m. We may write, therefore,

$$\mathbf{q} = [\mathbf{q}^1 | \mathbf{q}^2] \tag{1.62}$$

where, as already said, $\mathbf{q}^1$ has j components and $\mathbf{q}^2$ has m components.

Let us now put

$$\bar{\mathbf{q}} = \mathbf{q}\,\mathbf{M} \tag{1.63}$$

It then follows that

$$\bar{\mathbf{q}} = [\bar{\mathbf{q}}^1 | \mathbf{q}^2], \tag{1.64}$$

where clearly

$$\bar{\mathbf{q}} = \mathbf{q}^1 - \mathbf{q}^2\,\mathbf{T} \tag{1.65}$$

Similarly, we may consider the vector of prices $\mathbf{p}$ as partitioned into two sub-vectors of j and m components respectively, and we may write, on analogy with (1.62),

$$\mathbf{p} = [\mathbf{p}^1 | \mathbf{p}^2] \tag{1.66}$$

We may finally imagine that we have multiplied both sides of the fundamental equation of the model

$$\mathbf{p}\,\mathbf{A}(1+r) + w\,\mathbf{q} = \mathbf{p}\,\mathbf{B} \tag{1.67}$$

on the right by matrix $\mathbf{M}$.

Having done this, and after multiplication on the right by matrix $\mathbf{M}$, equation (1.67) may be replaced by the system of the following two equations:

$$\begin{cases} \mathbf{p}^1\,\overline{\mathbf{A}}_{11}(1+r) + w\,\bar{\mathbf{q}}^1 = \mathbf{p}^1\,\overline{\mathbf{B}}_{11} & (1.68) \\ \mathbf{p}^1\,\mathbf{A}_{12}(1+r) + \mathbf{p}^2\,\mathbf{A}_{22}(1+r) + w\,\mathbf{q}^2 = \mathbf{p}^1\,\overline{\mathbf{B}}_{11} + \mathbf{p}^2\,\mathbf{B}_{22} & (1.69) \end{cases}$$

The vector equation (1.69) is a translation of the system of equations given by Sraffa (1960, section 62). We should point out, however, that this system is not to be considered equivalent to the system which translates the fundamental vector equation (1.67) – at least, not if we wish to preserve for the term 'equivalent' the meaning that it has in the theory of the systems of linear equations. We need only point out that the system which translates equation (1.68) has a different number of equations and unknowns (to be exact, fewer) from the system that translates equation (1.69).

Strictly speaking, only the system of the pair of equations (1.68) and (1.69) is equivalent to equation (1.67), in the sense that every solution of the pair of equations (1.68) and (1.69) supplies a solution to equation (1.67) and vice versa. However, it should be pointed out that the pair of equations (1.68) and (1.69) can be solved in the order in which they have been written; indeed, equation (1.68) involves only vector $\mathbf{p}^1$, the only components of which are the prices of the basic commodities. Once such prices have been determined, it is also possible to solve equation (1.69), determining the prices of the other commodities – when, of course, the conditions allowing such solutions are satisfied. All remarks that we have made concerning the fundamental equation (1.67), when all the products are basic products, may now be made about equation (1.68). Indeed, not any choice of vector $\bar{\mathbf{q}}^1$ leads to a solution that includes all positive components of the price vector $\mathbf{p}^1$. On this particular point we should have to state hypotheses similar to UA 4 (see end of section 4). However, it may finally be pointed out that, in the case of the vector equation (1.68), the vector $\bar{\mathbf{q}}^1$ which appears there and is given by (1.65) may not have positive components. Now, for the purpose of constructing a standard product and in order to highlight the fact that some commodities may not be basic, Sraffa gives an interpretation of the fact that a linear combination of industries may yield coefficients that are not all positive (see the development of this argument in Sraffa, 1960, section 56). But it seems that he has not thought it necessary to interpret negative quantities of labour absorbed by industries. However, such a case needs to be justified or interpreted, and we willingly leave this task to the economists.

The construction of the standard product in the case of equation (1.68) must be carried out following the procedure examined in section 5. Consequently the possibility of such a construction must be ensured by a hypothesis similar to UA 5, since it is not ensured by hypotheses UA 1, UA 2, UA 3 and UA 4 alone.

References

Dominedò, V., 'Una teoria economica neo-ricardiana', *Giornale degli economisti*, XXI (1962) 710–31.

Leontief, W. W., *The Structure of American Economy* 1919–1939 (New York: Oxford University Press, 1951).

Manara, C. F. and Nicola, P. C., *Elementi di economia matematica* (Milan: Viscontea, 1967).

Newman, P., 'Production of Commodities by means of Commodities', *Schweizerische Zeitschrift für Volkswirtschaft und Statistik*, XCVIII (1962) 58–75.

Sraffa, P., *Production of Commodities by Means of Commodities* (Cambridge: Cambridge University Press, 1960).

CHAPTER TWO

The Notion of Vertical Integration in Economic Analysis[1]

LUIGI L. PASINETTI

Very few notions in economic analysis are so seldom explicitly mentioned as the notion of vertical integration and are at the same time so widely used, implicitly or without full awareness.[2] I came to this conviction during the discussions on a multi-sector model of economic growth which I presented a few years ago (Pasinetti, 1965). The synthetic notion of a 'vertically integrated sector' is used explicitly in that model, but within the simplified context of an economic system in which capital goods are made by labour alone; and I have always been faced with questions.[3]

An explicit and more general investigation of the meaning and relevance of vertical integration in economic analysis may therefore prove of some usefulness. Instead of starting from the synthetic notions and going back to their elementary components, I shall start here from these elementary components – i.e. from the now familiar schemes of inter-industry analysis – and go on to the synthetic notions. The crucial role played by vertical integration in the theories of value, income distribution and economic growth should emerge clearly as the investigation develops. The whole analysis will be carried out with reference to the general case of

[1] Originally published in *Metroeconomica*, XXV (1973) 1–29.

[2] The notion of vertical integration is implicit in all discussions on the theory of value of the classical economists. The same thing can be said of the marginalist economists. When, for example, Léon Walras adopted the device of eliminating intermediate commodities from his analysis of production, he was making use of the logical process of vertical integration. (See Walras, 1874; 1965 edn, pp. 241 ff.) Keynesian macroeconomic analysis is also generally carried out in terms of vertically integrated magnitudes (net national income, net savings, new investments, consumption, and so on). Very rarely, however, is the logical process of vertical integration explicitly discussed. Generally it is simply taken for granted.

[3] These questions have normally been concerned with the problem of how to construct the vertically integrated sectors in the general case. Some indications are given in Pasinetti (1965, Ch. 6), but in a too brief and incomplete manner.

production of all commodities by means of commodities. The simplified case of capital goods produced by labour alone will be shown at the end as a particular case.

1 Production of commodities by means of commodities

An economic system will be considered in which all commodities are produced by means of commodities, used as capital goods. Commodities enter the process of production at the beginning of each 'year' as inputs, jointly with labour services, and commodities come out at the end of the year as outputs. The economic system is supposed to be *viable*, in the sense that it is capable of producing larger quantities of commodities than those required to replace used-up capital goods.

The following notation will be used throughout.[4]

(i) Column vector $\mathbf{X}(t) \equiv [X_i(t)]$, $i = 1, 2, \ldots m$, to denote the physical quantities of the m commodities that are produced in year t.

(ii) Column vector $\mathbf{Y}(t) \equiv [Y_i(t)]$, $i = 1, 2, \ldots m$, to denote the physical net product of the economic system, i.e. what is available for consumption and new investments after deducting replacements from $\mathbf{X}(t)$. Of course, $\mathbf{Y}(t)$ may further be regarded as a sum of commodities devoted to consumption and of commodities devoted to investments, to be denoted by column vectors $\mathbf{C}(t) \equiv [C_i(t)]$ and $\mathbf{J}^{(d)}(t) \equiv [J_i^{(d)}(t)]$, $i = 1, 2, \ldots m$, respectively. By definition, $\mathbf{C}(t) + \mathbf{J}^{(d)}(t) \equiv \mathbf{Y}(t)$.

(iii) Column vector $\mathbf{S}(t) \equiv [S_i(t)]$, $i = 1, 2, \ldots m$, to denote the physical quantities of commodities that are required as capital goods (capital stocks), at the beginning of year t, in order to obtain quantities $\mathbf{X}(t)$ at the end of year t.

(iv) Row vector $\mathbf{p}(t) \equiv [p_i(t)]$, $i = 1, 2, \ldots m$, to denote prices of commodities $1, 2, \ldots m$.

(v) Scalar $L(t)$, to denote the labour force required by the economic system in year t, measured, let us say, in man-years.

(vi) Scalar π to denote the (uniform) rate of profit.

(vii) Scalar $w(t)$ to denote the (uniform) wage rate.

As far as technology is concerned, two successive analytical stages will be taken – a procedure which is by now customary in this type of analysis. Usually, as is well known, one begins by considering, first, production with circulating capital goods; then one goes on to production with fixed capital goods. The advantage of this procedure is that almost all basic concepts can

[4] Symbol $\equiv$ will be used to denote a definitional equality and in particular, as in all cases in this section, an equality of two different notations for the same thing.

be singled out at the first stage, where relatively few analytical complications arise. The second stage can then be devoted to pointing out which conclusions still hold and which conclusions are affected by generalisation. A slightly more general approach is taken in the present work. Fixed capital goods are introduced immediately at the first stage, but with a simplifying assumption on how they depreciate. The case of production with fixed-capital goods in general will, of course, be considered at a second stage.

2 Fixed capital goods with a simplifying assumption

We shall begin by considering a technology which requires both circulating capital goods (which are used up within one year) and fixed capital goods (which last for more than one year). The simplifying assumption will be made that in each industry j a constant proportion δ_j of all fixed capital goods drops out of the production process each year ($j = 1, 2, \ldots m$). Moreover, for the time being, all technical coefficients will be supposed to be constant through time.

The technique of the whole economic system will be represented by

(i) a row vector $\mathbf{a}_{[n]} \equiv [a_{nj}]$, $n = m+1, j = 1, 2, \ldots m$, all $a_{nj} \geq 0$, where each a_{nj} denotes the annual input of labour required by one physical unit of the commodity produced in industry j;

(ii) a square matrix $\mathbf{A} \equiv [a_{ij}]$; $i, j = 1, 2, \ldots m$, all $a_{ij} \geq 0$, in which each column j represents the physical stocks of capital goods (both circulating and fixed) required for the production of one physical unit of the commodity produced in industry j. Square matrix $\mathbf{A}$ may be regarded as the sum of two non-negative square matrices: $\mathbf{A}^{(C)} \equiv [a_{ij}^{(C)}]$ and $\mathbf{A}^{(F)} \equiv [a_{ij}^{(F)}]$; $i, j = 1, 2, \ldots m$, as representing the stocks of circulating-capital goods and the stocks of fixed capital goods respectively. Therefore $\mathbf{A} \equiv A^{(C)} + \mathbf{A}^{(F)}$, by definition. Of course, each year in each industry j, the economic system has to replace all circulating capital goods and a fraction δ_j of the fixed capital goods; $j = 1, 2, \ldots m$. If we call $\hat{\delta}$ a diagonal matrix with all the δ_js on the main diagonal, we may therefore define another square matrix $\mathbf{A}^{\ominus} \equiv [a_{ij}^{\ominus}] \equiv \mathbf{A}^{(C)} + \mathbf{A}^{(F)}\hat{\delta}$, as representing that part of the initial stocks of capital goods that are actually used up each year by the production process. By definition, $\mathbf{A}^{\ominus} + \mathbf{A}^{(F)}\ (\mathbf{I} - \hat{\delta}) \equiv \mathbf{A}$. The particular case in which all capital goods are circulating capital goods is represented by $\mathbf{A}^{(F)} = \mathbf{O}$, where $\mathbf{O}$ is the zero matrix, and, therefore, $\mathbf{A}^{\ominus} = \mathbf{A}$.

With this notation, the physical economic system may be represented by the following system of equations:

$$(\mathbf{I}-\mathbf{A}^{\ominus})\mathbf{X}(t) = \mathbf{Y}(t) \tag{2.1}$$

$$a_{[n]}\mathbf{X}(t) = L(t) \tag{2.2}$$

$$\mathbf{A}\mathbf{X}(t) = \mathbf{S}(t) \tag{2.3}$$

where (2.1), (2.2) represent the flows of commodities and labour services required in year t to produce net product $\mathbf{Y}(t)$, and (2.3) represents the stocks of capital goods required at the beginning of year t for production to be effected. At the same time, equilibrium prices are represented by the following system of equations:

$$\mathbf{p} = \mathbf{a}_{[n]}w + \mathbf{p}\mathbf{A}^{\ominus} + \mathbf{p}\mathbf{A}\pi \tag{2.4}$$

which determines all prices if one of these and the wage rate (or alternatively the rate of profit) are fixed exogenously.

3 An 'industry'

On the assumption just made concerning fixed capital goods, each industry j ($j = 1, 2, \ldots m$) produces only one good: commodity j; and in order to produce one physical unit of such a commodity, it needs a quantity of labour represented by the jth coefficient of vector $\mathbf{a}_{[n]}$ and a series of heterogeneous stocks of capital goods, represented by the jth column of matrix $\mathbf{A}$. Industry j may therefore be synthetically represented by a 'direct labour coefficient' – the jth component of vector $\mathbf{a}_{[n]}$ – and by what may be called a 'unit of direct productive capacity' – a composite commodity defined by the jth column of matrix $\mathbf{A}$.

In equations (2.1)–(2.3), the physical quantities of an economic system are classified precisely in this way, i.e. according to the criterion of the 'industry'. This classification has the advantage of being immediately observable; but it maintains our attention at a rather superficial level. A reclassification of the same physical quantities may be obtained on the basis of a conceptually more complex, but analytically far more powerful, criterion, which we shall now consider.

4 A 'vertically integrated sector'

We may define a new vector $\mathbf{Y}_i(t)$ as a column vector the components of which are all zeros except the ith one, defined here as $Y_i(t)$ – i.e. the ith component of vector $\mathbf{Y}(t)$. Moreover, we shall use scalar $L^{(i)}(t)$ to denote the quantity of labour required, column vector $\mathbf{X}^{(i)}(t)$ to denote the physical quantities of commodities to be produced, and column vector $\mathbf{S}^{(i)}(t)$ to denote the stocks of capital goods required, in the whole economic system, in order to obtain physical quantity $Y_i(t)$ of final good i ($i = 1, 2, \ldots m$).

For each particular net product $Y_i(t)$, we obtain from (2.1)–(2.3)

$$\mathbf{X}^{(i)}(t) = (\mathbf{I} - \mathbf{A}^{\ominus})^{-1}\mathbf{Y}_i(t) \tag{2.5}$$

$$L^{(i)}(t) = \mathbf{a}_{[n]}(\mathbf{I} - \mathbf{A}^{\ominus})^{-1}\mathbf{Y}_i(t) \tag{2.6}$$

$$\mathbf{S}^{(i)}(t) = \mathbf{A}(\mathbf{I} - \mathbf{A}^{\ominus})^{-1}\mathbf{Y}_i(t), \qquad i = 1, 2, \ldots m \tag{2.7}$$

i.e. in fact, m-sub-systems (as Piero Sraffa has called them – 1960, p. 89). From (2.5)–(2.7) and the definition of $\mathbf{Y}_i(t)$ it follows that

$$\sum_i^m \mathbf{Y}_i(t) = \mathbf{Y}(t), \qquad \sum_i^m \mathbf{X}^{(i)}(t) = \mathbf{X}(t) \tag{2.8}$$

$$\sum_i^m L^{(i)}(t) = L(t), \qquad \sum_i^m \mathbf{S}^{(i)}(t) = \mathbf{S}(t) \tag{2.9}$$

The m sub-systems add up to the original complete economic system.

The economic meaning of the coefficients appearing on the right hand side of (2.5) has been widely illustrated in the economic literature. Matrix $(\mathbf{I} - \mathbf{A}^{\ominus})^{-1}$ is known as the Leontief inverse matrix (after Leontief, 1951) – its ith column ($i = 1, 2, \ldots m$) contains the series of heterogeneous commodities that are directly and indirectly required in the whole economic system to obtain one physical unit of commodity i as a final good. On the other hand, less attention has been paid to the economic meaning of the coefficients that appear on the right-hand side of (2.6) and (2.7). (It is, again, Leontief [1953, 1956] who first applied these concepts.) More synthetically, we may define,

$$\mathbf{a}_{[n]}(\mathbf{I} - \mathbf{A}^{\ominus})^{-1} \equiv \mathbf{v} \equiv [v_i] \tag{2.10}$$

$$\mathbf{A}(\mathbf{I} - \mathbf{A}^{\ominus})^{-1} \equiv \mathbf{H} \equiv [\mathbf{h}_i], \qquad i = 1, 2, \ldots m \tag{2.11}$$

where each $\mathbf{h}_i$ is a column vector, and thus rewrite (2.6), (2.7) in a more compact way:

$$L^{(i)}(t) = \mathbf{v}\mathbf{Y}_i(t) \equiv v_i Y_i \tag{2.6a}$$

$$\mathbf{S}^{(i)}(t) = \mathbf{H}\mathbf{Y}_i(t) \equiv \mathbf{h}_i Y_i, \qquad i = 1, 2, \ldots m \tag{2.7a}$$

Each coefficient v_i in (2.6a) expresses in a consolidated way the quantity of labour directly and indirectly required in the whole economic system to obtain one physical unit of commodity i as a final good. We shall call it the *vertically integrated labour coefficient* for commodity i ($i = 1, 2, \ldots m$). Likewise, each column vector $\mathbf{h}_i$ in (2.7a) expresses in a consolidated way the series of heterogeneous physical quantities of commodities $1, 2, \ldots m$, which are directly and indirectly required as stocks, in the whole economic system, in order to obtain one physical unit of commodity i as a final good (i

= 1, 2, . . . m). This is another particular composite commodity, which we shall call *a unit of vertically integrated productive capacity* for commodity i (i = 1, 2, . . . m).

Scalar v_i and column vector $\mathbf{h}_i$, together, represent what we may call the *vertically integrated sector* for the production of commodity i as a final good (whether for consumption of for investment); i = 1, 2, . . . m. A vertically integrated sector is therefore a compact way of representing a sub-system, as it synthesises each sub-system into a single labour coefficient v_i and a single composite commodity $\mathbf{h}_i$. For an economic system with m commodities, we obviously obtain m labour coefficients (the m components of row vector $\mathbf{v}$) and m units of productive capacity (the m columns of matrix $\mathbf{H}$), i.e. m vertically integrated sectors for the production of the m commodities as final goods.

In comparison with the previous section, we may say that vector $\mathbf{a}_{[n]}$ and matrix $\mathbf{A}$ classify the total quantity of labour $L(t)$ and total quantities of stocks of capital goods $\mathbf{S}(t)$ according to the criterion of the industry in which they are required:

$$L(t) = \mathbf{a}_{[n]}\mathbf{X}(t), \qquad \mathbf{S}(t) = \mathbf{A}\mathbf{X}(t) \tag{2.12}$$

All these quantities are directly observable and directly quantifiable. Vector $\mathbf{v}$ and matrix $\mathbf{H}$ reclassify the same physical quantities according to the criterion of the vertically integrated sector for which they are directly and indirectly required:

$$L^{(i)}(t) = \mathbf{a}_{[n]}\,(\mathbf{I}-\mathbf{A}^{\ominus})^{-1}\,\mathbf{Y}_i\,(t) = \mathbf{v}\,\mathbf{Y}_i\,(t) \tag{2.6b}$$
$$\mathbf{S}^{(i)}\,(t) = \mathbf{A}\,(\mathbf{I}-\mathbf{A}^{\ominus})^{-1}\,\mathbf{Y}_i\,(t) = \mathbf{H}\,\mathbf{Y}_i\,(t), \qquad i = 1, 2, \ldots m \tag{2.7b}$$

$$L(t) = \sum_i^m L^{(i)}\,(t), \qquad \mathbf{S}(t) = \sum_i^m \mathbf{S}^{(i)}\,(t) \tag{2.13}$$

Neither $\mathbf{v}$ nor $\mathbf{H}$ is directly observable, but they can be obtained through post-multiplication by $(\mathbf{I}-\mathbf{A}^{\ominus})^{-1}$ from quantities $\mathbf{a}_{[n]}$ and $\mathbf{A}$, which are directly observable. They are therefore quantifiable in an indirect way.

To conclude, precisely the same physical quantities $L(t)$ and $\mathbf{S}(t)$ appear in both (2.12) and (2.13), but they are classified according to two different criteria – the more immediate criterion of the 'industry' in the former, the conceptually more complex criterion of the 'vertically integrated sector' in the latter. Both classifications are empirically quantifiable – the former directly and the latter through the indirect logical process of vertical integration.

5 Vertical integration in the theory of value and income distribution

When Adam Smith put forward (1776; 1904 edn, pp. 49 and 52) the proposition that every commodity finally resolves itself into wages, profits and rents, he rightly sensed that he had reached an important conclusion: he had (implicitly) grasped the basic concept of vertical integration.

In our analysis, neither the price system written in section 2 on the basis of directly observable magnitudes

$$\mathbf{p} = \mathbf{a}_{[n]} w + \mathbf{p}\,\mathbf{A}^{\ominus} + \mathbf{p}\,\mathbf{A}\,\pi \tag{2.4}$$

nor what may be called its 'solution'

$$\mathbf{p} = \mathbf{a}_{[n]} (\mathbf{I} - \mathbf{A}^{\ominus} - \mathbf{A}\,\pi)^{-1} w \tag{2.14}$$

can give us a clear idea of Adam Smith's theoretical insight.

But if we perform a few logical operations and rewrite (2.4) as

$$\mathbf{p}(\mathbf{I} - \mathbf{A}^{\ominus}) = \mathbf{a}_{[n]} w + \mathbf{p}\,\mathbf{A}\,\pi \tag{2.15}$$

$$\mathbf{p} = \mathbf{a}_{[n]} (\mathbf{I} - \mathbf{A}^{\ominus})^{-1} w + \mathbf{p}\,\mathbf{A}(\mathbf{I} - \mathbf{A}^{\ominus})^{-1} \pi \tag{2.16}$$

we can see the two notions characterising a vertically integrated sector reappear. After substitution from definitions (2.10) and (2.11), (2.16) may be written

$$\mathbf{p} = \mathbf{v} w + \mathbf{p}\,\mathbf{H}\,\pi \tag{2.17}$$

This is a remarkable expression, as it explicitly shows that each price is ultimately made up of only two components: wages and profits.[5] It is precisely the logical operation of vertical integration that makes this evident, by consolidating all the complex intermediate stages into one single labour coefficient and one single unit of productive capacity – the former being multiplied by the wage rate, and the latter (after being evaluated at current prices) by the rate of profit. It may be noticed that vector $\mathbf{p}\,\mathbf{H}$ is nothing but a vector of the m vertically integrated capital – output ratios multiplied by the price of the final commodity to which they refer. Hence, one alternative way of representing the m vertically integrated sectors might be that of using vector $\mathbf{v}$ (the m vertically integrated labour coefficients) and vector $\mathbf{p}\,\mathbf{H}$ (the m vertically integrated capital-per-unit-of-output ratios).[6]

Another property of (2.17) is that it exposes the antagonism of wages and profits in income distribution. When $\pi = 0$, the second addendum vanishes and prices become

$$\mathbf{p} = \mathbf{v} w \tag{2.18}$$

Wages are obviously at their maximum, as they absorb the whole purchasing power deriving from prices.

[5] No rents are considered in the present scheme.

[6] This is in fact the way suggested in Pasinetti (1965, Ch. 6), where the procedure to obtain them is also given (multiplication of direct labour coefficients and direct capital–output ratios by the inverse Leontief matrix).

Conversely, when $w = 0$, profits are at their maximum and (2.17) becomes a linear and homogeneous system of equations

$$\mathbf{p}(\mathbf{I} - \Pi\,\mathbf{H}) = \mathbf{0} \tag{2.19}$$

where Π stands for the rate of profit corresponding to $w = 0$, or maximum rate of profit. Since the economic system is viable *ex-hypothesi*, Π must be positive. Maximum rate of profit Π also emerges, from (2.19), as the reciprocal of the eigenvalues – which we may call λ – of matrix **H**. Non-trivial solutions require, of course,

$$\det(\lambda\,\mathbf{I} - \mathbf{H}) = 0 \tag{2.20}$$

an algebraic equation that yields m roots for λ. However, since **H** is a non-negative matrix,[7] we know on the basis of the Perron–Frobenius theorem (see, for example, Gantmacher, 1959) that its maximum eigenvalue, λ_{max}, (a) is a real and positive number; (b) has a non-negative eigenvector (i.e. non-negative prices) associated with it; (c) is also the eigenvalue which is maximum in modulus (i.e. $\lambda_{max} = |\lambda|_{max}$). This is the only root of (2.20) that is economically relevant[8] and we shall therefore straightaway define

$$\Pi = \frac{1}{\lambda_{max}} \tag{2.21}$$

For any positive π lower than Π, we also know on the basis of the Perron–Frobenius theorem that $(\mathbf{I} - \pi\,\mathbf{H})^{-1}$ is non-negative, so that the general solution of (2.17),

$$\mathbf{p} = \mathbf{v}(\mathbf{I} - \pi\,\mathbf{H})^{-1}\,w \tag{2.22}$$

yields non-negative prices and an inverse monotonic relation between π and w, whatever the standard in terms of which w is measured.[9]

The same problems may be looked at in a more 'classical' way if the wage rate itself is used as the *numéraire* of the price system, i.e. if we put $w = 1$. In this case all prices come to be expressed in terms of the wage rate, i.e. in terms of 'labour commanded'. But the components of **v**, the vertically integrated labour coefficients, express what classical economists called 'labour embodied' (and Marx simply called 'values'). Therefore, wages – by

[7] Both $\mathbf{A}^{\ominus}$ and **A** are non-negative *ex-hypothesi*; and, moreover, the technique is supposed to be viable, which implies that $(\mathbf{I} - \mathbf{A}^{\ominus})^{-1}$ is non-negative. It follows that **H** is also non-negative.

[8] The assumption is made, following Sraffa, that the internal rate of reproduction of non-basic commodities (if there are any) is higher than the internal rate of reproduction of basic commodities.

[9] Since no price can become negative in terms of *any* standard (within the interval, $0 \leq \pi \leq \Pi$), no price can fall faster than w as π is increased. It follows that π and w (in terms of *any* standard) must be inversely and monotonically related to each other. See the detailed proof given by Sraffa (1960, pp. 39–40).

being distributed in proportion to 'labour embodied', as appears from (2.17) – can 'command' only part of the purchasing power deriving from prices. The difference

$$\mathbf{p} - \mathbf{v} = \mathbf{p}\mathbf{H}\pi \tag{2.23}$$

is absorbed by profits. 'Solution' (2.22) becomes

$$\mathbf{p} = \mathbf{v}(\mathbf{I} - \pi\mathbf{H})^{-1} \tag{2.24}$$

and may also be regarded as expressing the 'transformation' of $\mathbf{v}$ into $\mathbf{p}$, i.e. of Marxian values into prices. The linear operator $(\mathbf{I} - \pi\mathbf{H})^{-1}$, where the m units of vertically integrated productive capacity are shown to play a crucial role, represents such 'transformation' in logical terms. Only when $\pi = 0$ does 'labour commanded' become equal to classical 'labour embodied' (and prices to Marxian 'values'), i.e.

$$\mathbf{p} = \mathbf{v} \tag{2.25}$$

while matrix $\mathbf{H}$ drops out of the picture altogether.

6 A particular unit of measurement for capital goods

We may go back to the physical quantity system. So far in this analysis, all commodities have been measured in terms of the physical units that are commonly used to measure them (for example, tons, bushels, numbers). But expressions (2.11) and (2.7a) suggest the possibility of an alternative physical unit of measurement for capital goods. More precisely, they suggest the possibility of measuring capital goods in terms of a particular composite commodity which we may call 'physical unit of vertically integrated productive capacity'.

There clearly exists one such physical unit for each final good that is produced. If there are m final goods, there exist m physical units of vertically integrated productive capacity, represented by the columns of matrix $\mathbf{H}$, i.e. by

$$\mathbf{h}_i = \mathbf{A}(\mathbf{I} - \mathbf{A}^{\ominus})^{-1}\mathbf{e}_i, \qquad i = 1, 2, \ldots m \tag{2.26}$$

where $\mathbf{e}_i$ is the ith unit column vector.

For the purpose of our analysis, a composite commodity does not present any conceptual difficulty. (As a matter of fact, any commodity – for instance, a pair of shoes – can always be considered as composed of various elementary commodities – such as leather, string, rubber – put together in fixed proportions.) Therefore, when such units are used, the existing stocks of capital goods may be represented by an m component column vector

$$\mathbf{K}(t) \equiv [K_i(t)], \qquad i = 1, 2, \ldots m \tag{2.27}$$

It follows by definition that, in equilibrium,

$$K_i(t) = Y_i(t), \qquad i = 1, 2, \ldots m \tag{2.28}$$

It is always possible to 'translate' capital goods expressed in terms of vertically integrated productive capacities into capital goods expressed in ordinary physical units by the transformation

$$\mathbf{S}(t) = \mathbf{H}\,\mathbf{K}(t) \tag{2.29}$$

Matrix $\mathbf{H}$ thereby appears as a linear operator which – when applied to a vector of physical quantities measured in terms of vertically integrated productive capacities – reclassifies them in terms of ordinary physical units. When $\mathbf{H}$ is a non-singular matrix, there even exists a unique inverse transformation

$$\mathbf{K}(t) = \mathbf{H}^{-1}\,\mathbf{S}(t) \tag{2.30}$$

But, of course, $\mathbf{H}^{-1}$ need not necessarily exist. (That is, there may be more than one way, or there may be no exhaustive way, of forming vertically integrated units of productive capacity from arbitrarily given existing stocks of ordinary capital goods.)

7 Vertically integrated sectors for investment goods expressed in physical units of vertically integrated productive capacity

When capital goods are measured in physical units of vertically integrated productive capacity, new investments (which are additions to the existing stocks of capital goods) must be measured in the same units. But new investments are considered to be final goods and we know that it is possible to construct conceptually a vertically integrated sector in correspondence to each final good. Such a logical construction has been obtained in section 4 for final goods measured in ordinary physical units. It now becomes possible to obtain similar logical constructions for investment goods measured in physical units of vertically integrated productive capacity.

We may denote by $\mathbf{J}^{(v)}(t) \equiv [J_i^{(v)}(t)]$, $i = 1, 2, \ldots m$, the column vector of new investments measured in units of vertically integrated productive capacity for the corresponding final goods $1, 2, \ldots m$; and by $\mathbf{J}_i^{(v)}(t)$, $i = 1, 2, \ldots m$, a column vector the components of which are all zeros excepting the ith one, which is equal to $J_i^{(v)}(t)$. Obviously, $\sum_i^m \mathbf{J}_i^{(v)}(t) = \mathbf{J}^{(v)}(t)$.

It follows from (2.29) that $\mathbf{J}^{(v)}(t)$ – new investments expressed in physical units of vertically integrated productive capacity – and $\mathbf{J}^{(d)}(t)$ – new investments expressed in ordinary (direct) physical units – are related by

$$\mathbf{J}^{(d)}(t) = \mathbf{H}\,\mathbf{J}^{(v)}(t) \tag{2.31}$$

Similarly to what has been done in section 4, we may denote by $L^{(k_i)}(t)$ the labour services and by $\mathbf{X}^{(k_i)}(t)$ *and* $\mathbf{S}^{(k_i)}(t)$, respectively, the column vectors of the physical quantities produced and of the stocks of capital goods required, in the whole economic system, for the production of final good $J_i^{(v)}(t)$. Of course, $i = 1, 2, \ldots$ m.

For each physical quantity $J_i^{(v)}(t)$ we may now write the corresponding sub-system,

$$\mathbf{X}^{(k_i)}(t) = (\mathbf{I} - \mathbf{A}^{\ominus})^{-1}\,\mathbf{H}\,\mathbf{J}_i^{(v)}(t) \tag{2.32}$$

from which, after substitution into (2.2), (2.3), we obtain

$$L^{(k_i)}(t) = \mathbf{a}_{[n]}(\mathbf{I} - \mathbf{A}^{\ominus})^{-1}\,\mathbf{H}\,\mathbf{J}_i^{(v)}(t) \equiv \mathbf{v}\,\mathbf{H}\,\mathbf{J}_i^{(v)}(t) \tag{2.33}$$

$$\mathbf{S}^{(k_i)}(t) = \mathbf{A}(\mathbf{I} - \mathbf{A}^{\ominus})^{-1}\,\mathbf{H}\,\mathbf{J}_i^{(v)}(t) \equiv \mathbf{H}^2\,\mathbf{J}_i^{(v)}(t), \qquad i = 1, 2, \ldots m \tag{2.34}$$

Here again scalar $L^{(k_i)}(t)$ is the quantity of labour and vector $\mathbf{S}^{(k_i)}(t)$ is the series of stocks of capital goods directly and indirectly required in the whole economic system in order to produce quantity $J_i^{(v)}(t)$ of the investment good (measured in units of vertically integrated productive capacity) required for final good *i*. Therefore vector $\mathbf{v}\,\mathbf{H}$ in (2.33), which we may call $\mathbf{v}_k$, i.e.

$$\mathbf{v}_k \equiv \mathbf{v}\,\mathbf{H} \equiv \mathbf{a}_{[n]}(\mathbf{I} - \mathbf{A}^{\ominus})^{-1}\,\mathbf{A}(\mathbf{I} - \mathbf{A}^{\ominus})^{-1} \tag{2.35}$$

is a vector of vertically integrated labour coefficients and matrix

$$\mathbf{H}^2 \equiv \mathbf{A}(\mathbf{I} - \mathbf{A}^{\ominus})^{-1}\,\mathbf{H} \equiv \mathbf{A}(\mathbf{I} - \mathbf{A}^{\ominus})^{-1}\,\mathbf{A}(\mathbf{I} - \mathbf{A}^{\ominus})^{-1} \tag{2.36}$$

in (2.34) is a matrix the columns of which represent units of vertically integrated productive capacity. Vector $\mathbf{v}_k$ and matrix $\mathbf{H}^2$ together represent the *m* vertically integrated sectors for the *m* investment goods expressed in units of vertically integrated productive capacity.

As was to be expected, the vertically integrated sectors for investment goods, expressed in physical units of vertically integrated productive capacity, have been obtained through a logical operation of vertical integration performed twice.

8 Prices of investment goods expressed in units of vertically integrated productive capacity

When investment goods are expressed in ordinary physical units, their prices are those found in section 5 (i.e. the prices of the commodities of system (2.1)–(2.4), whether they are used for consumption or for investment). But, when investment goods are expressed in physical units of vertically integrated productive capacity, their prices – which we may denote by row vector $\mathbf{p}_k \equiv [p_{k_i}]$, $i = 1, 2, \ldots m$ – are a weighted average of the prices $\mathbf{p}$ of their elementary components, namely

$$\mathbf{p}_k = \mathbf{p}\,\mathbf{H} \tag{2.37}$$

After substitution from (2.17) and (2.35), we obtain

$$\mathbf{p}_k = \mathbf{v}_k w + \mathbf{p}_k \mathbf{H}\pi \tag{2.38}$$

This is a new price system in which prices, instead of being referred to the m ordinary commodities as in system (2.17), are referred to m composite commodities obtained by reclassifying the m ordinary commodities of system (2.17) by the operation of vertical integration (i.e. by multiplication by $\mathbf{H}$). Of course, the price system (2.17) and the price system (2.38) are equivalent. They yield the same maximum rate of profit. (As may be seen, Π emerges here, as in (2.17), as the reciprocal of the maximum eigenvalue of $\mathbf{H}$). And they yield the same maximum wage rate in terms of any pre-assigned standard. If we put $\pi = 0$ and $w = 1$, the components of $\mathbf{p}_k$ again turn out to be equal to the corresponding vertically integrated labour coefficients ($\mathbf{v}_k$ in this case). For all intermediate cases in which $0 < \pi < \Pi$,

$$\mathbf{p}_k = \mathbf{v}_k (\mathbf{I} - \pi\,\mathbf{H})^{-1} w \tag{2.39}$$

which gives for $\mathbf{p}_k$ precisely the same general expression that (2.22) gives for $\mathbf{p}$. All remarks and elaborations made for $\mathbf{p}$ in section 5 could therefore be repeated here for $\mathbf{p}_k$.

9 Vertically integrated sectors of higher order

After performing the logical operation of vertical integration twice, it is natural to ask oneself whether there is any meaning in performing it a third time. The answer is straightforward. The units of vertically integrated productive capacity for investment goods, expressed in units of vertically integrated productive capacity, are themselves composite commodities. We may therefore conceptually construct the vertically integrated sectors for these newly found composite commodities. Such vertically integrated sectors clearly require a logical process of vertical integration to be performed three times. For analytical convenience, we may call such sectors 'vertically integrated sectors of the third order', and therefore we may now call vertically integrated sectors of the second order, and vertically integrated sectors of the first order, respectively, the logical constructions obtained in section 7 and in section 4.

After using subscript k to denote the vertically integrated labour coefficients of the second order, we shall for consistency use subscript k^2 to denote the vertically integrated labour coefficients of the third order, to be obtained from the second order vertically integrated labour coefficients through post-multiplication by **H**, i.e.

$$\mathbf{v}_{k^2} \equiv \mathbf{v}_k \mathbf{H} \equiv \mathbf{a}_{[n]}(\mathbf{I}-\mathbf{A}^{\ominus})^{-1}\mathbf{H}\mathbf{H} \tag{2.40}$$

No new notation is needed for the matrix of the vertically integrated productive capacities of the third order, which clearly is $\mathbf{H}^3$.

These definitions now allow us to generalise the logical process of vertical integration to any higher order we may like. We can proceed from the vertically integrated sectors of the third order to the vertically integrated sectors of the fourth order, and from those of the fourth order to those of the fifth order, of the sixth order, and so on, step by step to the vertically integrated sectors of the sth order, where s is any natural number, as high as we may choose. Analytically, each step in this process to a higher and higher order of vertical integration is simply represented by post-multiplication by matrix **H**. The m units of vertically integrated productive capacity thus play a crucial role in the whole process.

In other terms, we may characterise the m vertically integrated sectors of the sth order by (a) a vector,

$$\mathbf{v}_{k^{s-1}} \equiv \mathbf{a}_{[n]}(\mathbf{I}-\mathbf{A}^{\ominus})^{-1}\underbrace{\mathbf{H}\ldots\mathbf{H}}_{(s-1)\text{ times}} \equiv \mathbf{v}\mathbf{H}^{s-1} = \mathbf{v}_{k^{s-2}}\mathbf{H} \tag{2.41}$$

the components of which are the m sth order vertically integrated labour coefficients; and by (b) a matrix,

$$\mathbf{A}(\mathbf{I}-\mathbf{A}^{\ominus})^{-1}\underbrace{\mathbf{H}\ldots\mathbf{H}}_{(s-1)\text{ times}} \equiv \mathbf{H}\mathbf{H}^{s-1} \equiv \mathbf{H}^{s} \tag{2.42}$$

the columns of which represent the m sth order vertically integrated physical units of productive capacity.

Each series of m physical units of the sth order vertically integrated productive capacity has of course (associated with it) its own series of m prices, which for consistency we shall denote by row vector $\mathbf{p}_{k^{s-1}}$. We clearly have

$$\mathbf{p}_{k^{s-1}} = \mathbf{p}_{k^{s-2}}\mathbf{H} = (\mathbf{v}_{k^{s-2}}w + \mathbf{p}_{k^{s-2}}\mathbf{H}\pi)\mathbf{H} = \mathbf{v}_{k^{s-1}}w + \mathbf{p}_{k^{s-1}}\mathbf{H}\pi \tag{2.43}$$

from which we obtain

$$\mathbf{p}_{k^{s-1}} = \mathbf{v}_{k^{s-1}}(\mathbf{I}-\pi\mathbf{H})^{-1}w \tag{2.44}$$

a remarkable general expression, of which (2.39) and (2.22) may be regarded as particular cases. All the theoretical remarks and elaborations made for prices **p** in section 5 could now be referred to prices $\mathbf{p}_{k^{s-1}}$ in general.

10 Higher-order vertical integration and reduction of prices to a sum of weighted quantities of labour

The notion of higher-order vertical integration may at first appear to be a very highly abstract notion indeed, and one may wonder whether any application of it can be found at all. But let us analyse the price system more deeply.

By using first-order vertical integration, we have been able in section 5 to split up each price into its two basic components – wages and profits. When the wage rate itself is used as the *numéraire* – i.e. when w is put equal to unity – (2.17) actually becomes

$$\mathbf{p} = \mathbf{v} + \mathbf{p}\,\mathbf{H}\,\pi \tag{2.45}$$

which shows the two components of prices in yet another light. The total purchasing power of prices, in terms of 'labour commanded', is shown to be equal to 'labour embodied' plus a residual absorbed by profits. A solution for $\mathbf{p}$ may of course be obtained immediately:

$$\mathbf{p} = \mathbf{v}(\mathbf{I} - \pi\,\mathbf{H})^{-1} \tag{2.46}$$

as was done in section 5. But an alternative procedure may also be followed – a procedure of successive approximations, which is conceptually far more interesting from a theoretical point of view.

Residual $\mathbf{p}\,\mathbf{H}\,\pi$ contains the same prices as appear on the left-hand side of (2.45). It may therefore itself be further split up into two components. After substitution from (2.37) and (2.38) we obtain

$$\mathbf{p}\,\mathbf{H}\pi \equiv \mathbf{p}_k\pi \equiv \mathbf{v}_k\pi + \mathbf{p}_k\,\mathbf{H}\pi^2 \tag{2.47}$$

Second-order vertical integration has thereby come onto the scene. The two components of $\mathbf{p}\,\mathbf{H}\,\pi$ are shown to be (i) profits on the second-order vertically integrated labour coefficients and (ii) a second-order residual, itself containing $\mathbf{p}_k$. A chain argument has been started. Residual $\mathbf{p}_k\,\mathbf{H}\,\pi^2$ may itself be split up into two further components, by using the notion of third-order vertical integration. After substitution from (2.43) we obtain

$$\mathbf{p}_k\,\mathbf{H}\,\pi^2 \equiv \mathbf{p}_{k^2}\,\pi^2 \equiv \mathbf{v}_{k^2}\,\pi^2 + \mathbf{p}_{k^2}\,\mathbf{H}\,\pi^3 \tag{2.48}$$

which in turn shows the second-order residual as a sum of the rate of profit (at the second power) on third-order vertically integrated labour coefficients plus a third-order residual containing prices, and itself liable to be split up into two further components. This logical chain may be pursued, step by step, to whatever degree we may choose. By using the same recurring formula (2.43), we obtain

$$\begin{aligned} \mathbf{p}_{k^2}\,\mathbf{H}\,\pi^3 &\equiv \mathbf{p}_{k^3}\,\pi^3 \equiv \mathbf{v}_{k^3}\,\pi^3 + \mathbf{p}_{k^3}\,\mathbf{H}\,\pi^4 \\ &\ \vdots \\ \mathbf{p}_{k^{s-1}}\,\mathbf{H}\,\pi^s &\equiv \mathbf{p}_{k^s}\,\pi^s \equiv \mathbf{v}_{k^s}\pi^s + \mathbf{p}_{k^s}\mathbf{H}\,\pi^{s+1} \end{aligned} \tag{2.49}$$

where s is a natural number as high as we may choose. Each step may now be substituted back into the previous one, in (2.49), and then in (2.48), (2.47), and (2.45), so as to obtain

$$\mathbf{p} = \mathbf{v} + \mathbf{v}_k \pi + \mathbf{v}_{k^2} \pi^2 + \ldots \mathbf{v}_{k^s} \pi^s + \mathbf{p}_{k^s} \mathbf{H} \pi^{s+1} \tag{2.50}$$

There still remains an $(s+1)$th order residual, but this residual can be made as small as may suit one's purpose by making s as great as is necessary. In the limit, as $s \to \infty$, the residual vanishes [10] and prices entirely resolve themeselves into an infinite sum of weighted quantities of labour:

$$\mathbf{p} = \mathbf{v} + \mathbf{v}_k \pi + \mathbf{v}_{k^2} \pi^2 + \mathbf{v}_{k^3} \pi^3 + \ldots \tag{2.51}$$

The remarkable upshot of this succession is that at the first round of approximation we find the first-order vertically integrated labour coefficients, at the second round of approximation we find the second-order vertically integrated labour coefficients, at the third round the third-order vertically integrated labour coefficients, and so on. Since these rounds go on to infinity, *all* higher-order vertically integrated labour coefficients contribute to the logical process of finding the final solution.

The condition under which the infinite series (2.51) is convergent can be seen immediately upon substitution from (2.41). We obtain

$$\mathbf{p} = \mathbf{v}[\mathbf{I} + \pi\mathbf{H} + \pi^2\mathbf{H}^2 + \pi^3\mathbf{H}^3 + \ldots] \tag{2.52}$$

where within square brackets appear in succession all the higher-order units of vertically integrated productive capacity, appropriately weighted with the powers of the rate of profit. It is not difficult to see that the series is convergent provided that $\pi < (1/|\lambda|_{\max}) = \Pi$[11]. Only when $\pi = \Pi$, i.e. when all the purchasing power of prices is absorbed by profits, is the series not convergent, and prices can 'command' an infinite quantity of labour. To the

[10] The $(s+1)$th order residual, after substitution from recurring formula (2.43), may be written as

$$\mathbf{p}_{k^s} \mathbf{H} \pi^{s+1} = \mathbf{p}(\pi\mathbf{H})^{s+1}$$

Supposing $\mathbf{p} > \mathbf{0}$, a necessary and sufficient condition for this expression to vanish, as $s \to \infty$, is $\lim_{s \to \infty} (\pi\mathbf{H})^s = \mathbf{O}$. This is precisely the case if $\pi < 1/|\lambda|_{\max}$. A proof can be given by using the similarity transformation of matrix $\mathbf{H}$ called its *Jordan canonical form*, i.e. $\mathbf{F} = \mathbf{V}\mathbf{H}\mathbf{V}^{-1}$, where $\mathbf{V}$ is a square non-singular matrix and $\mathbf{F}$ is a matrix with all eigenvalues of $\mathbf{H}$ on its main diagonal and zero elsewhere, except some ones on the next diagonal. Clearly $\mathbf{F}^s = \mathbf{V}\mathbf{H}^s\mathbf{V}^{-1}$. It can now be seen that if $\pi < 1/|\lambda|_{\max}$, all elements of $(\pi\mathbf{F})^s$ tend to zero as s tends to infinity. This ensures the tendency of $(\pi\mathbf{H})^s$ to $\mathbf{O}$ as s tends to infinity.

[11] This result is an immediate consequence of what is shown in the previous footnote, the series being a geometric one. The convergence of the infinite series (2.52), when $\pi < 1/|\lambda|_{\max}$, is a particular case of a more general theorem concerning functions of matrices. For a rigorous proof of this more general theorem, see, for example, MacDuffee (1946, pp. 97ff.) and Cherubino (1957, Ch. 4).

opposite extreme is the case in which $\pi = 0$, which makes all profit-weighted addenda vanish; and prices (in terms of 'labour commanded') become equal to the only unweighted addendum in the series – classical 'labour embodied'. In between these two extremes, i.e. for $0 < \pi < \Pi$, the series is infinite and convergent. As may be noticed, the series actually corresponds to the well known iterative numerical method for obtaining the inverse of matrix $(\mathbf{I} - \pi\mathbf{H})$, which appears in (2.24). In other words, the sum of the infinite series converges to inverse matrix

$$(\mathbf{I} - \pi\mathbf{H})^{-1} \tag{2.53}$$

which means that step-by-step solution (2.51) converges to 'exact' solution (2.24).

The notions of higher-order vertically integrated labour coefficients have therefore the remarkable property of conferring an economic meaning of high theoretical relevance on each round of approximation to be carried out in the search for the price solution. They resolve the price of every commodity into a sum of profit-weighted quantities of labour.[12]

11 A 'dual' exercise

Matrix $\mathbf{H}$ and all its powers have a dual counterpart which, though not essential to the arguments of the present paper, will here be evinced explicitly, for the sake of completeness. The analytical framework of the previous pages enables us to proceed very quickly at this stage, as we can start directly with an application that brings out all the dual notions at once.

Suppose that in the economic system considered so far the labour force is growing in time at the steady percentage rate $g > 0$ per annum, i.e.

$$L(t) = L(0)\,[1 + g]^t \tag{2.54}$$

And suppose that average consumption per head is also constant through time, so that we may write $\mathbf{c}$ for the column vector of average per capita consumption coefficients. We have

$$\mathbf{C}(t) = \mathbf{c}\mu^{-1}L(t) \tag{2.55}$$

where μ is the (constant) proportion of active to total population.

We shall consider the problem of finding a solution for the equilibrium (full employment) composition of total production $\mathbf{X}(t)$ in each year t. Of course, $\mathbf{X}(t)$ must include commodities for consumption, commodities for

[12] As may be realised, expression (2.51), by being the iterative solution of (2.24), also represents an iterative solution of Marx's 'transformation problem'. So Marx was not off the track, after all, when he sensed he could start from 'values' and calculate profits directly on them. But he tried to settle the problem in one step, while what is needed is a long iterative process.

new investments (i.e. for the expansion at rate g of all fixed and circulating capital goods, whether used for the production of consumption or of investment goods) and commodities for the replacement of all used-up capital goods (whether used up by production of consumption or of investment goods), i.e.

$$\mathbf{X}(t) = \mathbf{C}(t) + g\mathbf{A}\mathbf{X}(t) + \mathbf{A}^{\ominus}\mathbf{X}(t) \tag{2.56}$$

This system of equations may of course be solved immediately for $\mathbf{X}(t)$. If we follow a slightly roundabout way, we obtain

$$\mathbf{X}(t) = (\mathbf{I} - \mathbf{A}^{\ominus})^{-1}\mathbf{C}(t) + g(\mathbf{I} - \mathbf{A}^{\ominus})^{-1}\mathbf{A}\mathbf{X}(t)$$
$$\mathbf{X}(t) = [\mathbf{I} - g(\mathbf{I} - \mathbf{A}^{\ominus})^{-1}\mathbf{A}]^{-1}(\mathbf{I} - \mathbf{A}^{\ominus})^{-1}\mathbf{C}(t) \tag{2.57}$$

We may now define a new matrix $\mathbf{G}$, i.e.

$$\mathbf{G} \equiv (\mathbf{I} - \mathbf{A}^{\ominus})^{-1}\mathbf{A} \tag{2.58}$$

which immediately appears as dual to $\mathbf{H}$. After substitution into (2.57) we may write

$$\mathbf{X}(t) = (\mathbf{I} - g\mathbf{G})^{-1}(\mathbf{I} - \mathbf{A}^{\ominus})^{-1}\mathbf{C}(t) \tag{2.59}$$

This expression concerning physical quantities is clearly dual to expression (2.24) concerning prices. In general, of course,

$$\mathbf{G} \equiv (\mathbf{I} - \mathbf{A}^{\ominus})^{-1}\mathbf{A} \neq \mathbf{A}(\mathbf{I} - \mathbf{A}^{\ominus})^{-1} \equiv \mathbf{H}$$

But $\mathbf{G}$ and $\mathbf{H}$ have exactly the same eigenvalues. In particular, $\lambda_{\max} = |\lambda|_{\max}$ is the maximum eigenvalue of both of them.

We may now proceed, as in the previous section, to finding the solution of (2.56) through the alternative procedure of successive approximations. Total production $\mathbf{X}(t)$ must certainly contain a batch of commodities, which we may call $\mathbf{X}^{I}(t)$, that provide for consumption goods $\mathbf{C}(t)$ and for all commodities that go to replace the used-up means of production for producing $\mathbf{C}(t)$, i.e.

$$\mathbf{X}^{I}(t) = \mathbf{C}(t) + \mathbf{A}^{\ominus}\mathbf{X}^{I}(t)$$
$$\mathbf{X}^{I}(t) = (\mathbf{I} - \mathbf{A}^{\ominus})^{-1}\mathbf{C}(t) \tag{2.60}$$

If the economic system were stationary (i.e. if $g = 0$), that would be all that is needed; $\mathbf{X}^{I}(t)$ would simply coincide with $\mathbf{X}(t)$ and that would be the end of the story. But we are supposing $g > 0$. Therefore, another batch of commodities, which we may call $\mathbf{X}^{II}(t)$, is needed for *expansion* of the capital goods needed for the production of $\mathbf{X}^{I}(t)$ and also for replacement of the capital goods to be used up for $\mathbf{X}^{II}(t)$, i.e.

$$\mathbf{X}^{II}(t) = g\mathbf{A}\mathbf{X}^{I}(t) + \mathbf{A}^{\ominus}\mathbf{X}^{II}(t)$$
$$\mathbf{X}^{II}(t) = g(\mathbf{I} - \mathbf{A}^{\ominus})^{-1}\mathbf{A}\mathbf{X}^{I}(t) \equiv g\mathbf{G}\mathbf{X}^{I}(t) \tag{2.61}$$

A chain argument has now been started. What has been said for $\mathbf{X}^{I}(t)$ must be repeated for $\mathbf{X}^{II}(t)$. A third batch of commodities, $\mathbf{X}^{III}(t)$, is needed for expansion at growth rate g of $\mathbf{X}^{II}(t)$ and replacement of the corresponding capital goods, i.e.

$$\mathbf{X}^{III}(t) = g\mathbf{G}\mathbf{X}^{II}(t) = g^2\mathbf{G}^2\mathbf{X}^{I}(t) \tag{2.62}$$

And so the chain argument goes on. A fourth batch of commodities, $\mathbf{X}^{IV}(t)$, is needed for the next round, and then a fifth batch of commodities, a sixth batch, a seventh, and so on to infinity:

$$\begin{aligned} \mathbf{X}^{IV}(t) &= g\mathbf{G}\mathbf{X}^{III}(t) \equiv g^3\mathbf{G}^3\mathbf{X}^{I}(t) \\ &\vdots \\ \mathbf{X}^{s}(t) &= g\mathbf{G}\mathbf{X}^{s-1}(t) \equiv g^{s-1}\mathbf{G}^{s-1}\mathbf{X}^{I}(t) \\ &\vdots \end{aligned} \tag{2.63}$$

Total production $\mathbf{X}(t)$ clearly consists of the conceptual sum of the infinite series

$$\mathbf{X}(t) = \mathbf{X}^{I}(t) + \mathbf{X}^{II}(t) + \mathbf{X}^{III}(t) + \ldots \tag{2.64}$$

or, after substitution from (2.60) – (2.63),

$$\mathbf{X}(t) = [\mathbf{I} + g\mathbf{G} + g^2\mathbf{G}^2 + \ldots](\mathbf{I} - \mathbf{A}^{\ominus})^{-1}\mathbf{C}(t) \tag{2.65}$$

where in square brackets appears the series of all the powers of matrix **G**, appropriately weighted with the powers of g. This series in clearly dual to the series in (2.52), while expression $(\mathbf{I} - \mathbf{A}^{\ominus})^{-1}\mathbf{C}(t)$ is dual to expression $\mathbf{a}_{[n]}(\mathbf{I} - \mathbf{A}^{\ominus})^{-1} \equiv \mathbf{v}$. Again, it is not difficult to see that the present series converges to inverse matrix

$$(\mathbf{I} - g\mathbf{G})^{-1} \tag{2.66}$$

provided only that $g < 1/|\lambda|_{max}$,[13] which is exactly the same condition required for convergence of the series in (2.52). As was to be expected, step-by-step solution (2.65) converges to exact solution (2.59).

The problem remains of giving matrix **G** an explicit economic interpretation. We have seen in the previous pages that the columns of matrix **H** represent the m units of vertically integrated productive capacity – each column i of **H** represents the series of heterogeneous commodities directly and indirectly required as *capital-good stocks* in the whole economic system in order to produce one physical unit of final good $i\,(i = 1, 2, \ldots m)$. The economic meaning of **G** is the exact dual counterpart. Each column j of matrix **G** represents the series of heterogeneous commodities directly and indirectly required as *flows* in the whole economic system in order to

[13] The proof may be given along the same lines as those indicated with reference to $\pi < 1/|\lambda|_{max}$ and matrix **H** in notes 10 and 11 above.

produce all the stocks of capital goods necessary for one physical unit of commodity j ($j = 1, 2, \ldots m$). While **H** is a matrix of stocks for the production of flows, **G** is a matrix of flows for the production of stocks.

And, of course, the logical process that leads to matrix **G** can be applied all over again, in the same way as the logical process leading to matrix **H** has been applied all over again in section 9. The flows represented by **G** themselves require stocks of capital goods, and the production of these stocks requires (directly and indirectly) the flows represented by $(\mathbf{I}-\mathbf{A}^{\ominus})^{-1}\,\mathbf{A}(\mathbf{I}-\mathbf{A}^{\ominus})^{-1}\,\mathbf{A} \equiv \mathbf{G}^2$. A further step back yields $\mathbf{G}^3$ and a still further step back yields $\mathbf{G}^4$, and so on. This logical process may be pursued to any higher order as we may choose, each step requiring premultiplication by **G**. All these higher-order notions represented by the powers of matrix **G**, appropriately weighted with the powers of g, then appear in the infinite series (2.65), where they confer a specific economic meaning on the successive rounds of approximation to be carried out in the search for the equilibrium growth solution.

12 Production with fixed capital goods in general

The whole analysis has been carried out so far on the simplifying assumption that a constant proportion of all fixed capital goods drops out of the production process each year. This assumption may now be relaxed. In general, the way in which fixed capital goods wear out may vary widely from one industry to another and from one type of equipment to another. But in principle there is no difficulty in representing analytically any pattern of capital-good wear and tear. All capital goods may be considered, at the beginning of each year, to be entering the production process as particular inputs. Then, when, at the end of the year, they come out of the production process one year older, they may be considered as different commodities jointly produced with the commodities they contribute to produce.

This procedure requires each industry to be decomposed into as many 'activities' as the there are 'years' in which the capital goods are used, each activity representing the same process of production but with a fixed capital good of a different age. Since each activity except one (the final one in which the capital good concerned drops out of the production process) produces jointly with the good that is produced also a capital good of a different age (which is considered as a different commodity), equality is maintained between the number of activities and the number of commodities.

Analytically, if technical coefficients remain constant through time, the technique for the whole economic system may be represented by

(i) a non-negative row vector of direct-labour coefficients $\mathbf{a}_{[n]} \equiv [a_{nj}]$, $n = m+1, j = 1, 2, \ldots m$, where j stands now for the jth activity and m

for the number of activities (and of commodities);

(ii) a non-negative square matrix of commodity-input coefficients $\mathbf{A} \equiv [a_{ij}]$, $i, j, = 1, 2, \ldots m$ (this matrix includes all capital goods, both circulating and fixed, since all of them are considered as entering the production process as inputs at the beginning of the year);

(iii) a non-negative square matrix of commodity-output coefficients $\mathbf{B} \equiv [b_{ij}]$, $i, j = 1, 2, \ldots m$ (this matrix represents all commodities existing at the end of each year – consumption goods, and capital goods of all types, new and old).

To complete the notation a convention must be chosen regarding the normalisation of all technical coefficients (i.e. regarding the scale to which each unit activity is referred). And the choice made here is to refer all the coefficients in each column (activity) j of $\mathbf{a}_{[n]}$, $\mathbf{A}$, $\mathbf{B}$, to the physical unit produced of commodity $i = j$ $(i, j = 1, 2, \ldots m)$. This procedure has the convenient property of making all elements on the main diagonal of $\mathbf{B}$ equal to unity (after suitable rearrangement of rows and columns), and therefore of allowing us to make use of all notation defined in section 2.

When production takes place with fixed capital goods in general, the physical economic system is thus represented by the system of equations

$$(\mathbf{B} - \mathbf{A})\mathbf{X}(t) = \mathbf{Y}(t) \tag{2.67}$$

$$\mathbf{a}_{[n]}\mathbf{X}(t) = L(t) \tag{2.68}$$

$$\mathbf{A}\mathbf{X}(t) = \mathbf{S}(t) \tag{2.69}$$

and prices by the system of equations

$$\mathbf{pB} = \mathbf{a}_{[n]}w + \mathbf{pA} + \mathbf{pA}\pi \tag{2.70}$$

In the particular case of constant proportion depreciation, the number of activities reduces to one in each industry; output matrix $\mathbf{B}$ reduces to identity matrix $\mathbf{I}$; and input matrix $\mathbf{A}$, which appears both in (2.67) and on the second addendum of (2.70), reduces to $\mathbf{A}^{\ominus}$. General system of production with fixed capital goods (2.67)–(2.70) reduces to the previously considered particular system (2.1)–(2.4).

13 Generalisations and restrictions

The complications of production with fixed capital goods in general make it no longer possible to give an unambiguous meaning to the notion of 'industry'. (Each industry may be made up of many activities each of which has its own labour coefficient and its own unit of direct productive capacity.) But the notion of vertically integrated sector remains unaffected by complications. The whole economic system remains susceptible to being conceptually decomposed into m sub-systems precisely in the same way as has been done in section 4. The only formal difference is that matrix $(\mathbf{B}-\mathbf{A})^{-1}$ takes the place of matrix $(\mathbf{I}-\mathbf{A}^{\ominus})^{-1}$ in expressions (2.5), (2.6) and (2.7). Therefore, for production with fixed capital goods in general, the vertically integrated labour coefficients and the physical units of vertically integrated productive capacity come to be defined respectively by the components and by the columns of

$$\mathbf{v} \equiv \mathbf{a}_{[n]}(\mathbf{B}-\mathbf{A})^{-1} \tag{2.71}$$

$$\mathbf{H} \equiv \mathbf{A}(\mathbf{B}-\mathbf{A})^{-1} \tag{2.72}$$

which represent a generalisation of (2.10) and (2.11). Similarly, the vertically integrated sectors of higher order come to be defined by

$$\mathbf{v}_{k^{s-1}} \equiv \mathbf{a}_{[n]}(\mathbf{B}-\mathbf{A})^{-1}\,\mathbf{H}^{s-1} \tag{2.73}$$

$$\mathbf{H}^{s} \equiv [\mathbf{A}(\mathbf{B}-\mathbf{A})^{-1}]^{s} \tag{2.74}$$

(where s is any positive natural number), which represent a generalisation of (2.41) and (2.42).

What becomes more difficult to do, in the case of production with fixed capital goods in general, is to devise a neat way of discriminating between the cases in which the above expressions have and the cases in which they do not have an economic meaning. In the simplified case of the previous pages the procedure is clear. Non-negativity of $\mathbf{A}^{\ominus}$ is sufficient to ensure non-negativity of $(\mathbf{I}-\mathbf{A}^{\ominus})^{-1}$. But here the fact that both $\mathbf{B}$ and $\mathbf{A}$ are non-negative *ex hypothesi* does not necessarily imply that $(\mathbf{B}-\mathbf{A})^{-1}$, and as a consequence $\mathbf{v}$, $\mathbf{H}$ and $\mathbf{G}$, should also be non-negative. Actually $\mathbf{v}$, $\mathbf{H}$ and $\mathbf{G}$ might indeed contain some negative elements and still make good economic sense. What we can say is that, since prices cannot be negative, $\mathbf{v}$ cannot be accepted as economically meaningful if it contains negative components when the rate of profit is zero. But there is nothing to prevent prices from all being positive, even if some components of $\mathbf{v}$ are negative, when the rate of profit is positive. And in this case a vector $\mathbf{v}$ with some negative components would make perfectly good economic sense. Similarly, we can say that if a particular column k of matrix $\mathbf{H}$ contains some negative components, the production of commodity k alone as a final good would require some activities to be run in reverse, and this would be impossible (and thus would have no economic sense). But commodity k might not be produced as a final good at all, or there might be no necessity to produce it alone (the sub-systems are only conceptual, not real, constructions). And in this case too a matrix $\mathbf{H}$ with some negative components would make perfectly good economic sense. A similar (but dual) argument can be developed for matrix $\mathbf{G}$.

In any case, the prices of the m commodities, expressed in ordinary physical units, continue to be given by the formulations of section 5 above, again with the only difference that more general matrix $(\mathbf{B} - \mathbf{A})$ is to replace $(\mathbf{I} - \mathbf{A}^{\ominus})$, and more general matrix $\mathbf{A}$ to replace $\mathbf{A}^{\ominus}$. Similarly, the prices of the *m* composite commodities, expressed in physical units of vertically integrated productive capacity of any order, continue to be expressed by (2.43) and (2.44), with the more general definitions of $\mathbf{v}$ and $\mathbf{H}$ given by (2.71) and (2.72). Actually, if both $\mathbf{v}$ and $\mathbf{H}$ happen to be non-negative, all remarks made in section 5 hold good in their entirety. In the case in which $\mathbf{v}$ and/or $\mathbf{H}$ do happen to contain some negative elements, what is no longer certain is that prices should remain all non-negative (i.e. economically meaningful) at *all* levels of the rate of profit; and as a consequence that the relation between w and π should always be inverse and monotonic in terms of *all* commodities. However, the remarks made in section 5 on the relationship between the classical notions of 'labour commanded' and 'labour embodied' continue to hold.

But the most interesting results of all refer to the elaborations of sections 10 and 11, which do continue to hold. The step-by-step solution for prices $\mathbf{p}$ continues to be represented by infinite series (2.51) or (2.52), with the vertically integrated units of productive capacity of all orders $\mathbf{H}$, $\mathbf{H}^2$, $\mathbf{H}^3, \ldots$, and with the vertically integrated labour coefficients of all orders, $\mathbf{v}, \mathbf{v}_k, \mathbf{v}_{k^2}, \ldots$, being defined by more general expressions (2.71)–(2.74). The condition of convergence of the series is again the same, i.e. $\pi < 1/|\lambda|_{\max}$.[14] Similarly, the step-by-step solution for total production $\mathbf{X}(t)$ continues to be expressed by the infinite series (2.65), with more general matrix $(\mathbf{B} - \mathbf{A})^{-1}$ in the place of $(\mathbf{I} - \mathbf{A}^{\ominus})^{-1}$. The series is again convergent for $g < 1/|\lambda|_{\max}$.

What must be added here is that we can no longer be certain that the eigenvalue of $\mathbf{H}$ and $\mathbf{G}$ which is maximum in modulus – i.e. $|\lambda|_{\max}$ – is also the eigenvalue which is economically relevant. If there exists a $|\lambda|_{\max} > \lambda_e$, where λ_e represents the economically relevant eigenvalue, the series (2.52) and (2.65) converge for all π and g smaller than $1/|\lambda|_{\max}$, but do not converge for π and $g \geq 1/|\lambda|_{\max}$. In other words (and with reference to π, for the sake of brevity, since the same thing can be repeated for g), if we define $\pi^* = 1/|\lambda|_{\max}$, the series (2.52) converges for all rates of profit within the range $0 < \pi < \pi^*$. In those cases in which λ in $|\lambda|_{\max}$ is a real and positive number, π^* coincides with Π, and (2.52) converges, as before, for all economically significant rates of profit up to Π (but not at, or beyond, Π). In other, more complicated cases in which $\pi^* < \pi_e$, where $\pi_e = 1/\lambda_e$, π^* becomes the new critical level of the rate of profit. The series (2.52) converges for all rates of profit up to π^*, but not at or beyond, π^*. It is, however, important to realise that $|\lambda|_{\max}$ is finite. Therefore π^* is in any case positive. This means that, from zero upwards (even in the most complicated cases of joint production!),

[14] See above, notes 10 and 11.

there always exists a range of positive rates of profit within which the series (2.52) is convergent.

The reduction of prices to a sum of weighted quantities of labour is thereby revealed to be a result of great generality. The series

$$\mathbf{p} = \mathbf{v} + \mathbf{v}_k\pi + \mathbf{v}_{k^2}\pi^2 + \mathbf{v}_{k^3}\pi^3 + \ldots \qquad (2.75)$$

where $\mathbf{v}_{k^s} \equiv \mathbf{v}[\mathbf{A}(\mathbf{B}-\mathbf{A})^{-1}]^s$, clearly represents a generalisation of Piero Sraffa's reduction of prices to *dated* quantities of labour (which is only possible in the case of single-product industries). The logical process of infinite successive vertical integration is thus revealed to be more general, and to go much deeper, than the logical process of infinite chronological decomposition. A generalisation of this type, with all its theoretical implications, is no doubt one of the most remarkable results of the present analysis.

14 Technical progress

So far in our analysis all technical coefficients have been supposed to be absolutely constant through time. But the notion of a vertically integrated sector is not only unaffected by technical change; it actually acquires greater relevance when technical change is present. In particular, the notion of a physical unit of productive capacity, by being defined with reference to the commodity that is produced, continues to make sense, as a physical unit, whatever complications technical change may cause to its composition in terms of ordinary commodities.

If there is technical progress in the economic system, we may suppose, for consistency with our previous analysis, that changes take place at discontinuous points in time. Technical coefficients may be supposed to change at the beginning of each year, and then remain constant during the year. With this convention, the whole previous analysis may simply be reinterpreted as referring to a particular year t. This means that all magnitudes considered in the previous pages must be *dated*. Not only physical quantities $\mathbf{X}(t)$, $\mathbf{Y}(t)$, $\mathbf{S}(t)$, and so on, but also prices $\mathbf{p}(t)$, technique $\mathbf{a}_{[n]}(t)$, $\mathbf{A}(t)$, $\mathbf{B}(t)$, and, as a consequence, vertically integrated sectors $\mathbf{v}(t)$, $\mathbf{H}(t)$; $\mathbf{v}_k(t)$, $\mathbf{H}^2(t)$; $\mathbf{v}_{k^2}(t)$, $\mathbf{H}^3(t)$, and so on, must be written with a time suffix.

A distinction, however, has to be made at this point between two types of technical progress.

(a) *Disembodied technical progress.* We may call 'disembodied' technical progress those improvements that do not affect the technical characteristics of capital goods, and simply enable production of larger physical quantities of commodities out of existing capital goods. Analytically this type of technical progress is expressed by the diminution of some technical coefficients and presents no difficulty. Capital goods, measured in ordinary physical units, remain the same, but their relations to capital goods measured in terms of vertically integrated productive capacities change as time goes on. This means that a particular matrix $\mathbf{H}(t)$ expressing the relation between the two types of units comes into existence for each particular year t; so that an appropriate $\mathbf{H}(t)$ has to be used in each year in order to go from the vertically integrated units to the ordinary ones.

(b) *Embodied technical progress.* We may call 'embodied' technical progress those improvements that need to be embodied into specific (new) capital goods. In particular, these improvements are supposed to be embodied into such new capital goods that render the old ones either entirely or partially obsolete, in the sense that the old capital goods, even if they continue to be used for the time being, will never be replaced by physical capital goods of the same type when they are replaced. It must therefore be specified that notation $\mathbf{a}_{[n]}(t)$, $\mathbf{A}(t)$, $\mathbf{B}(t)$ is to be understood as denoting the latest technique for the whole economic system, as this is known at the beginning of year t, so that $\mathbf{v}(t) \equiv \mathbf{a}_{[n]}(t)[\mathbf{B}(t)-\mathbf{A}(t)]^{-1}$, $\mathbf{H}(t) \equiv \mathbf{A}(t)[\mathbf{B}(t)-\mathbf{A}(t)]^{-1}$ represent the corresponding vertically integrated sectors *as they would be* if the technique of time t had been known in the past and the composition of the capital goods had thereby become evenly balanced. This means that technique $\mathbf{a}_{[n]}(t)$, $\mathbf{A}(t)$, $\mathbf{B}(t)$, and corresponding vertically integrated sectors $\mathbf{v}(t)$, $\mathbf{H}(t)$ represent *hypothetical* magnitudes in this case. The *actual* economic system, if it is to be represented in the same way, requires a different notation; for example, we may write $\bar{\mathbf{a}}_{[n]}(t)$, $\bar{\mathbf{A}}(t)$, $\bar{\mathbf{B}}(t)$, to denote the technique which is actually in operation in year t (a mixture of activities of different 'vintages'). Then $\bar{\mathbf{v}}(t) \equiv \bar{\mathbf{a}}_{[n]}(t)[\bar{\mathbf{B}}(t)-\bar{\mathbf{A}}(t)]^{-1}$, $\bar{\mathbf{H}}(t) \equiv \bar{\mathbf{A}}(t)[\bar{\mathbf{B}}(t)-\bar{\mathbf{A}}(t)]^{-1}$ will represent the corresponding *actual* vertically integrated sectors. It goes without saying that all cases considered so far, including that of embodied technical progress, may be regarded as particular cases in which hypothetical and actual vertically integrated sectors happen to coincide.

Of course, both the hypothetical and the actual vertically integrated sectors are relevant – when they are distinct from each other – but for different purposes. The *hypothetical* vertically integrated sectors are crucial to the determination of prices, as they express the latest technique. The *actual* vertically integrated sectors become relevant for the purpose of representing the physical economic system.

15 The particular case of capital goods produced by labour alone

It becomes rather simple at this point to go back to my multi-sector model of economic growth (Pasinetti, 1965) and view it as a particular case of the analysis of the previous pages. The assumption that all capital goods are made by labour alone, and that they wear out according to a constant proportion $1/T$, makes it a particular case of the analysis presented in the opening sections of the present paper. And the assumption that technical progress takes place by diminution of all labour coefficients makes it a particular case of disembodied technical progress.

Such a simplified economic system possesses many convenient properties. The vertically integrated labour coefficients for consumption goods are expressed by the sum of the direct-labour coefficients plus the quantities of labour required by replacements,[15] and the vertically integrated labour coefficients for investment goods are simply expressed by direct-labour coefficients. The vertically integrated units of productive capacity for consumption goods are expressed by unit vectors, and those for investment goods by zero vectors. Second-order vertical integration is even simpler. In consumption-good industries, the second-order vertically integrated labour coefficients for the capital goods (measured in units of vertically integrated productive capacity) coincide with their direct labour coefficients; and in investment-good industries the second-order vertically integrated labour coefficients are all zero. Finally, the second-order vertically integrated units of productive capacity are all represented by zero vectors. The vertically integrated sectors of any higher order are all zero.

In matrix notation, if we denote by $\mathbf{O}_i$ the null square matrix of the ith order, and by $\mathbf{I}_i$ the identity matrix of the ith order, the matrices defined in the previous pages (using the symbols adopted in Pasinetti, 1965) reduce to the following:

$$\mathbf{A} = \left[\begin{array}{c|c} \mathbf{O}_{n-1} & \mathbf{O}_{n-1} \\ \hline \mathbf{I}_{n-1} & \mathbf{O}_{n-1} \end{array}\right]; \qquad \mathbf{A}^{\ominus} = \left[\begin{array}{c|c} \mathbf{O}_{n-1} & \mathbf{O}_{n-1} \\ \hline \frac{1}{T}\mathbf{I}_{n-1} & \mathbf{O}_{n-1} \end{array}\right]$$

$$(\mathbf{I} - \mathbf{A}^{\ominus})^{-1} = \left[\begin{array}{c|c} \mathbf{I}_{n-1} & \mathbf{O}_{n-1} \\ \hline \frac{1}{T}\mathbf{I}_{n-1} & \mathbf{I}_{n-1} \end{array}\right];$$

$$\mathbf{H} \equiv \mathbf{A}(\mathbf{I} - \mathbf{A}^{\ominus})^{-1} = \left[\begin{array}{c|c} \mathbf{O}_{n-1} & \mathbf{O}_{n-1} \\ \hline \mathbf{I}_{n-1} & \mathbf{O}_{n-1} \end{array}\right];$$

[15] It may be useful, in this respect, to point out an oversight in Pasinetti (1965, p. 669). The vector on the left-hand side of equality (VI.3) is written with symbols a_{ni}, $i = 1, 2, \ldots n-1$, which – in the previous chapters – are used to indicate *direct* labour coefficients. What should have been done was to use a new symbol: for example, as in the present analysis, v_1, $v_2, \ldots v_{n-1}$.

$$\mathbf{H}^2 = \mathbf{O}; \qquad (\mathbf{I} - \pi\mathbf{H})^{-1} = \left[\begin{array}{c|c} \mathbf{I}_{n-1} & \mathbf{O}_{n-1} \\ \hline \pi\mathbf{I}_{n-1} & \mathbf{I}_{n-1} \end{array}\right];$$

$$\mathbf{a}_{[n]}(t) = [a_{n1}(t), a_{n2}(t), \ldots a_{n,n-1}(t); a_{nk_1}(t) \ldots a_{nk_{n-1}}(t)];$$

$$\mathbf{v}(t) \equiv \mathbf{a}_{[n]}(t)(\mathbf{I} - \mathbf{A}^{\ominus})^{-1} = [(a_{n1}(t) + \frac{1}{T}a_{nk_1}(t)) \ldots (a_{n,n-1}(t)$$

$$+ \frac{1}{T}a_{nk_{n-1}}(t)) \quad a_{nk_1}(t) \ldots a_{nk_{n-1}}(t)];$$

$$\mathbf{v}_k(t) \equiv \mathbf{v}(t)\mathbf{H} = [a_{nk_1}(t), a_{nk_2}(t), \ldots a_{nk_{n-1}}(t); 0, 0, \ldots 0];$$

$$\mathbf{v}_{k^2}(t) \equiv \mathbf{v}_k(t)\mathbf{H} = [0, 0, \ldots 0]$$

By substituting these particular expressions into (2.22) or (2.51), we obtain:

$$p_i(t) = \left[a_{ni}(t) + \left(\frac{1}{T} + \pi\right) a_{nk_i}(t) \right] w(t)$$

$$p_{k_i}(t) = a_{nk_i}(t) w(t), \qquad i = 1, 2, \ldots n-1$$

which are precisely the 'solutions' for prices given in the original formulation.[16]

[16] See Pasinetti (1965, p. 597). A more complex case is considered on pp. 598–601, in which the capital goods produced by the investment-good industries are supposed to be used both in the consumption-good industries and in the investment-good industries, given a proportion γ_i, $i = 1, 2, \ldots n-1$, between their productive capacities for the two types of industries. In this case, the matrices defined here (again by using the symbols of Pasinetti (1965), and supposing for notational simplicity that T_k, T, γ, π are all uniform) reduce to the following:

$$\mathbf{A} = \left[\begin{array}{c|c} \mathbf{O}_{n-1} & \mathbf{O}_{n-1} \\ \hline \mathbf{I}_{n-1} & \gamma\mathbf{I}_{n-1} \end{array}\right]; \qquad \mathbf{A}^{\ominus} = \left[\begin{array}{c|c} \mathbf{O}_{n-1} & \mathbf{O}_{n-1} \\ \hline \frac{1}{T}\mathbf{I}_{n-1} & \gamma\frac{1}{T_k}\mathbf{I}_{n-1} \end{array}\right];$$

$$(\mathbf{I} - \mathbf{A}^{\ominus})^{-1} = \left[\begin{array}{c|c} \mathbf{I}_{n-1} & \mathbf{O}_{n-1} \\ \hline \frac{1}{T}\frac{T_k}{T_k - \gamma}\mathbf{I}_{n-1} & \frac{T_k}{T_k - \gamma}\mathbf{I}_{n-1} \end{array}\right];$$

$$\mathbf{a}_{[n]}(t) = [a_{n1}(t), a_{n2}(t), \ldots a_{n,n-1}(t); a_{nk_1}(t) \ldots a_{nk_{n-1}}(t)];$$

$$\mathbf{A}(\mathbf{I} - \mathbf{A}^{\ominus})^{-1} \equiv \mathbf{H} = \left[\begin{array}{c|c} \mathbf{O}_{n-1} & \mathbf{O}_{n-1} \\ \hline \left(1 + \frac{1}{T}\gamma\frac{T_k}{T_k - \gamma}\right)\mathbf{I}_{n-1} & \gamma\frac{T_k}{T_k - \gamma}\mathbf{I}_{n-1} \end{array}\right];$$

$$(\mathbf{I} - \pi\mathbf{H}) = \left[\begin{array}{c|c} \mathbf{I}_{n-1} & \mathbf{O}_{n-1} \\ \hline -\pi\left(1 + \frac{1}{T}\gamma\frac{T_k}{T_k - \gamma}\right)\mathbf{I}_{n-1} & \left(1 - \pi\gamma\frac{T_k}{T_k - \gamma}\right)\mathbf{I}_{n-1} \end{array}\right];$$

16 New analytical possibilities for dynamic analysis

But the use of vertically integrated sectors is also aimed at the wider purpose of opening up new possibilities for dynamic analysis.

In the general case of production of all commodities by means of fixed capital goods and of technical progress of the most general type, the relation between ordinary physical capital goods and capital goods in units of productive capacity breaks down at the end of each period and the problem arises of what meaning one can give to the physical operation of replacement of the capital goods. Clearly, 'replacement' ceases to have any meaningful sense in terms of ordinary physical units. On the other hand, 'replacement' does continue to make sense in terms of physical units of productive capacity. Even in the midst of a maze of physical and qualitative changes, we may indeed continue to say that replacement of used-up capital goods has taken place if, at the end of each period, the economic system has recovered the same productive capacities as it had at the beginning.

The analytical consequences of these remarks are far-reaching. With technical progress, any relation in which capital goods are expressed in ordinary physical units becomes useless for dynamic analysis. But relations expressed in physical units of productive capacity continue to hold through time, and actually acquire an autonomy of their own, quite independently of their changing composition. At the same time, the elaborations of the previous pages provide the way for a return to the ordinary physical units any time that this is necessary, within each period t. Of course, a different result will be obtained for each single period.

This property seems to me to confer on the logical process of vertical integration an analytical relevance for dynamic investigations which perhaps has not been completely realised as yet. The vertically integrated sectors seem to belong to that category of synthetic notions which, once obtained, contribute to reduce in many directions the very order of magnitude of the analytical difficulties. An example of this is given after all by the multi-sector model of economic growth, from which the present

---

$$(\mathbf{I}-\pi\mathbf{H})^{-1} = \left[\begin{array}{c|c} \mathbf{I}_{n-1} & \mathbf{O}_{n-1} \\ \hline \frac{\pi}{T}\frac{\gamma T_k+(T_k-\gamma)T}{T_k-\gamma-\pi\gamma T_k}\mathbf{I}_{n-1} & \frac{T_k-\gamma}{T_k-\gamma-\pi\gamma T_k}\mathbf{I}_{n-1} \end{array}\right];$$

$$\mathbf{v} = \Big[\Big(a_{n1}(t)+\frac{1}{T}\frac{T_k}{T_k-\gamma}a_{nk_1}(t)\Big)\ldots\Big(a_{n,n-1}(t)+\frac{1}{T}\frac{T_k}{T_k-\gamma}a_{nk_{n-1}}(t)\Big)$$

$$\frac{T_k}{T_k-\gamma}a_{nk_1}(t)\ldots\frac{T_k}{T_k-\gamma}a_{nk_{n-1}}(t)\Big]$$

Here again, as can easily be checked, post-multiplication of $\mathbf{v}$ by $(\mathbf{I}-\pi\mathbf{H})^{-1}$, and by w, yields the expressions for prices given in Pasinetti (1965, p. 600).

analysis has started, which has permitted the investigation of a whole series of structural dynamic relations – something which would have been impossible to do with any traditional growth model.

It may not be too much to hope that a better understanding, and a more explicit utilisation, of the logical process of vertical integration will help to overcome the widely recognised failure of modern economic theory to come to grips with the analytical difficulties of technical change.

References

Cherubino, S., *Calcolo delle matrici* (Rome: Cremonese, 1957).

Gantmacher, F. R., *The Theory of Matrices* (New York: Chelsea, 1959).

Leontief, W. W., *The Structure of American Economy 1919–1939* (New York: Oxford University Press, 1951).

Leontief, W. W., 'Domestic Production and Foreign Trade: The American Capital Position Re-examined', *Proceedings of the American Philosophical Society*, XCVII, no. 4 (1953) 332–49.

Leontief, W. W., 'Factor Proportions and the Structure of American Trade: Further Theoretical and Empirical Analysis', *Review of Economics and Statistics*, XXXVIII (1956) 386–407.

MacDuffee, C. C., *The Theory of Matrices* (New York: Chelsea, 1946).

Pasinetti, L. L., 'A New Theoretical Approach to the Problems of Economic Growth', *Pontificiae academiae scientiarum scripta varia*, no. 28 (1965) 571–696; repr. in *The Econometric Approach to Development Planning* (Amsterdam: North-Holland, 1965).

Smith, Adam, *An Inquiry into the Nature and Causes of the Wealth of Nations* (1776), ed. E. Cannan (London: Methuen, 1904).

Sraffa, P., *Production of Commodities by Means of Commodities* (Cambridge: Cambridge University Press, 1960).

Walras, Léon, *Elements of Pure Economics* (1874–7), ed. W. Jaffé (London: Allen & Unwin, 1965).

CHAPTER THREE

Basics, Non-Basics and Joint Production[1]

IAN STEEDMAN

1 Introduction

The distinction between basic and non-basic commodities plays a central role in the analysis presented by Sraffa in his *Production of Commodities by Means of Commodities* (1960). Thus, the conditions of production of basics are said to play an essential part in the determination of prices and the rate of profit, while those of non-basics do not; it follows, in turn, that the effects of taxes and of changes in methods of production are said to depend on whether they relate to basic or to non-basic commodities (see, for example, ibid., sections 6 and 65). It may therefore be of interest to examine rather closely the general formulation of the distinction between basics and non-basics which Sraffa presents in the course of his discussion of joint production.

While Sraffa represents the inputs and outputs for a given productive process by the corresponding *rows* of the input and output matrices, the more common practice of representing them by the *columns* will be adopted here. Subject to this slight change, Sraffa's general formulation of the distinction between basic and non-basic commodities is as follows (ibid., section 60):

> In a system of k productive processes and k commodities (no matter whether produced singly or jointly) we say that a commodity or more generally a group of n linked commodities (where n must be smaller than k and may be equal to 1) are non-basic if of the k [columns] (formed by the $2n$ quantities in which they appear in each process) not more than n

[1] I should like to thank Professor L. L. Pasinetti for encouragement and helpful discussion concerning this essay. It may be noted here that the ideas contained in this essay were first presented to a Round Table at Trinity College, Cambridge, in September 1976, as part of a much longer paper. One version of the present note was then published in the original Italian edition of the present book, and a second version, in English, was published in the *Economic Journal* of June 1977. The present essay is slightly different from both these earlier versions.

[columns] are independent, the others being linear combinations of these.

2 Pasinetti's direct and indirect capital matrix

In his essay reprinted as Chapter 2 above, Pasinetti introduced the concept of a 'direct and indirect capital matrix', the jth column of which is the vector of capital stocks required, directly or indirectly, for the production of one unit of *net* output of commodity j (see Ch. 2, sections 4 and 13). If the inputs and outputs for a given productive process are represented by the corresponding columns of matrices **A** and **B** respectively, then it is easily shown (see Ch. 2, section 4) that the direct and indirect capital matrix, **H**, is given by[2]

$$\mathbf{H} \equiv \mathbf{A}(\mathbf{B}-\mathbf{A})^{-1} \tag{3.1}$$

3 Basics, non-basics and the H matrix

In a single-product system commodities can be so numbered that the **A** matrix takes the form

$$\mathbf{A} \equiv \begin{bmatrix} \mathbf{A}_1 & \mathbf{A}_2 \\ \mathbf{0} & \mathbf{A}_4 \end{bmatrix}$$

where matrix $\mathbf{A}_1$ refers to basics, and $\mathbf{B} \equiv \mathbf{I}$. Then the **H** matrix, since $\mathbf{H} \equiv \mathbf{A}(\mathbf{I}-\mathbf{A})^{-1} \equiv \mathbf{A}+\mathbf{A}^2+\mathbf{A}^3+\ldots$, here takes the form

$$\mathbf{H} \equiv \begin{bmatrix} \mathbf{H}_1 & \mathbf{H}_2 \\ \mathbf{0} & \mathbf{H}_4 \end{bmatrix}$$

where $\mathbf{H}_1 = \mathbf{A}_1(\mathbf{I}-\mathbf{A}_1)^{-1}$ and $\mathbf{H}_4 = \mathbf{A}_4(\mathbf{I}-\mathbf{A}_4)^{-1}$. While no comparable reordering can be done for the **A** and **B** matrices of a joint-production system, since they are commodity/process matrices and not commodity/commodity matrices, it is natural to ask whether the corresponding **H** matrix, which *is* a commodity/commodity matrix, might not exhibit the classification of commodities into basics and non-basics in just the same way as occurs with single products.

Following the argument of Manara (see above Ch. 1, section 6), reorder **A** and **B** so that the first j rows refer to basics and the last m rows to non-basics and so that the last m columns are linearly independent in their last m rows.[3]

[2] It will be assumed throughout that $(\mathbf{B}-\mathbf{A})$ is non-singular. See also note 3 and the appendix to this essay.

[3] Read strictly, Sraffa's general definition, quoted above, implies only that 'not more' than m of the last columns are linearly independent in their last m rows, and, indeed, in the footnote to his general definition, Sraffa says explicitly that 'less than' m columns could be linearly independent. There is good reason to think, however, that Manara is right to insist on there being *exactly* m such columns; see the appendix to this essay.

Now, writing

$$\mathbf{A} \equiv \begin{bmatrix} \mathbf{A}_1 & \mathbf{A}_2 \\ \mathbf{A}_3 & \mathbf{A}_4 \end{bmatrix}, \qquad \mathbf{B} \equiv \begin{bmatrix} \mathbf{B}_1 & \mathbf{B}_2 \\ \mathbf{B}_3 & \mathbf{B}_4 \end{bmatrix}$$

Sraffa's general definition of non-basics implies that there exists a matrix $\mathbf{T}$ such that $\mathbf{A}_3 = \mathbf{A}_4\mathbf{T}$ and $\mathbf{B}_3 = \mathbf{B}_4\mathbf{T}$. Defining

$$\mathbf{M} \equiv \begin{bmatrix} \mathbf{I}_j & \mathbf{0} \\ -\mathbf{T} & \mathbf{I}_m \end{bmatrix}$$

it follows that

$$\mathbf{A}\mathbf{M} = \begin{bmatrix} \mathbf{A}_1 - \mathbf{A}_2\mathbf{T} & \mathbf{A}_2 \\ \mathbf{0} & \mathbf{A}_4 \end{bmatrix}, \qquad \mathbf{B}\mathbf{M} = \begin{bmatrix} \mathbf{B}_1 - \mathbf{B}_2\mathbf{T} & \mathbf{B}_2 \\ \mathbf{0} & \mathbf{B}_4 \end{bmatrix}$$

Now, since $\mathbf{H}(\mathbf{B} - \mathbf{A}) \equiv \mathbf{A}$, we have $\mathbf{H}(\mathbf{BM} - \mathbf{AM}) \equiv \mathbf{AM}$, which leads easily to

$$\mathbf{H} \equiv \left[\begin{array}{c|c} (\mathbf{A}_1 - \mathbf{A}_2\mathbf{T})(\mathbf{C}_1 - \mathbf{C}_2\mathbf{T})^{-1} & [\mathbf{A}_2 - (\mathbf{A}_1 - \mathbf{A}_2\mathbf{T})(\mathbf{C}_1 - \mathbf{C}_2\mathbf{T})^{-1}\mathbf{C}_2]\mathbf{C}_4^{-1} \\ \hline \mathbf{0} & \mathbf{A}_4\mathbf{C}_4^{-1} \end{array}\right] \tag{3.2}$$

where $\mathbf{C}_i \equiv (\mathbf{B}_i - \mathbf{A}_i)$.

It will be seen immediately from (3.2) that Sraffa's general definition of basics and non-basics does indeed imply that, after suitable relabelling of commodities, the $\mathbf{H}$ matrix has an $m \times j$ block of zeros in the lower left-hand corner ($\mathbf{H}_3 = \mathbf{0}$). In this respect, then, the similarity with the $\mathbf{H}$ matrix for the single-product case is very strong.

The similarity is also strong with respect to the lower right-hand corner (the matrix $\mathbf{H}_4$), since $\mathbf{H}_4 \equiv \mathbf{A}_4\mathbf{C}_4^{-1}$ in both the single-products and the joint-products case. On the other hand, while $\mathbf{H}_1 \equiv \mathbf{A}_1\mathbf{C}_1^{-1}$ in the single-products case, this is *not* so, in general,[4] with joint production. In the general joint-production case, the sub-matrix $\mathbf{H}_1$ depends on $\mathbf{T}$ and it therefore depends on the conditions of production of the non-basic commodities.

In relation to joint production, Sraffa writes (1960, section 57) that 'The criterion previously adopted for distinguishing between basic and non-basic products (namely whether they do, or do not, enter directly or indirectly the means of production of all commodities) now fails. . . .' It seems natural at this point to suggest that that criterion *can be retained*,

[4] It will be clear that $(\mathbf{A}_1 - \mathbf{A}_2\mathbf{T})(\mathbf{C}_1 - \mathbf{C}_2\mathbf{T})^{-1} = (\mathbf{A}_1\mathbf{C}_1^{-1})$ if and only if $(\mathbf{A}_2\mathbf{T}) = (\mathbf{A}_1\mathbf{C}_1^{-1})\cdot(\mathbf{C}_2\mathbf{T})$: a sufficient but not necessary condition is thus obviously that $\mathbf{T} = 0$, i.e. $\mathbf{A}_3 = \mathbf{B}_3 = 0$.

provided only that it is thought of in terms of the **H** matrix. Indeed, one might perhaps *define* basics as those commodities which appear in the $\mathbf{H}_1$ sub-matrix when **H** has been reduced as far as possible by suitable relabelling of commodities. This definition reduces to that in terms of the sub-matrix $\mathbf{A}_1$ in the single-products case and surely has far greater intuitive appeal than Sraffa's formulation of the general definition in terms of linear dependence and independence.

4 Prices and the rate of profit

Sraffa's argument (1960, section 65) that, even with joint production, 'basics have an essential part in the determination of prices and the rate of profit, while non-basics have none' can now be considered.

Consider first the case in which wages are zero, so that the row vector of prices, **p**, and the rate of profit, R, must satisfy

$$(1+R)\mathbf{p}\,\mathbf{A} = \mathbf{p}\,\mathbf{B}$$

or $$R\,\mathbf{p}\,\mathbf{A} = \mathbf{p}(\mathbf{B}-\mathbf{A})$$

or $$R\,\mathbf{p}\,\mathbf{H} = \mathbf{p} \tag{3.3}$$

from (3.1). Dividing the price vector into two parts, referring to basics (*b*) and non-basics (*nb*) respectively, and partitioning **H** as in (3.2), (3.3) may be rewritten as

$$R(\mathbf{p}^b, \mathbf{p}^{nb})\begin{bmatrix}\mathbf{H}_1 & \mathbf{H}_2 \\ \mathbf{0} & \mathbf{H}_4\end{bmatrix} = (\mathbf{p}^b, \mathbf{p}^{nb}) \tag{3.4}$$

Now Sraffa considers (ibid.) a particular case which amounts to supposing that, *everything else being unaltered*, the output of some non-basic decreases in the same proportion in every process. In the terminology used above, one row in $\mathbf{B}_3$, $\mathbf{B}_4$ changes by a scalar multiple, with everything else constant, so that **T** is unchanged. Hence $\mathbf{H}_1$ is unchanged. It is then immediately apparent from (3.4) that R and $\mathbf{p}^b$ are unaltered.

However, to say that R and $\mathbf{p}^b$ do not *change* when a very *particular* change occurs in the production conditions of a non-basic is hardly to say that non-basics play no role in determining R and $\mathbf{p}^b$. Thus, **T** may not have *changed* but it is still present in $\mathbf{H}_1$, and the values of R and $\mathbf{p}^b$ most certainly do depend on **T** and thus on the production conditions of non-basics. Or, to put the same point somewhat differently, if the output of a given non-basic decreased in every process, but by a different proportionate amount process by process, then, *ceteris paribus*, **T** would change, in general, and hence $\mathbf{H}_1$, R and $\mathbf{p}^b$ would change. Thus, with joint production, it would appear that non-basics do have an essential part in the determination of prices and the rate of profits.

(Contrary to what Sraffa appears to suggest in the final sentence of section 65 of his book, the system of basic equations [section 62] *does* depend on the quantities of non-basics, since the linear transformations, by means of which the non-basics are eliminated, themselves so depend.)

It does not follow, however, that the distinction between basics and non-basics has become an empty one. It is still the case that, *given* the conditions of production (of both basics and non-basics), the relation between the prices of basics and the rate of profit can be considered independently of the relation between the prices of non-basics and the rate of profit, while the converse is not true. Thus, (3.4) can be generalised as follows: let wages be positive and paid at the end of the production cycle; let r be the rate of profit; let $\mathbf{p}$ be a row vector of labour-commanded prices and $\mathbf{v}$ a row vector of direct and indirect labour use (Marxian values). It can then be shown (see above, Ch. 2, sections 12 and 13) that, in partitioned form, (3.4) is generalised to[5]

$$(\mathbf{p}^b, \mathbf{p}^{nb}) = (\mathbf{v}^b, \mathbf{v}^{nb}) + r(\mathbf{p}^b, \mathbf{p}^{nb}) \begin{bmatrix} \mathbf{H}_1 & \mathbf{H}_2 \\ \mathbf{0} & \mathbf{H}_4 \end{bmatrix} \tag{3.5}$$

It will be seen from (3.5) that

$$\mathbf{p}^b = \mathbf{v}^b(\mathbf{I} - r\,\mathbf{H}_1)^{-1} \tag{3.6}$$

$$\mathbf{p}^{nb} = (\mathbf{v}^{nb} + r\,\mathbf{p}^b\,\mathbf{H}_2)(\mathbf{I} - r\,\mathbf{H}_4)^{-1} \tag{3.7}$$

Thus, the functional relation between $\mathbf{p}^b$ and r can be examined independently of that between $\mathbf{p}^{nb}$ and r (equation 3.6) but the latter depends on the former (equation 3.7): it is not, of course, implied that the relation between $\mathbf{p}^b$ and r is independent of the conditions of production of non-basics, since both $\mathbf{v}^b$ and $\mathbf{H}_1$ depend on $\mathbf{T}$.

5 Conclusion

It has been suggested that the intuitively appealing idea of a basic commodity as a commodity which enters, directly or indirectly, the production of every commodity can be retained, in the general joint-products case, provided that it is now interpreted in terms of the Pasinetti **H**

[5] Relation (3.5) can, of course, be written in unpartitioned form as:

$$\mathbf{p} = \mathbf{v} + r\,\mathbf{p}\,\mathbf{H}$$

It is interesting to note that this relation implies the existence of 'families' of joint-production systems, each member of a family having a different **A, B, a** (**a** being the row vector of direct-labour inputs) but the *same* **H, v** and hence the *same* economic properties. System j will belong to the same family as system 1 if and only if $\mathbf{A}_j\mathbf{B}_j^{-1} = \mathbf{A}_1\mathbf{B}_1^{-1}$ and $\mathbf{a}_j\mathbf{B}_j^{-1} = \mathbf{a}_1\mathbf{B}_1^{-1}$. (Cf. Schefold, 1971, theorem 3.1; Schefold also makes the point [ibid., p. 11] that the prices of basics have a logical priority over those of non-basics.)

matrix. After appropriate relabelling, the **H** matrix will exhibit the basic commodities in an irreducible square matrix in the top left-hand corner, while the lower left and right-hand sub-matrices, referring to non-basics, will be $\mathbf{H}_3 \equiv \mathbf{0}$ and $\mathbf{H}_4 \equiv \mathbf{A}_4 \mathbf{C}_4^{-1}$, just as in the single-products case. (It must be noted, however, that both $\mathbf{H}_1$ and $\mathbf{H}_2$ depend on the matrix **T** and hence on the production conditions of non-basics.) It has been shown, finally, that in general non-basics do have a role in the determination of prices and the rate of profit but that the prices of basics still have a logical priority over the prices of non-basics.

Appendix

The purpose of this appendix is to indicate why Manara was correct to postulate the existence of a number of linearly independent columns *exactly equal* to the number of non-basics, rather than allowing the number of such columns to be merely less than or equal to the number of non-basics, as is suggested by Sraffa.

Using the notation introduced above, consider the simple case in which $\mathbf{A}_3 = \mathbf{B}_3 = \mathbf{T} = \mathbf{0}$. Taking a feasible rate of profit, $\bar{r}$, as given, the labour-commanded prices must satisfy the relations

$$(1+\bar{r})\,\mathbf{p}^b \mathbf{A}_1 + \mathbf{a}_1 = \mathbf{p}^b \mathbf{B}_1 \qquad (3A.1)$$

$$(1+\bar{r})(\mathbf{p}^b \mathbf{A}_2 + \mathbf{p}^{nb} \mathbf{A}_4) + \mathbf{a}_2 = \mathbf{p}^b \mathbf{B}_2 + \mathbf{p}^{nb} \mathbf{B}_4 \qquad (3A.2)$$

where $\mathbf{a}_1$ refers to the first j processes and $\mathbf{a}_2$ to the last m. The prices $\mathbf{p}^b$ are determined by (3A.1) as

$$\mathbf{p}^b = \mathbf{a}_1 [\mathbf{B}_1 - (1+\bar{r})\,\mathbf{A}_1]^{-1}$$

and (3A.2) then yields

$$\mathbf{p}^{nb}[\mathbf{B}_4 - (1+\bar{r})\,\mathbf{A}_4] = \mathbf{a}_2 - \mathbf{p}^b [\mathbf{B}_2 - (1+\bar{r})\,\mathbf{A}_2] \qquad (3A.3)$$

Now, the matrix on the left-hand side of (3A.3) is, of course, a square $m \times m$ matrix. If, following Manara, we take that matrix to contain m linearly independent columns, then it can be inverted to solve (3A.3) for the prices $\mathbf{p}^{nb}$. On the other hand, if, following Sraffa, we allow the possibility that the rank of $[\mathbf{B}_4 - (1+\bar{r})\,\mathbf{A}_4]$ should be *less than m*, then either (3A.3) will have no solution at all for $\mathbf{p}^{nb}$, or solutions, if they do exist, will not be unique. Note, in particular, that if $[\mathbf{B} - (1+\bar{r})\,\mathbf{A}]$ were singular for $\bar{r} = 0$ – which is what Sraffa seems to allow – then neither the **H** matrix nor the values of non-basics, $\mathbf{v}^{nb}$, would be defined.

References

Schefold, B., *Theorie der Kuppelproduktion* (*Mr. Sraffa on Joint Production*) (Basel: privately printed, 1971).

Sraffa, P., *Production of Commodities by Means of Commodities* (Cambridge: Cambridge University Press, 1960).

CHAPTER FOUR

A Note on Basics, Non-Basics and Joint Production

LUIGI L. PASINETTI

1 The definitions of Manara and Steedman

The general definition of basic and non-basic commodities is given by Sraffa (1960, section 60) and has been formalised by Manara (Ch. 1, section 6).

Given the general price system

$$\mathbf{pB} = \mathbf{pA}(1+r) + \mathbf{a}_{[n]} w \tag{4.1}$$

(where $\mathbf{p}$ is the row vector of prices; $\mathbf{B}$ is the non-negative, square, output matrix of joint coefficients; $\mathbf{A}$ is the non-negative, square, input matrix of coefficients; $\mathbf{a}_{[n]}$ is the non-negative row vector of labour coefficients; and, finally, r and w are scalars representing, respectively, the rate of profit and the unit wage rate), Manara has demonstrated that, if we imagine the matrices $\mathbf{A}$ and $\mathbf{B}$ to be partitioned into four sub-matrices,

$$\mathbf{A} = \begin{bmatrix} \mathbf{A}_{11} & \mathbf{A}_{12} \\ \mathbf{A}_{21} & \mathbf{A}_{22} \end{bmatrix}, \qquad \mathbf{B} = \begin{bmatrix} \mathbf{B}_{11} & \mathbf{B}_{12} \\ \mathbf{B}_{21} & \mathbf{B}_{22} \end{bmatrix} \tag{4.2}$$

(where $\mathbf{A}_{11}, \mathbf{B}_{11}$ are square sub-matrices of order j, and $\mathbf{A}_{22}, \mathbf{B}_{22}$ are square sub-matrices of order m), the commodities corresponding to the last m rows of the two matrices $\mathbf{A}$ and $\mathbf{B}$ are non-basic if there exists a matrix $\mathbf{T}$, of order $m \times j$, such that

$$\mathbf{A}_{21} = \mathbf{A}_{22}\mathbf{T}, \qquad \mathbf{B}_{21} = \mathbf{B}_{22}\mathbf{T} \tag{4.3}$$

The demonstration given by Manara is based on the definition of an auxiliary matrix $\mathbf{M}$, defined as follows:

$$\mathbf{M} = \begin{bmatrix} \mathbf{I}_j & \mathbf{0} \\ -\mathbf{T} & \mathbf{I}_m \end{bmatrix} \tag{4.4}$$

where $\mathbf{I}_j$ and $\mathbf{I}_m$ are identity matrices of orders j and m respectively (see Ch. 1, section 6).

Steedman has subsequently demonstrated, by means of the same auxiliary matrix, that it is possible to give an alternative definition of basic and non-basic commodities by making use of the matrix **H**, which in Chapter 2 above I have defined as

$$\mathbf{H} = \mathbf{A}(\mathbf{B} - \mathbf{A})^{-1} \tag{4.5}$$

This, as demonstrated above (Ch. 2, section 4), has a well defined economic meaning – namely, the meaning of matrix of the vertically integrated units of productive capacity. Steedman points out (Ch. 3, section 3) that, if by means of the appropriate interchanges of rows and corresponding columns, it is possible to reduce the matrix **H** to the form

$$\mathbf{H} = \begin{bmatrix} \mathbf{H}_{11} & \mathbf{H}_{12} \\ \mathbf{0} & \mathbf{H}_{22} \end{bmatrix} \tag{4.6}$$

(where $\mathbf{H}_{11}$ is square of order j and $\mathbf{H}_{22}$ is square of order m), then the commodities corresponding to the last m rows of **H** are non-basic commodities, while the others are basic commodities.

However, matrix **H** is not the sole matrix, in the general scheme of joint production, that permits the definition of basic and non-basic commodities by means of the simple notion of a reducible matrix. I shall now demonstrate that there exists another matrix which possesses that property.

2 A third definition

By post-multiplying system (4.1) by inverse matrix $\mathbf{B}^{-1}$, we obtain[1]

$$\mathbf{p} = \mathbf{p}\,\mathbf{A}\,\mathbf{B}^{-1}(1+r) + \mathbf{a}_{[n]}\,\mathbf{B}^{-1}\,\mathbf{w} \tag{4.7}$$

i.e. a system which is formally similar to the price system for the case of single production (with the substantial, but not formal, difference that matrix $\mathbf{AB}^{-1}$ takes the place of matrix **A** and vector $\mathbf{a}_{[n]}\,\mathbf{B}^{-1}$ takes the place of vector $\mathbf{a}_{[n]}$; $\mathbf{AB}^{-1}$ and $\mathbf{a}_{[n]}\,\mathbf{B}^{-1}$ each reducing to **A** and $\mathbf{a}_{[n]}$, respectively, in the special case in which $\mathbf{B} = \mathbf{I}$).

Suppose now that that last m commodities of the matrices **A** and **B** are non-basic. Using matrix **M**, we can write

$$\mathbf{A}\,\mathbf{B}^{-1}\mathbf{BM} = \mathbf{AM}$$

$$\mathbf{A}\,\mathbf{B}^{-1} = \mathbf{AM}\,(\mathbf{BM})^{-1}$$

[1] The sole condition required is that matrix **B** is non-singular, which is normally the case. (Only in the case of really unusual joint production would the columns of **B** be linearly dependent.) Yet, this is a slightly more restrictive condition than the analogous condition – i.e. non-singularity of the matrix $(\mathbf{B} - \mathbf{A})$ – required in the case of the matrix **H**.

Then, by using the method of inversion by parts, we have

$$\mathbf{AM} = \begin{bmatrix} \mathbf{A}_{11} - \mathbf{A}_{12}\mathbf{T} & \mathbf{A}_{12} \\ \mathbf{0} & \mathbf{A}_{22} \end{bmatrix}$$

$$(\mathbf{BM})^{-1} = \begin{bmatrix} (\mathbf{B}_{11} - \mathbf{B}_{12}\mathbf{T})^{-1} & -(\mathbf{B}_{11} - \mathbf{B}_{12}\mathbf{T})^{-1}\mathbf{B}_{12}\mathbf{B}_{22}^{-1} \\ \mathbf{0} & \mathbf{B}_{22}^{-1} \end{bmatrix}$$

and, finally,

$$\mathbf{AB}^{-1} = \left[\begin{array}{c|c} (\mathbf{A}_{11} - \mathbf{A}_{12}\mathbf{T})(\mathbf{B}_{11} - \mathbf{B}_{12}\mathbf{T})^{-1} & [\mathbf{A}_{12} - (\mathbf{A}_{11} - \mathbf{A}_{12}\mathbf{T})(\mathbf{B}_{11} - \mathbf{B}_{12}\mathbf{T})^{-1}\mathbf{B}_{12}]\mathbf{B}_{22}^{-1} \\ \hline \mathbf{0} & \mathbf{A}_{22}\mathbf{B}_{22}^{-1} \end{array}\right] \tag{4.8}$$

Hence, matrix $\mathbf{AB}^{-1}$ is a reducible matrix containing a null sub-matrix of order $m \times j$ in the lower left-hand corner. Inserting (4.8) into (4.7), we can see immediately that the prices of the first j commodities do not depend on the prices of the subsequent m commodities, while the contrary is not true.

We may therefore conclude that, in the general case, the distinction between basic and non-basic commodities may alternatively be presented in the following way. If, by means of appropriate interchanges of rows and corresponding columns, it is possible to reduce the matrix $\mathbf{AB}^{-1}$ to the form

$$\mathbf{AB}^{-1} = \begin{bmatrix} (\mathbf{AB}^{-1})_{11} & (\mathbf{AB}^{-1})_{12} \\ \mathbf{0} & (\mathbf{AB}^{-1})_{22} \end{bmatrix} \tag{4.9}$$

(where $(\mathbf{AB}^{-1})_{11}$ is a square sub-matrix of order j and $(\mathbf{AB}^{-1})_{22}$ is a square sub-matrix of order m), then the commodities corresponding to the last m rows of $\mathbf{AB}^{-1}$ are non-basic commodities, and the others are basic commodities.

3 Comparisons with the case of single production

All these elaborations are clearly of interest to the extent that they allow the extension to the general case of joint production of the simple rules and properties that hold for the case of single production.

Now, both matrix $\mathbf{AB}^{-1}$ and matrix $\mathbf{H}$ allow the extension to the case of joint production of the simple rule (valid for the matrix $\mathbf{A}$ in the case of single production) according to which the distinction between basic and non-basic commodities can be reduced to the property of reducibility of the matrix in question. In this way, the two types of commodities correspond to the first j rows and the subsequent m rows respectively of the matrix itself; $m \times j$ being the order of the null sub-matrix that appears in its bottom left-hand corner ($j+m > m \geq 0$). In other words, we may simply say that (as for matrix **A** in the case of single production), if the matrix $\mathbf{AB}^{-1}$ – or the matrix **H** – can be reduced, by means of appropriate interchanges of rows and corresponding columns, to the reducible form, where $m \times j$ is the order of the null sub-matrix in the bottom left-hand corner, then the various commodities are ordered so that the first j commodities are basic and the following m commodities are non-basic commodities.

The economic interpretation of this distinction is, however, not equally evident in the three cases. In the case of single production, the reducible form of the matrix **A** immediately implies that the basic commodities enter and the non-basic commodities do not enter (either directly or indirectly) in the production processes of all commodities.

In the case of joint production, the matrix **H** has the notable property of retaining this same economic interpretation, with the sole condition that the entry or non-entry into production of all commodities is no longer interpreted with reference to the direct production processes of the various commodities, but with reference to the corresponding vertically integrated sectors.

The case of the matrix $\mathbf{AB}^{-1}$ is more complex. If the matrix $\mathbf{AB}^{-1}$ is reducible, it is still possible to talk in abstract terms of commodities that enter and commodities that do not enter (directly or indirectly) all production processes, exactly as for the matrix **A**. However, in this case we are dealing with very particular production processes, resulting from the transformation that the matrix $\mathbf{B}^{-1}$ operates on **A**. The economic meaning of each production process thus 'transformed' remains that of inputs, per unit of output. However, these are no longer inputs in a real and observable sense, but are so only in a logical sense, to which it is not easy to give an immediate economic interpretation, except in very special cases.

It should be added that the matrix $\mathbf{AB}^{-1}$ (and for that matter also the matrix **H**) is not necessarily a non-negative matrix, despite the fact that **A** and **B** are both non-negative. For elaborations in terms of the matrix $\mathbf{AB}^{-1}$ (and for that matter in terms of the matrix **H**) it is therefore not possible to use Perron–Frobenius theorems for non-negative matrices.

Reference

Sraffa, P., *Production of Commodities by Means of Commodities* (Cambridge: Cambridge University Press, 1960).

CHAPTER FIVE

Prices, Rate of Profit and Life of Machines in Sraffa's Fixed-Capital Model[1]

PAOLO VARRI

1 Introduction

Means of production are traditionally classified as durable (fixed capital) and non-durable (circulating capital), according to whether their technical characteristics allow them to be reused several times in the productive process or not. This particular characteristic of the means of production is relevant to a great number of economic problems.

Economists have almost always been reluctant, however, to involve themselves in the analytical complications connected with the introduction into their models of fixed capital along with circulating capital. The main reason for this widespread phenomenon has probably been the tendency to simplify problems as much as possible and the traditional lack of interest in economic growth and technical progress.

Indeed, most of the essential features of an economic system are already present in schemes involving only circulating capital. One of the most convincing proofs of this is given by the results recently obtained for the theory of capital (see Sraffa, 1960, pt I; and Pasinetti *et al.*, 1966); however, this is not sufficient justification for the scarce interest so far shown in the problem at theoretical level.

In recent years the most important contribution towards the introduction of durable means of production into economic analysis, and especially into the theory of value and income distribution, has been Sraffa's

[1] Originally published as 'Prezzi, saggio del profitto e durata del capitale fisso nello schema teorico di Piero Sraffa', *Studi economici*, XXIX, no. 1 (1974) 5–44. Subsequent discussions in the same journal have stressed the point that the possibility of trade of old machines is excluded from the model here analysed.

(1960, pt II). The solution that he reproposes[2] is to treat *machines* as a special case of joint production. We propose to continue in this direction.

From a theoretical point of view, this method has the great advantage of allowing an 'economic' rather than a 'technical' solution to the problem of depreciation. Indeed, in most cases it permits the determination of depreciation quotas at the same time as relative prices.

This has allowed us, first of all, to highlight certain serious limitations in the solutions previously proposed. The analysis we carry out here aims to overcome what we regard as one of the bigger obstacles to a wider adoption of the method proposed by Sraffa: the possible emergence of negative prices. This is the problem we tackle in this paper, trying to define the economic significance of the mathematical conditions that exclude the possibility of negative prices.

2 The problem of machines in traditional economic theory

The first attempts at the analysis of an economic system containing machines, along with labour and circulating capital, to produce commodities go back to the beginning of the nineteenth century.

Ricardo (1821) was specifically involved in two problems connected with the introduction of machines into the productive process. He first considered the effects of this on his theory of value, and then he considered the effects on the process of economic growth and in particular on the level of employment. However, only recently has the work of Ricardo been adequately revalued by scholars. For many years the most well known contributions on the subject belonged to a later theoretical stream originating in the work of Böhm-Bawerk.[3] The most well known of these contributions is probably Wicksell's review article of the book by G. Akerman (cf. Wicksell, 1934, Appendices I and II).

Wicksell's intellectual background was strictly marginalistic, and this obviously influenced his approach to the problem. He constructed an *ad hoc* model of the economic system in which it is possible to construct machines that are in all ways identical except that they last different periods of time, according to the quantity of labour employed in their production. The relationship is perfectly in line with the law of diminishing marginal returns. Hence, the only problem that arises consists in identifying the optimum life of the machine according to the variations of the cost of the labour factor.

However, as is well known, the marginal approach to economic problems has been heavily criticised for its failure to provide useful information on the working of a real economic system.

[2] On the historical precedents of the method in question see 'Reference to the Literature', appendix D of Sraffa (1960).

[3] For our purposes, the most important is Böhm Bawerk (1891).

First of all, it has been shown that the results obtainable from aggregate models do not retain their validity if the analysis is transferred to disaggregated schemes.

Secondly, the shift to multisector schemes has made it more difficult in analysis, and, above all, less reasonable in interpretation, to maintain the traditional approach originally conceived in aggregate terms.

This has provided the opportunity to question the very basis of the marginal construction and to take up the analysis at the point at which Ricardo left it.[4]

3 Multisector schemes

Sraffa's approach to the problem of machines which we wish to analyse is definitely part of this new line of development of economic thought. In order to be able better to understand the fundamental features of his definition of the problem, we need to recall the scheme involving circulating capital alone.

This scheme represents the economic system as a set of interdependent industries that produce commodities by means of labour and other commodities. Sraffa's starting point is the table of the physical flows of goods between the various industries of the economic system. He considers it as given, and independent from the other variables taken into consideration.[5]

From this point of view, there is therefore a notable analogy between Sraffa's scheme and the possibly better-known linear models of production. This is the reason why certain theoretical problems can be dealt with in the same terms in both schemes, as we shall do below for the problem of the introduction of durable means of production into the analysis.

The economic system thus represented is viable if it is, on the whole, able to produce commodities in larger quantities than they are consumed. We may therefore suppose that all the outcoming net product is divided between wages and profits in such a way that the wage rate and the rate of profit on the value of the means of production are uniform in all the different industries. On the basis of these hypotheses, and given one of the two distributive variables, we can define a set of exchange values which, if adopted, allows the various industries to restore the initial stocks of means of production for the repetition of the productive operations in the next period.

[4] A very clear example of this particular development of contemporary economic thought, in no way affected by marginalistic influences, is the collection of essays by Pasinetti (1974).

[5] It is easy to see that, in the case of a stationary economic system using only circulating capital, the description of the structure of the economic system given by the table of inter-industry flows of commodities is independent of the length of the period of time chosen as a reference.

Mathematically, the above system of prices may be written in matrix form as follows:[6]

$$(1+r)\mathbf{A}\mathbf{p} + w\mathbf{L} = \mathbf{p} \tag{5.1}$$

where

r and w are the rate of profit and the wage rate,
$\mathbf{p}$ is the vector of prices,
$\mathbf{A}$ is the matrix of commodities input into the various industries, and
$\mathbf{L}$ is the vector of labour input.

It is well known, and so it is unnecessary to go into detail here, that there is an interval of non-negative values of r (or of w) corresponding to which the solutions for prices are positive.[7]

For this reason, the scheme, though based on simple hypotheses, is economically significant and possesses, we should stress, a theoretical significance independent of that of the linear models of production mentioned above. Indeed, in the first case, prices are determined on the basis of the table of total flows of goods. In the second case, on the other hand, the significance of the prices of goods is tied to the hypothesis that the technical coefficients are constant, i.e. that the relations of proportionality inferrable from the table remain unchanged even if the levels of production in the system are changed.[8]

4 Fixed capital in linear multisector schemes

Durable means of production may be introduced in many different ways into the linear multisector model so far considered.[9]

[6] The normalisation adopted for the elements of **A** and **L** is that illustrated in the note 10 below.

[7] The most frequent reference for these demonstrations is Newman (1962).

[8] It is perhaps worth pointing out that the coefficients in the system of equations (5.1) have been normalised according to the less common of the two rules usually adopted. According to one convention, used for linear models, the elements of matrix **A** and vector **L** are referred to a level of unitary production of the industry under consideration and are normally defined as 'technical coefficients'. Alternatively, the same elements may be referred to the quantity available overall, in the economic system, of the means of production under consideration. They then become 'proportions', i.e. pure numbers independent of any unit of measure whatsoever. Either normalisation may be followed, according to the circumstances and within the limits defined above. The second method, the one adopted here, has the advantage of giving a standard expression to the viability conditions of the system.

[9] By 'linear multisector models' we mean not only the linear models usually considered but also Sraffian schemes, which are not economically linear though they have the same analytical structure as linear models.

Generally, each method adopted tries to reach a double objective. First of all, it aims at offering a sufficiently general solution to the problem; secondly, it tries to preserve, as far as possible, the analytical simplicity of the schemes with circulating capital only.

One quite large and well developed group of solutions originates in the studies of Leontief (1951). His model manages, by means of certain simplifying hypotheses, to retain the simplicity of the scheme involving circulating capital only. It is therefore worth making a brief analysis of these developments, on the basis of the system of equations (5.1).

(5.1) may also be written as follows:

$$\mathbf{Ap} + r\mathbf{Ap} + \mathbf{L}w = \mathbf{p} \tag{5.2}$$

The two new terms have an obvious economic significance: **Ap** represents the value of consumed means of production, while $r\mathbf{Ap}$ is the amount of profits on capital used, which in this case coincides with that consumed in the productive processes.[10]

From this point of view, the main effect of the introduction of durable means of production into the scheme is to make the value of means of production consumed in production different from the value of means of production involved in production. Moreover, many special cases may be reduced to this scheme and receive a uniform treatment.

Let us suppose, for example, that certain quantities of raw materials, proportional to the quantity of goods produced, must be stocked in excess of the amount used in production. Their contribution to the price of the product will in this case be realised on the basis of the interest involved in the permanent anticipation of their value. If the generic element s_{ij} of matrix **S** represents the quantity of the jth commodity held as stock in the ith industry, equation (5.2) may be easily modified in the following way, in order to take into account the new element of cost:

$$\mathbf{Ap} + r(\mathbf{Ap} + \mathbf{Sp}) + \mathbf{L}w = \mathbf{p} \tag{5.3}$$

From this point of view, those special kinds of fixed capital that, once built, do not deteriorate in production, and the use of which may therefore be indefinitely protracted in time, are very similar to stocks. On the analogy of s_{ij}, we may define such (rather strange) equipment as k_{ij}, and we obtain the new system of prices:

$$\mathbf{Ap} + r(\mathbf{Ap} + \mathbf{Sp} + \mathbf{Kp}) + \mathbf{L}w = \mathbf{p} \tag{5.4}$$

In the overwhelming majority of cases, however, machines cannot be used

[10] It might be useful for the reader to reinterpret matrix **A** and vector **L** in this section as Leontief technical coefficients. Since we are interested here in the structure of commodity flows only from a qualitative point of view, such a reinterpretation is not strictly necessary for the development of the argument.

indefinitely. Year by year, they pass a part of their value to the goods which they contribute to produce, until the moment when they are eliminated and replaced.

This is in rather general terms the standard story of depreciation. Hence, on analogy with the previous cases, the set of machines used in production has been indicated by matrix **M**, and the part assumed to be consumed in production during the period by matrix **D**.

The above system of prices may now therefore be further modified and adapted to the new situation as follows:

$$\mathbf{Ap} + \mathbf{Dp} + r(\mathbf{Ap} + \mathbf{Sp} + \mathbf{Kp} + \mathbf{Mp}) + \mathbf{L}w = \mathbf{p} \tag{5.5}$$

Clearly, however, this is merely a formal adaptation. Indeed, this approach to depreciation has little economic sense and has to face two substantial criticisms, which seriously limit its relevance.

The first point concerns the arbitrary way in which the rates of depreciation are determined. Even if we leave out of consideration their interpretation in physical or value terms, we are still left with the fact that, apart from special cases of general interest, the use of machines for successive periods involves maintenance and repair, and also the joint consumption of heterogeneous means of production (raw materials, fuel, labour, and so on) in different quantities for the different periods of the machine's use. This makes a merely technical solution (i.e. independent of the system of prices) to the problem of the determination of the rate of depreciation quite inconceivable. Indeed, it is in no way possible to obtain any general indication of the economic return of the machine from the technical data (consumption of the machine in its different years of activity, number of pieces produced each year, specification of the maintenance and repair operations technically recommended).

In the general case, therefore, the rates of depreciation and, as we shall see, the year in which the machine will be eliminated cannot be determined independently of prices, as, on the contrary, the system of equations (5.5) requires.

There is another, lesser aspect of this solution which does not convince. It does not seem to take any account of an important difference between fixed and circulating capital: the former's indivisibility.

This problem is so well known in the literature that a simple clarification is all that is needed here. Any type of input–output relationship involving fixed capital expressed in physical terms (expressed either as technical coefficient or as proportion) strictly speaking loses the operative significance it normally has in the presence of circulating capital alone, since it seems to us that there is no sense in referring to fractions of fixed capital (i.e. to fractions of machines, plants, assembly lines, and so on).

Moreover, the fact that machines may, and usually are, used below their full capacity, creates obvious difficulties when we attempt to introduce them *sic et simpliciter* in a theory of production characterised by constant returns to scale.

All this leads us to conclude that the representation of the productive system formulated in the system of prices (5.5) is inadequate and misleading for a theory of value – i.e. for a correct solution to the problem of relative prices in the presence of durable means of production.

It is, however, not difficult to understand the reasons for its enormous success in the literature, if we consider the simplicity of the equations it produces and the fact that their analytical structure remains unchanged throughout the different cases mentioned above. This is evidently a significant example of how the economic sense of a problem is occasionally sacrificed for one of its analytical variants producing an easier and more elegant solution.

5 Fixed capital and joint production

The approach to the problem we have just considered is by far the most frequent in economic literature. However, it is not the only one. An alternative solution has been put forward, independently, by von Neumann (1937) and Sraffa (1960). This consists in the consideration of fixed capital as a special case of joint production.

According to this method, durable means of production used in production are represented both as input, along with the other means of production, and as joint product, together with the goods produced by them. This arrangement implies that the same machine is considered as a different commodity at its different ages. Each year of the machine's activity is represented by a particular equation of joint production up till the time when the machine becomes unusable and is eliminated or sold as scrap.

If we wish to isolate the problem of fixed capital from the more general problem of joint production, then we may suppose that the machines are the only element of joint production characterising the productive system under consideration. This means that a single equation will no longer be sufficient to represent each productive process. We shall clearly have to introduce as many equations as there are years of production of the durable means of production used in each process.[11]

[11] This means that, in the case of production with fixed capital, the observation of physical flows of goods in the economic system during just one period may provide insufficient data for the construction of the matrix of our system of equations. We shall, however, return to this point at the end of the essay.

We shall indicate by activities[12] 1, 2, . . . *s*, respectively, the successive individual equations of the productive process considered. Before going any further, however, let us examine briefly how the alternative scheme we have just outlined satisfies the criticism advanced previously.

We can say straight away that no difficulty arises for the problem of depreciation. Any technical pattern of machine use can be represented in the model, and, since the description contained in the equations of the individual activities is exclusively in terms of physical requisites of commodities and labour present in the system, no arbitrary element is introduced into the price system to be discussed.

As for the problem of the divisibility and variability in the degree of utilisation of machines, some caution is needed. The schemes of von Neumann and Sraffa have important differences on this point, though they treat fixed capital in a similar way. Von Neumann's dynamic scheme cannot leave out of the analysis the effects of variations in the production levels of the system. Hence, a hypothesis on returns to scale becomes essential. Sraffa's stationary scheme, on the other hand, does not raise questions of variations of production levels from the given initial position. The problem of returns does not arise and can therefore (as in what follows) be simply ignored.

6 The general system of prices

As we saw in section 4, the formal structure of system (5.1) has remained more or less unchanged through the successive elaborations aimed at introducing durable means of production into the scheme. We need only call $\mathbf{C} = \mathbf{A} + \mathbf{D}$ the matrix of consumed-goods flow and call $\mathbf{F} = \mathbf{A} + \mathbf{S} + \mathbf{K} + \mathbf{M}$ the matrix of the stocks of goods used (but not consumed) in the productive system, and we are able to rewrite system (5.5) in the following alternative form:

$$\mathbf{Cp} + r\mathbf{Fp} + \mathbf{L}w = \mathbf{p} \tag{5.6}$$

which is very similar to (5.2), and so can be analysed on analogous lines to those mentioned in section 3.

If, on the contrary, fixed capital is represented according to the scheme of joint production, the system of price equations will be the following:

$$(1 + r)\mathbf{Ap} + \mathbf{L}w = \mathbf{Bp} \tag{5.7}$$

[12] The term 'activity' therefore retains the same meaning in this context as in Chapter 2 above.

where **A** is the matrix of inputs, **B** is the matrix of outputs and **L** is the vector of requirements of direct labour.[13]

If we make the reasonable assumption that each productive process of the economic system is organised in the complete series of its activities (i.e. assuming that the technical description of the productive system in terms of the two matrices **A** and **B** and the vector **L** is complete), the system of equations will be determined, but for two degrees of freedom, which, as is well known, can be eliminated by fixing one price and one of the two distributive variables.

The formal solution for $(1/w)\mathbf{p}$ (with $w \neq 0$) is immediate:

$$(1/w)\mathbf{p} = [\mathbf{B} - (1+r)\mathbf{A}]^{-1}\mathbf{L} \tag{5.8}$$

Unfortunately, however, the conditions sufficient to guarantee the existence of economically meaningful solutions for the single-product system cannot be transferred to this more complicated case. Hence, it is much more difficult to make an *a priori* distinction between the cases which (giving non-negative solutions) are economically significant and those which are economically irrelevant.

In other words, it does not seem that the mere fact that the system is viable, i.e. that $\mathbf{s}(\mathbf{B}-\mathbf{A}) \geq \mathbf{0}$, is a sufficient basis on which to establish that prices and distributive variables are non-negative (the same point is made by Pasinetti–see above, Ch. 2, section 13). As mentioned at the beginning, this is probably one of the main reasons why the method of representing fixed capital reproposed by Sraffa has not been more widely used in economic models. We shall examine the origin of this difficulty more closely, with the aid, to begin with, of a simplified model.

7 A simplified model

Let us consider an economic system composed of n industries, in which each industry produces a single commodity using labour and other means of production. All the commodities produced are also means of production, and one of them is a durable means of production. Let us suppose, for the sake of simplicity, that it is used in only one industry: that which produces the nth commodity.

If, technically, the longer duration of utilisation of this means of production is s years, then the observations made in section 5 above allow us to define the following system of prices for our productive system:

[13] It is not worth introducing a special normalisation for the quantities of goods and labour that occur in this system of prices. We suppose simply that all the quantities that appear there are expressed in absolute physical terms.

$$
t\overbrace{}^{C}\overbrace{}^{c}\overbrace{}^{M_1}\overbrace{}^{M_2}\overbrace{}^{M_s}
\begin{bmatrix}
\mathbf{A}_{n-1} & \mathbf{a}_{1n} & \mathbf{0} & \mathbf{0} & \ldots\mathbf{0} \\
\mathbf{a}_{n1} & a_{nn} & 0 & 0 & \ldots 0 \\
\mathbf{a}_{n+1,1} & a_{n+1,n} & a_{n+1,n+1} & 0 & \ldots 0 \\
\mathbf{a}_{n+2,1} & a_{n+2,n} & 0 & a_{n+2,n+2} & \ldots 0 \\
\vdots & \vdots & \vdots & \vdots & \vdots \\
\mathbf{a}_{n+s,1} & a_{n+s,n} & 0 & 0 & \ldots a_{n+s,n+s}
\end{bmatrix}
\begin{bmatrix}
\mathbf{p}_{n-1} \\ p_n \\ p_{m1} \\ p_{m2} \\ \vdots \\ p_{ms}
\end{bmatrix}
+
\begin{bmatrix}
\mathbf{l}_{n-1} \\ l_n \\ l_{n+1} \\ l_{n+2} \\ \vdots \\ l_{n+s}
\end{bmatrix} w
$$

$$
=\begin{bmatrix}
\mathbf{I}_{n-1} & \mathbf{0} & \mathbf{0} & \mathbf{0} & \ldots\mathbf{0} \\
\mathbf{0} & b_{nn} & b_{n,n+1} & 0 & \ldots 0 \\
\mathbf{0} & b_{n+1,n} & 0 & b_{n+1,n+2} & \ldots 0 \\
\mathbf{0} & b_{n+2,n} & 0 & 0 & \ldots 0 \\
\vdots & \vdots & \vdots & \vdots & \vdots \\
\mathbf{0} & b_{n+s,n} & 0 & 0 & \ldots 0
\end{bmatrix}
\begin{bmatrix}
\mathbf{p}_{n-1} \\ p_n \\ p_{m1} \\ p_{m2} \\ \vdots \\ p_{ms}
\end{bmatrix} \tag{5.9}
$$

This has been appropriately partitioned into blocks.

The first block, of $n-1$ equations, includes the productive processes relative to the first $n-1$ commodities produced in the system, among which is also the durable means of production. The coefficients referring to these $n-1$ goods, i.e. those appearing in the first column of the two matrices in relation (5.9), have been normalised in terms of proportions by making their quantity produced overall equal to unity.

The second block consists solely of the nth equation; it refers to the productive process that produces the nth commodity using the new machine (its input coefficient is here not distinguished, being represented as one of the elements of the row vector $\mathbf{a}_{n1}$). In this case, the normalisation rule consists in making the quantity of the nth commodity produced by this activity equal to unity. As a result, if the machine is employed in successive activities, this quantity does not represent the total production of this commodity in the whole economic system.

The following s blocks represent the S activities, which produce further quantities of the nth commodity, using machines that are increasingly older. These quantities are expressed as proportions of the quantity of the same commodity produced by activity 0, which uses the new machine and is represented by the nth equation.

The quantities of old machines jointly produced in the respective activities are made equal to unity ($b_{n,n+1} = b_{n+1,n+2} = \ldots = 1$).

The system of prices written in this way has an interesting property. Every successive reduced system, starting from that of order n, which includes the first n equations and n unknowns (in addition to the rate of profit $r = t - 1$ and the wage rate w), is itself an autonomous system of prices that can be analysed independently of the whole one of which it is a part. Therefore, the number of reduced systems that can be considered is $s + 1$, i.e. the maximum number of activities of which the nth process is composed.

It is worth saying here that it is precisely through the reciprocal comparison of such reduced systems that we shall be able to clarify the mechanism of the formation of negative prices. Hence, this property of the system of prices (5.9) is of fundamental importance for our further analysis.

The first of these reduced systems is obtained by limiting the activity of the machine to its first year of age. It will therefore be composed of the first $n - 1$ processes and of the activity 0 of the nth process; i.e. it is a system of n equations in $n + 2$ unknowns: the n prices and the two distributive variables.

The viability conditions of this first reduced system are as follows:

$$\mathbf{s}_{n-1}\mathbf{A}_{n-1} + \mathbf{a}_{n1} \leq \mathbf{s}_{n-1} \tag{5.10}$$

$$\mathbf{s}_{n-1}\mathbf{a}_{1n} + a_{nn} \leq 1 \tag{5.11}$$

Relation (5.10) refers to the first $n - 1$ commodities, among which, as already pointed out, is the new machine. This relation shows that the quantity of each commodity that is employed overall is not greater than the quantity of it that is produced. On the other hand, (5.11) concerns the nth commodity produced in the first activity of the productive process by means of the new machine. Its significance is similar to that of (5.10), except that it will not necessarily hold, since there is no reason to believe that the quantity of the nth commodity produced by this activity (excluding the quantities produced in the successive employments of the old machine) is sufficient to cover the quantity of this commodity utilised in the entire productive system.

As for the reduced schemes of order greater than n, it is useful first of all to perform a re-elaboration, suggested by Sraffa himself (1960, section 76), which brings them back to a formal structure similar to that of single-production schemes. This consists in a suitable series of capitalisations which add up the various activities of the last industry in a single equation.

In our case, such operations are performed by premultiplying the system of equations (5.9) by a suitable transformation matrix, the structure of which depends on the number of periods of use of the machine under consideration. In the extreme case of s years, the transformation matrix will be of order $n + s$ and its structure will be as follows:

$$\begin{bmatrix} \mathbf{I}_{n-1} & \mathbf{0} & \mathbf{0} & \mathbf{0} & \cdots & \mathbf{0} \\ \mathbf{0} & t^s & t^{s-1} & t^{s-2} & \cdots & t^0 \\ \mathbf{0} & 0 & 0 & 0 & \cdots & 0 \\ \mathbf{0} & 0 & 0 & 0 & \cdots & 0 \\ \vdots & \vdots & \vdots & \vdots & & \vdots \\ \mathbf{0} & 0 & 0 & 0 & \cdots & 0 \end{bmatrix} = \mathbf{E}(t^s) \qquad (5.12)$$

For shorter durations it will be proportionately reduced both in the degree of the elements in t and in its order. In the opposite extreme case, where the machine is used exclusively in its first year of activity, no transformation is necessary and the transformation matrix is simply the identity matrix: $\mathbf{E}(t^0) = \mathbf{I}$.

In general terms, the system obtained after premultiplication is the following:

$$t\mathbf{E}(t^s)\mathbf{A}\mathbf{p} + \mathbf{E}(t^s)\mathbf{L}w = \mathbf{E}(t^s)\mathbf{B}\mathbf{p} \qquad (5.13)$$

After the elimination of terms common to both sides, its non-zero part may be explicitly written as follows:

$$t\begin{bmatrix} \mathbf{A}_{n-1} & \mathbf{a}_{1n} \\ \sum_{j=0}^{s} t^{s-j}\mathbf{a}_{n+j,1} & \sum_{j=0}^{s} t^{s-j}a_{n+j,n} \end{bmatrix}\begin{bmatrix} \mathbf{p}_{n-1} \\ p_n \end{bmatrix} + \begin{bmatrix} \mathbf{l}_{n-1} \\ \sum_{j=0}^{s} t^{s-j}l_{n+j} \end{bmatrix} w$$

$$= \begin{bmatrix} \mathbf{I}_{n-1} & \mathbf{0} \\ \mathbf{0} & \sum_{j=0}^{s} t^{s-j}b_{n+j,n} \end{bmatrix}\begin{bmatrix} \mathbf{p}_{n-1} \\ p_n \end{bmatrix} \qquad (5.14)$$

This allows us to obtain a solution for the first n prices immediately, according to the usual procedure for this type of systems. By fixing one price and one of the two distributive variables – the rate of profit for example – we obtain the following relation, which is perfectly determinate:

$$\begin{bmatrix} \mathbf{p}_{n-1} \\ p_n \end{bmatrix} = \left\{\begin{bmatrix} \mathbf{I}_{n-1} & \mathbf{0} \\ \mathbf{0} & \sum_{j=0}^{s} t^{s-j}b_{n+j,n} \end{bmatrix}\right.$$

$$\left. - t\begin{bmatrix} \mathbf{A}_{n-1} & \mathbf{a}_{1n} \\ \sum_{j=0}^{s} t^{s-j}\mathbf{a}_{n+j,1} & \sum_{j=0}^{s} t^{s-j}a_{n+j,n} \end{bmatrix}\right\}^{-1}\begin{bmatrix} \mathbf{l}_{n-1} \\ \sum_{j=0}^{s} t^{s-j}l_{n+j} \end{bmatrix} w \qquad (5.15)$$

By means of algebraic transformations this may be formally brought to have the same structure as the solution of the price system for single production:

$$\begin{bmatrix} \mathbf{p}_{n-1} \\ p_n \end{bmatrix} = \begin{bmatrix} \mathbf{I}_{n-1} & \mathbf{0} \\ \mathbf{0} & 1 \Big/ \sum_{j=0}^{s} t^{s-j} b_{n+j,\,n} \end{bmatrix} \left\{ \begin{bmatrix} \mathbf{I}_{n-1} & \mathbf{0} \\ \mathbf{0} & 1 \end{bmatrix} \right.$$

$$\left. - t \begin{bmatrix} \mathbf{A}_{n-1} & \mathbf{a}_{1n} \left(\sum_{j=0}^{s} t^{s-j} b_{n+j,\,n} \right)^{-1} \\ \sum_{j=0}^{s} t^{s-j} \mathbf{a}_{n+j,\,1} & \left(\sum_{j=0}^{s} t^{s-j} a_{n+j,\,n} \right) \Big/ \left(\sum_{j=0}^{s} t^{s-j} b_{n+j,\,n} \right) \end{bmatrix} \right\}^{-1}$$

$$\begin{bmatrix} \mathbf{l}_{n-1} \\ \sum_{j=0}^{s} t^{s-j} l_{n+j} \end{bmatrix} w \tag{5.16}$$

and it is convenient to refer the viability conditions to this particular version of the price system.

These conditions are defined, as usual, in relation to the sum of the elements on the columns of the commodity input matrix, which in this case is an appropriate transformation of the matrix of the initial system, (5.9).

$$\mathbf{s}_{n-1} \mathbf{A}_{n-1} + \sum_{j=0}^{s} \mathbf{a}_{n+j,\,1} \leq \mathbf{s}_{n-1} \tag{5.17}$$

$$\mathbf{s}_{n-1} \mathbf{a}_{1n} \left(\sum_{j=0}^{s} b_{n+j,\,n} \right)^{-1} + \sum_{j=0}^{s} a_{n+j,\,n} \Big/ \sum_{j=0}^{s} b_{n+j,\,n} \leq 1 \tag{5.18}$$

Clearly, both relations depend on the number of activities considered on each occasion. Hence, the effective upper limit of the interval of variation over which the summations are spread will lie between 0 and s.

As the number of activities considered increases, the quota of overall reuse of commodities used as means of production in the succession of activities included in the nth productive process will also increase. Consequently, the margins of validity of (5.17) will be restricted.

On the other hand, the overall quota of reuse of the nth commodity ought to diminish as a consequence of the additional quantities of it produced, using increasingly old machines. This, consequently, reduces the possible overall net deficit of this commodity to the point of converting it into a surplus, thereby verifying relation (5.18).

In neither case, however, can anything precise be said about the laws of variation in the orders of magnitude, since they do not necessarily vary in a regular way. Consequently, a productive system will be economically significant only if the viability conditions (5.17) and (5.18) are fulfilled for at least one of its reduced systems.

8 Solutions of the system with one productive activity using machines

All the reduced systems obtained from the complete system (5.9) have the property of being formally convertable, by means of transformation (5.12), to a scheme similar to those for single production using only circulating capital. This fact is particularly useful when we wish to analyse the solutions: it implies that we can face the problem in two successive phases: first with reference to the price of the first n commodities (including, therefore, the price of the new machine) and to the distributive variables; then with reference only to the price of the old machines.

We have already mentioned that in what follows we shall call for the comparison of the successive reduced systems obtainable from the initial one. The fact that the viability conditions are not necessarily verified for such reduced systems means that we have to analyse a wider range of variation of the rate of profit, r, than is usually considered for single production. We shall therefore analyse the various price systems for values of $r \geq -1$, and we shall go beyond the maximum rate of profit of the reduced systems considered.

The first reduced system that it is useful to analyse is that which results from the elimination of all the activities of the last productive process with the exception of the first: the machine is therefore used as if it were a non-durable means of production. We shall use the prefix 0 to indicate all the variables referring to this special system.

$$t\begin{bmatrix} \mathbf{A}_{n-1} & \mathbf{a}_{1n} \\ \mathbf{a}_{n1} & a_{nn} \end{bmatrix}\begin{bmatrix} {}_0\mathbf{p}_{n-1} \\ {}_0p_n \end{bmatrix}+\begin{bmatrix} \mathbf{l}_{n-1} \\ l_n \end{bmatrix}{}_0w=\begin{bmatrix} \mathbf{I}_{n-1} & \mathbf{0} \\ \mathbf{0} & 1 \end{bmatrix}\begin{bmatrix} {}_0\mathbf{p}_{n-1} \\ {}_0p_n \end{bmatrix} \tag{5.19}$$

Since, according to the hypothesis, no old machine is present, we shall consider the solution to the system of prices straightaway, without any preliminary transformation.

For $r = -1$, i.e. for $t = 1 + r = 0$, we have simply

$$\begin{bmatrix} {}_0\mathbf{p}_{n-1} \\ {}_0p_n \end{bmatrix}=\begin{bmatrix} \mathbf{l}_{n-1} \\ l_n \end{bmatrix}{}_0w$$

If a suitable *numéraire* is chosen, a positive wage rate will be obtained and relative prices will be non-negative.

For values of $r > -1$, the solution of the price system will have the usual form:

$$\begin{bmatrix} {}_0\mathbf{p}_{n-1} \\ {}_0p_n \end{bmatrix} = \left\{ \begin{bmatrix} \mathbf{I}_{n-1} & \mathbf{0} \\ \mathbf{0} & 1 \end{bmatrix} - t \begin{bmatrix} \mathbf{A}_{n-1} & \mathbf{a}_{1n} \\ \mathbf{a}_{n1} & a_{nn} \end{bmatrix} \right\}^{-1} \begin{bmatrix} \mathbf{l}_{n-1} \\ l_n \end{bmatrix} {}_0w \quad (5.20)$$

which is equal to (5.16) in the special case in which $s = 0$. An alternative, more compact expression of relation (5.20) that we shall use below is

$${}_0\mathbf{p} = [\mathbf{I} - t_0\mathbf{A}]^{-1}\, {}_0\mathbf{L}_0 w \quad (5.21)$$

If we fix the ith commodity as *numéraire*, the expression of w can be obtained immediately from the ith component of the vector ${}_0\mathbf{p}$:

$${}_0w = \frac{1}{[\mathbf{I} - t\,{}_0\mathbf{A}]^{-1}_{(i)}\, {}_0\mathbf{L}} \quad (5.22)$$

where $[\mathbf{I} - t\,{}_0\mathbf{A}]^{-1}_{(i)}$ $(i = 1, 2, \ldots n)$ is the ith row of the inverse matrix.

As is known, for values of r such that dom ${}_0\mathbf{A} < 1/t$,[14] the inverse matrix in question is positive.[15] If we have dom ${}_0\mathbf{A} = 1/T({}_0\mathbf{A}) = 1/[1 + R({}_0\mathbf{A})]$, this implies that the inverse matrix will be positive for $r < R({}_0\mathbf{A})$ or, correspondingly, for $t < T({}_0\mathbf{A})$. Then it follows that also ${}_0\mathbf{p}$ and ${}_0w$ in (5.21) and (5.22) will be positive.

If the viability condition (5.11) holds, that would be sufficient to confirm that dom ${}_0\mathbf{A} < 1$,[16] and therefore that $T({}_0\mathbf{A}) > 1$ and $r > 0$. However, we have already remarked that relation (5.11) is not necessarily verified for a reduced system obtained from the initial one. This therefore requires further considerations.

We have to analyse the behaviour of our system of prices, and in particular the behaviour of its inverse matrix, $[\mathbf{I} - t\,{}_0\mathbf{A}]^{-1}$, for values of $r > R({}_0\mathbf{A})$. With this end in view, we can calculate the inverse of the matrix that appears in the solution of our system in the following partitioned form. Let us define

$$\begin{bmatrix} \mathbf{I}_{n-1} - t\,\mathbf{A}_{n-1} & -t\,\mathbf{a}_{1n} \\ -t\,\mathbf{a}_{n1} & 1 - t\,a_{nn} \end{bmatrix}^{-1} = \begin{bmatrix} \alpha_{11} & \alpha_{12} \\ \alpha_{21} & \alpha_{22} \end{bmatrix}$$

14 Following widespread practice, 'dom' followed by the indication of a matrix is used to indicate the matrix's maximum eigenvalue.

15 For the sake of simplicity, it is implicitly assumed that matrix ${}_0\mathbf{A}$ is irreducible. The theorem which allows this conclusion is that of Perron–Frobenius, to be found in almost all texts on matrix algebra. See, for example, Gantmacher (1959, vol. II, p. 53).

16 This conclusion derives from a well known corollary of the Perron–Frobenius theorem. Cf. ibid., p. 63.

Then, expressions for α_{ij} can be easily obtained as functions of $[\mathbf{I}-t\mathbf{A}_{n-1}]^{-1}$ as follows:[17]

$$\alpha_{22} = \{1 - t\,a_{nn} - t\,\mathbf{a}_{n1}[\mathbf{I} - t\,\mathbf{A}_{n-1}]^{-1}\,t\,\mathbf{a}_{1n}\}^{-1} \tag{5.23}$$

$$\alpha_{21} = -\alpha_{22}(-t\,\mathbf{a}_{n1})[\mathbf{I} - t\,\mathbf{A}_{n-1}]^{-1} \tag{5.24}$$

$$\alpha_{12} = -[\mathbf{I} - t\,\mathbf{A}_{n-1}]^{-1}(-t\,\mathbf{a}_{1n})\alpha_{22} \tag{5.25}$$

$$\alpha_{11} = [\mathbf{I} - t\,\mathbf{A}_{n-1}]^{-1} - [\mathbf{I} - t\,\mathbf{A}_{n-1}]^{-1}(-t\,\mathbf{a}_{1n})\alpha_{21} \tag{5.26}$$

This allows us to take advantage of a notable property of non-negative square matrices: the maximum eigenvalue of a non-negative square matrix is always greater than that of any principal minor (cf. Gantmacher, 1959, vol. II, p. 69, proposition 4). In our case, this means that

$$\text{dom}\,\mathbf{A}_{n-1} < \text{dom}\,{}_0\mathbf{A} \tag{5.27}$$

In other words, the maximum eigenvalue of $\mathbf{A}_{n-1}$ constitutes a lower limit to the maximum eigenvalue of ${}_0\mathbf{A}$.

If, then, we denote the value of t corresponding to dom $\mathbf{A}_{n-1}$ by $T(\mathbf{A}_{n-1})$, i.e. if we write that

$$\text{dom}\,\mathbf{A}_{n-1} = 1/T(\mathbf{A}_{n-1}) = 1/[1 + R(\mathbf{A}_{n-1})] \tag{5.28}$$

it will be evident that $T(\mathbf{A}_{n-1}) > T({}_0\mathbf{A})$ or, correspondingly, $R(\mathbf{A}_{n-1}) > R({}_0\mathbf{A})$.

In this case too we can say that $[\mathbf{I} - t\,\mathbf{A}_{n-1}]^{-1}$ is positive if $t < T(\mathbf{A}_{n-1})$. In addition, since $\mathbf{a}_{n1} \geq \mathbf{0}$ in (5.10), it is certainly true that

$$\mathbf{s}_{n-1}\,\mathbf{A}_{n-1} \leq \mathbf{s}_{n-1} \tag{5.29}$$

and therefore that dom $\mathbf{A}_{n-1} < 1$,[18] from which it follows that $T(\mathbf{A}_{n-1}) > 1$ and that $R(\mathbf{A}_{n-1}) > 0$.

This allows us to analyse, as proposed, the sign of the inverse matrix $[\mathbf{I} - t\,{}_0\mathbf{A}]^{-1}$ in a wider interval than that previously considered, i.e. also for values of r included between $R({}_0\mathbf{A})$ (the sign of which is generally indeterminate) and $R(\mathbf{A}_{n-1})$ (which, on the other hand, is always positive).

We shall begin with the sign of α_{22}, of which, for the sake of simplicity, it is more convenient to analyse the reciprocal α_{22}^{-1}, i.e. the part of relation (5.23) (repeated here for the reader's convenience) which lies within braces:

$$\alpha_{22} = \{1 - t\,a_{nn} - t\,\mathbf{a}_{n1}[\mathbf{I} - t\,\mathbf{A}_{n-1}]^{-1}\,t\,\mathbf{a}_{1n}\}^{-1} \tag{5.23}$$

[17] The inversion of a matrix by partitioning is quite a widespread technique of calculus. See, for example, Hadley (1961, pp. 107 ff.).

[18] See above, note 16.

In the open interval $[0, T(\mathbf{A}_{n-1})]$, $\alpha_{22}{}^{-1}$ is a continuous and decreasing function of t.[19]

When $t = 0$, $\alpha_{22}{}^{-1} = 1$. Successively, $\alpha_{22}{}^{-1}$ decreases as t increases until it vanishes for $t = T({}_0\mathbf{A})$, where $[\mathbf{I} - t\,{}_0\mathbf{A}]^{-1}$ and α_{22} are not definite. Finally, for $T({}_0\mathbf{A}) < t < T(\mathbf{A}_{n-1})$ we shall have $\alpha_{22}^{-1} < 0$.[20]

We see straightaway from (5.24) and (5.25) that, in correspondence with the above interval of values of t, α_{21} and α_{12} have the same sign as α_{22}, while the sign of α_{11} in (5.26) remains imprecise.

In other words, for $T({}_0\mathbf{A}) < t < T(\mathbf{A}_{n-1})$ we shall have

$$\begin{bmatrix} \mathbf{I}_{n-1} - t\,\mathbf{A}_{n-1} & -t\,\mathbf{a}_{1n} \\ -t\,\mathbf{a}_{n1} & 1 - t\,a_{nn} \end{bmatrix}^{-1} = \begin{bmatrix} (\pm) & (-) \\ (-) & (-) \end{bmatrix}$$

This suggests that we should adopt the nth commodity, i.e. that produced by the machine, as the *numéraire* of our system of prices. In this case, in fact, the wage rate ${}_0w$ defined by (5.22) will be positive for $0 \le t < T({}_0\mathbf{A})$, will vanish for $t = T({}_0\mathbf{A})$, and will then be negative up to $t = T(\mathbf{A}_{n-1})$ exclusive. The vector of prices $\mathbf{p}_{n-1}$ will have the same sign as ${}_0w$ up to $T({}_0\mathbf{A})$ exclusive, will be positive for $t = T({}_0\mathbf{A})$, while its sign will remain imprecise in the open interval $[T({}_0\mathbf{A}), T(\mathbf{A}_{n-1})]$.

9 Solutions of the system with two productive activities using machines

We are now in the best position to tackle the problem we put at the

[19] To prove this we need only to derive $\alpha_{22}{}^{-1}$ with respect to t. We obtain:

$$d\alpha_{22}{}^{-1}/dt = -a_{nn} - \{\mathbf{a}_{n1}[\mathbf{I} - t\mathbf{A}_{n-1}]^{-1} t\mathbf{a}_{1n} + t\mathbf{a}_{n1}[\mathbf{I} - t\mathbf{A}_{n-1}]^{-1}\mathbf{A}_{n-1} [\mathbf{I} - t\mathbf{A}_{n-1}]^{-1} t\mathbf{a}_{1n} + t\mathbf{a}_{n1}[\mathbf{I} - t\mathbf{A}_{n-1}]^{-1}\mathbf{a}_{1n}\}$$

which, in the interval under consideration, is less than zero.

[20] We should note, incidentally, that this is another way to obtain simple confirmation of the fact that, if the viability condition (5.11) is satisfied for $t = 1$, $\alpha_{22}{}^{-1}$ is positive. Therefore, the function being monotonic, we may deduce that $R({}_0\mathbf{A}) > 0$. From (5.10) we obtain, in fact,

$$\mathbf{s}_{n-1}\mathbf{A}_{n-1} + \mathbf{a}_{n1} \le \mathbf{s}_{n-1}$$

$$\mathbf{a}_{n1} \le \mathbf{s}_{n-1}[\mathbf{I} - \mathbf{A}_{n-1}]$$

Postmultiplying both sides by $[\mathbf{I} - t\mathbf{A}_{n-1}]^{-1}$, which, in the interval of t considered, is positive, we have

$$\mathbf{a}_{n1}[\mathbf{I} - \mathbf{A}_{n-1}]^{-1} \le \mathbf{s}_{n-1}$$

and then, postmultiplying by $\mathbf{a}_{1n}$:

$$\mathbf{a}_{n1}[\mathbf{I} - t\mathbf{A}_{n-1}]^{-1}\mathbf{a}_{1n} < \mathbf{s}_{n-1}\mathbf{a}_{1n}$$

Finally, since we see from (5.11) that $\mathbf{s}_{n-1}\mathbf{a}_{1n} \le 1 - a_{nn}$, we may write that

$$\mathbf{a}_{n1}[\mathbf{I} - \mathbf{A}_{n-1}]^{-1}\mathbf{a}_{1n} < 1 - a_{nn}$$

from which it emerges that for $t = 1$, $\alpha_{22} > 0$.

beginning. It arises as soon as we go to analyse the reduced system immediately following the one just dealt with. Its system of equations is characterised by the fact that the nth productive process consists of two distinct activities: the first uses the new machine and supplies, jointly with the product, the same machine one year older; the second reuses this one-year-old machine for another cycle of production.

The price system of this second reduced scheme is as follows:

$$t\begin{bmatrix} \mathbf{A}_{n-1} & \mathbf{a}_{1n} & \mathbf{0} \\ \mathbf{a}_{n1} & a_{nn} & 0 \\ \mathbf{a}_{n+1,1} & a_{n+1,n} & a_{n+1,n+1} \end{bmatrix}\begin{bmatrix} {}_1\mathbf{p}_{n-1} \\ {}_1p_n \\ {}_1p_{m1} \end{bmatrix}+\begin{bmatrix} \mathbf{l}_{n-1} \\ l_n \\ l_{n+1} \end{bmatrix}{}_1w$$
$$=\begin{bmatrix} \mathbf{I}_{n-1} & \mathbf{0} & \mathbf{0} \\ \mathbf{0} & 1 & b_{n,n+1} \\ \mathbf{0} & b_{n+1,n} & 0 \end{bmatrix}\begin{bmatrix} {}_1\mathbf{p}_{n-1} \\ {}_1p_n \\ {}_1p_{m1} \end{bmatrix} \tag{5.30}$$

To remain consistent with previous notation, we shall also refer to it in the alternative compact form

$$t\,{}_1\mathbf{A}\,{}_1\mathbf{p}+{}_1\mathbf{L}\,{}_1w={}_1\mathbf{B}\,{}_1\mathbf{p} \tag{5.31}$$

As mentioned at the beginning, we shall deal with the solution to this system of equations in two successive phases. First we shall find the solution for ${}_1\mathbf{p}_{n-1}$, ${}_1p_n$, ${}_1w$ and r; then we shall find the solution for ${}_1p_{m1}$, i.e. for the price of the one-year-old machine.

The transformation matrix that allows this particular procedure is, in this case,

$$\mathbf{E}(t^1)=\begin{bmatrix} \mathbf{I} & \mathbf{0} & \mathbf{0} \\ \mathbf{0} & t & 1 \\ \mathbf{0} & 0 & 0 \end{bmatrix} \tag{5.32}$$

As previously mentioned, this allows us to express the nth process as the sum of the second activity and the first capitalised at the rate $1+r=t$.

In this way the solution of the transformed system will simply be a special case of relation (5.16):

$$\begin{bmatrix} {}_1\mathbf{p}_{n-1} \\ {}_1p_n \end{bmatrix}=\begin{bmatrix} \mathbf{I}_{n-1} & \mathbf{0} \\ \mathbf{0} & 1/(tb_{nn}+b_{n+1,n}) \end{bmatrix}\left\{\begin{bmatrix} \mathbf{I}_{n-1} & \mathbf{0} \\ \mathbf{0} & 1 \end{bmatrix}\right.$$
$$\left.-t\begin{bmatrix} \mathbf{A}_{n-1} & \mathbf{a}_{1n}(tb_{nn}+b_{n+1,n})^{-1} \\ t\mathbf{a}_{n1}+\mathbf{a}_{n+1,1} & (ta_{nn}+a_{n+1,n})/(tb_{nn}+b_{n+1,n}) \end{bmatrix}\right\}^{-1}\begin{bmatrix} \mathbf{l}_{n-1} \\ tl_n+l_{n+1} \end{bmatrix}{}_1w \tag{5.33}$$

This may also be written in the compact form[21]

$$ {}_1\bar{\mathbf{p}} = \mathbf{D}[\mathbf{I} - t\,{}_1\bar{\mathbf{A}}]^{-1}\,{}_1\bar{\mathbf{L}}_1 w \tag{5.34}$$

The viability conditions (referring to matrix ${}_1\bar{\mathbf{A}}$) of this reduced system are, in their turn, a special case of (5.17) and (5.18):

$$ \mathbf{s}_{n-1}\mathbf{A}_{n-1} + \sum_{j=0}^{1} \mathbf{a}_{n+j,1} \leq \mathbf{s}_{n-1} \tag{5.35}$$

$$ \mathbf{s}_{n-1}\mathbf{a}_{1n}\left(\sum_{j=0}^{1} b_{n+j,n}\right)^{-1} + \left(\sum_{j=0}^{1} a_{n+j,n} \Big/ \sum_{j=0}^{1} b_{n+j,n}\right) \leq 1 \tag{5.36}$$

Again, we shall analyse the solutions starting from $t = 0$ (i.e. from $r = -1$).

From (5.33) we immediately obtain that for $t = 0$

$$ \begin{bmatrix} {}_1\mathbf{p}_{n-1} \\ {}_1 p_n \end{bmatrix} = \begin{bmatrix} \mathbf{I}_{n-1} & \mathbf{0} \\ \mathbf{0} & 1/b_{n+1,n} \end{bmatrix} \begin{bmatrix} \mathbf{l}_{n-1} \\ l_{n+1} \end{bmatrix} {}_1 w \tag{5.37}$$

If, in order to retain uniformity with the preceding system, we choose the nth commodity as *numeraire*, then we easily obtain a general relation for ${}_1 w$:

$$ \begin{aligned} {}_1 w &= 1/\{\mathbf{D}[\mathbf{I} - t\,{}_1\bar{\mathbf{A}}]^{-1}\}_{(n)}\,{}_1\bar{\mathbf{L}} \\ &= 1/\{[\mathbf{I} - t\,{}_1\bar{\mathbf{A}}]_{(n)}^{-1}\,{}_1\bar{\mathbf{L}}(tb_{nn} + b_{n+1,n})^{-1}\} \end{aligned} \tag{5.38}$$

Although here ${}_1\bar{\mathbf{A}}$ is a matrix the elements of which are functions of t, it still remains a non-negative matrix for $t > 0$. Therefore, although dom ${}_1\bar{\mathbf{A}}$ is variable as function of t, it is a real and positive number in the interval that is relevant to us. In particular, for any $t > 0$, we shall have, for the same reasons as given for relation 5.26,

$$ \text{dom}\,\mathbf{A}_{n-1} < \text{dom}\,{}_1\bar{\mathbf{A}} \tag{5.39}$$

which, as we already know, means that $T(\mathbf{A}_{n-1}) > T({}_1\bar{\mathbf{A}})$.

The special feature of this case with respect to the previous one is that, although $T({}_1\bar{\mathbf{A}})$ is a continuous function of t, it is not easy to establish if it is a monotonic function. Hence, we cannot exclude *a priori* that the roots of the characteristic equation, according to which $t = T(\bar{\mathbf{A}})$, are multiples, as the example in Figure 5.1 shows.[22]

[21] We have placed a line above the symbols referring to the transformed system to distinguish them from those of the initial reduced system. This distinction was not necessary for the system, discussed in the previous section, with just one activity, because it did not require any transformation.

[22] See below, note 30 however.

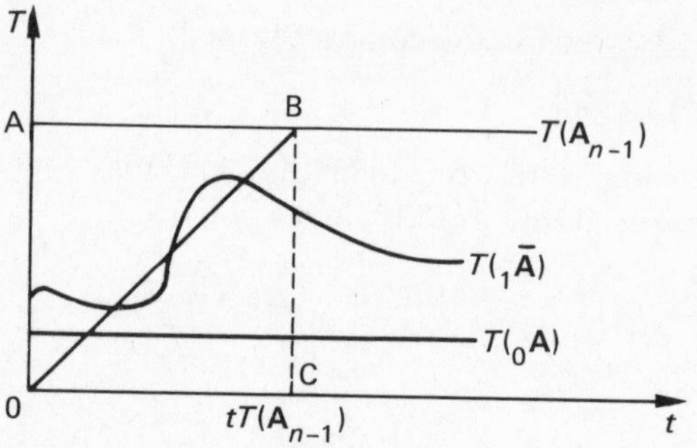

FIGURE 5.1

In the figure we have represented T (i.e. the reciprocal of the dominant eigenvalue of the various matrices examined so far) as a function of t; $T({}_0\mathbf{A})$ and $T(\mathbf{A}_{n-1})$, which are independent of t, have been shown as straight horizontal lines. In addition, we know from (5.39) that $T({}_1\mathbf{A})$ is certainly smaller than $T(\mathbf{A}_{n-1})$, and, since we are not interested in values of $t > T(\mathbf{A}_{n-1})$, our investigation will be limited to the square OABC. The triangle OAB clearly represents the set of points for which $T > t$, which are therefore able to supply an inverse matrix $[\mathbf{I} - t({}_1\overline{\mathbf{A}})]^{-1}$, which is positive.[23] The fact that $T({}_1\overline{\mathbf{A}})$ and, more generally, $T({}_i\overline{\mathbf{A}})$, with $2 \le i \le s$, is not necessarily a single root does not, therefore, create particular analytical difficulties. It does, however, raise the problem of how to evaluate the economic significance of this peculiar feature, which is not to be found in single-production schemes. This will be dealt with at the end, however, when discussing the economic significance of the whole analysis performed.

We have seen above that, in the interval $(0, T(\mathbf{A}_{n-1}))$, every time that $t < T({}_1\overline{\mathbf{A}})$, $[\mathbf{I} - t\,{}_1\overline{\mathbf{A}}]^{-1} > \mathbf{0}$. We now have to analyse the sign of the same matrix for values of t that are greater than $T({}_1\overline{\mathbf{A}})$, in the interval previously mentioned.

Once again, the easiest way to do this seems to be the computation of the inverse by partitioning. Using a notation similar to that used previously, we can say that:

$$\begin{bmatrix} \mathbf{I}_{n-1} - t\,\mathbf{A}_{n-1} & -t\mathbf{a}_{1n}\left(\sum_{j=0}^{1} t^{1-j} b_{n+j,n}\right)^{-1} \\ -t\sum_{j=0}^{1} t^{1-j}\mathbf{a}_{n+j,1} & 1 - t\left(\sum_{j=0}^{1} t^{1-j} a_{n+j,n} \Big/ \sum_{j=0}^{1} t^{1-j} b_{n+j,n}\right) \end{bmatrix} = \begin{bmatrix} {}_1\alpha_{11} & {}_1\alpha_{12} \\ {}_1\alpha_{21} & {}_1\alpha_{22} \end{bmatrix} \tag{5.40}$$

[23] These general observations refer to any of the $s+1$ reduced systems. The index i of the inverse matrix therefore varies from 0 to s.

In the same way as before, we obtain

$$ {}_1\alpha_{22} = \left\{1 - t\left(\sum_{j=0}^{1} t^{1-j} a_{n+j,n} \Big/ \sum_{j=0}^{1} t^{1-j} b_{n+j,n}\right)\right. $$
$$ \left. - t\left(\sum_{j=0}^{1} t^{1-j}\mathbf{a}_{n+j,1}\right)[\mathbf{I} - t\,\mathbf{A}_{n-1}]^{-1}\, t\mathbf{a}_{1n} \Big/ \sum_{j=0}^{1} t^{1-j} b_{n+j,n}\right\}^{-1} \quad (5.41) $$

$$ {}_1\alpha_{21} = -{}_1\alpha_{22}\left[-t\left(\sum_{j=0}^{1} t^{1-j}\mathbf{a}_{n+j,1}\right)\right][\mathbf{I} - t\,\mathbf{A}_{n-1}]^{-1} \quad (5.42) $$

$$ {}_1\alpha_{12} = -[\mathbf{I} - t\,\mathbf{A}_{n-1}]^{-1}\left[-t\mathbf{a}_{1n}\left(\sum_{j=0}^{1} t^{1-j} b_{n+j,n}\right)^{-1}\right]{}_1\alpha_{22} \quad (5.43) $$

$$ {}_1\alpha_{11} = [\mathbf{I} - t\,\mathbf{A}_{n-1}]^{-1} - [\mathbf{I} - t\,\mathbf{A}_{n-1}]^{-1}\left[-t\mathbf{a}_{1n}\left(\sum_{j=0}^{1} t^{1-j} b_{n+j,n}\right)^{-1}\right]{}_1\alpha_{21} \quad (5.44) $$

Once again, for the sake of simplicity, we shall analyse the reciprocal of ${}_1\alpha_{22}$, i.e. the expression within braces in (5.41). We know that in the interval $(0, T(\mathbf{A}_{n-1}))$ it will vanish each time that $t = T({}_1\overline{\mathbf{A}})$. For $t = 0$, ${}_1\alpha_{22}{}^{-1} = 1$. For reasons of continuity, ${}_1\alpha_{22}$ will remain positive until the first point in which $t = T({}_1\overline{\mathbf{A}})$ and afterwards will be negative or positive according to whether t is greater or smaller than $T({}_1\overline{\mathbf{A}})$.[24]

It is interesting to observe that, every time that ${}_1\alpha_{22} > 0$, the remaining blocks are also positive; if, however, ${}_1\alpha_{22} < 0$, ${}_1\alpha_{21}$ and ${}_1\alpha_{12}$ will be also negative, while the sign of ${}_1\alpha_{11}$ will remain indeterminate.

We now have all the elements allowing us to describe with sufficient precision the behaviour of ${}_1w$ and ${}_1\bar{\mathbf{p}}$ as r varies. For $t = 0$, we shall have ${}_1w > 0$. Subsequently ${}_1w$ will remain positive up till the first point at which r equals the corresponding $R({}_1\overline{\mathbf{A}})$. Obviously, if the viability conditions (5.35) and (5.36) are satisfied for $r = 0$, the wage rate at that point will be positive.[25] The prices of all the commodities, except those of old machines, will also be positive in correspondence to positive values of ${}_1w$, while nothing definite can be said of the other cases.

[24] Contrary to what is maintained in the text, ${}_1\alpha_{22}{}^{-1}$ turns out to be not only a continuous, but also a monotonically decreasing, function of t; from (5.41) in fact we obtain:

$$ \begin{aligned} d({}_1\alpha_{22}{}^{-1})/dt = & -[(2ta_{nn} + a_{n+1,n})(tb_{nn} + b_{n+1,n}) - (t^2 a_{nn} + ta_{n+1,n})b_{nn}] \\ & -\{(2t\mathbf{a}_{n1} + \mathbf{a}_{n+1,1})(\mathbf{I} - t\mathbf{A}_{n-1})^{-1} t\mathbf{a}_{1n}/(tb_{nn} + b_{n+1,n}) \\ & + (t^2\mathbf{a}_{n1} + t\mathbf{a}_{n+1,1})[(d/dt[\mathbf{I} - t\mathbf{A}_{n-1}]^{-1})t\mathbf{a}_{n1}/(tb_{nn} + b_{n+1,n}) \\ & + [\mathbf{I} - t\mathbf{A}_{n-1}]^{-1}[\mathbf{a}_{n1}(tb_{nn} + b_{n+1,n}) - t\mathbf{a}_{n1}b_{nn}]]\} \end{aligned} $$

which in the interval $[0, T(\mathbf{A}_{n-1})]$ is always negative. However, this result does not hold for all the subsequent reduced systems, since already in the case of a system with three activities the sign of $d({}_1\alpha_{22}{}^{-1})/dt$ is not definite. In order to keep the exposition brief, we have therefore preferred to conduct the discussion on the basis of the general rule.

[25] The demonstration of the result is completely analogous with that given in note 20 above.

The information collected so far allow us to identify the sign of ${}_1p_{m1}$ rather easily. To do this, we should go back to the complete version, (5.30), of the reduced system now under consideration. The particular structure of the system of equations allows us to obtain a solution for ${}_1p_{m1}$ by partitioning in few operations. From the first n equations of (5.30) in fact we obtain

$$t\begin{bmatrix} \mathbf{A}_{n-1} & \mathbf{a}_{1n} \\ \mathbf{a}_{n1} & a_{nn} \end{bmatrix}\begin{bmatrix} {}_1\mathbf{p}_{n-1} \\ {}_1p_n \end{bmatrix}+\begin{bmatrix} \mathbf{l}_{n-1} \\ l_n \end{bmatrix}{}_1w$$

$$=\begin{bmatrix} \mathbf{I}_{n-1} & \mathbf{0} \\ \mathbf{0} & 1 \end{bmatrix}\begin{bmatrix} {}_1\mathbf{p}_{n-1} \\ {}_1\mathrm{p}_n \end{bmatrix}+\begin{bmatrix} \mathbf{0} \\ b_{n,\,n+1} \end{bmatrix}{}_1p_{m1}, \tag{5.45}$$

which, using the notation of the previous section, can also be written as

$$[\mathbf{I}-t_0\mathbf{A}]^{-1}{}_0\mathbf{L}_1w-[\mathbf{I}-t_0\mathbf{A}]^{-1}\begin{bmatrix} \mathbf{0} \\ b_{n,\,n+1} \end{bmatrix}{}_1p_{m1}=\begin{bmatrix} \mathbf{p}_{n-1} \\ p_n \end{bmatrix} \tag{5.46}$$

If we explicitly consider the nth equation of system (5.46), i.e. that related to the *numéraire*, we have

$$[\mathbf{I}-t_0\mathbf{A}]_{(n)}^{-1}{}_0\mathbf{L}_1w-[\mathbf{I}-t_0\mathbf{A}]_{(n)}^{-1}\begin{bmatrix} \mathbf{0} \\ b_{n,\,n+1} \end{bmatrix}{}_1p_{m1}=1 \tag{5.47}$$

Substituting (5.22) for $i=n$ in (5.47), we easily obtain

$$[\mathbf{I}-t_0\mathbf{A}]_{(n)}^{-1}\begin{bmatrix} \mathbf{0} \\ b_{n+1,\,n} \end{bmatrix}{}_1p_{m1}=({}_1w-{}_0w)/{}_0w \tag{5.48}$$

Since the coefficient of ${}_1p_{m1}$ and ${}_0w$ always have the same sign, we may therefore definitely conclude that ${}_1p_{m1} \lesseqgtr 0$, depending on whether ${}_1w \lesseqgtr {}_0w$.

This has a precise economic significance. It shows that the price of the machine will be positive if, and only if, the extension in the use of the machine from the first to the second year of activity involves, with an equal rate of profit, higher wages in the whole economic system.

Before we further evaluate the significance and the economic relevance of this result, we should like to define a more general formulation, valid for a scheme with old machines of different ages.

10 Solutions of the system with three or more productive activities with machines

The reader will already have realised that the observations made so far have a recursive nature. Analysing the productive system when there are three rather than two activities in the nth process means simply repeating all the observations made in the previous section for the new situation. The only new point concerns the price of old machines. It is worth considering this briefly before finally concluding the subject.

The system of prices is evidently the following:

$$t\begin{bmatrix} \mathbf{A}_{n-1} & \mathbf{a}_{1n} & \mathbf{0} & \mathbf{0} \\ \mathbf{a}_{n1} & a_{nn} & 0 & 0 \\ \mathbf{a}_{n+1,1} & a_{n+1,n} & a_{n+1,n+1} & 0 \\ \mathbf{a}_{n+2,1} & a_{n+2,n} & 0 & a_{n+2,n+2} \end{bmatrix} \begin{bmatrix} {}_2\mathbf{p}_{n-1} \\ {}_2p_n \\ {}_2p_{m1} \\ {}_2p_{m2} \end{bmatrix} + \begin{bmatrix} \mathbf{l}_{n-1} \\ l_n \\ l_{n+1} \\ l_{n+2} \end{bmatrix} {}_2w = \begin{bmatrix} \mathbf{I}_{n-1} & \mathbf{0} & \mathbf{0} & \mathbf{0} \\ \mathbf{0} & b_{nn} & b_{n,n+1} & 0 \\ \mathbf{0} & b_{n+1,n} & 0 & b_{n+1,n+2} \\ \mathbf{0} & b_{n+2,n} & 0 & 0 \end{bmatrix} \begin{bmatrix} {}_2\mathbf{p}_{n-1} \\ {}_2p_n \\ {}_2p_{m1} \\ {}_2p_{m2} \end{bmatrix} \quad (5.49)$$

Let us suppose that we have already analysed the solutions for ${}_2\mathbf{p}_{n-1}$, ${}_2p_n$, ${}_2w$ and r and that we have therefore identified the economically relevant intervals of variation of r. The solutions to be considered are then those for ${}_2p_{m1}$ and ${}_2p_{m2}$. As previously, we have to deal with system (5.49) in its partitioned form.

From the first two rows of (5.49) we obtain

$$t\begin{bmatrix} \mathbf{A}_{n-1} & \mathbf{a}_{1n} \\ \mathbf{a}_{n1} & a_{nn} \end{bmatrix} \begin{bmatrix} {}_2\mathbf{p}_{n-1} \\ {}_2p_n \end{bmatrix} \begin{bmatrix} \mathbf{l}_{n-1} \\ l_n \end{bmatrix} {}_2w = \begin{bmatrix} \mathbf{I}_{n-1} & \mathbf{0} \\ \mathbf{0} & 1 \end{bmatrix} \begin{bmatrix} {}_2\mathbf{p}_{n-1} \\ {}_2p_n \end{bmatrix} + \begin{bmatrix} \mathbf{0} \\ b_{n,n+1} \end{bmatrix} {}_2p_{m1} \quad (5.50)$$

It is easy to see that this is the same system as (5.44) in the previous section. Thus, the same conclusions as made there will apply to ${}_2p_{m1}$: ${}_2p_{m1} \lesseqqgtr 0$ depending on whether ${}_2w \lesseqqgtr {}_0w$.

The sign of ${}_2p_{m2}$ may be determined in a completely analogous way. Once again we have to solve system (5.49) by partitioning, this time using the first three equations. In this way we obtain

$$t\begin{bmatrix} \mathbf{A}_{n-1} & \mathbf{a}_{1n} & \mathbf{0} \\ \mathbf{a}_{n1} & a_{nn} & 0 \\ \mathbf{a}_{n+1,1} & a_{n+1,n} & a_{n+1,n+1} \end{bmatrix} \begin{bmatrix} {}_2\mathbf{p}_{n-1} \\ {}_2p_n \\ {}_2p_{m1} \end{bmatrix} + \begin{bmatrix} \mathbf{l}_{n-1} \\ l_n \\ l_{n+1} \end{bmatrix} {}_2w = \begin{bmatrix} \mathbf{I}_{n-1} & \mathbf{0} & \mathbf{0} \\ \mathbf{0} & 1 & b_{n,n+1} \\ \mathbf{0} & b_{n+1,n} & 0 \end{bmatrix} \begin{bmatrix} {}_2\mathbf{p}_{n-1} \\ {}_2p_n \\ {}_2p_{m1} \end{bmatrix} + \begin{bmatrix} \mathbf{0} \\ 0 \\ b_{n+1,n+2} \end{bmatrix} {}_2p_{m2} \quad (5.51)$$

which, in order to remain consistent with relation (5.31) above, may alternatively be written as

$$t_1\mathbf{A}\begin{bmatrix} {}_2\mathbf{p}_{n-1} \\ {}_2p_n \\ {}_2p_{m1} \end{bmatrix} + {}_1\mathbf{L}\,{}_2w = {}_1\mathbf{B}\begin{bmatrix} {}_2\mathbf{p}_{n-1} \\ {}_2p_n \\ {}_2p_{m1} \end{bmatrix} + \begin{bmatrix} \mathbf{0} \\ 0 \\ b_{n+1,\,n+2} \end{bmatrix} {}_2p_{m2} \quad (5.52)$$

With simple transformations we obtain

$$[{}_1\mathbf{B}-t_1\mathbf{A}]^{-1}\,{}_1\mathbf{L}_2w-[{}_1\mathbf{B}-t_1\mathbf{A}]^{-1}\begin{bmatrix} \mathbf{0} \\ 0 \\ b_{n+1,\,n+2} \end{bmatrix} {}_2p_{m2} = \begin{bmatrix} {}_2\mathbf{p}_{n-1} \\ {}_2p_n \\ {}_2p_{n-1} \end{bmatrix} \quad (5.53)$$

in which the nth equation, which refers to the *numéraire*, gives us

$$[{}_1\mathbf{B}-t_1\mathbf{A}]_{(n)}^{-1}\,{}_1\mathbf{L}_2w-[{}_1\mathbf{B}-t_1\mathbf{A}]_{(n)}^{-1}\begin{bmatrix} \mathbf{0} \\ 0 \\ b_{n+1,\,n+2} \end{bmatrix} {}_2p_{m2} = 1 \quad (5.54)$$

But $[{}_1\mathbf{B}-t_1\mathbf{A}]_{(n)}^{-1}\,{}_1\mathbf{L}$ is simply an expression of $1/{}_1w$ alternative to (5.38) and would have been obtained by operating directly on the reduced and non-transformed system (5.31), instead of, as we did, on the transformed system.[26]

We can therefore substitute it in (5.54), thereby obtaining

$$[{}_1\mathbf{B}-t_1\mathbf{A}]_{(n)}^{-1}\begin{bmatrix} \mathbf{0} \\ 0 \\ b_{n+1,\,n+2} \end{bmatrix} {}_2p_{m2} = ({}_2w-{}_1w)/{}_1w \quad (5.55)$$

In this case too, the sign of the coefficient of ${}_2p_{m2}$ is equal to that of ${}_1w$. In fact,

$${}_1w = 1/\{\mathbf{D}[\mathbf{I}-t_1\overline{\mathbf{A}}]^{-1}\}_{(n)}\,{}_1\overline{\mathbf{L}} = 1/[{}_1\mathbf{B}-t_1\mathbf{A}]_{(n)}^{-1}\,{}_1\mathbf{L} \quad (5.56)$$

for any $\mathbf{L}$, and therefore, since $\mathbf{D} \geq \mathbf{0}$, the sign of $[{}_1\mathbf{B}-t_1\mathbf{A}]_{(n)}^{-1}$

[26] From (5.31) we obtain the following solution for the price vector: ${}_1\mathbf{p} = [{}_1\mathbf{B}-t_1\mathbf{A}]^{-1}\,{}_1\mathbf{L}_1w$. The nth component of ${}_1p$, i.e. that corresponding to the price of the commodity chosen as *numéraire* gives the expression of ${}_1w$ in which we are interested: ${}_1w = 1/[\mathbf{B}-t_1\mathbf{A}]_{(n)}^{-1}\,{}_1\mathbf{L}$.

$[\mathbf{0}, 0, b_{n+1,\,n+2}]'$ cannot be different from that of ${}_1w$. From (5.55), therefore, it follows, in complete analogy with ${}_2p_{m1}$ that ${}_2p_{m2} \lesseqgtr 0$ according to whether ${}_2w \lesseqgtr {}_1w$.

From all this we can definitely make the general conclusion that the sign of the prices of old machines, at a given level of the rate of profit, will depend on the relative magnitude of wage rates in the previous reduced systems. To exemplify this, we can summarise in the following table the various possible cases for a scheme including up to three activities.

	System with 2 activities	*System with 3 activities*
(1) ${}_0w < {}_1w < {}_2w$	$p_{m1} > 0$	$p_{m1} > 0$; $p_{m2} > 0$
(2) ${}_0w < {}_2w < {}_1w$	$p_{m1} > 0$	$p_{m1} > 0$; $p_{m2} < 0$
(3) ${}_2w < {}_1w < {}_0w$	$p_{m1} < 0$	$p_{m1} < 0$; $p_{m2} < 0$
(4) ${}_2w < {}_0w < {}_1w$	$p_{m1} > 0$	$p_{m1} < 0$; $p_{m2} < 0$
(5) ${}_1w < {}_0w < {}_2w$	$p_{m1} < 0$	$p_{m1} > 0$; $p_{m2} > 0$
(6) ${}_1w < {}_2w < {}_0w$	$p_{m1} < 0$	$p_{m1} < 0$; $p_{m2} > 0$

This clearly shows that, in the two-activity system, the sign of the price of the one-year-old machine does not give any information about the sign of the price of the same machine when it is used for a further year in a three-activity system. In the same way, the fact that p_{m2} is positive in the three-activity system does not at all mean that p_{m1} will also be positive.

11 Some economic implications of the preceding analysis

The special features of the analysis made so far, with respect to schemes with only circulating capital, suggest that some comments on its economic significance may be useful.

An observation worth making straightaway concerns the procedure used in the previous sections. It consists in the analysis of the solutions of each of the productive systems in two successive moments. This does not at all mean that the system of equations in the case of production with fixed capital is composed of two groups of equations that are in some way separated and therefore liable to be analysed independently of one another. The transformation of the original system to make it formally similar to a scheme of single production does not eliminate the expressions referring to the activities: they are simply combined in a single equation summarising all the information contained in the individual equations.

The transformed system is therefore an algebraic elaboration of the original system and not a part of it. Its interest derives from the fact that it is formally analogous to a scheme of single production and so allows one to refer its characteristic properties alternatively to one or the other of its analytic expressions, thereby facilitating the economic interpretation.

A concrete example of this is seen when, in a scheme of production with fixed capital, we analyse the behaviour of the relation $w-r$. The previous analysis has shown us that in this case w is not generally a monotonic function of r.

This means, for example, that *a priori* we cannot exclude behaviours such as those illustrated in Figures 5.2 and 5.3. The conclusions we have reached allow us to affirm that even these cases, although they seem abnormal from the point of view of single production, are economically significant, at least in the sense of allowing a strictly positive solution for the vector of prices of commodities produced (except those of old machines) for *all* parts of the relation $w-r$ included in the positive quadrant and such that $r < R(\mathbf{A}_{n-1})$.[27]

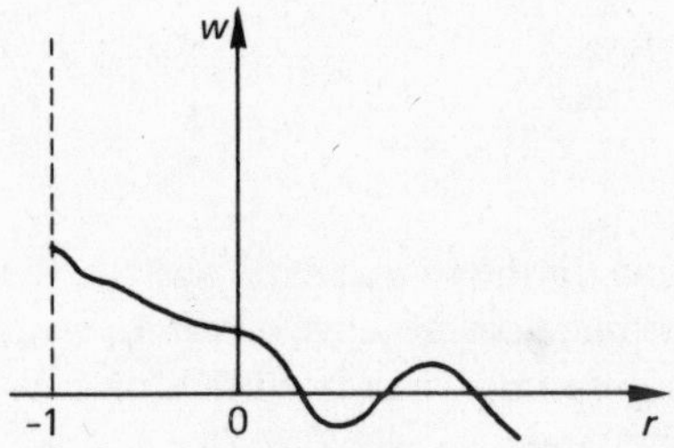

FIGURE 5.2

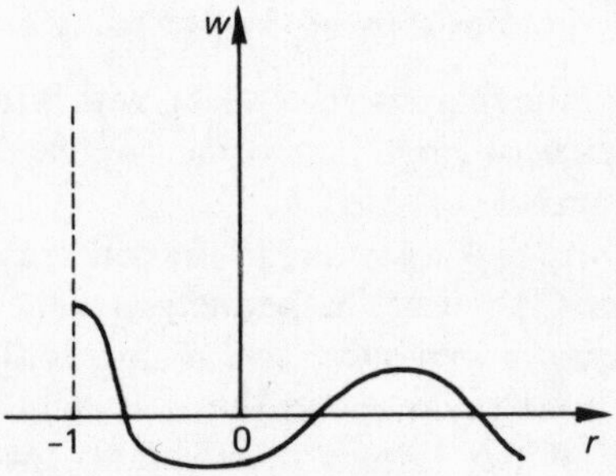

FIGURE 5.3

The same cases considered with reference to a transformed system (and therefore made formally analogous to a scheme of single production) appear very much more 'normal'. This is simply because we observe that all

[27] Figure 5.3 in particular corresponds to a system that is not viable with a zero rate of profit but which subsequently becomes economically significant.

the points of intersection between w and the axis of the abscissae are actually dominant eigenvalues of the transformed matrix of commodity inputs. The only special feature is that the matrix is itself a function of r and therefore does not supply a single maximum rate of profit (and thus no single dominant eigenvalue), as in the scheme of single production. Instead it gives a set of multiple roots.

On the other hand, the fact that parts of the $w-r$ relation belong to the positive quadrant is not sufficient to guarantee positive solutions for the *entire* vector of prices of our system of equations. A new condition, independent of the previous one, must be satisfied for the price of old machines to be positive. At the level of r considered, wages must be higher than those which could be obtained from the same productive system by reducing the period of utilisation of the machine. The negative price of old machines simply indicates that the productive system, or, rather, the number of periods of utilisation of the machine, is inefficient, in the sense that, if the number of periods were reduced then the system, with the same rate of profit, could allow higher wages.

This condition is independent of the previous one concerning the price of all commodities apart from old machines. This is confirmed by the fact that it is valid even outside the positive quadrant, i.e. even for non-positive values of w and r. Although in these cases we cannot determine the sign of the whole price vector, we can certainly affirm that the price of old machines is positive.

12 The case of negative prices in Sraffa's scheme

The discussion, in the previous sections, on the possible emergence of negative prices for old machines in a scheme of production with fixed capital has brought us, by a different route, to well known developments in the modern theory of production.

We have, in fact, defined a criterion which is substantially the same, though presented in a different context, as that proposed by Sraffa for the evaluation of the economic profitability of alternative productive techniques at the various levels of the rate of profits, in the case of single production (cf. Sraffa, 1960, Ch. 12).

It is worth analysing further why this convergence of results occurs. The explanation is connected with a fundamental difference between the scheme of single production and the scheme of production with fixed capital.

In the scheme of basic single-product industries, every industry is strictly necessary for the existence of the entire economic system (the elimination of one single basic industry means the loss of the commodity it produces and of all the other commodities in the system, because all of them are produced, directly or indirectly, with its help). With fixed capital, however, the industry which uses the machines is, as we have seen, composed of a series of productive activities, which can theoretically be lengthened or shortened at will without affecting the existence of the entire economic system.

Indeed, this situation is analogous to that which we find in a single-production system when non-basic commodities are produced in addition to basic commodities. Here, too, the basic industries alone can have an existence independent of the whole system, and also the possible emergence of negative solutions for the prices of the non-basic commodities cannot generally be excluded *a priori* (cf. Sraffa, 1960, Appendix B; Newman, 1962; Bharadwaj, 1970; Varri, 1973). In both cases (fixed capital and non-basic commodities) the possibility of negative prices seems to be closely connected with the system's potentiality to undergo a change in the number of its equations without ceasing to be determinate.

As a matter of fact, this occurs every time that the 'subsidiary' equations (i.e. those referring to non-basic industries or productive activities employing old machines) place a limit, given the rate of profit (or wage rate), on the wage rate (or rate of profit) which in their absence would have been obtained from the remaining equations of the system.

The problem becomes more important when we consider levels of the rate of profits (and wage rates) that are, *ceteris paribus*, different from those supposed to be uniformly present in the economic system described in the table of commodity flows. If negative prices emerge in a situation of this type, it merely indicates that the productive processes adopted at the initial level of the distributive variables are not those that, *ceteris paribus*, would have been chosen if the different distribution under consideration had prevailed initially.

This could provide an opportunity for easy and inopportune criticisms of Sraffa's entire analytical construction, so let us further clarify this point.

It is useful to remember here that one of the basic objectives of Sraffa's book is to clarify certain aspects of the functioning of a theoretical scheme for the simultaneous determination of relative prices in a system of interdependent industries. He aims to do this by isolating the effects of notional variations in the rate of profits (or wage rate) on prices and wages (or profits), on the hypothesis that all the other variables of the economic system remain unchanged. In this way, it is not of great concern if some prices are negative in relation to particular levels of the rate of profit.

From this point of view, therefore, it is important not to attribute any direct practical relevance to an analysis of this kind concerning the effects of variations in distributive parameters. This is because, being limited to the computational level and therefore entirely abstract, it is not in itself sufficient for the purpose of interpreting reality.

13 Life of machines and rate of profit: the 'reswitching' of activities

In the previous section we examined the fundamental reasons for the connection between the problem of the choice of technique and the problem of defining necessary and sufficient conditions to guarantee the existence of economically meaningful prices in the scheme of production with fixed capital. This gives us the opportunity to try to transfer to the problem of the machines, and to reinterpret accordingly, the results obtained in the recent debate on reswitching of techniques.

If in our simplified model we equalise in pairs the relations obtained for ${}_0w$, ${}_1w$ and ${}_2w$, we get polynomials of a degree higher than the second, the roots of which supply the so-called 'switchpoints' where two different periods of machine use are equally profitable. If the relation $w-r$ is constructed for each successive period of activity of the machine, the most external parts of the different curves will indicate the most profitable durations of the machine for each different level of the rate of profits. If those durations are respected, both the prices of machines and of commodities produced will be positive.

There is therefore no *a priori* regularity in the relationship between the economic life of a machine and the rate of profit. What we can say in general is that, given the system of economically profitable equations at a certain level of the rate of profit, the presence of negative prices at different rates of profit indicates that a shorter utilisation of the machines, all other things being equal, would be more profitable. On the other hand, positive prices do not exclude that a possible lengthening of the use of the machine, involving the insertion of new equations into the system, might increase wages without decreasing the rate of profit.

This allows us to reach another important conclusion. It is logically incorrect to assume that the duration of utilisation of the machines is generally independent of the distribution of income, and it is also incorrect to assume that any kind of monotonic relation exists between the two variables.

This incidentally adds another argument to the criticism recently made against the theories that require the measurement of capital in terms of an aggregate quantity. Indeed, this is one more reason why the rate of profit should be relevant for the determination of such a quantity.

14 Two particular solutions for the system of prices: the 'standard system' and the 'labour values'

Two solutions of Sraffa's general price system are of particular analytical interest: that in which $w = 0$, and the opposite one, in which $r = 0$. The first supplies the prices when the rate of profit equals the Standard ratio, while in the second the prices are proportional to the quantity of labour directly and indirectly used in production.

There are, however, some difficulties connected with these special solutions when fixed capital is taken into consideration. It is worth mentioning them here, if only in passing.

The first difficulty is linked with the possible emergence of negative prices in relation to these two extreme levels of the distributive variables. As far as this is concerned, we need only apply the observations previously made.

The other two problems involve the price system less directly, and for this reason we shall not deal with them here. They are concerned with the non-uniqueness of R, i.e. the possibility that with $w = 0$ there is more than one intersection between r and the axis of the abscissae, and the possibility that, when $r = 0$, the corresponding value of w is not necessarily the maximum and might even be negative. Both cases require special analysis, which we shall not attempt here.

15 Extensions and concluding remarks

So far, all the elaborations have been based on a highly simplified productive system in which a single machine is used for the production of a single commodity. However, there is no difficulty in principle about extending the analysis to cases that are more complicated and therefore more interesting.

For the purpose of better defining the limits of validity of the simplified scheme we have adopted, we shall mention a few of these cases before passing on to our final remarks about the economic significance of the scheme.

One economically important extension to the simplified scheme is that in which more than one single industry uses a particular durable means of production. All we need do to adapt the model to this extension is to add the equations corresponding to the new activities. The structure of the system, however, will remain substantially unaltered and we need only adapt our previous considerations. If all commodities produced are basic commodities, the only difference with respect to the simplified system previously adopted is that the number of reductions to be carried out on the initial system in order to obtain the reduced one will be equal to the number of machines used in the system, and the number of relations $w - r$ to be examined in order to verify the sign of the price of the old machines is equal to the product of the physical durations of the various machines. This does not involve any difficulty in principle.

Neither is there any difficulty in the special case in which the same machine is used in more than one process. As Sraffa points out, while the price of the new machine is uniform for all industries, it will then depend on the particular use made of the machine in the industry concerned (cf. Sraffa, 1960, section 78). In particular, it may happen that a machine is directly used for the production of other machines of the same type. Once again, we have to insert the equations corresponding to this special case into the system and follow the same procedure as previously adopted.[28]

In conclusion, since all these cases do not involve substantial changes in the system of equations they have no independent economic interest. Of more interest is the case in which the productive processes supply a single product while contemporaneously using more than one machine.

At first glance, it could seem that the analytical complications of the general scheme of joint production are inevitable in this case. We can set apart the cases in which the machines are actually used singly in succession: here we can represent the overall process as a succession of individual subprocesses, whose semifinished goods are treated as goods. However, we are still left with the case in which this separation cannot be made, and the initial problem is still with us.

The same case is also discussed by Roncaglia (1971). He correctly points out that, if the price of the old machine also depends on the age of the machines employed jointly with it, the system of prices cannot generally be determined with a finite number of equations. He finds a way out of this embarrassing situation by simply assuming that the technical efficiency of the machines is reciprocally independent, so that the analysis can be stopped when the last of the machines originally adopted is eliminated. However, the hypothesis is clearly arbitrary and, hence, logically unsatisfactory.

In fact, the main difficulty in this case is not the system of prices but the very concept of stationary state at the basis of the particular theory of prices of production which we are examining here. We need to be able to identify a regularly repeating period in the uninterrupted succession of productive operations if the notion of stationary equilibrium is to be used. We may then define a system of price equations and calculate its equilibrium solution with reference to this regularly repeating period. This is another respect in which the analysis of productive systems with only circulating capital differs from that of cases with fixed capital.

In the particular system under examination (where two or more machines are jointly used to produce a single commodity and their return depends on the state of the other machines) it may even happen that such a period can not be identified. This would require that a moment exists in which, at the

[28] What we have to do here is to combine the activities of two productive processes: first of all the process that produces the new machine, and then that which produces the commodity in the production of which this machine plays a part.

same time, all the machines under consideration stop being used, and, clearly, this may not occur. This is therefore the essential hypothesis for the analysis, and not that suggested by Roncaglia, which eliminates the problem *tout court*.

Having established the limits within which the case of several machines used jointly is compatible with the theoretical scheme under examination, it could be of interest to discover if the conclusions reached on the basis of our simplified model may also be extended to this case, which is analytically more complex but substantially very near to the general scheme of joint production.

With this end in view, we can use a procedure which is analytically very useful and also economically significant. It consists in considering the set of machines under consideration as a new, independent 'machine' which is 'composed' of the various individual machines. This 'machine', which we might quite reasonably define as a 'plant', will have a life equal to the period within which all the individual machines are simultaneously eliminated, while the substitution of the individual machines of which it is composed will appear as simple operations of repair and maintenance of the 'plant'.[29]

It is not necessary to point out that the nature of this procedure is not simply analytical. It has a precise economic and technological basis in a large number of concrete cases. An assembly line and the equipment of a workshop are simple examples of fixed capitals which are more significant as a whole than in terms of their individual components.

So far as our previous analysis is concerned, we need only note that this brings us to a scheme which is qualitatively identical with the simplified scheme initially adopted. At the same time, the general scheme of joint production is made less relevant.

In this sense the above analysis seems to be useful in overcoming some of the difficulties preventing more widespread inclusion of machines in economic models. This, I believe, could be a significant step towards dynamic analysis.

References

Bharadwaj, K., 'On the Maximum Number of Switches between Two Production Systems', *Schweizerische Zeitschrift für Volkswirtschaft und Statistik*, CVI (1970) 409–28.

Böhm-Bawerk, E. von, *The Positive Theory of Capital*, trans. W. Smart (London: Macmillan, 1891). (Original German edition published in 1889).

[29] In this case, the component machines, unless employed individually in other productive processes, will not be considered as durable means of production, since once they take their place in the plant they lose their individuality.

Gantmacher, F. R., *The Theory of Matrices* (New York: Chelsea, 1959).
Hadley, G., *Linear Algebra* (Reading, Mass.: Addison-Wesley, 1961).
Leontief, W., *The Structure of American Economy 1919–39* (New York: Oxford University Press, 1951).
Neumann, J. von, 'A Model of General Economic Equilibrium' (first published in 1937), *Review of Economic Studies*, XIII (1945–6) 1–9.
Newman, P., 'Production of Commodities by means of Commodities', *Schweizerische Zeitschrift für Volkswirtschaft und Statistik*, , XCVIII (1962) 58–75.
Pasinetti, L. L., *Growth and Income Distribution: Essays in Economic Theory* (Cambridge: Cambridge University Press, 1974).
Pasinetti, L. L. *et al.*, 'Paradoxes in Capital Theory: A Symposium', *Quarterly Journal of Economics*, XXX (1966) 503–83.
Ricardo, D., *On the Principles of Political Economy and Taxation* (first published in 1821), vol. I of *The Works and Correspondence of David Ricardo*, ed. P. Sraffa (Cambridge: Cambridge University Press, 1951).
Roncaglia, A., 'Il capitale fisso in uno schema di produzione circolare', *Studi economici*, XXVI (1971) 1–14.
Sraffa, P., *Production of Commodities by Means of Commodities* (Cambridge: Cambridge University Press, 1960).
Varri, P., 'Basic and Non Basic Commodities in Mr. Sraffa's Production System' (1973), mimeo.
Wicksell, K., *Lectures on Political Economy* (first published in 1901), ed. L. Robbins (London: Routledge and Kegan Paul, 1934).

CHAPTER SIX

Fixed Capital in Sraffa's Theoretical Scheme[1]

SALVATORE BALDONE

1 Introduction

In this essay the analysis of fixed capital in terms of joint production, as proposed by Sraffa and extensively developed by him in the case of 'constant efficiency' of machines, will be formalised for the more general case in which the pattern of varying efficiency of machines is not definable in physical terms.

We shall suppose, therefore, that the productive process using the machine is divided into as many separate activities as are the years of the working life of the machine. Each of these activities produces the particular commodity of the process in question and also the machine one year older – the only element of joint production.

By treating fixed capital in these terms we generally obtain some results that are not completely in conformity with those obtained from the case of single production with circulating capital alone. We intend to analyse such results and in particular to try to find the reasons behind negative prices for old machines and to identify the relationship between the positivity of such prices and the economic life of the machines themselves.

2 Some remarks on the problem of fixed capital

Capital, even in its simplest form of circulating capital, can be seen as a collection of heterogeneous commodities entering into production. But, when we take durable means of production into consideration (i.e. instruments which can be used for more than one year[2] in production), it takes on a new, temporal dimension, which links together flows of commodities employed and produced in different periods. The individual elements that go to make up capital therefore seem in general to be

[1] Originally published as 'Il capitale fisso nello schema teorico di Piero Sraffa', *Studi economici*, XXIX, no. 1 (1974) 45–106, here translated with slight modifications by the author.

[2] The 'year' is the conventional unit period of production.

characterised by two dimensions: quantity and duration.

The introduction of the temporal dimension of fixed capital into the analysis gives rise to another element of heterogeneity, in the sense that it is no longer possible unequivocably to define the relative efficiency of the same machine used in production at different ages. In fact, two activities producing the same commodity–using commodities, labour and a machine which is the same but of different ages, are generally not comparable, since there are usually changes in the proportions of the various inputs and also in the dimension of the output.

If such a comparison is not generally possible, we cannot identify a law of equivalence in physical terms between the new machine and the machine which has been used in production for a certain number of years. The consequent effects are on two levels: the periodic contribution to production of such a machine cannot be determined in physical terms, and consequently the corresponding depreciation quotas in purely technical terms cannot be determined either. Since the temporal dimension of durable means of production cannot generally be reduced to a quantitative equivalent, the problem arises of how to accommodate it correctly in schemes of economic analysis.

It is clear at this point that it is possible to resolve the difficulties over the life, or the age structure, of the different durable means of production by considering the machines at different stages of their life as commodities which are 'qualitatively' different. A machine of a certain age is simply the output, along with the marketable commodity which is the primary object of the process, of a productive activity that uses, as part of the annual intakes, the same machine one year less old. It is therefore possible to treat fixed capital satisfactorily simply in terms of joint production. And von Neumann (1937) and Sraffa (1960) insert fixed capital into a scheme of this type, though they have profoundly different methodologies and aims.

The introduction into the analysis of the temporal dimension of durable means of production, which are not generally reducible to a quantitative equivalent, highlights the important problem of determining their 'economic life', i.e. their most profitable period of use. This is an operation that logically precedes that of the choice of productive technique. In addition, as we shall see later, the temporal dimension characterising durable instruments of production has an important role to play in the context of the theory of value.

There is a further element that makes the approach in terms of joint production a completely general method with which to tackle the problem of fixed capital. Consider the case in which it is possible to define the pattern of efficiency variation of a machine on a technical level, and suppose that this efficiency is falling. If the physical life of the machine is given, then it is possible to use financial tables to determine the depreciation plan for the machine. This does not mean, however, that the most economically profitable period of utilisation coincides with the physical life of the machine. It might happen, in fact, that, before the machine comes to the end of its physical life, the negative effect in terms of average intakes per unit of output, owing to the machine's fall in efficiency, offsets the positive effect of the reduction of the depreciation charge per unit of output, resulting from the increase in the years of machine utilisation. Here too we cannot avoid an economic evaluation, which alone is able to determine the economic life of the machine. The joint-production approach alone permits this type of evaluation in every case; in addition, as we shall see later on, it is able to show elements which automatically give information about the profitability or not of every particular arrangement of the working life of a machine.

Economists have not omitted to give importance to the problem of durable means of production in their works, even though the solutions put forward have not generally been very satisfactory from a theoretical point of view. Without going into analytic details, we can say that even the classical economists – Ricardo (1821) in particular – and Marx (1867–94) dealt with the problem of machines, on the one hand drawing attention to the importance of the phenomenon of depreciation in relation to the theory of value, and on the other stressing the aspects (more rightly to be seen as dynamic) that are relative to the effects that their introduction produces on the level of income and employment.

Passing to later schools of thought and in particular to those expressing a theory of production and distribution based on the concept of 'quantity of capital' (understood as aggregate quantity independent of distribution), we have to recognise that they were intrinsically unable to deal with the durability of fixed capital in a satisfactory way: the need to reduce the temporal dimension to a quantitative equivalent eliminates the problem without solving it.

The type of durable instrument that has been most dealt with in such theories is that with 'constant efficiency'. This gives a constant flow of output in time until the moment when it suddenly collapses. If maintenance costs exist, they are supposed to be constant so that they have no significant influence on the problem. Clearly, the life of such a machine is technically determined. The economic problem therefore consists in choosing between a certain number of machines, perfectly equal apart from their life, which is in direct functional relation to the sum of investments made for the production of each machine. There is no problem of economic evaluation of the duration: this is reduced to a problem of determining the optimum quantity of capital.

In these terms the problem is no longer that of determining the profitable life of a given instrument, but is rather that of choosing the most profitable productive technique: this is the type of problem that authors such as

Böhm–Bawerk (1889) and Wicksell (1901) tried to solve when they turned their attention to the problem of duration.

More recent versions of such theoretic schemes have also tackled the case of decreasing efficiency of capital.

In this case treatment has been in terms of 'evaporation' or 'radioactive decay' of fixed capital, as a result of which non-new capital is supposed to be equivalent to a smaller quantity of new capital of the same type. But this is completely unsatisfactory. In fact, it is equivalent to supposing that it is possible to identify *a priori* the law according to which the efficiency of the durable means of production is renewed. It has the same limitations as the situation with capital of constant efficiency, of which it is effectively a special case.

Not even Walras (1874–7), even though working in a disaggregate scheme, succeeds in offering a logically acceptable solution to the problem of how to deal with durable means of production. This is owing to the substantial limitation of Walras's analysis to a single period and to the 'non-circular' nature of the productive process, which imposes a homogenisation of the machines of different ages by means of the identification of the periodic contribution to production in physical terms.

The recent spread of formal schemes allowing consideration of the characteristics of heterogeneity of the commodities has not generally led to a correct solution of the difficulties involved in the introduction of fixed capital. For example, that part of the economic literature headed by the works of Leontief (see, for example, Leontief 1951 and 1953), though many times it explicitly faces the problem of durable means of production, still has an approach similar to that of the theories mentioned above. In fact, the temporal dimension of the durable means of production is resolved in quantitative terms, on the assumption that it is possible to identify in physical terms the contribution by such instruments to production in each year. As already pointed out, not only is such a position lacking in generality, but, in addition, such a treatment of fixed capital is inadequate for the purpose of determining the economic life of the durable means of production.

3 Fixed capital and joint production: the price system

Consider an economic system producing h marketable commodities, the first of which, which we shall call the machine, has the characteristic of being able to play a part in the production of the hth commodity for n years at most.

We shall call n the physical life of the machine.[3]

[3] Rather than of physical life, it would be better to talk of technical life of the machine. It is in fact always possible to prolong the life of the machine by suitable repairs. There is, however, very probably a limit beyond which repairs would become so many and so frequent that the machine would certainly be no longer profitable.

If we suppose that the machine is used until the limit of its physical life, the industry producing the hth commodity will be divided into n different activities, each one employing non-durable means of production and also the machine at a particular age in order to produce the hth commodity and, jointly, also the machine itself one year older. If there are no residual scraps, as we suppose, the activity employing the n-year-old machine will produce only the hth commodity, since the machine exhausts its contribution to production at that age.

Suppose in addition that the $h-1$ commodities produced without the use of durable instruments are made available singly by the respective industries.

The structure of the economic system may therefore be represented by the following arrangement of the elements of the matrices of inputs and outputs and of the vector of labour requirements, where a, b, l indicate the elements which can be positive.

$$
\mathbf{A}_n = \left[\begin{array}{ccccc|c|c|c|c|c|c}
0 & a & a & \cdots & a & a & 0 & 0 & \cdots & 0 & 0 \\
0 & a & a & \cdots & a & a & 0 & 0 & \cdots & 0 & 0 \\
\vdots & \vdots & \vdots & & \vdots & \vdots & \vdots & \vdots & & \vdots & \vdots \\
0 & a & a & \cdots & a & a & 0 & 0 & \cdots & 0 & 0 \\
\hdashline
a & a & a & \cdots & a & a & 0 & 0 & \cdots & 0 & 0 \\
\hdashline
0 & a & a & \cdots & a & a & a & 0 & \cdots & 0 & 0 \\
\hdashline
0 & a & a & \cdots & a & a & 0 & a & \cdots & 0 & 0 \\
\hdashline
\vdots & \vdots & \vdots & & \vdots & \vdots & \vdots & \vdots & & \vdots & \vdots \\
\hdashline
0 & a & a & \cdots & a & a & 0 & 0 & \cdots & a & 0 \\
\hdashline
0 & a & a & \cdots & a & a & 0 & 0 & \cdots & 0 & a
\end{array}\right]
$$

$$
= \left[\begin{array}{ccccccc}
\mathbf{a} & \mathbf{a.} & \mathbf{0} & \mathbf{0} & \cdots & \mathbf{0} & \mathbf{0} \\
\mathbf{a}_{00} & a._0 & 0 & 0 & \cdots & 0 & 0 \\
\mathbf{a}_{10} & a._1 & a_1 & 0 & \cdots & 0 & 0 \\
\mathbf{a}_{20} & a._2 & 0 & a_2 & \cdots & 0 & 0 \\
\vdots & \vdots & \vdots & \vdots & & \vdots & \vdots \\
\mathbf{a}_{n-1,0} & a._{n-1} & 0 & 0 & \cdots & a_{n-1} & 0 \\
\mathbf{a}_{n,0} & a._n & 0 & 0 & \cdots & 0 & a_n
\end{array}\right]
$$

$$
\mathbf{B}_n = \left[\begin{array}{ccccc|c|c|c|c|c|c}
b & 0 & 0 & \cdots & 0 & 0 & 0 & 0 & 0 & \cdots & 0 \\
0 & b & 0 & \cdots & 0 & 0 & 0 & 0 & 0 & \cdots & 0 \\
0 & 0 & b & \cdots & 0 & 0 & 0 & 0 & 0 & \cdots & 0 \\
\vdots & \vdots & \vdots & & \vdots & \vdots & \vdots & \vdots & \vdots & & \vdots \\
0 & 0 & 0 & \cdots & b & 0 & 0 & 0 & 0 & \cdots & 0 \\
\hline
0 & 0 & 0 & \cdots & 0 & b & b & 0 & 0 & \cdots & 0 \\
\hline
0 & 0 & 0 & \cdots & 0 & b & 0 & b & 0 & \cdots & 0 \\
\hline
0 & 0 & 0 & \cdots & 0 & b & 0 & 0 & b & \cdots & 0 \\
\hline
\vdots & \vdots & \vdots & & \vdots & \vdots & \vdots & \vdots & \vdots & & \vdots \\
\hline
0 & 0 & 0 & \cdots & 0 & b & 0 & 0 & 0 & \cdots & b \\
\hline
0 & 0 & 0 & \cdots & 0 & b & 0 & 0 & 0 & \cdots & 0
\end{array}\right]
$$

$$
= \begin{bmatrix}
\mathbf{b} & \mathbf{0} & \mathbf{0} & \mathbf{0} & \mathbf{0} & \cdots & \mathbf{0} \\
\mathbf{0} & b_{\cdot 0} & b_1 & 0 & 0 & \cdots & 0 \\
\mathbf{0} & b_{\cdot 1} & 0 & b_2 & 0 & \cdots & 0 \\
\mathbf{0} & b_{\cdot 2} & 0 & 0 & b_3 & \cdots & 0 \\
\vdots & \vdots & \vdots & \vdots & \vdots & & \vdots \\
\mathbf{0} & b_{\cdot n-1} & 0 & 0 & 0 & \cdots & b_n \\
\mathbf{0} & b_{\cdot n} & 0 & 0 & 0 & \cdots & 0
\end{bmatrix}
$$

$$
\mathbf{L}_n = \left[\begin{array}{c}
l \\ l \\ \vdots \\ l \\ \hline l \\ l \\ l \\ \vdots \\ l \\ l
\end{array}\right]
= \begin{bmatrix}
\mathbf{l} \\ l_0 \\ l_1 \\ l_2 \\ \vdots \\ l_{n-1} \\ l_n
\end{bmatrix}
$$

On the basis of the representation of the activities given above, the first $h-1$ rows of matrices $\mathbf{A}_n$ and $\mathbf{B}_n$, together with the corresponding elements of the column vector $\mathbf{L}_n$, represent the productive processes that do not employ the machine. Consequently, $\mathbf{a}$ is a non-negative square matrix of order $h-1$, and its elements indicate the inputs of commodities, apart from that produced with the use of the machine, that enter into the various processes of single production to produce the outputs indicated by the corresponding elements of the diagonal matrix $\mathbf{b}$, which clearly is also of dimension $h-1$.

$\mathbf{a}.$ is a column vector the $h-1$ components of which indicate the inputs of the hth commodity in the processes that do not employ the machine.

The $h-1$ components of the row vector $\mathbf{a}_{00}$ and the scalar $a._0$ indicate the inputs of the various commodities into the mechanised activity that produces the quantity $b._0$ of the hth commodity together with b_1 machines of one year of age.

The elements that identify the activities employing old machines to produce the hth commodity are now subject to an obvious interpretation: $\mathbf{a}_{i0}$ is the row vector the components of which, together with the scalar $a._i$, indicate the non-durable inputs into the activities that employ a_i machines of i years of age together with l_i labour units to produce the quantity of the hth commodity indicated by the scalar $b._i$ together with b_{i+1} machines of $i+1$ years of age.

Suppose that in addition the system is in a stationary state, which, as far as the durable instruments are concerned, means that the corresponding temporal sequence of outputs and inputs always involves the same number of machines.

The system could be standardised by dividing the inputs and the output – or outputs – of each commodity by the corresponding total production. The result would be that all the inputs and outputs of machines would be equal to unity, as would total production of the various non-durable commodities. Clearly, the meaning of such ratios would not be that of technical coefficients of production, but simply that of rates of participation of each commodity to the production in the different activities. In the pages that follow, however, absolute sizes will be used and no assumption on returns to scale will be formulated.

Let r be the annual rate of profit. Then, starting from the general system of prices

$$(1+r)\mathbf{A}_n\mathbf{p}^n + w\mathbf{L}_n = \mathbf{B}_n\mathbf{p}^n \qquad (6.1)$$

and expressing the prices themselves in terms of the price of the hth commodity, adopted as *numéraire*, we can construct by substitution the functional relationship between the rate of profits and the wage rate.

Indicating the prices of the new machine and of the other marketable commodities (with the exception of the hth) by the components of vector $\mathbf{p}$, from the last equation of system (6.1) we can obtain the following expression for the price ${}_m p^n{}_n$[4] of the machine of n years of age:

$$ {}_m p^n{}_n = (b._n - ta._n - t\mathbf{a}_{n0}\mathbf{p} - wl_n)/ta_n \tag{6.2}$$

where $t = 1 + r$ is the factor of profit. Substituting (6.2) in the penultimate equation of system (6.1), we can similarly obtain the price of the machine of $n-1$ years of age and so on until we obtain the price of the one-year-old machine.

Remembering that the assumption of a stationariness means that $b_i = a_i$ $(i = 1, 2, \ldots n)$, i.e. that the number of machines of i years of age employed is equal to the number of machines produced of this age, we substitute the expression of $\mathbf{p}$ obtained from the first $h-1$ equations of system (6.1) in the hth equation, which corresponds to the activity using the new machine. We thereby obtain the following expression for the wage–profit relationship corresponding to the system employing the machine in production up to n years of age:

$$w^n = \frac{[t^n b._0 + t^{n-1} b._1 + \ldots + b._n - t(t^n a._0 + t^{n-1} a._1 + \ldots + a._n)]}{[t(t^n \mathbf{a}_{00} + t^{n-1}\mathbf{a}_{10} + \ldots + \mathbf{a}_{n0})[\mathbf{b} - t\mathbf{a}]^{-1}\mathbf{1} + (t^n l_0 + t^{n-1} l_1 + \ldots + l_n)]}$$

$$- \frac{[t^2(t^n \mathbf{a}_{00} + t^{n-1}\mathbf{a}_{10} + \ldots + \mathbf{a}_{n0})[\mathbf{b} - t\mathbf{a}]^{-1}\mathbf{a}.]}{[t(t^n \mathbf{a}_{00} + t^{n-1}\mathbf{a}_{10} + \ldots + \mathbf{a}_{n0})[\mathbf{b} - t\mathbf{a}]^{-1}\mathbf{1} + (t^n l_0 + t^{n-1} l_1 + \ldots + l_n)]} \tag{6.3}$$

If we say that

$$\begin{aligned} t^n b._0 + t^{n-1} b._1 + \ldots + b._n &= \hat{b}._n(t) \\ t^n a._0 + t^{n-1} a._1 + \ldots + a._n &= \hat{a}._n(t) \\ t^n \mathbf{a}_{00} + t^{n-1}\mathbf{a}_{10} + \ldots + \mathbf{a}_{n0} &= \hat{\mathbf{a}}_{n0}(t) \\ t^n l_0 + t^{n-1} l_1 + \ldots + l_n &= \hat{l}_n(t) \end{aligned}$$

then we can rewrite (6.3) as follows:

$$\begin{aligned} w^n(t) = \{&[\hat{b}._n(t) - t\hat{a}._n(t)] - t^2 \hat{\mathbf{a}}_{n0}(t)[\mathbf{b} - t\mathbf{a}]^{-1}\mathbf{a}.\}/ \\ &\{t\hat{\mathbf{a}}_{n0}(t)[\mathbf{b} - t\mathbf{a}]^{-1}\mathbf{1} + \hat{l}_n(t)\} \end{aligned} \tag{6.4}$$

The sequence of operations used to construct (6.4) is equivalent to the application to system (6.1) of the following operator

$$\begin{bmatrix} \mathbf{I} & \mathbf{0} & \mathbf{0} & \ldots \mathbf{0} & \mathbf{0} \\ \mathbf{0} & t^n & t^{n-1} & \ldots t & 1 \end{bmatrix} \tag{6.5}$$

where $\mathbf{I}$ is a unit matrix of dimension $h-1$. If we indicate the price of the commodity produced by means of the machine with p_0, we are able to pass

[4] In the present model, ${}_m p^i{}_j$ indicates the price of the machine of j years of age in the system that employs the machine up to i years of age $(i, j = 1, 2, \ldots n; j \le i)$.

from the original scheme to the following:

$$t\begin{bmatrix} \mathbf{a} & \mathbf{a}. \\ \hat{\mathbf{a}}_{n0} & \hat{a}._n \end{bmatrix}\begin{bmatrix} \mathbf{p} \\ p_0 \end{bmatrix} + t\begin{bmatrix} 0 & 0 & \dots 0 \\ t^{n-1}a_1 & t^{n-2}a_2 & \dots a_n \end{bmatrix}\begin{bmatrix} {}_mp_1 \\ \vdots \\ {}_mp_n \end{bmatrix} + w\begin{bmatrix} \mathbf{l} \\ \hat{l}_n \end{bmatrix}$$

$$= \begin{bmatrix} \mathbf{b} & \mathbf{0} \\ \mathbf{0} & \hat{b}._n \end{bmatrix}\begin{bmatrix} \mathbf{p} \\ p_0 \end{bmatrix} + \begin{bmatrix} \mathbf{0} & \mathbf{0} & \dots & \mathbf{0} \\ t^n b_1 & t^{n-1}b_2 & \dots & tb_n \end{bmatrix}\begin{bmatrix} {}_mp_1 \\ \vdots \\ {}_mp_n \end{bmatrix} \tag{6.6}$$

As a result of the assumptions formulated about the economic system, the second addend in the first member and the last addend in the second member are equal, and therefore cancel out. Making $p_0 = 1$, we immediately obtain (6.4).

An examination of (6.5) allows us to see clearly the meaning of the operations carried out: they make the various activities into which, on account of the presence of the machine, the hth productive process is divided comparable from a temporal point of view.

The operation of capitalisation of the mechanised activities, at the date of the employment of the oldest machine, does not affect the processes using circulating capital only, since they are simultaneous with all unit periods of production.

We may call this operation 'vertical integration in a temporal sense' of the activities employing the machine in its various years of age; it allows us formally to eliminate the joint-production component and bring the analysis back to the forms of single production with only circulating capital. In fact, let it be assumed that

$$\hat{\mathbf{A}}_n(t) = \begin{bmatrix} \mathbf{a} & \mathbf{a}. \\ \hat{\mathbf{a}}_{n0}(t) & \hat{a}._n(t) \end{bmatrix}$$

$$\hat{\mathbf{B}}_n(t) = \begin{bmatrix} \mathbf{b} & \mathbf{0} \\ \mathbf{0} & \hat{b}._n(t) \end{bmatrix}$$

$$\hat{\mathbf{L}}_n(t) = \begin{bmatrix} \mathbf{l} \\ \hat{l}_n(t) \end{bmatrix}, \qquad \hat{\mathbf{p}} = \begin{bmatrix} \mathbf{p} \\ p_0 \end{bmatrix}$$

Then (6.6) may be rewritten as follows:

$$t\hat{\mathbf{A}}_n(t)\,\hat{\mathbf{p}} + w\,\hat{L}_n(t) = \hat{\mathbf{B}}_n(t)\,\hat{\mathbf{p}} \tag{6.7}$$

where $\hat{\mathbf{B}}_n(t)$ is a diagonal matrix. We shall call such a transformation of (6.1) an 'integrated system'.

4 Positivity of the maximum wage rate

Clearly, for the system under examination to be economically meaningful, the condition of productivity[5] must be satisfied. Therefore, the total quantity produced of at least one commodity (apart from the durable instrument, since we have supposed that the system is stationary) should be greater than that used as input in the system itself.

We may therefore prove the following.

Proposition 1

If system $\mathbf{A}_n$, $\mathbf{B}_n$, $\mathbf{L}_n$ is productive, then $w^n(t)$ is positive for $t = 1$.

Proof

Calling **s** the sum vector of suitable dimension, according to the assumption of productivity, we can write,

$$\mathbf{s}(\mathbf{B}_n - \mathbf{A}_n) \geq \mathbf{0}^6 \qquad (6.8)$$

Disregarding the columns of matrices $\mathbf{B}_n$ and $\mathbf{A}_n$ corresponding to the inputs and outputs of old machines (for which there is no surplus), (6.8) may

[5] Here we shall use a different terminology from that adopted by Sraffa (1960, section 3). Hence we shall say that system (6.1) is productive if the total quantity produced of each commodity is not inferior to the global quantity employed and if it is greater for at least one commodity, i.e. if

$$\mathbf{s}(\mathbf{B}_n - \mathbf{A}_n) \geq \mathbf{0} \qquad (1)$$

where $\mathbf{s} = [1, 1, \ldots 1]$ is the sum vector of appropriate size. Since the economy under examination is stationary, (1) may also be referred to the integrated system (6.7):

$$\mathbf{s}[\hat{\mathbf{B}}_n(1) - \hat{\mathbf{A}}_n(1)] \geq \mathbf{0}$$

The present definition of a productive system corresponds, therefore, to Sraffa's definition of a system in a self-replacing state with surplus. Moreover, we shall say that the integrated economic system is viable in relation to a determined value of the rate of profit and of nominal wage, if, whatever the requirements of labour are, there is a non-negative system of prices able to support such a distribution of income.

It is easy to prove that, if the system satisfies the assumption of productivity, there is a set of distributive configurations in correspondence with which the integrated system is viable. On the other hand, if the dominant eigenvalue of matrix $t\hat{\mathbf{B}}_n^{-1}(t)\,\hat{\mathbf{A}}_n(t)$ is less than 1, the integrated system is viable.

[6] In comparing matrices or vectors we shall use the following symbolism:

$\mathbf{a} = \mathbf{b}$ if each component of $\mathbf{a}$ is equal to the corresponding component of $\mathbf{b}$,
$\mathbf{a} \geqq \mathbf{b}$ if each component of $\mathbf{a}$ is greater than or equal to the corresponding component of $\mathbf{b}$,
$\mathbf{a} \geq \mathbf{b}$ if $\mathbf{a} \geqq \mathbf{b}$ and $\mathbf{a} \neq \mathbf{b}$.

be partitioned into the following inequalities:

$$\mathbf{sb} - [\mathbf{sa} + \hat{\mathbf{a}}_{n0}(1)] \geq \mathbf{0} \tag{6.8a}$$

$$\hat{b}._n(1) - [\mathbf{sa}. + \hat{a}._n(1)] \geq 0 \tag{6.8b}$$

From (6.8a) we obtain,

$$\mathbf{s}[\mathbf{b} - \mathbf{a}] \geq \hat{\mathbf{a}}_{n0}(1)$$

Hence, on the basis of the assumption of productivity of the system, of the structure of matrix **a** and of well known theorems on non-negative matrices, it emerges that $[\mathbf{b} - \mathbf{a}]^{-1} \geq \mathbf{0}$ and therefore that

$$\mathbf{s} \geq \hat{\mathbf{a}}_{n0}(1)[\mathbf{b} - \mathbf{a}]^{-1} \tag{6.9}$$

(6.8b) may be rewritten as follows:

$$\hat{b}._n(1) - \hat{a}._n(1) \geq \mathbf{sa}. \tag{6.10}$$

But, according to the assumption of productivity, either (6.10) is satisfied with the sign of strict inequality, or this is verified for at least one of the inequalities (6.9). Consequently, substituting the right-hand side of (6.9) for **s** in (6.10), we obtain

$$\hat{b}._n(1) - \hat{a}._n(1) > \hat{\mathbf{a}}_{n0}(1)[\mathbf{b} - \mathbf{a}]^{-1}\mathbf{a}.$$

We have thus proved that the numerator of $w^n(1)$ is positive, so that consequently $w^n(1) > 0$. *q.e.d.*

In the above proof, the assumption of productivity of the system is essential for the positivity of the maximum wage rate. The fact that this condition is satisfied when the use of the machine is extended up to the limit (as in the case just examined) of its physical life does not necessarily mean that it is satisfied with another productive configuration obtained by varying the working life of the machine. For example, consider the economic system when only the new machine is employed in production: it could happen that the quantity of the marketable commodity produced with the machine is less than the quantity of that commodity used in the economic system. In other words, it is not to be assumed that the system is productive when the working life of the machine is not, for example, extended beyond a minimum number of years.

5 Existence and positivity of the maximum rate of profit

In the present section we propose to prove the existence and the positivity of a maximum value of the rate of profit for system (6.1), i.e. of a rate of profit in relation to which the share of surplus that is allotted to labour is zero.

To this end, we shall proceed to prove the following proposition.

Proposition 2

If matrix $\begin{bmatrix} \mathbf{a} & \mathbf{a}_{\cdot} \\ \mathbf{a}_{00} & a_{\cdot 0} \end{bmatrix}$ is indecomposable[7] and if the system satisfies the assumption of productivity, then there exists a value of the factor of profit $t = T_n$, $T_n > 1$, which is a root of the equation $\det[\hat{\mathbf{B}}_n(t) - t\hat{\mathbf{A}}_n(t)] = 0$.

Proof

Since $\hat{\mathbf{B}}_n(t)$ is a non-singular diagonal matrix, the equation $\det[\hat{\mathbf{B}}_n(t) - t\hat{\mathbf{A}}_n(t)] = 0$ is equivalent to $\det[\mathbf{I} - t\hat{\mathbf{B}}_n^{-1}(t)\hat{\mathbf{A}}_n(t)] = 0$.

In addition, since matrix $\hat{\mathbf{B}}_n(t)$ is non-negative and matrix $\hat{\mathbf{A}}_n(t)$ is non-negative and indecomposable,[8] then also $t\hat{\mathbf{B}}_n^{-1}(t)\hat{\mathbf{A}}_n(t)$ will be non-negative and indecomposable. On the basis of well known theorems, we can state that the matrix in question possesses a dominant eigenvalue $\lambda_M(t) > 0$ for every value of t.

We may therefore write

$$\lambda_M(t)\hat{\mathbf{p}}(t) = t\hat{\mathbf{B}}_n^{-1}(t)\hat{\mathbf{A}}_n(t)\hat{\mathbf{p}}(t)^9 \tag{6.11}$$

On the basis of the theorems referred to above, we have $\hat{\mathbf{p}}[\lambda_M(t)] > \mathbf{0}$.

Since system (6.11) is homogeneous in $\hat{\mathbf{p}}(t)$, we can normalise the eigenvector and obtain

$$\lambda_M(t)\mathbf{s}\hat{\mathbf{p}}(t) = \lambda_M(t) = \mathbf{s}t\,\hat{\mathbf{B}}_n^{-1}(t)\hat{\mathbf{A}}_n(t)\hat{\mathbf{p}}(t) \tag{6.12}$$

But, on account of the assumption of indecomposability, $\mathbf{s}t\hat{\mathbf{B}}_n^{-1}(t)\hat{\mathbf{A}}_n(t)$ is a vector of rational functions in t, in which each component tends to a finite or infinite positive value as t increases, since the degree of the numerator is

[7] The assumption of indecomposability of matrix $\begin{bmatrix} \mathbf{a} & \mathbf{a}_{\cdot} \\ \mathbf{a}_{00} & a_{\cdot 0} \end{bmatrix}$ is introduced to simplify the proof. Apart from the obvious economic interpretation, in the system under examination this assumption excludes also the existence of commodities which are produced in the first h processes and are used exclusively in the activities employing the old machines. These would be commodities filling the function of simple 'spare parts', needed exclusively for the maintenance or repair of old machines. For the consequences of the presence of such commodities, see note 10.

[8] $\hat{\mathbf{A}}_n(t)$ is obtained by adding non-negative matrices to the matrix $\begin{bmatrix} \mathbf{a} & \mathbf{a}_{\cdot} \\ t^n\mathbf{a}_{00} & t^n a_{\cdot 0} \end{bmatrix}$, which according to our assumption is indecomposable.

[9] The components of vector $\hat{\mathbf{p}}(t)$ clearly indicate the prices of all the commodities except those of the old machines.

at least equal to that of the denominator.[10] Consequently, $\lambda_M(t) \to \infty$ when $t \to \infty$.

In addition, $\lambda_M(t)$ is a continuous function of t, since the elements of $t\,\hat{\mathbf{B}}_n^{-1}(t)\,\hat{\mathbf{A}}_n(t)$ are continuous functions of t and the dominant eigenvalue is a continuous function of the elements of the matrix.

Consequently, since the assumption of productivity of the system means that $\lambda_M(1) < 1$, there exists a value $t = T_n$, $T_n > 1$, in relation to which we have $\lambda_M(T_n) = 1$.

In correspondence to such a value of t we have,

$$T_n\,\hat{\mathbf{A}}_n(T_n)\hat{\mathbf{p}}(T_n) = \hat{\mathbf{B}}_n(T_n)\hat{\mathbf{p}}(T_n) \qquad \textit{q.e.d.}$$

We have therefore been able to identify the interval $[1, T_n)$[11] of the factor of profit, in correspondence with which matrix $t\hat{\mathbf{B}}_n^{-1}(t)\,\hat{\mathbf{A}}_n(t)$ possesses a dominant eigenvalue less than one. The system is therefore able to provide a positive share of surplus which can be allotted to labour for values of t belonging to such an interval.

In addition, the prices $\hat{\mathbf{p}}(t)$ of the new machine and of the other marketable commodities are positive for $t \in [1, T_n]$.

On the basis of the observations made above, and on the strength of certain properties of non-negative matrices, it is possible to prove the following corollary.

Corollary 1

There exists a value of the factor of profit $t = \overline{T}$, $\overline{T} > T_n$ that is a root of the equation $\det[\mathbf{b} - t\mathbf{a}] = 0$.

Proof

Since $t\hat{\mathbf{B}}_n^{-1}(t)\hat{\mathbf{A}}_n(t)$ is an indecomposable matrix, for $t = T_n$ we have $\lambda_M(t\mathbf{b}^{-1}\mathbf{a}) < 1$ (cf. Gantmacher, 1959, p. 69, proposition 4); consequently T_n cannot be a root of $\det[\mathbf{b} - t\mathbf{a}] = 0$.

Since $\lambda_M(t\mathbf{b}^{-1}\mathbf{a})$ is always less than $\lambda_M[t\hat{\mathbf{B}}_n^{-1}(t)\hat{\mathbf{A}}_n(t)]$ for $t \in [1, T_n]$, we can state that there exists a $\overline{T} > T_n$ for which

$$\lambda_M(\overline{T}\mathbf{b}^{-1}\mathbf{a}) = 1. \qquad \textit{q.e.d.}$$

[10] This result is obtained on the basis of the indecomposability of the matrix $\begin{bmatrix} \mathbf{a} & \mathbf{a}_{.} \\ \mathbf{a}_{00} & a_{.0} \end{bmatrix}$, since this excludes the existence of commodities used exclusively in the activities that employ old machines. Results similar to those of the present proposition can, however, be obtained even if we leave out such an assumption, since the elements of vector $\mathbf{s}t\,\hat{\mathbf{B}}_n^{-1}(t)\,\hat{\mathbf{A}}_n(t)$, which would be rational functions with the denominator of a degree higher than the numerator, would be lower bounded when $t \to \infty$.

[11] We shall call $[y, z)$ the interval of the real line with extremes y and z, closed on the left and open on the right.

In other terms, we have $[\mathbf{b}-t\mathbf{a}]^{-1} \geq \mathbf{0}$ for $t \in [1, T)$. This result will be used in section 7 in order to identify the conditions that guarantee the positivity of the prices of old machines.

6 Remarks about the wage–profit relationship in the case of production with fixed capital

We cannot at this point prove the uniqueness of the maximum factor of profit or, more generally, the monotonicity of $w^n(t)$ for $t \in [1, T_n]$, since, in contrast to the case of single production, the condition which assures the negativity of the derivative of $w^n(t)$ with respect to the factor of profit does not necessarily occur in the case of production with fixed capital.

In fact, differentiating (6.4) with respect to t, we obtain,[12]

$$d/dt[w^n(t)] = \frac{d/dt[\hat{b}_{\cdot n}(t) - t\hat{a}_{\cdot n}(t)][t\hat{\mathbf{a}}_{n0}(t)[b-t\mathbf{a}]^{-1}\mathbf{1}+\hat{l}_n(t)]}{[\hat{t\mathbf{a}}_{n0}(t)[\mathbf{b}-t\mathbf{a}]^{-1}\mathbf{1}+\hat{l}_n(t)]^2}$$
$$-\frac{d/dt[t^2\hat{\mathbf{a}}_{n0}(t)[\mathbf{b}-t\mathbf{a}]^{-1}\mathbf{a}.][t\hat{\mathbf{a}}_{n0}(t)[\mathbf{b}-t\mathbf{a}]^{-1}\mathbf{1}+\hat{l}_n(t)]}{[t\hat{\mathbf{a}}_{n0}(t)[\mathbf{b}-t\mathbf{a}]^{-1}\mathbf{1}+\hat{l}_n(t)]^2}$$
$$-\frac{[[\hat{b}_{\cdot n}(t) - t\hat{a}_{\cdot n}(t)] - t\hat{\mathbf{a}}_{n0}(t)[\mathbf{b}-t\mathbf{a}]^{-1}\mathbf{a}.]d/dt[t\hat{\mathbf{a}}_{n0}(t)[\mathbf{b}-t\mathbf{a}]^{-1}\mathbf{1}+\hat{l}_n(t)]}{[t\hat{\mathbf{a}}_{n0}(t)[\mathbf{b}-t\mathbf{a}]^{-1}\mathbf{1}+\hat{l}_n(t)]^2} \quad (6.13)$$

We may easily verify that the last two addends to the right-hand side of (6.13) are positive for $t \in [1, T_n]$. A sufficient condition for the negativity of (6.13) would be given by $d/dt[\hat{b}_{\cdot n}(t) - t\hat{a}_{\cdot n}(t)] < 0$: a condition which always occurs in the case of single production with circulating capital alone, since $\hat{b}_{\cdot n}(t)$ and $\hat{a}_{\cdot n}(t)$ are two constants.

Such a derivative could be positive in the case under examination, and for particular values of the coefficients this could make the whole expression (6.13) positive. There could therefore be increasing sections of the wage–profit curve. However, we shall see later on why such sections are economically irrelevant.

[12] If $\mathbf{V}(x)$ is a non-singular square matrix the elements of which are differentiable function of x,

$$d/dx(\mathbf{V}^{-1}) = -\mathbf{V}^{-1}d/dx(\mathbf{V})\mathbf{V}^{-1} \quad (1)$$

By definition, we have

$$\mathbf{V}\mathbf{V}^{-1} = \mathbf{1}$$

and differentiating both sides of the equation we obtain

$$d/dx(\mathbf{V})\mathbf{V}^{-1} + \mathbf{V}d/dx(\mathbf{V}^{-1}) = \mathbf{0} \quad (2)$$

Premultiplying (2) by $\mathbf{V}^{-1}$ we obtain (1).

If we go back for a moment to the proof of Proposition 2, it is easy to understand mathematically why the wage-profit curve behaves in this way. The fact that the elements of matrix $t\hat{\mathbf{B}}_n^{-1}(t)\hat{\mathbf{A}}_n(t)$ are rational functions in t, in which the degree of the numerator is at least equal to that of the denominator, does not guarantee at all that they are increasing monotonic functions of t for $t \in [1, T_n]$.[13] The behaviour of the dominant eigenvalue may therefore be decisively influenced by the decreasing elements and may diminish as the factor of profit increases within a certain range, thereby giving rise to the phenomenon identified above.

If this were to happen for values of the factor of profit greater than T_n, we could have more than one economically meaningful solution for system (6.11). In this case, the wage–profit curve would once more assume positive values for intervals of the factor of profit, in relation to which the economic system would be viable once more. If we assume that T_n represents the smallest economically meaningful value of t in relation to which $w^n(t) = 0$, then such behaviour can only occur for $t \in [T_n, \overline{T}]$. Indeed, the dominant root of matrix $t\mathbf{b}^{-1}\mathbf{a}$ is a strictly increasing function of t; and, since $\lambda_M(t\mathbf{b}^{-1}\mathbf{a}) = 1$ for $t = \overline{T}$, we may say, on the basis of Corollary 1, that the economic system cannot be viable for values of the factor of profit greater than $\overline{T}$.

7 Conditions for the positivity of prices of old machines

The fact that a durable instrument may be used in production for more than one year means that we can identify different productive configurations using the same machine, each of these configurations referring to a different working life of the machine itself. If, as supposed, the physical life of the machine is n years, we have n possible productive configurations.

The technique under examination therefore allows us to construct a family of n wage–profit curves, which we can obtain by successively adding to the preceding activities each new activity using a machine a year older, or by successively eliminating the activities employing the oldest machines.

In what follows, we shall call the outermost contour of the family of curves mentioned above the 'wage–profit frontier'.

Since the frontier may consist of connected sections of different curves, it may have angular points and therefore may not be differentiable over the whole range of economic definition.

We shall prove below that the comparison of all the wage–profit curves allows us to determine for which values of the exogenous distributive

[13] It can easily be shown that such a possibility can occur only if the use of the machine is prolonged beyond the first year of age, and only for the elements of the matrix of the integrated system which refers to the mechanised industry.

variable the use of the machine up to a certain age gives rise to positive prices, even for old machines.

The sections of the curves composing the wage–profit frontier indicate, for the corresponding values of the exogenous distributive variable, the most profitable temporal dimension for the productive employment of the machine. The technique thus temporally dimensioned determines a solution for prices which is positive in all its components for values of the exogenous distributive variable belonging to the relevant interval.

Consider system (6.1) extended to the point of employing the machine of n years of age. Leaving aside the last equation, i.e. that referring to the activity employing the oldest machine, we can construct the wage–profit curve as a function of the price ${}_mp^n{}_n$ of that machine. Leaving aside the last two equations we proceed similarly to construct the curve as a function of ${}_mp^n{}_{n-1}$; and so on, until we reach ${}_mp^n{}_1$.

Carrying out the required substitutions, we obtain,

$$\left\{\begin{array}{l} w^n[t\hat{\mathbf{a}}_{n-1,0}(t)[\mathbf{b}-t\mathbf{a}]^{-1}\mathbf{l}+\hat{l}_{n-1}(t)] = \hat{b}._{n-1}(t)-t\hat{a}._{n-1}(t) \\ \quad -t^2\hat{\mathbf{a}}_{n-1,0}(t)[\mathbf{b}-t\mathbf{a}]^{-1}\mathbf{a}.+b_{nm}p^n{}_n \\ w^n[t\hat{\mathbf{a}}_{n-2,0}(t)[\mathbf{b}-t\mathbf{a}]^{-1}\mathbf{l}+\hat{l}_{n-2}(t)] = \hat{b}._{n-2}(t) \\ \quad -t\hat{a}._{n-2}(t)-t^2\hat{\mathbf{a}}_{n-2,0}(t)[\mathbf{b}-t\mathbf{a}]^{-1}\mathbf{a}. \\ \quad +b_{n-1\,m}p^n{}_{n-1} \\ \vdots \\ w^n[t\mathbf{a}_{00}(t)[\mathbf{b}-t\mathbf{a}]^{-1}\mathbf{l}+l_0] = b._0-ta._0 \\ \quad -t^2\mathbf{a}_{00}[\mathbf{b}-t\mathbf{a}]^{-1}\mathbf{a}.+b_{1\,m}p^n{}_1 \end{array}\right. \tag{6.14}$$

If

$$t\hat{\mathbf{a}}_{j,0}(t)[\mathbf{b}-t\mathbf{a}]^{-1}\mathbf{l}+\hat{l}_j(t) = D^j$$

$$\hat{b}._j(t)-t\hat{a}._j(t)-t^2\hat{\mathbf{a}}_{j,0}(t)[\mathbf{b}-t\mathbf{a}]^{-1}\mathbf{a}. = N^j$$

then (6.14) may be rewritten as follows:

$$w^nD^j = N^j+b_{j+1\,m}p^n{}_{j+1} \qquad (j=0,1,\ldots n-1) \tag{6.15}$$

In correspondence to values of the rate of profit for which $D^j > 0$, we can divide both sides of (6.15) by D^j, thereby obtaining

$$(w^n-w^j) = (b_{j+1}/D^j)_m p^n{}_{j+1} \qquad (j=0,1,\ldots n-1) \tag{6.16}$$

It is therefore possible to relate to each other the various wage–profit curves corresponding to the n possible working lives of the machine by means of the prices of the old machines themselves. In particular, we may compare the frontier of the system with the curves or parts of curves which are dominated.

If, therefore, we call w^n the curve relative to the system using the machine up to n years of age and we call w^j that relative to a shorter working life, using the notation introduced above, we may prove the following proposition.

Proposition 3

The prices of old machines associated with the system using the durable instrument up to n years of age are positive if, and only if, $w^n(t) > w^j(t)$ ($j = 0, 1, \ldots n-1$).

In particular, zero prices for machines of $j+1$ years of age ($j = 0, 1, \ldots n-1$) correspond to values of t where $w^n(t) = w^j(t)$, i.e. to the intersections of the wage–profit curves.

Proof

On the basis of the results of Corollary 1 and of the remarks made in the above section, we can affirm that the value $\overline{T}$ of the factor of profit constitutes an upper boundary to all possible values of t that are maximum roots of the system for the different working lives of the machine, since $[\mathbf{b} - t\mathbf{a}]$ is a minor of order $h-1$ which is common to all the matrices $[\hat{\mathbf{B}}_j(t) - t\hat{\mathbf{A}}_j(t)]$ ($j = 0, 1, \ldots n$) of the integrated systems. Since $T_j < \overline{T}$ ($j = 1, \ldots n$) we therefore have $[\mathbf{b} - t\mathbf{a}]^{-1} \geq \mathbf{0}$ and, consequently, $D^j > 0$ for $t \in [1, \overline{T})$.

On the strength of what is stated in (6.16), we can immediately derive the proposition.

q.e.d.

Now consider the case in which, having fixed the factor of profit, w^n is not dominant with respect to all values of the wage corresponding to shorter working life of the machine; some of the differences $w^n - w^j$ ($j = 0, 1, \ldots n-1$) will be negative. It is therefore not profitable to employ in production old machines with a negative price, since their use, for the same rate of profit, results in a lower wage rate. If they are eliminated, the productive structure can be rearranged so that, with the factor of profit given, the wage rate will be higher than could be obtained by further reducing the working life of the machine.

In other words, the prices of old machines in the system using the machine up to a given age are positive if, and only if, the wage–profit curve corresponding to such an utilisation of the durable instrument dominates all the other curves corresponding to shorter working lives of the machine.

We should point out that, should the curves all be arranged in increasing age order,[14] the prices of old machines are all positive no matter how long

[14] For instance, this is the case when the efficiency of machine can be defined as constant or increasing in physical terms over its whole lifetime.

the machine is used in production. In this case, in fact, the dominance with respect to shorter lives is valid for each of the wage–profit curves and not only for that which forms the frontier at the prefixed value of the rate of profit.

In any case, the curve forming the frontier and corresponding to the physical life of the machine should be regarded as relevant, since for an equal rate of profit it allows a higher wage.

As the factor of profit varies within its economic range, so, in most cases, does the working life of the machine producing the highest wage rate. Consequently, the economic life of the machine can be identified, for the different values of the factor of profit, from the sections of curves composing the wage–profit frontier.

We may therefore state the following corollary.

Corollary 2

The profitable employment of the machine can be obtained for the different values of the exogenous distributive variable by making the technique conform to the age which corresponds to the wage–profit frontier.

Such employment produces positive prices for the old machines; in addition, if the matrix $\begin{bmatrix} \mathbf{a} & \mathbf{a}. \\ \mathbf{a}_{00} & a._0 \end{bmatrix}$ is indecomposable, the prices of the new machine and of the non-durable commodities will be the lowest, in terms of the wage.

Proof

The first part of the corollary is an immediate derivation of Proposition 2, proved above.

To prove the second part we need only consider two systems corresponding to two different working lives of the machine, f and j years respectively. Considering the first $h-1$ equations of the two systems, we obtain,

$$(1/w^f)\mathbf{p}^f = (1/w^f)t[\mathbf{b}-t\mathbf{a}]^{-1}\mathbf{a}. + [\mathbf{b}-t\mathbf{a}]^{-1}\mathbf{l}$$
$$(1/w^j)\mathbf{p}^j = (1/w^j)t[\mathbf{b}-t\mathbf{a}]^{-1}\mathbf{a}. + [\mathbf{b}-t\mathbf{a}]^{-1}\mathbf{l}$$

If we subtract the second relation from the first, then, using $\mathbf{p}^*$ to indicate prices in terms of the wage rate, we obtain,

$$\mathbf{p}^{f*} - \mathbf{p}^{j*} = [(1/w^f) - (1/w^j)]t[\mathbf{b}-t\mathbf{a}]^{-1}\mathbf{a}.$$

If matrix $\begin{bmatrix} \mathbf{a} & \mathbf{a}. \\ \mathbf{a}_{00} & a._0 \end{bmatrix}$ is indecomposable, then vector $[\mathbf{b}-t\mathbf{a}]^{-1}\mathbf{a}.$ is positive for $t \in [1, \overline{T})$;[15] we therefore obtain $\mathbf{p}^{f*} < \mathbf{p}^{j*}$ if, and only if, $w^f > w^j$. Since $1/w^j$ is simply the price of the *numéraire* in terms of the wage in the corresponding system, the corollary is proved. *q.e.d.*

8 Distribution of income and economic life of the machine

If we exclude certain special cases, such as when the machine's physical efficiency is constant or increasing over its life, then the economic life of a machine will depend on the level of the exogeneous distributive variable – in our case, the rate of profit.

Once we have chosen, therefore, a possible profitable life for the machine, corresponding to a particular distributive structure, we may find that it is no longer profitable, as the rate of profit varies within its economic range. If this occurs, there will then be a value of the rate of profit in correspondence with which the price of some of the old machines will become zero and then negative; there will therefore be an intersection between the wage–profit curve corresponding to the life initially considered and the curve relating to a different life, which now becomes dominant.

We cannot generally exclude the possibility that these two curves may intersect each other again as the rate of profit varies in its economic range. The easiest way to show this phenomenon is to give a numerical illustration: the appendix to this essay gives such an example of the model formulated above. We can see from this that the use of only the new machine is profitable for values of the rate of profit that are rather low or are near their upper limit, while for intermediate values the economic life of the machine is longer.

[15] This property may be easily proved by carrying out the same block partition on the inverse of the matrix

$$\hat{\mathbf{B}}_n - t\,\hat{\mathbf{A}}_n = \begin{bmatrix} \mathbf{b} - t\mathbf{a} & -t\,\mathbf{a}. \\ -t\,\hat{\mathbf{a}}_{n0} & \hat{b}_{\cdot n} - t\hat{a}_{\cdot n} \end{bmatrix} \tag{1}$$

Let $\begin{bmatrix} \mathbf{A} & \mathbf{B} \\ \mathbf{C} & D \end{bmatrix} > \mathbf{0}$ be such a matrix. By definition, we obtain

$$\begin{bmatrix} \mathbf{A} & \mathbf{B} \\ \mathbf{C} & D \end{bmatrix} \cdot \begin{bmatrix} \mathbf{b} - t\mathbf{a} & -t\mathbf{a}. \\ -t\hat{\mathbf{a}}_{\cdot 0} & \hat{b}_{\cdot n} - t\hat{a}_{\cdot n} \end{bmatrix} = \begin{bmatrix} \mathbf{1} & \mathbf{0} \\ \mathbf{0} & 1 \end{bmatrix} \tag{2}$$

Multiplying and making the necessary substitutions in (2), we obtain:

$$t[\mathbf{b} - t\mathbf{a}]^{-1}\mathbf{a}. = \mathbf{B}[[\hat{b}_{\cdot n} - t\hat{a}_{\cdot n}] - t^2\hat{\mathbf{a}}_{n0}[\mathbf{b} - t\mathbf{a}]^{-1}\mathbf{a}.]$$

On the account of the assumption of indecomposability of matrix $\hat{\mathbf{B}}_n - t\hat{\mathbf{A}}_n$, for $t \in [1, T_n)$, we have $\mathbf{B} > \mathbf{0}$ and $\{[\hat{b}_n - t\hat{a}_{\cdot n}] - t^2\hat{\mathbf{a}}_{n0}[\mathbf{b} - t\mathbf{a}]^{-1}\mathbf{a}.\} > 0$; consequently, we have $[\mathbf{b} - t\mathbf{a}]^{-1}\mathbf{a}. > \mathbf{0}$. Since the elements of the matrix $[\mathbf{b} - t\mathbf{a}]^{-1}$ are continuous and non-decreasing functions of t for $t \in [1, \overline{T})$, we obtain $[\mathbf{b} - t\mathbf{a}]^{-1}\mathbf{a}. > \mathbf{0}$ for $t \in [1, \overline{T})$.

This is a phenomenon that is very similar to what in the economic literature goes under the name of 'reswitching of techniques'. As the income distribution varies, so do the relative prices and consequently the value of the capital per unit of labour. In this way, the profitability of the individual activities varies, which, as a consequence, changes the profitability in the use of the machines.

Here, too, changes are linked to the particular structure of the technology and it is not generally possible to establish *a priori* how the economic life of the machine varies with the level of the exogenous distributive variable.

9 A different machine for every productive sector

Up to this point the analysis concerning the positivity of old-machine prices (and, therefore, the economic life of the machine itself) has been pursued on the simplifying assumption that only one of the productive sectors of the economic system under examination employs a durable instrument.

The special nature of this case lies not so much in the fact that only one productive sector is mechanised as in the fact that the model thus formulated has the nature of a partial analysis. In other terms, the identification of an 'economic life' for the machine in the mechanised sector does not produce any quantitative effect on the productive structure of the remaining sectors. Consequently, no feedback effect occurs in the sector using the machine.

When, however, more than one sector uses machines in production, then clearly the sectoral choices (made on the supposition that the remaining structure of the productive system is given) may influence the profitability of the choices made by the other mechanised sectors. This is so because a change in the productive structure caused by a certain sectoral choice may alter the profitable life of machines in another sector, and may then generate a feedback effect in the first sector by means of a new structural change.

For this case, therefore, we need to analyse the effect of sectoral choices in the light of the interactions of the whole economic system.

Let us suppose, for the sake of simplicity, that h commodities are produced in the system, each with the use of a machine; in turn, the machines are produced by m industries using only circulating capital and labour.

It is clear that generally we have $m \leq h$, since the same type of machine may be employed in different industries. Such machines will evidently have the same price when new, but once used in production they will assume as many identities as there are different industries in which they have been employed. Two technically identical machines should be considered as different machines once they have been used in different industries. Hence, if we call the different mechanised industries (overall, h in number) α, β, $\gamma, \ldots \eta$, then the economically different machines are also implicitly identified in the same way.

On the basis of what we have said so far, we can formalise the model adopting the same symbols as previously. We shall, however, use the symbol of the respective industry to identify each input and output vector related to the use and production of old machines.

If we take the non-durable commodity produced by machine ε as the *numéraire*, the price system may be written out as in (6.17).

$$t\begin{bmatrix}
\mathbf{a} & {}_{\varepsilon}\mathbf{a}_{.} & 0 & \cdots & 0 & \cdots & 0 & \cdots & 0 & \cdots & 0 & \cdots & 0 \\
{}_{\varepsilon}\mathbf{a}_{00} & {}_{\varepsilon}a_{.0} & 0 & \cdots & 0 & \cdots & 0 & \cdots & 0 & \cdots & 0 & \cdots & 0 \\
{}_{\alpha}\mathbf{a}_{10} & {}_{\alpha}a_{.1} & {}_{\alpha}a_{1} & \cdots & 0 & \cdots & 0 & \cdots & 0 & \cdots & 0 & \cdots & 0 \\
\vdots & \vdots & \vdots & & \vdots & & \vdots & & \vdots & & \vdots & & \vdots \\
{}_{\varepsilon}\mathbf{a}_{10} & {}_{\varepsilon}a_{.1} & 0 & \cdots & {}_{\varepsilon}a_{1} & \cdots & 0 & \cdots & 0 & \cdots & 0 & \cdots & 0 \\
\vdots & \vdots & \vdots & & \vdots & & \vdots & & \vdots & & \vdots & & \vdots \\
{}_{\alpha}\mathbf{a}_{n-1,0} & {}_{\alpha}a_{.n-1} & 0 & \cdots & 0 & \cdots & {}_{\alpha}a_{n-1} & \cdots & 0 & \cdots & 0 & \cdots & 0 \\
\vdots & \vdots & \vdots & & \vdots & & \vdots & & \vdots & & \vdots & & \vdots \\
{}_{\varepsilon}\mathbf{a}_{n-1,0} & {}_{\varepsilon}a_{.n-1} & 0 & \cdots & 0 & \cdots & 0 & \cdots & {}_{\varepsilon}a_{n-1} & \cdots & 0 & \cdots & 0 \\
{}_{\alpha}\mathbf{a}_{n0} & {}_{\alpha}a_{.n} & 0 & \cdots & 0 & \cdots & 0 & \cdots & 0 & \cdots & {}_{\alpha}a_{n} & \cdots & 0 \\
\vdots & \vdots & \vdots & & \vdots & & \vdots & & \vdots & & \vdots & & \vdots \\
{}_{\varepsilon}\mathbf{a}_{n0} & {}_{\varepsilon}a_{.n} & 0 & \cdots & 0 & \cdots & 0 & \cdots & 0 & \cdots & 0 & \cdots & {}_{\varepsilon}a_{n}
\end{bmatrix}
\begin{bmatrix}
\mathbf{p} \\ 1 \\ {}_{\alpha}p_{1} \\ \vdots \\ {}_{\varepsilon}p_{1} \\ \vdots \\ {}_{\alpha}p_{n-1} \\ \vdots \\ {}_{\varepsilon}p_{n-1} \\ {}_{\alpha}p_{n} \\ \vdots \\ {}_{\varepsilon}p_{n}
\end{bmatrix}
+ w \begin{bmatrix}
1 \\ {}_{\varepsilon}l_{0} \\ {}_{\alpha}l_{1} \\ \vdots \\ {}_{\varepsilon}l_{1} \\ \vdots \\ {}_{\alpha}l_{n-1} \\ \vdots \\ {}_{\varepsilon}l_{n-1} \\ {}_{\alpha}l_{n} \\ \vdots \\ {}_{\varepsilon}l_{n}
\end{bmatrix} =$$

$$
= \begin{bmatrix}
\mathbf{b} & \mathbf{0} & {}_{\alpha}\mathbf{b}_1 & \cdots & \mathbf{0} & \mathbf{0} & \cdots & \mathbf{0} & \cdots & \mathbf{0} & \cdots & \mathbf{0} \\
\mathbf{0} & {}_{\varepsilon}b_{\cdot 0} & 0 & \cdots & {}_{\varepsilon}b_1 & 0 & \cdots & 0 & \cdots & 0 & \cdots & 0 \\
{}_{\alpha}\mathbf{b}_{10} & 0 & 0 & \cdots & 0 & {}_{\alpha}b_2 & \cdots & 0 & \cdots & 0 & \cdots & 0 \\
\vdots & \vdots & \vdots & & \vdots & \vdots & & \vdots & & \vdots & & \vdots \\
\mathbf{0} & {}_{\varepsilon}b_{\cdot 1} & 0 & \cdots & 0 & 0 & \cdots & {}_{\varepsilon}b_2 & \cdots & 0 & \cdots & 0 \\
\vdots & \vdots & \vdots & & \vdots & \vdots & & \vdots & & \vdots & & \vdots \\
{}_{\alpha}\mathbf{b}_{n-1,0} & 0 & 0 & \cdots & 0 & 0 & \cdots & 0 & \cdots & {}_{\alpha}b_n & \cdots & 0 \\
\vdots & \vdots & \vdots & & \vdots & \vdots & & \vdots & & \vdots & & \vdots \\
\mathbf{0} & {}_{\varepsilon}b_{\cdot n-1} & 0 & \cdots & 0 & 0 & \cdots & 0 & \cdots & 0 & \cdots & {}_{\varepsilon}b_n \\
{}_{\alpha}\mathbf{b}_{n0} & 0 & 0 & \cdots & 0 & 0 & \cdots & 0 & \cdots & 0 & \cdots & 0 \\
\vdots & \vdots & \vdots & & \vdots & \vdots & & \vdots & & \vdots & & \vdots \\
\mathbf{0} & {}_{\varepsilon}b_{\cdot n} & 0 & \cdots & 0 & 0 & \cdots & 0 & \cdots & 0 & \cdots & 0
\end{bmatrix}
\begin{bmatrix}
\mathbf{p} \\ 1 \\ {}_{\alpha}p_1 \\ \vdots \\ {}_{\varepsilon}p_1 \\ {}_{\alpha}p_2 \\ \vdots \\ {}_{\varepsilon}p_2 \\ \vdots \\ {}_{\alpha}p_n \\ \vdots \\ {}_{\varepsilon}p_n
\end{bmatrix}
\tag{6.17}
$$

Of course, the maximum technical life of the machines, τ_δ, $\delta \in \{\alpha, \beta, \gamma, \ldots \eta\}$, will generally differ from industry to industry. Consequently, not all the activities employing old machines reach the same maximum index, but each will find its limit in the corresponding technical life. After this section we shall generally indicate the maximum technical life of machine ε by τ without an index, in order to avoid excessively weighing down the notations.

In system (6.17) the components of the column vector ${}_{\varepsilon}\mathbf{a}_{\cdot}$ still indicate the quantities of the *numéraire* that are employed in the production of new machines and absorbed by the activities that use the durable instruments (with the exclusion of industry ε) when new. ${}_{\varepsilon}\mathbf{a}_{00}$ is the row vector the components of which indicate the number of new machines and the quantities of non-durable inputs that enter into the production of the *numéraire* together with ${}_{\varepsilon}a_{\cdot 0}$ units of the commodity in question. $\mathbf{a}$ and consequently $\mathbf{b}$ are square matrices referring to processes which produce the new machines and to the activities that employ them with the exclusion of that which uses machine ε when new. Hence, if new machines emerge from m industries and if they take a part in the production of h different commodities, the dimension of $\mathbf{a}$ and $\mathbf{b}$ is $m+h-1$; the activities are then arranged such that matrix $\mathbf{b}$ is diagonal.

The components of vector ${}_{\varepsilon}\mathbf{a}_{r0}$ and the scalars ${}_{\delta}a_{\cdot r}$ and ${}_{\delta}a_{r}$, $\delta \in \{\alpha, \beta, \gamma, \ldots \eta\}$, $r = 1, 2, \ldots \tau_{\delta}$, indicate respectively the inputs of non-durable means of production and new machines, of the *numéraire*, and of the number of machines δ of r years of age employed in the respective activities. As for output, there is a completely symmetrical meaning for the corresponding vector and scalars. We should point out, however, that as a result of the assumption we have formulated on the nature of production, all the components of vectors ${}_{\delta}\mathbf{b}_{r0}$ are zero, except for that corresponding to the output of the marketable commodity δ which is produced by the activity under examination.

All the components of the column vectors ${}_{\delta}\mathbf{b}_{1}$, $\delta \in \{\alpha, \beta, \gamma, \ldots \eta\} \delta \neq \varepsilon$ also are zero, except for that corresponding to the activity that produces commodity δ employing the corresponding new machine, defined as machine δ. This component indicates the output of machines of one year of age. Scalar ${}_{\varepsilon}b_{1}$ has a completely analogous meaning.

We can extend the criterion suggested above for the determination of the conditions of positivity for the prices of old machines, with the necessary adaptation, to the case under examination.

In fact, as briefly mentioned at the beginning of this section, when we consider more than one industry employing machines in production we must face two conceptually different problems: that of the determination of the most profitable life of the machine for each industry (i.e. a correct plan of depreciation); and that of the identification of a profitable employment structure for the various machines at the level of the whole economy. We shall see later that, despite the different nature of these two problems, the solution of the first in the scheme under examination supplies us with the means to solve the second.

If we denote by

$w_{(.)}(t)$ the wage–profit curve obtained in correspondence with the employment of all the machines up to the limit of their technical lives;

$w_{(.)\varepsilon(j)}(t)$ the curve corresponding to the use of all the machines up to the limit of their technical lives (with the exception of machine ε, which is used only until j years of age); and

${}_{\varepsilon}p_{j}^{(.)}$ the price of machine ε when it is j years old in the system that employs all the machines until their technical limit,

then we can prove the following proposition.

Proposition 4

The prices of the old machines ${}_{\varepsilon}p_j^{(\cdot)}, j = 1, 2, \ldots \tau$, in industry ε are positive if, and only if,

$$w_{(.)}(t) > w_{(\cdot)\varepsilon(j-1)}(t) \qquad (j = 1, 2, \ldots \tau)$$

Proof

Supposing that the use of machines in the industries is extended to the limit of their technical lives, we construct the curve $w_{(.)}(t)$ with reference to system (6.17) as a function of each of $w_{(.)\varepsilon(j-1)}(t), j = 1, 2, \ldots \tau$.

This can be done in the usual way, starting from the system of prices and constructing the wage–profit curve leaving out of consideration the equation relative to the activity using machine ε of τ years of age. We thereby obtain $w_{(.)}(t)$ in terms of $w_{(.)\varepsilon(\tau-1)}(t)$ and of ${}_{\varepsilon}p_{\tau}^{(\cdot)}$:

$$w_{(.)}(t) = w_{(.)\varepsilon(\tau-1)}(t) + [{}_{\varepsilon}b_{\tau}/\text{denominat. } w_{(.)\varepsilon(\tau-1)}(t)]\,{}_{\varepsilon}p_{\tau}^{(\cdot)} \qquad (6.18)$$

Repeating the construction, and leaving aside each time a further equation, we obtain as many relations similar to (6.19) as there are possible years in the use of machine:

$$\begin{cases} w_{(.)}(t) = w_{(.)\varepsilon(\tau-1)}(t) + [{}_{\varepsilon}b_{\tau}/\text{denominat. } w_{(.)\varepsilon(\tau-1)}(t)]\,{}_{\varepsilon}p_{\tau}^{(\cdot)} \\ \vdots \\ w_{(.)}(t) = w_{(.)\varepsilon(0)}(t) + [{}_{\varepsilon}b_{1}/\text{denominat. } w_{(.)\varepsilon(0)}(t)]\,{}_{\varepsilon}p_{\tau}^{(\cdot)} \end{cases} \qquad (6.19)$$

where denominat. $w_{(\cdot)\varepsilon(j)}(t)$ is

$$t[t^j\,{}_{\varepsilon}\mathbf{a}_{00} + t^{j-1}\,{}_{\varepsilon}\mathbf{a}_{10} + \ldots + {}_{\varepsilon}\mathbf{a}_{j0}][\hat{\mathbf{B}}_{(.)\varepsilon} - t\,\hat{\mathbf{A}}_{(.)\varepsilon}]^{-1}\,\hat{\mathbf{L}}_{(.)}$$
$$+ [t^j\,{}_{\varepsilon}l_0 + t^{j-1}\,{}_{\varepsilon}l_1 + \ldots + {}_{\varepsilon}l_j]$$

Since $[\hat{\mathbf{B}}_{(.)\varepsilon} - t\,\hat{\mathbf{A}}_{(.)\varepsilon}]$, which is a principal sub-matrix of the corresponding integrated system,[16] depends only on the working life of the machines other than ε, we obtain, as a result of Corollary 2, that the multiplicative coefficients of the old machine prices in (6.19) are all positive for $t \in [1, \overline{\mathbf{T}}_{(.)\varepsilon})$, since $\overline{\mathbf{T}}_{(.)\varepsilon} > 1$ is a root of the equation $\det[\hat{\mathbf{B}}_{(.)\varepsilon} - t\,\hat{\mathbf{A}}_{(.)\varepsilon}] = 0$. Consequently, the prices we are considering will be positive if, and only if,

[16] Matrix $[\hat{\mathbf{B}}_{(\cdot)\varepsilon} - t\,\hat{\mathbf{A}}_{(\cdot)\varepsilon}]$, which is common to all the productive configurations obtainable by varying the working life of machine ε is the formal equivalent of matrix $[\mathbf{b} - t\mathbf{a}]$ in the scheme with only one mechanised industry. It is obtained from the matrix of the corresponding integrated system by eliminating the row corresponding to industry ε which produces the *numéraire* and the column corresponding to the inputs of this commodity. In this case, the elements of matrices $\hat{\mathbf{A}}_{(\cdot)\varepsilon}$ and $\hat{\mathbf{B}}_{(\cdot)\varepsilon}$, corresponding to the mechanised industries, are functions of the factor of profit; this results from the operation of temporal integration carried out on system (6.17).

$w_{(\cdot)} > w_{(\cdot)\varepsilon(j-1)}$, $j = 1, 2, \ldots \tau$. If the equals sign applies to any relation, then the corresponding prices are zero. *q.e.d.*

If, one by one, we take the price of the commodities produced by the various mechanised industries as the *numéraire* and repeat the demonstration we have just made, then it is possible to identify the most profitable life for the corresponding machine, for each industry and for every fixed value for the factor of profit, assuming that the structure of use of the other machines remains unchanged.

All the results so far obtained now permit us to face the second problem we raised: the determination of the conditions which guarantee the positivity of old machine prices for the economy as a whole.

We should point out straightaway that it is possible for our purposes to make an overall examination of the data gained from the partial analyses just made, even though these data are quantitatively heterogeneous as a result of using a different *numéraire* for each industry. This we can do because the relations of dominance within the family of wage–profit curves for each industry are invariable with respect to the *numéraire* adopted.[17]

Consequently, if the price of an old machine is negative in terms of the price of the commodity produced with its use, it remains negative even if a different *numéraire* is adopted. Given, therefore, a certain working life for the machines in the various industries, the prices of the old machines, at the level of the whole economy, will be positive if, and only if, sector by sector the wage–profit curve dominates all the others corresponding to different working lives of the machine concerned. If one of the prices is negative, then it is not profitable to employ the corresponding old machine. This leads to a change of the age structure in the employment of machines. We therefore need to analyse the economic system thus redimensioned and proceed once more to compare the various wage–profit curves. This procedure is repeated until we find an age structure for which the relative curve in each industry dominates all the curves obtained by varying the working life of the corresponding machine. Clearly, the elimination of the old machines with negative prices will allow us to give the employment of old machines the most profitable structure.

[17] Consider the family of curves ε, $\varepsilon \in \{\alpha, \beta, \ldots \eta\}$. In the economic range of the factor of profit $[1, \overline{T}_{(\cdot)\varepsilon})$ the prices of the new machines and of the non-durable commodities corresponding to two different lives of machine ε are equal, in terms of the wage rate, if and only if there is an intersection of the corresponding wage–profit curves (cf. Corollary 2). Since the wage–profit curve is given by the reciprocal of the price taken as *numéraire* expressed in terms of the wage, the result is that, whatever *numeraire* is adopted, the values of the factor of profit, where there are intersections of the various wage–profit curves, do not vary. In addition, since the maximum values of the factor of profit relating to the different lives of the machines are technological data, it follows that, as a result of the continuity of the curves with respect to t, the relationships of dominance are also invariable with respect to whatever *numeraire* is adopted.

Calling the prices of the old machines in a given industry 'internal prices' when they are expressed in terms of the specific *numéraire*, we can state the following proposition.

Proposition 5

The prices of the old machines in the whole economic system are positive if, and only if, the internal prices of each sector are also positive. A wage–profit curve for the whole economy which dominates those of different structures in the employment of machines corresponds to such a productive configuration.

It may be of interest to note that it is not possible for a family of curves completely to dominate another over the whole economic range of the rate of profit, i.e. it is not possible for all the curves of a family to be above the curves of which the second family is composed. Indeed, the curve corresponding to the use of machines prolonged to the limit of their respective physical lives is common to all the families. Although these latter curves generally differ from one another on account of the different *numéraire* by which prices and wage are measured, they have the same maximum factor of profit. This occurs because this factor is determined exclusively by technology and therefore is invariable with respect to the choice of *numéraire*. We can therefore extend the previous analysis to values of the factor of profit which correspond to a situation where only one family has one or several curves in the positive quadrant. In this case, in fact, it might happen that the value of the factor of profit considered is superior to the minimum of values $\overline{T}_{(\cdot)\delta}$, $\delta \in \{\alpha, \beta, \gamma, \ldots \eta\}$, relative to the families of curves lying under the abscissae. It is sufficient, therefore, to make the age structure of machine use in the various sectors follow the outermost curve. All the families of curves, in relation to the new structure of employment, become economically meaningful in correspondence to the particular value of the factor of profit considered. The coefficients of the old-machine prices in relation (6.19) will be positive and the analysis may be carried on following the procedure previously illustrated.

10 Further generalisations: joint use of different types of machines and mechanisation of the industries producing durable instruments

In the previous section we examined the case in which every mechanised sector uses only one machine, at its different ages, for the production of the corresponding commodity.

At first sight it may seem that the model thus formulated results from an extremely restrictive hypothesis, as far as the nature and functioning of the productive structure are concerned. However, the model just outlined is actually of completely general application, on the assumption that the only joint products are machines that are one year older.

In fact, this model represents the situation of sequential production, where a suitably chosen length for the unit period of production allows the subdivision of the effective production process into many partial processes each using one machine (in addition to the other means of production), and it also represents the much more general situation where machines of different types are used together in the production of some commodity. All we need do, in fact, is to adopt the simple procedure of considering each collection of machines, once they have been used in production, as a single composite instrument.

Clearly, the new 'composite machine' will consist of a collection of new machines, each one supplied by a particular productive process. The value of such a composite machine will be the sum of the values of its individual components; it will subsequently assume its own identity and it will have a book value that cannot in general be divided among its single components.

In this way, it is possible for the number of activities in the model and the number of different products to remain equal. This is a prerequisite for determining the prices of the commodities.

The physical life, or rather, the technical life[18] of a composite machine does not generally coincide with that of its individual components. Indeed, if we exclude the situation where all the individual component machines simultaneously reach the limit of their physical capacity to produce, the physical life of the composite machine can normally be prolonged by replacing the components that have exhausted their productive capacity. Consequently, new machines may now be employed as spare parts in activities using aged composite machines: the new machines are substituted for exhausted elements of the composite machine.

So far we have analysed a model in which machines are produced with the intake of circulating capital and labour alone. However, it is possible to extend the scheme in the present direction by supposing that machines themselves are produced with the use of machines, or, rather, of collections of machines. Once again, no substantially new problems arise that have not been dealt with in the previous section.

Clearly, the analysis, which before was limited to industries using machines, must now be extended also to industries that produce machines, since, in addition to other commodities, they also use durable means of production. In this way all the productive sectors are in perfect formal symmetry.

The machine-producing industries are also divided into as many activities as there are years of use for their respective durable means of

[18] Cf note 2 above.

production. If we suppose that all industries employ durable means of production, then we can isolate a nucleus of single-product sectors by considering the production of new machines and other commodities using only new machines. In this way we obtain a single-production sub-system using only circulating capital, which can then be gradually expanded by the addition of further activities employing old machines and concerned with the production both of durable instruments and of other commodities.

We can therefore also apply to this scheme the analytic technique illustrated above.

11 Monotonicity of the wage–profit frontier

We have made it clear in previous sections that, in the case of production with fixed capital, the wage–profit curves are not necessarily monotonic decreasing functions of the rate of profit in its economic range. We shall shortly prove that this phenomenon is to be ascribed to the fact that, even if the wage–profit curve has positive values, some prices for old machines could be negative.

An increase in the rate of profit could therefore increase the weight of this negative component to such an extent that it diminishes instead of increases the value of the means of production. Consequently, the amount of surplus that can be allotted to labour increases and allows a raising of the wage rate.

However, this phenomenon cannot occur when the prices of old machines are non-negative. We prove this using the following lemma.

Lemma 1

With $\hat{\mathbf{p}}^*(t) = 1/w \begin{bmatrix} \mathbf{p} \\ p_0 \end{bmatrix} = \begin{bmatrix} \mathbf{p}^* \\ p_0{}^* \end{bmatrix}$ we indicate the vector the components of which give the price of the new machine and the price of non-durable commodities in terms of the wage rate. Now consider a range of the factor of profit in relation to which prices $\hat{\mathbf{p}}^*(t)$ are positive. If, for such values of the factor of profit, old machines have non-negative prices, then prices $\hat{\mathbf{p}}^*(t)$ are increasing functions of the factor of profit in the considered range.

In formulaic terms, $d/dt\,[\hat{\mathbf{p}}^*(t)] > \mathbf{0}$.

Proof

Consider system (6.1); using the above notation we can express $\hat{\mathbf{p}}^*(t)$ in the following form:

$$\hat{\mathbf{p}}^*(t) = \left\{ \mathbf{I} - t \begin{bmatrix} \mathbf{b}^{-1} & \mathbf{0} \\ \mathbf{0} & \hat{b}_{\cdot n}{}^{-1}(t) \end{bmatrix} \begin{bmatrix} \mathbf{a} & \mathbf{a}. \\ \hat{\mathbf{a}}_{n0}(t) & \hat{a}_{\cdot n}(t) \end{bmatrix} \right\}^{-1} \cdot \begin{bmatrix} \mathbf{b}^{-1} & \mathbf{0} \\ \mathbf{0} & \hat{b}_{\cdot n}{}^{-1}(t) \end{bmatrix} \begin{bmatrix} \mathbf{l} \\ \hat{l}_n(t) \end{bmatrix} \qquad (6.20)$$

Differentiating (6.20) with respect to t and arranging factors opportunely, we obtain,

$$d/dt[\hat{\mathbf{p}}^*(t)] = \left\{\mathbf{I} - t\begin{bmatrix}\mathbf{b}^{-1} & \mathbf{0}\\ \mathbf{0} & \hat{b}_{\cdot n}^{-1}(t)\end{bmatrix}\begin{bmatrix}\mathbf{a} & \mathbf{a}.\\ \hat{\mathbf{a}}_{n0}(t) & \hat{a}_{\cdot n}(t)\end{bmatrix}\right\}^{-1}$$

$$\cdot\left\{d/dt.\left[t\begin{bmatrix}\mathbf{b}^{-1} & \mathbf{0}\\ \mathbf{0} & \hat{b}_{\cdot n}^{-1}(t)\end{bmatrix}\begin{bmatrix}\mathbf{a} & \mathbf{a}.\\ \hat{\mathbf{a}}_{n0}(t) & \hat{a}_{\cdot n}(t)\end{bmatrix}\right]\hat{\mathbf{p}}^*(t)\right.$$

$$\left.+\,d/dt\left[\begin{bmatrix}\mathbf{b}^{-1} & \mathbf{0}\\ \mathbf{0} & \hat{b}_{\cdot n}^{-1}(t)\end{bmatrix}\begin{bmatrix}\mathbf{l}\\ \hat{l}_n(t)\end{bmatrix}\right]\right\} \tag{6.21}$$

Since matrix

$$\left\{\mathbf{I} - t\begin{bmatrix}\mathbf{b}^{-1} & \mathbf{0}\\ \mathbf{0} & \hat{b}_{\cdot n}^{-1}(t)\end{bmatrix}\begin{bmatrix}\mathbf{a} & \mathbf{a}.\\ \hat{\mathbf{a}}_{n0}(t) & \hat{a}_{\cdot n}(t)\end{bmatrix}\right\}^{-1}$$

is positive, a sufficient condition for (6.21) to be positive is that the expression within the second pair of braces in (6.21) is positive.

With this end in view, by multiplying out the expression in braces may be reduced to the following form:

$$d/dt\begin{bmatrix}t\mathbf{b}^{-1}\mathbf{a} & t\mathbf{b}^{-1}\mathbf{a}.\\ t\hat{b}_{\cdot n}^{-1}(t)\hat{\mathbf{a}}_{n0}(t) & t\hat{b}_{\cdot n}^{-1}(t)\hat{a}_{\cdot n}(t)\end{bmatrix}\hat{\mathbf{p}}^*(t)$$

$$+\,d/dt\begin{bmatrix}\mathbf{b}^{-1}\mathbf{l}\\ \hat{b}_{\cdot n}^{-1}(t)\hat{l}_n(t)\end{bmatrix} \tag{6.22}$$

Differentiating every element with respect to t, we obtain

$$\left[\begin{array}{c|c}\mathbf{b}^{-1}\mathbf{a} & \mathbf{b}^{-1}\mathbf{a}.\\ \hline \hat{b}_{\cdot n}^{-2}(t)[\hat{b}_{\cdot n}(t)\hat{\mathbf{a}}_{n0}(t) - t\,d/dt\,\hat{b}_{\cdot n}(t)\hat{\mathbf{a}}_{n0}(t) + t\hat{b}_{\cdot n}(t)d/dt\,\hat{\mathbf{a}}_{n0}(t)] & \hat{b}_{\cdot n}^{-2}(t)[\hat{b}_{\cdot n}(t)\hat{a}_{\cdot n}(t) - t\,d/dt\,\hat{b}_{\cdot n}(t)\hat{a}_{\cdot n}(t) + t\hat{b}_{\cdot n}(t)d/dt\,\hat{a}_{\cdot n}(t)]\end{array}\right]\cdot\hat{\mathbf{p}}^*(t)$$

$$+\left[\begin{array}{c}\mathbf{0}\\ \hline \hat{b}_{\cdot n}^{-2}(t)[-d/dt\,\hat{b}_{\cdot n}(t)\hat{l}_n(t) + \hat{b}_{\cdot n}(t)d/dt\,\hat{l}_n(t)]\end{array}\right]$$

For $\hat{\mathbf{p}}^*(t) > \mathbf{0}$ the first $h-1$ elements of the vector of the derivatives are positive, while the sign of the remainder depends on that of

$$[\hat{b}_{\cdot n}(t)\hat{\mathbf{a}}_{n0}(t) - t\,d/dt\,\hat{b}_{\cdot n}(t)\hat{\mathbf{a}}_{n0}(t) + t\hat{b}_{\cdot n}(t)d/dt\,\hat{\mathbf{a}}_{n0}(t)]\,\mathbf{p}^*(t)$$

$$+[b_{\cdot n}(t)\hat{a}_{\cdot n}(t) - t\,d/dt\,\hat{b}_{\cdot n}(t)\hat{a}_{\cdot n}(t) + t\hat{b}_{\cdot n}(t)d/dt\,\hat{a}_{\cdot n}(t)]\,p_0^*(t)$$

$$+[-d/dt\,\hat{b}_{\cdot n}(t)\hat{l}_n(t) + \hat{b}_{\cdot n}(t)d/dt\,\hat{l}_n(t)] \tag{6.23}$$

Multiplying out, (6.23) can be written as follows:

$$\sum_{i=0}^{n}\sum_{k=0}^{n}(1+n-k-i)t^{n+k-i}b_{\cdot n-k}\mathbf{a}_{i0}\mathbf{p}^*(t)$$

$$+\sum_{i=0}^{n}\sum_{k=0}^{n}(1+n-k-i)t^{n+k-i}b_{\cdot n-k}a_{\cdot i}p_0{}^*(t)$$

$$+\sum_{i=0}^{n}\sum_{k=0}^{n}(n-k-i)t^{n+k-i-1}b_{\cdot n-k}l_i$$

Substituting the respective values obtainable from the equation relative to the activities employing old machines for l_i, the above expression is equivalent to

$$\sum_{i=0}^{n}\sum_{k=0}^{n}t^{n+k-i}b_{\cdot n-k}\mathbf{a}_{i0}\mathbf{p}^*(t)+\sum_{i=0}^{n}\sum_{k=0}^{n}t^{n+k-i}b_{\cdot n-k}a_{\cdot i}p_0{}^*(t)$$

$$+\sum_{i=0}^{n}\sum_{k=0}^{n}(n-k-i)t^{n+k-i-1}b_{\cdot n-k}b_{\cdot i}p_0{}^*(t)$$

$$+\sum_{i=1}^{n}\sum_{k=0}^{n}t^{n+k-i}b_{\cdot n-k}a_{im}p_i^{n*}$$

The third addend is equal to zero, as can be easily proved. Therefore, on the basis of the assumptions that we have made, if the prices of old machines are non-negative, then expression (6.23) is positive. Consequently,

$$d/dt[\hat{\mathbf{p}}^*(t)] > \mathbf{0} \qquad \textit{q.e.d.}$$

As $\hat{\mathbf{p}}^*(t)$ is the price vector in terms of the wage rate, we know by definition that

$$p_0{}^*(t) = \frac{p_0(t)}{w(t)} = 1\bigg/\frac{w(t)}{p_0(t)}$$

But $w(t)/p_0(t)$ is nothing but the expression of the wage–profit curve as constructed in the previous sections. Consequently,

$$d/dt[w^n(t)] = -\frac{d/dt[p_0{}^*(t)]}{[p_0{}^*(t)]^2}$$

We have therefore proved the following proposition.

Proposition 6

If all commodities included old machines have non-negative prices then the wage–profit curve is a decreasing function of the rate of profit.

Since the prices of old machines are non-negative in correspondence with the wage–profit frontier, if we call T_{max} the value of the factor of profit corresponding to the intersection of the wage–profit frontier with the axis of the abscissae, we may immediately deduce the validity of the following corollary.

Corollary 3

The wage–profit frontier is a decreasing function of the rate of profit for $t \in [1, T_{max}]$.

When we suppose that more than one productive sector uses machines in production, the proof is completely similar and the results remain unaltered.

We may observe in this case how the prices of commodities produced by machines may be non-increasing functions of the rate of profit when expressed in terms of the wage rate only as a result of an unprofitable employment of the machine in the corresponding sector. Consequently, it is not possible for a wage–profit curve to have increasing sections in correspondence to ranges of the rate of profit for which this curve dominates the other curves in the same family, whether the use of the other machines, in their respective sectors, is profitable or not.

Since the employment of machines corresponding to the frontier is that which is profitable in each of the sectors that use them, it follows that the frontier is a decreasing function of the rate of profit.

On the basis of the remarks just made, we can define the economically relevant range of the factor of profit with greater accuracy. Given a particular age structure in the employment of machines, we can limit the analysis to values of $t \in [1, T_{max}]$. In fact, it is within this range that the phenomenon of multiple roots referred to in section 5 may occur. If the system corresponding to a particular employment of machines becomes vital again for $t > T_{max}$, the corresponding wage–profit curve should have an increasing section around its intersection with the axis of the abscissae. But in this case there should be another curve which dominates it and which corresponds to a different employment of the machines. In its turn, this other curve should correspond to a particular system that has become productive again; in this case, it would also have an increasing section and should therefore be dominated. By repeating this reasoning, we deduce that no curve can first have an increasing section, and therefore that no system can become productive again for $t > T_{max}$.

12 The standard system and the standard commodity

Contrary to what one may believe, the construction and the analysis of the standard system do not present substantial difficulties, and the existence of non-negative multipliers for the various industries and activities may be easily deduced from the nucleus of the analysis made in the previous sections.

The aim of the standard system is clearly the determination of the standard commodity, i.e. that particular *numéraire* that is independent of distribution.

Following Sraffa (1960, Ch. 8) and using the symbols already adopted, the standard system may be represented in the following way:

$$(1+R)[\mathbf{x}, x_0, x_1, \ldots x_n] \begin{bmatrix} \mathbf{a} & \mathbf{a}. & \mathbf{0} & \ldots & \mathbf{0} & \mathbf{0} \\ \mathbf{a}_{00} & a._0 & 0 & \ldots & 0 & 0 \\ \mathbf{a}_{10} & a._1 & a_1 & \ldots & 0 & 0 \\ \vdots & \vdots & \vdots & & \vdots & \vdots \\ \mathbf{a}_{n-1,0} & a._{n-1} & 0 & \ldots & a_{n-1} & 0 \\ \mathbf{a}_{n,0} & a._n & 0 & \ldots & 0 & a_n \end{bmatrix}$$

$$= [\mathbf{x}, x_0, x_1, \ldots x_n] \begin{bmatrix} \mathbf{b} & \mathbf{0} & \mathbf{0} & \mathbf{0} & \ldots & \mathbf{0} \\ \mathbf{0} & b._0 & b_1 & 0 & \ldots & 0 \\ \mathbf{0} & b._1 & 0 & b_2 & \ldots & 0 \\ \vdots & \vdots & \vdots & \vdots & & \vdots \\ \mathbf{0} & b._{n-1} & 0 & 0 & \ldots & b_n \\ \mathbf{0} & b._n & 0 & 0 & \ldots & 0 \end{bmatrix}$$

or, multiplying, as

$$\begin{cases} (1+R)(\mathbf{xa}+x_0\mathbf{a}_{00}+x_1\mathbf{a}_{10}+\ \ldots\ +x_n\mathbf{a}_{n0}) = \mathbf{xb} \\ (1+R)(\mathbf{xa}.+x_0a._0+x_1a._1+\ \ldots +x_na._n) = x_0b._0 \\ \qquad +\ \ldots + x_nb._n \\ (1+R)x_1a_1 = x_0b_1 \\ (1+R)x_2a_2 = x_1b_2 \\ \cdot \\ \cdot \\ \cdot \\ (1+R)x_na_n = x_{n-1}b_n \end{cases} \tag{6.24}$$

where R indicates the standard ratio and the components of the vector $[\mathbf{x}, x_0, x_1, \ldots, x_n]$ are the multipliers of the different activities.

By examining (6.24) we can immediately deduce that the multipliers of activities employing old machines are positive if, and only if, the multiplier of the activity employing the new machine also is positive.

Using the last n equations of system (6.24), it is possible to express the corresponding multipliers in terms of the multiplier x_0 relative to the activity employing the new machine. If we substitute the values thus obtained in the second equation, we can reduce (6.24) to the following equivalent system:

$$\begin{cases} (1+R)[(1+R)^n \mathbf{x}\mathbf{a} + x_0 \hat{\mathbf{a}}_{n0}(1+R)] = (1+R)^n \mathbf{x}\mathbf{b} \\ (1+R)[(1+R)^n \mathbf{x}\mathbf{a}. + x_0 \hat{a}._n(1+R)] = x_0 \hat{b}._n(1+R) \end{cases}$$

or, in a compact form, as

$$(1+R)[\mathbf{x}\ x_0]\begin{bmatrix} (1+R)^n \mathbf{a} & (1+R)^n \mathbf{a}. \\ \hat{\mathbf{a}}_{n0}(1+R) & \hat{a}._n(1+R) \end{bmatrix}$$

$$= [\mathbf{x}\ x_0]\begin{bmatrix} (1+R)^n \mathbf{b} & \mathbf{0} \\ \mathbf{0} & \hat{b}._n(1+R) \end{bmatrix} \qquad (6.25)$$

We can see straight away that the determinant of the matrix of the coefficients in the homogeneous system (6.25) has the same functional form as the determinant of the matrix of the corresponding integrated system of prices. Hence, on the basis of Proposition 2, we can prove the following proposition.

Proposition 7

There is a $R > 0$ corresponding to which the determinant of the matrix of the coefficients of the system (6.25) is zero and to which corresponds, following the Perron–Frobenius theorem, an eigenvector which is strictly positive if the system is indecomposable. It follows immediately that $R = T_n - 1$.

Sraffa's statement (1960, section 84) that the multipliers of the standard system are generally positive is therefore valid. Hence it is possible to construct a standard commodity with positive components.

We should point out, however, that it is not generally possible to establish the uniqueness of the standard ratio[19] and therefore of the standard

[19] On the basis of the remarks made in previous sections, by non-uniqueness of the standard ratio we mean the existence of several positive and distinct values for R that are roots of the equation $\det[\hat{\mathbf{B}}(R) - (1+R)\hat{\mathbf{A}}(R)] = 0$ and which are associated with non-negative eigenvectors.

commodity. Concerning the general case of joint production, Sraffa suggests that we should take as standard ratio the smallest of the economically meaningful values of R for which the determinant of system (6.25) vanishes, and to take as standard commodity that which corresponds to such a value, in order to eliminate the possibility of certain phenomena that from an economic point of view are to be considered anormal (cf. ibid., section 64).

This point deserves a little more attention. Let us suppose that the values of the standard ratio are i in number and are ranked in increasing order according to an index j. If we express the wage in terms of the standard net product (for definition, see ibid., section 26) corresponding to the standard ratio R_i, in order that a zero wage be compatible with more than one 'maximum' level of the rate of profit, then it is necessary for the wage to be the share of a net product the value of which is zero in correspondence with the prices calculated on the basis of a rate of profit equal to R_j ($j = 1, 2, \ldots i-1$). If the only element of joint production is old machines, the multipliers are positive; consequently, some of the prices will be negative. Since this can only happen for the prices of old machines, the condition deduced by Sraffa implicitly shows that the employment of the machine is not the most profitable at such values of the rate of profit. The corresponding wage–profit curve is therefore dominated by at least one other curve, corresponding to a different working life of the machine.

On the other hand, when the wage is expressed in terms of the standard product, the wage–profit relation becomes linear. Consequently, if the chosen standard product is that which corresponds to R_i, the wage–profit line assumes positive values, even when corresponding to those intermediate values of the rate of profit according to which the system is not viable. This fact explains why prices measured in terms of the standard product become infinite in correspondence to the values R_j ($j = 1, 2, \ldots i - 1$) of the rate of profit. For such values of r, the system ends (or begins) to be viable, the prices pass from positive to negative values (or *vice versa*) and there is a point of discontinuity.

Even if the uniqueness of the standard ratio and of the standard commodity can be established by a device such as that proposed by Sraffa, we should remember that in the present scheme of analysis the most profitable productive structure is identified as a function of the exogenous distributive variable. Hence, the standard ratio and the standard commodity are relative to each of the productive structures thus identified.

A maximum standard ratio may, however, be associated with the economic system. Such a ratio corresponds to the maximum of those determined by productive configurations that assure an economically meaningful system of prices for values of the rate of profit equal to the corresponding standard ratios. Obviously, this maximum standard ratio equals the maximum rate of profit of the wage–profit frontier.

Indeed, given a certain working life of the machine, we may well find that, for a value of the rate of profit equal to the greatest of the corresponding values of R, the price of some old machines will be negative. This means that, if we eliminate activities employing machines with negative prices, it will be possible to obtain a greater wage rate corresponding to the same rate of profit. The wage–profit curve corresponding to the new productive configuration will possess an intercept on the axis of the abscissae which is greater than the previous one. If, in correspondence with the new maximum rate of profit, the price system gives a positive solution, and if it is not possible or profitable[20] to increase the working life of the machine, then this new rate would also constitute the maximum value of the standard ratio for the system under consideration. This is not to say, however, that the technological dimension that determines it is that which is profitable when the rate of profit assumes values smaller than it.

13 Remarks on the asymmetry of prices and multipliers

The analysis of the standard system has allowed us to make clear the asymmetry of behaviour existing between prices and multipliers. When we consider the system of prices corresponding to a zero wage and that of the multipliers in their integrated forms, we note that the assumption of productivity is able to guarantee the existence of economically meaningful solutions for both models. If the system is indecomposable, it will therefore be possible to determine positive prices and multipliers for the sectors producing new machines, for the integrated industries employing them as well as for the industries producing non-durable commodities by the use of circulating capital alone.

Symmetry disappears when we expressly consider the activities that employ old machines among the means of production. While the multipliers of such activities are all positive if that of the activity using the new machine is also positive, the prices of the corresponding old machines may not be.

In this case, in fact, we lose the complete identity between commodities and activities that produce them which we find in the case of single production, though the identity of marketable commodities and their corresponding industries, which is formally reproduced in the integrated system, still remains valid.

[20] In fact, if the efficiency of the machine can be defined as constant or increasing over its whole lifetime, and if commodities are all basic, the corresponding prices will be positive, no matter how many years the machine is employed. In this case the maximum standard ratio will be that corresponding to the employment of the machine extended to the limit of its physical life.

Since the condition of productivity is defined at the aggregate level for each commodity its fulfilment guarantees that the system is reproducible on the level of industries, in the sense that every industry produces a quantity of the corresponding commodity which is not smaller than that totally employed in the economic system. This allows us directly to deduce no more than the existence of a positive standard ratio and of positive multipliers for the different industries. Since the standard ratio also measures the value of the maximum rate of profit for the corresponding productive configuration, we can also deduce that the industries are able to supply a uniform rate of profit equal to R, together with positive prices for the commodities they produce.

The assumption of productivity, however, does not supply any information concerning the possible limits that the single activities, into which the machine-using industries are divided, may place on the dimension of the standard ratio. In other words, the standard ratio corresponding to a given productive configuration is not necessarily the maximum uniform rate of surplus for the economic system under examination. It could, for example, increase if the working life of machines were varied. This would mean that the activities the elimination of which allows the uniform ratio between physical surplus and total intake of each commodity to increase are not, when prices correspond to a zero wage, able to supply a uniform rate of profit equal to the standard ratio.

Since the condition of productivity assures that the prices of new machines and non-durable commodities and the maximum rate of profit will be positive, whenever the phenomenon just mentioned occurs for activities employing old machines, it must of necessity show itself in the negativity of the prices of such machines.[21]

On the other hand, it is possible to reproportion the various activities within each mechanised industry without introducing negative multipliers, because each old machine, although produced jointly with the non-durable commodity, has the characteristic of being supplied by a single activity and

[21] In system (6.1), consider the equations relative to the activities which use the machine. If, in this note, we denote by the scalar a_0 the number of new machines employed in the production of the hth commodity, by the components of vector $\mathbf{a}'_{i0} (i = 0, 1, \ldots n)$ the inputs of non-durable means of production, by $\mathbf{p}$ the vector of the corresponding prices, by the non-zero component of vector $\mathbf{b}'_{i0} (i = 0, 1, \ldots n)$ the production of the above-mentioned commodity in the corresponding activities, and by ${}_m p_0$ the price of the new machine, we obtain the following system:

$$\begin{cases} Ta_{0m}p_0 + T\mathbf{a}'_{00}\mathbf{p} = \mathbf{b}'_{00}\mathbf{p} + b_{1m}p_1 \\ Ta_{1m}p_1 + T\mathbf{a}'_{10}\mathbf{p} = \mathbf{b}'_{10}\mathbf{p} + b_{1m}p_2 \\ \vdots \\ Ta_{nm}p_n + T\mathbf{a}'_{n0}\mathbf{p} = \mathbf{b}'_{n0}\mathbf{p} \end{cases} \qquad (1)$$

is connected to it by a causal relationship of production–use. In this way, each multiplier relative to these activities depends in a strictly causal way on the activity employing the machine at its immediately preceding age, since the number of machines of i years of age (and consequently the relative multiplier) depends on the number of machines of $i-1$ years of age.

The asymmetry found in the standard system reoccurs in a completely analogous form for prices and quantities when we consider any situation in which the table of potential physical flows is compared with a system of prices associated with hypothetical configurations of the exogenous distributive variable. In fact it is clear that the division of an industry into a number of activities which are within certain limits eliminable, gives rise to a sort of technological choice. Therefore, even if the fulfilment of the assumption of productivity assures the technical feasibility of a certain productive configuration, this does not mean to say that, after assigning a certain distribution of income between profits and wages, such a configuration is economically profitable.

14 The problem of the reduction of prices to dated quantities of labour in the case of production with fixed capital

We now wish to draw attention to the nature of the problem of the reduction of prices to dated quantities of labour as dealt with and solved in the case of production with circulating capital alone. At the same time we shall make some critical remarks concerning the parallel transposition of

---

Since $a_0 = a_1 = \ldots = a_n = b_1 = \ldots = b_n = \alpha$, if we solve (1) with respect of the prices of the machines, we obtain

$$\begin{bmatrix} {}_mp_0 \\ \\ \vdots \\ \\ {}_mp_n \end{bmatrix} = 1/\alpha \begin{bmatrix} 1/T & 1/T^2 & 1/T^3 & \cdots & 1/T^n & 1/T^{n+1} \\ 0 & 1/T & 1/T^2 & \cdots & 1/T^{n-1} & 1/T^n \\ \vdots & \vdots & \vdots & \cdots & \vdots & \vdots \\ 0 & 0 & 0 & \cdots & 1/T & 1/T^2 \\ 0 & 0 & 0 & \cdots & 0 & 1/T \end{bmatrix} \begin{bmatrix} \mathbf{b}'_{n0}\mathbf{p} - T\mathbf{a}'_{n0}\mathbf{p} \\ \\ \vdots \\ \\ \mathbf{b}'_{00}\mathbf{p} - T\mathbf{a}'_{00}\mathbf{p} \end{bmatrix} \quad (2)$$

System (2) is determined once values have been assigned to T and $\mathbf{p}$.

If the activity employing the machine of n years of age cannot supply at prices $\mathbf{p}$ a rate of profit $R = T-1$, the price of the corresponding machine is negative. Since ${}_mp_0$ is positive as a result of the assumption of viability, at least one of the components of the vector

$$\begin{bmatrix} \mathbf{b}'_{00}\mathbf{p} - T\mathbf{a}'_{00}\mathbf{p} \\ \vdots \quad \vdots \quad \vdots \quad \vdots \\ \mathbf{b}'_{n0}\mathbf{p} - T\mathbf{a}'_{n0}\mathbf{p} \end{bmatrix}$$

must be positive; that is, at least one of the activities must allow a gross rate of profit greater than R.

the problem to the case in which the use of a commodity in production does not end after one year only, and continues for more than one unit period of production.

In the case of single production with circulating capital only, the reduction is performed by going backwards round by round through the productive process, and resolving prices, generally, in the form of an infinite series of labour requirements. Each labour term is weighted by a power of the factor of profit appropriate to the round of production in which the amount of labour is required. The properties of the system make the addends positive and the series convergent for $t \in [1, T)$, where T indicates the maximum factor of profit.

It is also possible for the case of production with fixed capital to reduce prices to dated quantities of labour, by applying to system (6.1) the same device employed for the case of production with circulating capital alone.

However, the reduction made in this way does have certain anomalies. Above all, it is generally not possible to give an immediate proof of the convergence of the series of dated quantities of labour. It is true that this is assured for values of the rate of profit within the circle of convergence, but we cannot show the economic meaning of this interval, which, for single production with circulating capital only, coincides with the economic range of variation of the rate of profit.[22]

And then, although we assume that the series converges in a certain range of the rate of profit, some terms of the reduction generally have negative components, even if the working life of the machine is the most profitable.

The above-mentioned anomalies are very probably owing to the immediate transposition of the reduction technique adopted for production with only circulating capital to the case of production with fixed capital. Although this transposition is correct from a purely formal point of view, it is not necessarily so from a conceptual one. As we have seen, the treatment of fixed capital as a joint product necessarily introduces a new

[22] Consider system (6.1) in the case in which $w = 0$:

$$t\mathbf{A}\mathbf{p} = \mathbf{B}\mathbf{p} \tag{1}$$

As can be easily proved, we always have det $\mathbf{B} \neq 0$. Hence (1) may be written in the following way:

$$t\mathbf{B}^{-1}\mathbf{A}\mathbf{p} = \mathbf{p}$$

from which we obtain

$$[\mathbf{I} - t\mathbf{B}^{-1}\mathbf{A}]\mathbf{p} = \mathbf{0}$$

Since matrix $\mathbf{B}$ is not of a diagonal type, its inverse will generally contain some negative elements. This is also true for matrix $\mathbf{B}^{-1}\mathbf{A}$. Consequently, it is not possible to extend the properties of the non-negative matrices directly to $\mathbf{B}^{-1}\mathbf{A}$. Hence the difficulties mentioned in the text.

temporal dimension into the productive process, since machines may be used in production for more than one year. Clearly, this temporal dimension can be observed within a single year by the simultaneous presence of different activities that produce the same commodity, using the same type of machine but at different ages.

At this point it is useful to analyse briefly some characteristics of the activities employing aged machines. First of all, we should observe that aged machines, since they emerge as a joint product, do not require specific inputs to be produced; they simply are the result of using a durable instrument in production. Consequently, their price is not properly linked to the costs of production but is a book expression which is determined by means of the technological structure for making annual allowance for depreciation; this makes possible the replacement of the means of production and the payment of a uniform rate of profit in each activity.

In fact, as has been pointed out, the treatment of fixed capital in terms of joint production has the result that every commodity produced by use of a machine is obtained by as many activities as years for which the machine is in use. The necessity of determining a uniform price of production for every individual commodity means that the price must be fixed in terms of 'average' inputs in the production of the commodity.

The problem can be solved by attempting to change it to a situation that is formally analogous to that of single production. This can be done by integrating the activities that produce the same commodity using machines at different ages. This clearly requires that the various productive activities be made temporally 'homogeneous'.

On the basis of the remarks just made, a correct process of reduction should be carried out as follows: homogenisation, from a temporal point of view, of the productive activities; addition of the activities, with the elimination of old machines the prices of which cannot be reduced and can be determined only in a derivative way; and reduction of the prices of new machines and non-durable commodities in terms of dated quantities of labour.

The first phase of the process is that which is followed by the construction of the integrated system. Consider once more the simplified case of the system illustrated in the section 3, with reference to its integrated version

$$t\hat{\mathbf{A}}(t)\hat{\mathbf{p}} + w\hat{\mathbf{L}}(t) = \hat{\mathbf{B}}(t)\hat{\mathbf{p}}$$

If we make $w = 1$, then, since $\hat{\mathbf{B}}(t)$ is a diagonal matrix, we can write

$$\hat{\mathbf{p}} = t\hat{\mathbf{B}}^{-1}(t)\hat{\mathbf{A}}(t)\hat{\mathbf{p}} + \hat{\mathbf{B}}^{-1}(t)\hat{\mathbf{L}}(t) \tag{6.26}$$

Carrying out the reduction of (6.26) by the usual method, we obtain

$$\hat{\mathbf{p}} = \hat{\mathbf{B}}^{-1}\hat{\mathbf{L}} + t(\hat{\mathbf{B}}^{-1}\hat{\mathbf{A}})\hat{\mathbf{B}}^{-1}\hat{\mathbf{L}} + t^2(\hat{\mathbf{B}}^{-1}\hat{\mathbf{A}})^2\hat{\mathbf{B}}^{-1}\hat{\mathbf{L}} + \ldots \tag{6.27}$$

Since, by construction, $\hat{\mathbf{B}}(t)$ is a diagonal matrix with elements $b_{ii} > 0$, $\hat{\mathbf{B}}^{-1}(t)$ is also a diagonal matrix, with analogous characteristics; it follows immediately that all the terms on the right-hand side of (6.27) are positive.

If we remember that we have called T the smallest meaningful value of the factor of profit, so that $w(T) = 0$ in system (6.26), we can therefore prove the following proposition.

Proposition 8

The series on the right-hand side of (6.27) is convergent for $t \in [1, T)$.

Proof

Proof is quite obvious when we remember that every matrix $[\mathbf{I} - \mathbf{K}]^{-1}$ can be expressed as a series of powers if the dominant eigenvalue of $\mathbf{K}$ is less than one.

For every $\bar{t} \in [1, T)$, matrix $\bar{t}\hat{\mathbf{B}}^{-1}(t)\hat{\mathbf{A}}(\bar{t})$ is a numerical non-negative matrix which, by construction, has a dominant eigenvalue which is positive and less than one. Therefore, the series converges for $t = \bar{t}$. Since this is true for every $t \in [1, T)$, the proposition is proved. *q.e.d.*

Whenever the case referred to in section 6 occurs – whenever, that is, the dominant eigenvalue of matrix $t\hat{\mathbf{B}}^{-1}(t)\hat{\mathbf{A}}(t)$ could become less than one for values of t belonging to the interval $(T, \bar{T})$ – then there will be a further interval, or further intervals, of the factor of profit assuring the convergence of (6.27).

The effects produced on the original system by this phenomenon probably constitute one of the reasons why the analysis of the problem of convergence is difficult when introduced directly into system (6.1).

We should point out that, unlike the case of single production with circulating capital alone, matrices $\hat{\mathbf{A}}(t)$ and $\hat{\mathbf{B}}(t)$ and vector $\hat{\mathbf{L}}(t)$ are not the technological elements of the system but are obtained by partial aggregation of these data by means of the rate of profit.

It follows that the requisites which we can formally define as the amounts of labour which are required in each conceptual round of the reduction are functions of t. The elements of the reduction therefore depend in two ways on the rate of profit: first of all, the rate of profit determines the economic life of the machine, and therefore also the average technical requirements per unit of output, and consequently the elements of the reduction. In turn, each element of the reduction is a function of the rate of profit, so that a variation of the latter changes the elements of the reduction, even if the economic life of the machine remains unaltered.

The proposition according to which in a given technology a productive process may be represented by a series of inputs of labour in different periods – to be taken as a datum independent of distribution – runs into some difficulties, therefore, when we take fixed capital into consideration.

This representation – the biunivocal correspondence of the table of physical flows and the series of dated inputs of labour – in fact only occurs for single production with circulating capital alone. If, on the contrary, fixed capital is used in the system, we cannot make a similar representation of the productive process independent of the exogenous distributive variable. In fact, as has been pointed out, even in the context of the same productive configuration the labour requisites of each round are functions of the rate of profit and therefore vary as it varies.

15 Concluding remarks on the problem of depreciation

The results so far obtained allow us to make a few remarks about the introduction of fixed capital into the schemes of economic analysis.

We have seen that there are two fundamental problems involved in this case: the identification of the economic life of the machine, and the determination of the annual allowance for depreciation. The two problems are clearly not independent of each other and are simultaneously solved if we determine a suitable system of prices.

At this point we can see very well the logical limits of solutions directly or indirectly based on the assumption that it is possible to identify the economic life of the machines from a purely technological point of view. In an economic system in which commodities are produced by means of a multiplicity of commodities, some of which are durable, such solutions are restricted to very special cases.[23] It is therefore not realistically possible to identify a law based on technical considerations that measures the contribution of machines to production within each year in order to reconstitute their original value over the working life.

This means that there is no possibility of identifying an operator capable of transforming fixed capital into circulating capital. Nor can we solve the associated problem of economic evaluation through solutions to schemes that can be taken back to models of production with circulating capital only.

By analysing some results of the scheme illustrated in this essay, we can demonstrate, as previously seen, how it is generally logically incorrect and anyway completely arbitrary to solve the problem of depreciation on the supposition that it is possible to determine in purely technical terms the contribution of the machine to the various stages of production. Traditional schemes see in the participation of the machine in production,

[23] We refer here to cases where the efficiency of the machine can be determined on the basis of a simple comparison, in physical terms, of the different activities.

an absorption of part of its overall capacity to contribute to it; the annual depreciation quota is simply identified in terms of a suitable reduction in the original value of the machine. Consequently, these depreciation quotas must be positive; negative or zero quotas should therefore be limited to those periods in which maintenance or improvement operations on the machine allow its capacity to produce to be greater or identical to that of the previous period. The sign of the depreciation quotas should therefore be obtained from the technical law that measures the contribution of the machine to production.

In the scheme we have proposed, the generic allowance to be made for depreciation will be determined by the difference between the price of the machine of j years of age and that of the machine of $j+1$ years of age.

From (6.15) we obtain

$$b_{j+1}\,{}_mp^n_{j+1} = w^n D^j - N^j$$

$$b_j\,{}_mp^n_j = w^n D^{j-1} - N^{j-1}$$

Subtracting the first relation from the second, and remembering that $b_j = b_{j+1} = \alpha$, we obtain

$$\alpha({}_mp^n_j - {}_mp^n_{j+1}) = -w^n(D^j - D^{j-1}) + (N^j - N^{j-1})$$

If all mechanised activities use labour or at least a commodity different from that produced, then $D^j - D^{j-1} > 0$. We may therefore write

$$\frac{\alpha}{D^j - D^{j-1}}({}_mp^n_j - {}_mp^n_{j+1}) = -w^n + \frac{N^j - N^{j-1}}{D^j - D^{j-1}}$$

It is not always possible to determine *a priori* the sign of the jth depreciation allowance. It is certainly negative if $N^j - N^{j-1} < 0$, which implies that $w^i < w^{j-1}$, i.e. that the employment of the machine up to j years of age will not be profitable. The contrary is not true, however.

The presence of negative depreciation allowances should not cause surprise, however. If the jth allowance is negative, this simply means that, given the distribution of income, the budget of the activity using the n-year-old machine is not enough to give a positive allowance for depreciation. It might still be profitable to operate this activity, since this would allow the machine of $j+1$ years of age to be made available and the depreciation of the machine to be completed.

A numerical example illustrating this phenomenon is given in the appendix to this essay. We can see, in fact, that in the interval of the rate of profit between, for example, 6 and 54 per cent, in relation to which it is profitable to extend the employment of the machine until its second year of age, the allowance for depreciation ${}_mp^2_1 - {}_mp^2_2$ is negative, for whatever relative position of w^1 and w^0.

The objection could be made that this behaviour is owing to the particularity of the numerical example, since this could correspond to the very case where the machine, when passing from its second to its third year of employment, is repaired or improved so that it increases its residual capacity to produce (a situation which could also be treated by the schemes mentioned at the beginning). This doubt is completely unfounded, however, since a negative allowance for depreciation is a phenomenon linked with a particular level of distribution of income between wages and profits.

In fact, we need only examine Table 6A.4, which shows the behaviour of prices for one- and two-year-old machines at a rate of profit varying between 54 and 56 per cent. The depreciation allowance passes from negative to positive values as the rate of profit grows within the range under consideration.

The results just illustrated seem to prove that it cannot be correct to consider the single depreciation allowances as an index, in value terms, of the dynamic with which the machine gradually exhausts itself from period to period. In other words, these results show the arbitrariness of formulas of depreciation based on the concept of physical deterioration of the machine.

Appendix: numerical example

The numerical example reproduces a system in which a commodity, wheat, is produced, employing wheat, labour and a machine with a physical life of three years. The machine, in turn, is produced by means of wheat and labour.

The system of prices is expressed by the following equations:

$$t\begin{bmatrix} 0 & 0{\cdot}1 & 0 & 0 \\ 1 & 0{\cdot}4 & 0 & 0 \\ 0 & 0{\cdot}578 & 1 & 0 \\ 0 & 0{\cdot}6 & 0 & 1 \end{bmatrix} \begin{bmatrix} p \\ p_0 \\ {}_mp_1 \\ {}_mp_2 \end{bmatrix} + w \begin{bmatrix} 0{\cdot}4 \\ 0{\cdot}2 \\ 0{\cdot}6 \\ 0{\cdot}4 \end{bmatrix}$$

$$= \begin{bmatrix} 1 & 0 & 0 & 0 \\ 0 & 1 & 1 & 0 \\ 0 & 1 & 0 & 1 \\ 0 & 1 & 0 & 0 \end{bmatrix} \begin{bmatrix} p \\ p_0 \\ {}_mp_1 \\ {}_mp_2 \end{bmatrix}$$

Using the exponents 0, 1, 2 to refer respectively to the variables relative to the systems employing only the new machine, the machine up to one year of age, and the machine up to two years of age, we obtain the following expressions for the respective wage–profit curves in terms of the price p_0 of wheat:

$$w^0 = \frac{1 - 0{\cdot}4t - 0{\cdot}1t^2}{0{\cdot}2 + 0{\cdot}4t}$$

$$w^1 = \frac{1 + 0{\cdot}422t - 0{\cdot}4t^2 - 0{\cdot}1t^3}{0{\cdot}6 + 0{\cdot}2t + 0{\cdot}4t^2}$$

$$w^2 = \frac{1 + 0{\cdot}4t + 0{\cdot}422t^2 - 0{\cdot}4t^3 - 0{\cdot}1t^4}{0{\cdot}4 + 0{\cdot}6t + 0{\cdot}2t^2 + 0{\cdot}4t^3}$$

Table 6A.1–3 give, respectively for the three systems, the numerical values of the wage–profit curves, and of prices for the various rates of profit, the latter

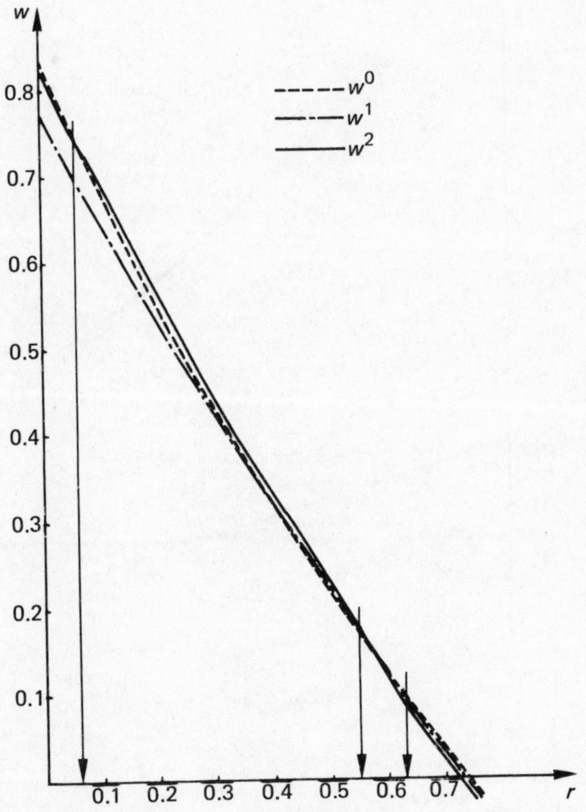

FIGURE 6A.1

being expressed in terms both of the price of wheat and of the wage rate. The same results are summarised in graph form in Figures 6A.1–3.

From inspection of Table 6A.1 and Figure 6A.1, we can see immediately that, for $0 \leq r < 0{\cdot}05$, it is only profitable to use the new machine; for $0{\cdot}05 < r < 0{\cdot}55$ it is best to use the machine until its physical exhaustion;

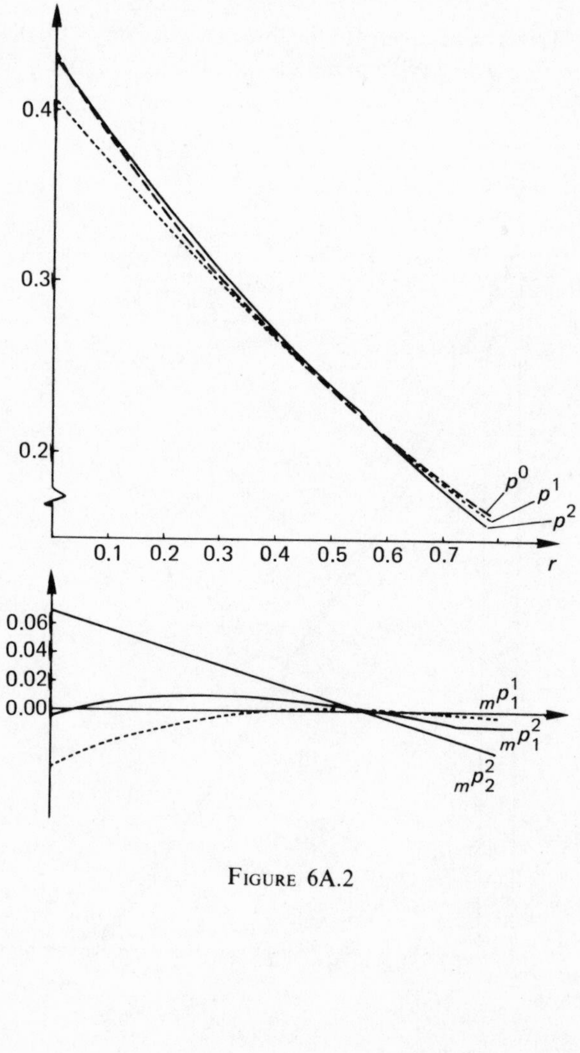

FIGURE 6A.2

and for $0{\cdot}55 < r < 0{\cdot}63$ profitable employment is limited at one year of age, while for higher values of the rate of profit it is profitable to use only the new machine.

The prices of old machines behave in a way that conforms to the rules enunciated in the course of the present work.

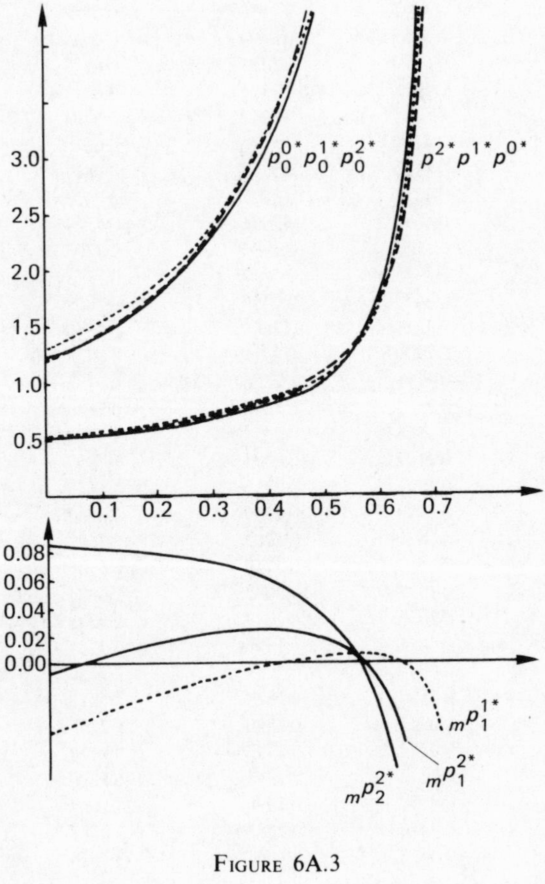

FIGURE 6A.3

TABLE 6A.1

r	w^0	p^0	p^{0*}	$p^{0*}{}_0$
0·00	0·8333	0·4333	0·5200	1·2000
0·02	0·8025	0·4230	0·5270	1·2460
0·04	0·7724	0·4129	0·5346	1·2945
0·06	0·7430	0·4032	0·5426	1·3458
0·08	0·7141	0·3936	0·5512	1·4002
0·10	0·6859	0·3843	0·5603	1·4578
0·12	0·6582	0·3753	0·5701	1·5191
0·14	0·6311	0·3664	0·5806	1·5843
0·16	0·6045	0·3578	0·5918	1·6540
0·18	0·5785	0·3494	0·6039	1·7285
0·20	0·5529	0·3411	0·6170	1·8085
0·22	0·5278	0·3331	0·6311	1·8944
0·24	0·5032	0·3252	0·6464	1·9872
0·26	0·4790	0·3176	0·6630	2·0875
0·28	0·4552	0·3101	0·6811	2·1964
0·30	0·4319	0·3027	0·7009	2·3151
0·32	0·4090	0·2956	0·7227	2·4449
0·34	0·3864	0·2885	0·7467	2·5875
0·36	0·3643	0·2817	0·7733	2·7449
0·38	0·3425	0·2750	0·8029	2·9197
0·40	0·3210	0·2684	0·8360	3·1147
0.42	0·2999	0·2619	0·8734	3·3339
0·44	0·2791	0·2556	0·9158	3·5819
0·46	0·2587	0·2494	0·9643	3·8651
0·48	0·2385	0·2434	1·0203	4·1913
0·50	0·2187	0·2375	1·0857	4·5714
0·52	0·1992	0·2316	1·1630	5·0198
0·54	0·1799	0·2259	1·2557	5·5570
0·56	0·1609	0·2203	1·3691	6·2123
0·58	0·1422	0·2149	1·5106	7·0294
0·60	0·1238	0·2095	1·6923	8·0769
0·62	0·1056	0·2042	1·9338	9·4685
0·64	0·0876	0·1990	2·2707	11·4072
0·66	0·0699	0·1939	2·7729	14·2951
0·68	0·0524	0·1889	3·6013	19·0559
0·70	0·0352	0·1840	5·2258	28·3870
0·72	0·0181	0·1792	9·8514	54·9504
0·74	0·0013	0·1745	126·1290	722·5806
0·76	−0·0152	0·1699	−11·1627	−65·6976
0·78	−0·0316	0·1653	−5·2288	−31·6227
0·80	−0·0478	0·1608	−3·3636	−20·9090

TABLE 6A.2

r	w^1	p^1	$_mp^1{}_1$	p^{1*}	$p^{1*}{}_0$	$_mp^{1*}{}_1$
0·00	0·7683	0·4073	−0·0390	0·5301	1·3015	−0·0507
0·02	0·7442	0·3997	−0·0354	0·5370	1·3435	−0·0476
0·04	0·7203	0·3921	−0·0320	0·5443	1·3881	−0·0445
0·06	0·6966	0·3846	−0·0289	0·5521	1·4354	−0·0415
0·08	0·6730	0·3772	−0·0259	0·5604	1·4857	−0·0386
0·10	0·6496	0·3698	−0·0232	0·5693	1·5393	−0·0357
0·12	0·6263	0·3625	−0·0206	0·5788	1·5965	−0·0330
0·14	0·6032	0·3553	−0·0183	0·5889	1·6576	−0·0303
0·16	0·5803	0·3481	−0·0161	0·5998	1·7231	−0·0277
0·18	0·5575	0·3410	−0·0140	0·6116	1·7934	−0·0252
0·20	0·5350	0·3340	−0·0121	0·6242	1·8690	−0·0227
0·22	0·5126	0·3270	−0·0104	0·6379	1·9506	0·0203
0·24	0·4904	0·3201	−0·0088	0·6528	2·0388	−0·0180
0·26	0·4684	0·3133	−0·0074	0·6689	2·1345	−0·0158
0·28	0·4466	0·3066	−0·0061	0·6865	2·2387	−0·0137
0·30	0·4250	0·3000	−0·0049	0·7058	2·3525	−0·0116
0·32	0·4036	0·2934	−0·0039	0·7270	2·4773	−0·0096
0·34	0·3824	0·2869	−0·0029	0·7503	2·6148	−0·0077
0·36	0·3614	0·2805	−0·0021	0·7763	2·7669	−0·0059
0·38	0·3405	0·2742	−0·0014	0·8051	2·9361	−0·0042
0·40	0·3199	0·2679	−0·0008	0·8375	3·1254	−0·0026
0·42	0·2995	0·2618	−0·0003	0·8740	3·3387	−0·0011
0·44	0·2792	0·2557	0·0000	0·9156	3·5806	0·0002
0·46	0·2592	0·2496	0·0003	0·9632	3·8575	0·0015
0·48	0·2393	0·2437	0·0006	1·0182	4·1774	0·0026
0·50	0·2197	0·2378	0·0007	1·0826	4·5512	0·0035
0·52	0·2002	0·2321	0·0008	1·1590	4·9936	0·0042
0·54	0·1809	0·2263	0·0008	1·2509	5·5254	0·0046
0·56	0·1618	0·2207	0·0007	1·3636	6·1769	0·0046
0·58	0·1429	0·2151	0·0006	1·5049	6·9933	0·0042
0·60	0·1242	0·2097	0·0003	1·6874	8·0463	0·0031
0·62	0·1057	0·2043	0·0001	1·9318	9·4561	0·0011
0·64	0·0874	0·1989	−0·0002	2·2763	11·4409	−0·0025
0·66	0·0692	0·1936	−0·0006	2·7974	14·4425	−0·0089
0·68	0·0512	0·1885	−0·0010	3·6778	19·5107	−0·0208
0·70	0·0334	0·1833	−0·0015	5·4830	29·9001	−0·0469
0·72	0·0158	0·1783	−0·0021	11·2786	63·2480	−0·1340
0·74	−0·0016	0·1733	−0·0027	−105·0550	−606·0633	1·6475
0·76	−0·0189	0·1684	−0·0033	−8·8926	−52·7991	0·1774
0·78	−0·0360	0·1635	−0·0040	−4·5361	−27·7312	0·1122
0·80	−0·0530	0·1587	−0·0047	−2·9953	−18·8628	0·0900

TABLE 6A.3

r	w^2	p^2	${}_mp^2{}_1$	${}_mp^2{}_2$	p^{2*}	$p^{2*}{}_0$	${}_mp^{2*}{}_1$	${}_mp^{2*}{}_2$
0·00	0·8262	0·4305	−0·0042	0·0695	0·5210	1·2102	−0·0051	0·0841
0·02	0·7991	0·4216	−0·0020	0·0669	0·5276	1·2512	−0·0025	0·0838
0·04	0·7723	0·4129	−0·0000	0·0644	0·5346	1·2947	−0·0000	0·0834
0·06	0·7457	0·4043	0·0017	0·0619	0·5421	1·3408	0·0023	0·0830
0·08	0·7194	0·3957	0·0033	0·0594	0·5501	1·3900	0·0046	0·0826
0·10	0·6933	0·3873	0·0047	0·0569	0·5586	1·4423	0·0068	0·0821
0·12	0·6674	0·3789	0·0059	0·0544	0·5678	1·4982	0·0089	0·0816
0·14	0·6418	0·3707	0·0069	0·0519	0·5776	1·5580	0·0109	0·0810
0·16	0·6164	0·3625	0·0078	0·0494	0·5881	1·6221	0·0127	0·0802
0·18	0·5913	0·3545	0·0086	0·0470	0·5995	1·6010	0·0145	0·0794
0·20	0·5664	0·3465	0·0091	0·0445	0·6118	1·7653	0·0162	0·0785
0·22	0·5418	0·3387	0·0096	0·0420	0·6251	1·8455	0·0177	0·0775
0·24	0·5174	0·3309	0·0099	0·0395	0·6396	1·9324	0·0191	0·0763
0·26	0·4933	0·3233	0·0100	0·0370	0·6553	2·0268	0·0204	0·0750
0·28	0·4695	0·3158	0·0101	0·0345	0·6726	2·1298	0·0215	0·0735
0·30	0·4459	0·3083	0·0100	0·0320	0·6915	2·2425	0·0225	0·0718
0·32	0·4225	0·3010	0·0098	0·0295	0·7123	2·3664	0·0233	0·0698
0·34	0·3994	0·2937	0·0095	0·0270	0·7354	2·5033	0·0239	0·0676
0·36	0·3766	0·2866	0·0091	0·0245	0·7611	2·6551	0·0243	0·0651
0·38	0·3540	0·2796	0·0086	0·0220	0·7897	2·8246	0·0244	0·0622
0·40	0·3316	0·2726	0·0080	0·0195	0·8220	3·0149	0·0243	0·0588
0·42	0·3095	0·2658	0·0074	0·0170	0·9004	3·4754	0·0239	0·0549
0·44	0·2877	0·2590	0·0066	0·0145	0·8586	3·2301	0·0230	0·0504
0·46	0·2661	0·2524	0·0057	0·0120	0·9486	3·7576	0·0217	0·0451
0·48	0·2447	0·2459	0·0048	0·0095	1·0046	4·0857	0·0199	0·0389
0·50	0·2236	0·2394	0·0039	0·0070	1·0707	4·4716	0·0174	0·0314
0·52	0·2027	0·2330	0·0028	0·0045	1·1497	4·9324	0·0140	0·0224
0·54	0·1820	0·2268	0·0017	0·0020	1·2457	5·4918	0·0095	0·0112
0·56	0·1616	0·2206	0·0005	−0·0004	1·3649	6·1855	0·0035	−0·0026
0·58	0·1414	0·2145	−0·0006	−0·0029	1·5168	7·0683	−0·0046	−0·0205
0·60	0·1215	0·2086	−0·0019	−0·0053	1·7167	8·2295	−0·0158	−0·0442
0·62	0·1017	0·2027	−0·0032	−0·0078	1·9917	9·8255	−0·0319	−0·0770
0·64	0·0822	0·1969	−0·0046	−0·0103	2·3936	12·1564	−0·0562	−0·1253
0·66	0·0629	0·1911	−0·0060	−0·0127	3·0363	15·8816	−0·0958	−0·2026
0·68	0·0438	0·1855	−0·0074	−0·0152	4·2279	22·7856	−0·1706	−0·3465
0·70	0·0250	0·1800	−0·0089	−0·0176	7·1938	39·9636	−0·3588	−0·7054
0·72	0·0063	0·1745	−0·0105	−0·0200	27·4053	157·0081	−1·6492	−3·1536
0·74	−0·0120	0·1691	−0·0120	−0·0225	−14·0081	−82·8057	0·9986	1·8640
0·76	−0·0303	0·1638	−0·0136	−0·0249	−5·4053	−32·9848	0·4501	0·8222
0·78	−0·0483	0·1586	−0·0152	−0·0273	−3·2810	−20·6802	0·3155	0·5633
0·80	−0·0661	0·1535	−0·0168	−0·0297	−2·3192	−15·1070	0·2552	0·4492

TABLE 6A.4

r	${}_mp^2{}_1$	${}_mp^2{}_2$	${}_mp^2{}_1 - {}_mp^2{}_2$
0·540	0·0017	0·0020	−0·0003
0·541	0·0016	0·0019	−0·0003
0·542	0·0016	0·0018	−0·0002
0·543	0·0015	0·0016	−0·0001
0·544	0·0015	0·0015	0·0000
0·545	0·0014	0·0014	0·0000
0·546	0·0013	0·0013	0·0000
0·547	0·0013	0·0011	0·0002
0·548	0·0012	0·0010	0·0002
0·550	0·0011	0·0008	0·0003
0·551	0·0011	0·0006	0·0005
0·552	0·0010	0·0005	0·0005
0·553	0·0009	0·0004	0·0005
0·554	0·0009	0·0003	0·0006
0·555	0·0008	0·0001	0·0007
0·556	0·0008	0·0000	0·0008
0·557	0·0007	−0·0000	−
0·558	0·0006	−0·0001	−
0·559	0·0006	−0·0003	−
0·560	0·0005	−0·0004	−

References

Böhm-Bawerk, E. von, *The Positive Theory of Capital*, trans. W. Smart (London: Macmillan, 1891). (Original German edition published in 1889.)

Gantmacher, F. R., *The Theory of Matrices* (New York: Chelsea, 1959).

Leontief, W., *The Structure of American Economy 1919–1939* (New York: Oxford University Press, 1951).

Leontief, W., *et al.*, *Studies in the Structure of the American Economy* (New York: Oxford University Press, 1953).

Marx, K., *Capital* (Moscow: Progress Publishers, 1965–7). (Original German text published in 1867–94.)

Neumann, J. von, 'A Model of General Economic Equilibrium' (first published in 1937), *Review of Economic Studies*, XIII (1945–6) 1–9.

Ricardo, D., *On the Principles of Political Economy and Taxation* (first published in 1821), vol. I of *The Works and Correspondence of David Ricardo*, ed. P. Sraffa (Cambridge: Cambridge University Press, 1951).

Sraffa, P., *Production of Commodities by Means of Commodities* (Cambridge: Cambridge University Press, 1960).

Walras, L., *Elements of Pure Economics* (first published in 1874–7), ed. W. Jaffé (London: George Allen and Unwin, 1965).

Wicksell, K., *Lectures on Political Economy* (first published in 1901), ed. L. Robbins (London: Routledge and Kegan Paul, 1934).

CHAPTER SEVEN

Fixed Capital as a Joint Product and the Analysis of Accumulation with Different Forms of Technical Progress[1]

BERTRAM SCHEFOLD

1 Introduction

Since the reswitching debate, the point has become familiar that the means of production in a capitalist society represent different 'quantities of capital', depending on the prevailing rate of profit. But, because these discussions have been about a critique of the neoclassical theory of value and distribution and not about a comprehensive new theory of capital, they have been conducted either in terms of circulating capital without machines or in terms of the production of one consumption good by means of one machine, with input prices assumed to be given, or with no physical inputs except labour (cf. Hicks, 1970; Nuti, 1970). Although von Neumann and Sraffa revived the 'old classical idea' (Sraffa) of treating what is left at the end of the year's process of production as an *economically different* good[2] from the one which entered the process, very few[3] have tried to construct

[1] The original English version of this essay was first circulated in 1974 as a mimeograph. The main mathematical results of parts I and II are based on the chapter on fixed capital in my thesis of 1971, a second edition of which is in preparation. Different sections of this essay have appeared and in part have been further developed in Schefold (1976a–c; 1978a, b).

[2] This point has not always been understood correctly. Precisely when dealing with the von Neumann model, Dorfman, Samuelson and Solow wrote (1958, p. 383), in order to illustrate its advantages, that 'it can handle capital goods without fuss and bother. A non-depreciating capital good simply enters both as input and as output in the corresponding process. If the capital good depreciates three per cent per unit of time, one unit of the good may appear as input, and 0 97 unit as output.' An economically depreciating machine is not a physically shrinking balloon!

[3] The most notable exception is Mirrlees (1969), who obtains some of the results contained in this paper by starting from different assumptions, including the rather mysterious '*R*-efficiency'.

models where fixed capital goods are explicitly distinguished from other kinds of joint products.

It is true that the common approach of dealing with the problem of fixed capital in special one-machine models and of dealing with the interaction between industries in special circulating-capital models seems to correspond to economic intuition. While joint production of the mutton–wool kind creates a multitude of difficult problems, it is indeed the peculiarity of fixed capital as a joint product that it has properties similar to those of circulating capital in so far as inter-industry relations are concerned, while some of the problems of the evaluation of machines can be discussed in models with one consumption good produced by means of one machine. But there are essential problems of the choice of technique in the presence of machines that can only be understood in a more comprehensive and more complex model.

I shall try to prove this below both intuitively and mathematically. In part I of this essay I want to contrast the somewhat paradoxical characteristics of joint-production systems with the familiar ones of circulating-capital systems. It will become clear that fixed-capital systems lie half way between the straightforward single-product systems and the intricacies of joint production proper.

Part II, the longest part, is devoted to a discussion of the more formal properties of fixed capital and in particular to the relationship between inter-industry relations and the efficiency pattern of individual machines. The analysis uses an extension of the reduction to dated quantities of labour. Switching of techniques and truncation are also discussed, and a new formalisation of 'roundabout processes' is proposed. It turns out (contrary to what might have been expected on the basis of Nuti, 1973) that the same truncation may return at different levels of the rate of profit, if the product of the machine is produced by means of a basic raw material.

Parts I and II of this essay are thus concerned with the formal properties of the model. In Part III, the most ambitious, I shall try to use the same framework for an analysis of accumulation with technical progress along Marxian and Ricardian lines. The central idea consists in distinguishing simple forms of technical progress at the microeconomic level and analysing them at the macroeconomic level by means of the classical theory of prices of production. The distinction of various forms of technical progress rests on the distinction between consumption goods, raw materials and machines. It is therefore dependent on the assumption of a fixed-capital model with several industries. The theory of prices of production will turn out to be 'correct' but more refined than really necessary: the main thrust of capitalist progress takes forms which can be analysed quite adequately in terms of the labour theory of value. To the extent that the latter is inadequate, capitalism itself is 'unreliable': it either conforms to the 'law of value' or technical progress may be no progress at all.

It must be admitted, however, that even in Part III only a few allusions concerning the forces behind capitalist accumulation, the wage struggle, and so on, are made. The modern rigour in the theory of capital and value has been achieved at the cost of making the integration of theory and of accounts of real historical processes more difficult.

PART I

2 Circulating-capital and joint-production systems

We consider the classical model of a capitalist economy in a self-replacing state. Occasionally, constant returns to scale will be assumed. There are n commodities being produced by m processes, which can be distinguished by the proportions in which they each use a positive amount of homogeneous labour and some of the produced commodities as inputs and by the proportions in which they produce commodities as outputs. Even if the output of some processes consists of several joint products, competition will ensure in most cases that, given a wide range of alternative techniques, the number of processes actually employed equals the number of commodities produced – the most obvious reason being that in general it will not otherwise be possible to produce the net output of commodities in the proportions socially required. For our present purposes it suffices to *assume* that $n = m$, so that with a given rate of profit r, calculated on the basic period of production, relative prices are determined by

$$(1+r)\mathbf{Ap} + w\mathbf{l} = \mathbf{Bp}$$

where $\mathbf{A}, \mathbf{B}$ are semi-positive square matrices whose elements a_i^j, b_i^j ($i, j = 1, 2, \ldots n$) denote the quantity of good j used (produced) in process i, where the column vectors $\mathbf{l} > \mathbf{0}$ and $\mathbf{p}$ are the labour vector and the price vector respectively, and where w is the wage rate. In order to exclude cases which would be meaningless in the context of our discussions, we shall assume throughout that no row of $\mathbf{A}$ or column of $\mathbf{B}$ vanishes and that $\det(\mathbf{B}-\mathbf{A}) \neq 0$. We measure goods in terms of total output by putting the column sum of each output equal to one (i.e. $\mathbf{eB} = \mathbf{e}$ where $\mathbf{e} = (1, 1, \ldots 1)$). We normalise $\mathbf{el} = 1$.

If $\mathbf{B}$ is the identity matrix, we are dealing with single-product industries, i.e. with circulating capital. We know, then, that if the single-product system is productive, i.e. if it is capable of producing a surplus, the following properties hold.

(i) Since we assume constant returns to scale, all products are then *separately producible*, i.e. it is possible to produce a net output consisting of a unit of any one commodity with non-negative activity levels.

(ii) It is possible to define *basic goods* as those goods which enter directly or indirectly the production of all the goods in the system. One assumes that the system contains at least one basic good. The subsystem composed of all the basic goods taken together with the processes producing them is then called the *basic system* and it is well known that this part of the system coincides with the part corresponding to the smallest indecomposable matrix $\mathbf{A}_1^1$ obtained after simultaneous permutations of rows and columns of the input matrix $\mathbf{A}$ such that

$$\mathbf{A} = \begin{bmatrix} \mathbf{A}_1^1 & \mathbf{A}_1^2 \\ \mathbf{A}_2^1 & \mathbf{A}_2^2 \end{bmatrix}$$

where $\mathbf{A}_1^1$ is quadratic and $\mathbf{A}_1^2$ equals zero. It is less often remarked but vital for the understanding of joint-production systems that the basic system coincides also with the set of *indispensable processes*, i.e. with the set of those processes which have to be activated for whatever net output there is to be produced. (In formulas: process i is not indispensable if a net output $\mathbf{s} = (s_1, \ldots s_n)$, $\mathbf{s} \geqq \mathbf{0}$, $\mathbf{s} \neq \mathbf{0}$, and non-negative activity levels $\mathbf{q} = (q_1, \ldots q_n)$ exist such that $\mathbf{q}(\mathbf{B} - \mathbf{A}) = \mathbf{s}$ and $q_i = 0$.) The main economic interest in the distinction between basics and non-basics derives, however, from a fourth property: if the price of a non-basic is changed because of a tax on it or because its method of production is changed, only the price of this and possibly some other non-basics is affected, whereas a change in the method of production of a basic affects all prices. It follows that the theory of distribution will mainly be concerned with basics in this latter sense.

(iiia) There is a unique maximum rate of profit which is numerically equal to the maximum rate of balanced growth of the basic system. Relative prices of production of basics are defined and positive for all rates of profit.

(iiib) The same can be assumed to be true for the prices of non-basics, for, if it is not the case for some non-basics, its method of production has to be changed at those rates of profit where its price is not positive. For this rather subtle point, see Bharadwaj, 1970.)

(iv) Sraffa's standard commodity exists and may be used to express prices and to reveal the known straight-line relationship between the real wage and the rate of profit.

(v) If prices are measured instead in terms of the wage rate (labour commanded $\hat{\mathbf{p}} = (1/w)\mathbf{p}$), prices will be equal to labour values at $r = 0$, rise monotonically with r, and tend to infinity at the maximum rate of profit, R.

(vi) If an alternative method of production for one of the commodities in a basic single-product system is introduced, all prices in terms of the wage rate are simultaneously raised or lowered (or stay the same, if the two methods happen to be introduced at a switchpoint). Supposing that the alternative technique (an invention, say) is superior, the real wage (whatever its standard) will be raised by the new technique at a given rate of profit, and the entrepreneurs who are the first to make the transition, while the old prices are still ruling, will make surplus profits, while those who are last and still use the old technique when the new price system has come into use will make losses (see section 9(2) below and Schefold, 1978 b, c).

None of these properties holds in all joint-production systems, but all hold in a modified form for fixed-capital systems. Take, for example, the first property: if there are two kinds of farmers breeding sheep (cf. Marshall, 1966, p. 322), the first (in Scotland) breeding sheep yielding mainly the consumption good mutton and some wool, while the second (in Australia) produce mainly the consumption good wool and some mutton, there are two equations determining relative prices of wool and mutton, and it will be possible to vary the proportions of total net output of wool and mutton in some range. But it will not be feasible to produce a net output of, say, mutton alone; hence, wool and mutton are not separately producible.

As a result, negative prices may appear as formal solutions of the price system, indicating that the methods of production are economically not compatible. However, this cannot be the case for the labour values of goods which are separately producible, for, if a good i is separately producible, the equation

$$\mathbf{q}_i(\mathbf{B} - \mathbf{A}) = \mathbf{e}_i$$

where $\mathbf{e}_i$ is the ith unit vector, has a non-negative activity vector $\mathbf{q}_i = (q_i^1, \ldots q_i^n)$ as its solution, so that u_i, the ith of the labour values $\mathbf{u} = (\mathbf{B} - \mathbf{A})^{-1}\mathbf{l}$[4] is positive:

$$u_i = \mathbf{e}_i\mathbf{u} = \mathbf{e}_i(\mathbf{B} - \mathbf{A})^{-1}\mathbf{l} = \mathbf{q}_i\mathbf{l} > 0$$

Moreover, if all values in the system are positive, the price $\hat{p}_i = p_i/w$ of commodity i in terms of the wage rate will rise monotonically with r in a

[4] That $\mathbf{u} = (\mathbf{B} - \mathbf{A})^{-1}\mathbf{l}$ represents labour values can be shown by means of Sraffa's sub-systems approach, which is implicit in the above equations. If $\mathbf{e}_i$ is the net output of the system, $\mathbf{q}_i\mathbf{l}$ is the amount of labour required to produce it directly and indirectly.

neighbourhood of $r = 0$, for by differentiating the price equations we obtain

$$\mathbf{B}\frac{d}{dr}\hat{\mathbf{p}} = \mathbf{A}\hat{\mathbf{p}} + (1+r)\mathbf{A}\frac{d}{dr}\hat{\mathbf{p}}$$

Hence,

$$\frac{d}{dr}\hat{p}_i(0) = \mathbf{e}_i\frac{d}{dr}\hat{\mathbf{p}}(0) = \mathbf{e}_i(\mathbf{B}-\mathbf{A})^{-1}\mathbf{A}\hat{\mathbf{p}}(0) = \mathbf{q}_i\mathbf{A}\mathbf{u} > 0$$

But negative labour values can quite easily occur, for they may be compatible with positive prices at the ruling rate of profit. They give rise to a curious paradox (see Sraffa, 1960, section 70): if good i is produced by a negative amount of labour ($\mathbf{q}_i\mathbf{l} < 0$), and if $\mathbf{s}$ is the net output of the economy at the normal activity levels $\mathbf{e} = (1, 1, \ldots 1)$,

$$\mathbf{e}(\mathbf{B}-\mathbf{A}) = \mathbf{s} \geq \mathbf{0}$$ [5]

the total net output can be *increased* by a small amount δ of commodity i using a *diminished* quantity of labour. For, if δ is small, $\mathbf{e}+\delta\mathbf{q}_i$ is feasible (non-negative) activity levels and

$$(\mathbf{e}+\delta\mathbf{q}_i)(\mathbf{B}-\mathbf{A}) = \mathbf{s}+\delta\mathbf{e}_i \geq \mathbf{s}$$

In the case of fixed capital this paradox is easily resolved, as will be seen later on. But, before we turn to the fixed capital model, let us isolate the fundamental reason why negative values are possible.

Theorem 1

If some labour values of a joint-production system are not positive, some processes are not indispensable.

Proof

If $u_i \leq 0$, $\mathbf{e}_i(\mathbf{B}-\mathbf{A})^{-1} = \mathbf{q}_i \ngtr 0$. If $q_i^j = 0$, the ith process is not indispensable. If all q_i^j are either > 0 or < 0, take

$\lambda = \min_j q_i^j$. Then we have

$$|\lambda|\mathbf{e}(\mathbf{B}-\mathbf{A}) + \mathbf{q}_i(\mathbf{B}-\mathbf{A}) = |\lambda|\mathbf{s}+\mathbf{e}_i \geq \mathbf{0}$$

while $|\lambda|\mathbf{e}+\mathbf{q} \geq 0$ with $|\lambda| + q_i^j = 0$ for at least one j.

Hence, if all processes are indispensable, values must be positive, as they

[5] If all elements of a matrix or vector $\mathbf{A}$ are greater than those of $\mathbf{B}$, we write $\mathbf{A} > \mathbf{B}$; if they are greater or equal, we write $\mathbf{A} \geqq \mathbf{B}$; if $\mathbf{A} \geqq \mathbf{B}$ and $\mathbf{A} \neq \mathbf{B}$, we write $\mathbf{A} \geq \mathbf{B}$.

must be if all commodities are separately producible. If both conditions are fulfilled simultaneously, we are almost back at a single-product system, for on the one hand prices behave then as in single-product systems (see Theorem 2 below), and on the other it is clear that no real joint-production system can possess both these properties. We have seen that joint production almost excludes separate producibility (not completely, though), and it is plain that, if there are several processes each of which produces the same set of goods, it will mostly be possible to produce a net output (albeit not in the required proportions) without activating all the processes.

As a consequence, the notion of the basic system is also called into question. Indeed, no two of the four properties of the basic part of a single-product system mentioned above are strictly equivalent for joint-production systems. The list of characteristics of basics in single-product systems is in fact even longer, and they all give rise to alternative definitions of 'basics' in the joint-production case. A meaningful definition can be chosen only with regard to the theory in which the concept is to be used.

In order to avoid getting lost in a discussion which is only of marginal importance for the subject of fixed capital,[6] we choose to extend the notion of decomposability which is the most appropriate for a theory of accumulation. In obvious direct generalisation of the single-product case we define: a joint-production system **A**, **B** is indecomposable if no permutation of rows and columns can be found which transform **A** and **B** simultaneously into almost triangular matrices:

$$\begin{bmatrix} \mathbf{A}_1^1 & \mathbf{0} \\ \mathbf{A}_2^1 & \mathbf{A}_2^2 \end{bmatrix} \qquad \begin{bmatrix} \mathbf{B}_1^1 & \mathbf{0} \\ \mathbf{B}_2^1 & \mathbf{B}_2^2 \end{bmatrix}$$

where $\mathbf{A}_1^1$, $\mathbf{B}_1^1$ are quadratic matrices of the same order. Completely decomposable systems with $\mathbf{A}_2^1 = \mathbf{B}_2^1 = \mathbf{0}$ will be excluded by assumption.

Clearly, any method of production in the decomposable part $(\mathbf{A}_2^2, \mathbf{B}_2^2)$ can be changed without affecting the indecomposable part $(\mathbf{A}_1^1, \mathbf{B}_1^1)$, but one cannot say that the commodities produced in the former do not enter indirectly the production of the commodities produced in the latter if the relevant elements of $\mathbf{A}_2^1$ and $\mathbf{B}_2^1$ are positive.

We now prove the following theorem.

Theorem 2

If all products of a joint production system are separately producible and if all processes are indispensable, the system is indecomposable and possesses the above-listed qualities (iii), (iv), and (v) of a basic single-product system.

[6] A more detailed exposition is in preparation. For its mathematical basis see Schefold (1971).

Proof

Since all products are separately producible, $\mathbf{e}_i\ (\mathbf{B}-\mathbf{A})^{-1} \geq \mathbf{0}$ for all i, and, since all processes are indispensable, $\mathbf{e}_i(\mathbf{B}-\mathbf{A})^{-1} > \mathbf{0}$ for all i, hence $(\mathbf{B}-\mathbf{A})^{-1} > \mathbf{0}$, $\mathbf{q}_i = \mathbf{e}_i(\mathbf{B}-\mathbf{A})^{-1} > \mathbf{0}$, $i = 1, 2, \ldots n$. If any of the columns of $\mathbf{A}$ were to vanish, say $\mathbf{a}^n = \mathbf{0}$, we should have $\mathbf{q}_i(\mathbf{b}^n - \mathbf{a}^n) = 0$ for $i < n$, which contradicts $\mathbf{q}_i(\mathbf{b}^n - \mathbf{a}^n) = \mathbf{q}_i\mathbf{b}^n > 0$, because $\mathbf{q}_i > \mathbf{0}$, $\mathbf{b}^n \geq \mathbf{0}$. Thus $\mathbf{a}^i \geq \mathbf{0}$ for all i and $(\mathbf{B}-\mathbf{A})^{-1}\mathbf{A} > \mathbf{0}$.

Now, if $\mathbf{A}$, $\mathbf{B}$ were a decomposable system, $(\mathbf{B}-\mathbf{A})^{-1}\mathbf{A}$ would be a decomposable matrix, for (ignoring trivial permutations) $\mathbf{A}$, $\mathbf{B}$, $\mathbf{B}-\mathbf{A}$; hence, $(\mathbf{B}-\mathbf{A})^{-1}$ and $(\mathbf{B}-\mathbf{A})^{-1}\mathbf{A}$ would all be almost triangular matrices of the same order. This contradicts $(\mathbf{B}-\mathbf{A})^{-1}\mathbf{A} > \mathbf{0}$; therefore $\mathbf{A}$, $\mathbf{B}$ is an indecomposable system.

By virtue of the Perron–Frobenius theorem there is a unique $R > 0$ and a column vector $\mathbf{p} > \mathbf{0}$ so that $R(\mathbf{B}-\mathbf{A})^{-1}\mathbf{A}\mathbf{p} = \mathbf{p}$, hence $(1+R)\mathbf{A}\mathbf{p} = \mathbf{B}\mathbf{p}$, and there is a unique row vector $\mathbf{q}$ with $(1+R)\mathbf{q}\mathbf{A} = \mathbf{q}\mathbf{B}$. $\mathbf{q}$ must also be positive, by virtue of the Frobenius theorem, for $R\mathbf{q}\mathbf{A}(\mathbf{B}-\mathbf{A})^{-1} = \mathbf{q}$, and $\mathbf{A}(\mathbf{B}-\mathbf{A})^{-1} > \mathbf{0}$, since we have assumed that the rows $\mathbf{a}_i$ of $\mathbf{A}$ are semi-positive. $\mathbf{q}$ provides the standard commodity.

Now consider prices $\hat{\mathbf{p}} = (1/w)\mathbf{p}$ in terms of the wage rate. That they have the required properties is obvious from the transformation ($\mathbf{I}$ is the unit matrix)

$$\begin{aligned}\hat{\mathbf{p}} &= [\mathbf{B}-(1+r)\mathbf{A}]^{-1}\mathbf{l} = [(\mathbf{B}-\mathbf{A})(\mathbf{I}-r(\mathbf{B}-\mathbf{A})^{-1}\mathbf{A}]^{-1}\mathbf{l}\\ &= [\mathbf{I}-r(\mathbf{B}-\mathbf{A})^{-1}\mathbf{A}]^{-1}(\mathbf{B}-\mathbf{A})^{-1}\mathbf{l}.\end{aligned}$$

PART II

3 Machines

The comparative ease with which fixed-capital systems as we shall define them are handled is owing to the fact that new machines are separately producible within them and that the prices of old machines appear as derived from those of the new ones once their prices are known. If the system is indecomposable, this will be reflected in the fact that only processes using old machines will not be indispensable.

In order to define what we mean by a pure fixed-capital system, we distinguish between *finished goods* (circulating capital and new machines) and *intermediate goods* (old machines of various ages). In order to isolate our problem from that of joint production in general, we assume that each process produces one and only one finished good (no superimposed joint production). The processes engaged in the production of a finished good taken together will be said to form a group. We assume not only that no transfer of intermediate goods between groups takes place, but also that within each group only one machine at various ages is used. (The latter assumption is fairly easily relaxed, the former only under additional restrictions – see below.) There is always one *primary* process which uses exclusively finished goods as inputs, among them the new machine. After the end of the year the new machine leaves the process as a one-year-old machine together with the output of the finished good and enters the first *intermediate* process, by which it is used and also reproduced as a two-year-old machine. The latter enters a second intermediate process, and so on, until the machine is worn out.

Our preliminary assumptions of admitting only one aging machine in each group allows that the same kind of new machine may enter different groups. But, as a consequence, each new machine will gradually turn into a different set of intermediate goods. Each machine is characterised by the group in which it is used, since no trade of old machines between groups takes place. The point is that the efficiency of the machines will vary to different degrees with age in that the amounts of finished good produced, of raw material, spare parts, and so on, used up, and of labour employed, will vary with the age of the machine. Efficiency may rise because of 'learning by doing' or, more importantly, because the period of construction of the machine is longer than that of circulating capitals (for instance, the machine could be a ship which takes two years to be built). The efficiency may be falling – for example, because an increasing number of spare parts has to be used to keep the output of the finished good constant. Constant efficiency is not ruled out either, but is of lesser interest in so far as it excludes a meaningful treatment of the most characteristic problem of fixed capital, i.e. the problem of determining the economic lifetime of a machine as distinct from its 'maximum' physical lifetime. If the efficiency of a machine consisting of many parts is constant, there is no reason why it should not last forever, if it is properly maintained, i.e. if those parts which are of fairly constant efficiency but finite duration (valves, light bulbs, and so forth) are periodically replaced. We shall not discuss everlasting machines explicitly, however, although they can be included in the framework of our analysis without great difficulty. We are mainly interested in machines the efficiency of which varies because, for economic or technical reasons or both, not all their parts are capable of periodic replacement.[7]

[7] Each of usually thousands of parts of a machine (springs, axles, boilers, and so on) has under normal operation a lifetime determined by a certain probability distribution, which may be known. Engineers try to specify expensive and vital parts which can be made to last longer at greater expense in such a way that most of them begin to fail at roughly the same time; the machine as a whole has then to be replaced. This is the physical lifetime of the machine; its choice is a matter of the choice of techniques. Given a physical lifetime, it may turn out to be

We now turn to the formal definition: there is a total number of n commodities in the system, of which, say, the first f are finished, the rest intermediate, goods. If the machine involved in the production of finished good i has a maximum physical lifetime of T_i years, the group of processes producing good i may be written as follows:

$$(1+r)\left[\mathbf{a}_i(t)\mathbf{p}_1+\mathbf{m}_i(t-1)\mathbf{p}_2\right]+wl_i(t)=\mathbf{b}_i(t)\mathbf{p}_1+\mathbf{m}_i(t)\mathbf{p}_2, \qquad t=1,\ 2,\dots T_i$$

where $\mathbf{p}_1$ is the f vector of relative prices of finished goods, $\mathbf{p}_2$ the $(n-f)$ vector of prices of intermediate goods. $l_i(t)$ is the input of labour, $\mathbf{a}_i(t)$, $\mathbf{b}_i(t)$ are f vectors for inputs and outputs of finished goods, $\mathbf{m}_i(t-1)$ and $\mathbf{m}_i(t)$ are $(n-f)$ vectors for input and output of intermediate goods, all to the tth of T_i processes for the production of good i.

Only the ith element of $\mathbf{b}_i(t)$ is not necessarily zero. Since the total output of each commodity equals one, we have

$$\sum_{t=1}^{T_i} b_i^{\,i}(t)=1, \qquad i=1,2,\dots f$$

Our main assumption is that the system is productive, i.e.

$$\sum_{i,t} a_i^{\,j}(t)\le 1, \qquad j=1,2,\dots f$$

The first process uses finished goods exclusively, i.e. $\mathbf{m}_i(0)=\mathbf{0}$, $i=1, 2,\dots f$, and all primary processes use some finished goods as inputs, hence $\mathbf{a}_i(1)\geq\mathbf{0}$; $i=1,2,\dots f$. Since the machine is used up after the last process, $\mathbf{m}_i(T_i)=\mathbf{0}$. If no machine is involved in the production of good i, so that the process uses circulating capital only, then, put formally, $T_i=1$, $\mathbf{m}_i(0)=\mathbf{m}_i(1)=\mathbf{0}$. Finally, since each machine is both a different good at a different age and characterised by the process in which it is used (no trade between groups), the $(T_1-1)+\dots+(T_f-1)=n-f$ vectors $\mathbf{m}_i(t)$, $i=1, 2,\dots f$; $t=1,2,\dots T_i-1$, are all different unit vectors. All equations taken together can be written in matrix form as

$$(1+r)\mathbf{Ap}+w\mathbf{l}=\mathbf{Bp}$$

economically advantageous to 'truncate' the machine before the technical necessity to replace it arises. This is the problem of truncation, of which more later on. The technical lifetime of a machine is in reality seldom well defined and not independent of economic considerations, but we assume it to be given. Before its end approaches the number of spare parts needed increases in characteristic fashion, and the efficiency of the machine deteriorates, inviting truncation. The lower the wage of the repair man, the longer it pays to keep the car, but matters are not always that simple, at least in theory [see section 9 (1)]. The efficiency of the newly born machine is not constant either (for instance, again in the case of a car, because the mesh of the gear is not optimal before the car has been run in). The variation of efficiency is reminiscent of the laws of returns on land, but the neoclassical conclusions cannot be drawn, because 'efficiency' depends on prices.

where

$$\mathbf{A} = \begin{bmatrix} \mathbf{a}_1(1), \mathbf{m}_1(0) \\ \mathbf{a}_1(2), \mathbf{m}_1(1) \\ \cdot \\ \cdot \\ \cdot \\ \mathbf{a}_f(T_f), \mathbf{m}_f(T_f - 1) \end{bmatrix}, \qquad \mathbf{B} = \begin{bmatrix} \mathbf{b}_1(1), \mathbf{m}_1(1) \\ \mathbf{b}_1(2), \mathbf{m}_1(2) \\ \cdot \\ \cdot \\ \cdot \\ \mathbf{b}_f(T_f), \mathbf{m}_f(T_f) \end{bmatrix}$$

$$\mathbf{l} = \begin{bmatrix} l_1(1) \\ l_1(2) \\ \cdot \\ \cdot \\ \cdot \\ l_f(T_f) \end{bmatrix}, \qquad \mathbf{p} = \begin{bmatrix} \mathbf{p}_1 \\ \mathbf{p}_2 \end{bmatrix}$$

By a familiar procedure (see Sraffa, 1960, section 76) the intermediate goods can be eliminated from the system: one combines the equations of each group i by multiplying the tth equation by a factor $(1+r)^{T_i - t}$ and summing over t for each group i to get the reduced system

$$(1+r)\tilde{\mathbf{A}}(r)\mathbf{p}_1 + w\tilde{\mathbf{l}}(r) = \tilde{\mathbf{B}}(r)\mathbf{p}_1$$

where

$$\tilde{\mathbf{A}}(r) = \begin{bmatrix} \tilde{\mathbf{a}}_1(r) \\ \cdot \\ \cdot \\ \cdot \\ \tilde{\mathbf{a}}_f(r) \end{bmatrix}, \qquad \tilde{\mathbf{B}}(r) = \begin{bmatrix} \tilde{\mathbf{b}}_1(r) \\ \cdot \\ \cdot \\ \cdot \\ \tilde{\mathbf{b}}_f(r) \end{bmatrix}, \qquad \tilde{\mathbf{l}}(r) = \begin{bmatrix} \tilde{l}_1(r) \\ \cdot \\ \cdot \\ \cdot \\ \tilde{l}_f(r) \end{bmatrix}$$

$$\tilde{\mathbf{a}}_i(r) = \sum_{t=1}^{T_i} (1+r)^{T_i - t}\, \mathbf{a}_i(t)$$

$$\tilde{\mathbf{b}}_i(r) = \sum_{t=1}^{T_i} (1+r)^{T_i - t}\, \mathbf{b}_i(t)$$

$$\tilde{\mathbf{l}}_i(r) = \sum_{t=1}^{T_i} (1+r)^{T_i - t}\, l_i(t)$$

This system will be called the *integrated system*, because of the following intuitive interpretation: instead of thinking of the T_i processes of group i as of T_i separate activities running side by side at the same time, imagine an entrepreneur producing finished good i in T_i successive years. At the beginning of the first period he will have to buy a bundle $\mathbf{a}_i(1)$ of finished goods (including his new machine); at the end of the period he obtains $\mathbf{b}_i(1)$ as an output to be sold. He will have to buy $\mathbf{a}_i(2)$ to start production with the one-year-old machine and produce during the second period – and so on till his machine is worn out, at the end of the T_ith period. Hence, T_i is the total turnover period of group i. Considering it as a whole, the entrepreneur may strike the balance by multiplying each input and output by that power of $(1+r)$ which indicates the number of full periods that have passed by since it has been bought or sold. The resulting equation is the *integrated process*. As one should expect, it is identical with the equation for group i in the integrated system which we obtained above by mathematical elimination of the intermediate goods.

Before we consider its mathematical properties, let us discuss the integrated system in greater detail from an economic point of view.

If activity levels were such that at some time all integrated processes with turnover periods $T_1, \ldots T_f$ could start simultaneously, they would all simultaneously end again after a time equal to the smallest common multiple of $T_1, \ldots T_f$, which we denote by T. Obviously, if the rate of profit were calculated on the basis of T periods, we should then be back at a single-product system, since no net output of intermediate goods would appear explicitly in the equations. Since the way in which the rate of profit is calculated does not affect the technical characteristics of the system, it is therefore intuitively plausible that finished goods are separately producible and have positive values which are equal to those obtained in the original system. When the rate of profit is zero, it does not matter at which time the products appear. But, if the rate of profit is positive, the subdivision of the 'long period' T into the unit period of production matters. To disregard the dating of inputs and outputs within the 'long period' T would mean adding up all inputs used during the 'long period' and treating them as if they had to be available at its beginning, and, similarly, adding all outputs and treating them as if they were to be available only at its end.

By so doing one would obtain a system equal to the integrated system at $r = 0$. The construction of the integrated system at $r = 0$ amounts simply to adding up the equations for each group so that intermediate goods cancel out. The integrated system at $r = 0$ provides, therefore, an approximation for prices at low rates of profit. Since $\tilde{\mathbf{B}}(0) = \mathbf{I}$, the prices determined by

$$(1+r)\mathbf{F}\mathbf{p}_1 + w\mathbf{h} = \mathbf{p}_1$$

where $\mathbf{F} = \tilde{\mathbf{A}}(0)$, $\mathbf{h} = \tilde{\mathbf{l}}(0)$, approximate for small rates of profit the correct prices given by

$$(1+r)\tilde{\mathbf{A}}(r)\mathbf{p}_1 + w\tilde{\mathbf{l}}(r) = \tilde{\mathbf{B}}(r)\mathbf{p}_1$$

The quality of the approximation depends on the evenness of the distribution of inputs and outputs during the 'long period', i.e. on the efficiency pattern of inputs and outputs to integrated processes. Looking at it this way, one should make the following guesses. Prices of finished goods are positive at least at low rates of profit. If all inputs and outputs are evenly distributed over the 'long period', i.e. if all machines are of 'constant physical efficiency', the system should essentially behave like a single-product system: prices in terms of the wage rate are positive and monotonically rising up to some maximum rate of profit. But, if the distribution of inputs is uneven, i.e. if the machines are of variable efficiency, the situation may get more complicated. For example, if most of the output of an integrated process is produced at its beginning, this may be of no effect at low rates of profit, while high rates of profit may cause the value of the product to fall, even relative to wages.

4 Integrated systems and finished goods

This section is in the main only a mathematical proof of the statements just made.

Theorem 3

(i) $\tilde{\mathbf{B}}(0)$ is equal to the identity matrix.

(ii) $\det[\tilde{\mathbf{B}}(0) - \tilde{\mathbf{A}}(0)] \neq 0, \quad \sum_{i=1}^{f} [\tilde{\mathbf{b}}_i(0) - \tilde{\mathbf{a}}_i(0)] \geq \mathbf{0}.$

(iii) If $\mathbf{A}$, $\mathbf{B}$ form an indecomposable system, $\tilde{\mathbf{A}}(r)$ is an indecomposable matrix for $r \geq 0$.

(iv) If all primary processes are indispensable, $\mathbf{A}$, $\mathbf{B}$ form an indecomposable system.

(v) $[\tilde{\mathbf{B}}(0) - \tilde{\mathbf{A}}(0)]^{-1} > \mathbf{0}$, if $\mathbf{A}$, $\mathbf{B}$ form an indecomposable system.

Proof

(i) and (ii) are trivial consequences of the corresponding assumptions about $\mathbf{A}$ and $\mathbf{B}$, and (v) follows from (i), (ii) and (iii). To prove (iii), suppose $\tilde{\mathbf{A}}$ was decomposable, having s rows of zeros in columns $s+1, s+2, \ldots f$ above the diagonal. $\mathbf{A}$ and $\mathbf{B}$ would then each have zeros in $T_1 + \ldots + T_s$ rows in $f-s$ columns $s+1, \ldots f$, i.e. there would be no inputs of finished goods $s+1, \ldots f$ to any of the first s groups. On the same rows only $(T_1 - 1) + \ldots + (T_s - 1) = T_1 + \ldots + T_s - s$ intermediate goods would be used or produced, hence $n-f-(T_1+\ldots+T_s)+s$ columns of intermediate goods would have zeros in these rows, or, taken together, there would be $n-f-(T_1+\ldots+T_s)+s+f-s=n-(T_1+\ldots+T_s)$ columns with zeros in the $T_1+\ldots+T_s$ rows, which proves that **A**, **B** would form a decomposable system.

To prove (iv): if the system were decomposable, there would be a subsystem of s – say, processes and goods – such that

$$\mathbf{A}=\begin{bmatrix}\mathbf{A}_1^1 & \mathbf{0}\\ \mathbf{A}_2^1 & \mathbf{A}_2^2\end{bmatrix},\qquad \mathbf{B}=\begin{bmatrix}\mathbf{B}_1^1 & \mathbf{0}\\ \mathbf{B}_2^1 & \mathbf{B}_2^2\end{bmatrix}$$

where $\mathbf{A}_1^1$, $\mathbf{B}_1^1$ are quadratic matrices of the same order. Suppose the output of the ith finished good in the tth process appeared (after the permutations) in $\mathbf{B}_1^1$. The ith machine at age $t-1$ would then have to appear in $\mathbf{A}_1^1$, the ith machine at age t in $\mathbf{B}_1^1$. In like way, the positive outputs and inputs of the entire ith group would be found in $\mathbf{A}_1^1$, $\mathbf{B}_1^1$; hence, if the ith process of group i appears in either $(\mathbf{A}_1^1, \mathbf{B}_1^1)$ or $(\mathbf{A}_2, \mathbf{B}_2)$, the entire group appears in either $(\mathbf{A}_1^1, \mathbf{B}_1^1)$ or $(\mathbf{A}_2, \mathbf{B}_2)$. Therefore there are neither finished nor intermediate products produced in $\mathbf{B}_2^1$, $\mathbf{B}_2^1=\mathbf{0}$, and it follows that $\mathbf{e}(\mathbf{B}_1^1-\mathbf{A}_1^1)\geq\mathbf{0}$, where $\mathbf{e}=(1,1\ldots1)$, in contradiction to the assumption.

To shorten the exposition, we shall assume from now on that **A**, **B** form an indecomposable system, hence that $\tilde{\mathbf{A}}(0)$ is an indecomposable matrix.

The following lemma is crucial, but may be omitted, with its proof, by the non-mathematical reader (cf. Schefold, 1971, section 13).

Lemma 1

There is a root $R>0$ of the equation $\det[\tilde{\mathbf{B}}(r)-(1+r)\tilde{\mathbf{A}}(r)]=0$ such that

(i) $\det[\tilde{\mathbf{B}}(r)-(1+r)\mathbf{A}(r)]\neq 0,\quad 0\leq r<R;$

(ii) $[\tilde{\mathbf{B}}(r)-(1+r)\tilde{\mathbf{A}}(r)]^{-1}>\mathbf{0},\quad 0\leq r<R;$

(iii) the 'eigenvector' $\tilde{\mathbf{q}}$ with

$$\tilde{\mathbf{q}}[\tilde{\mathbf{B}}(R)-(1+R)\tilde{\mathbf{A}}(R)]=\mathbf{0}$$

is positive and unique.

Proof

(i) $\tilde{\mathbf{B}}(r)$ is a diagonal matrix with positive elements for all non-negative r. The matrix $\hat{\mathbf{A}}(r)=[\tilde{\mathbf{B}}(r)]^{-1}\tilde{\mathbf{A}}(r)$ is a semi-positive indecomposable matrix for any given r. There is therefore for each given $r>0$ a unique $\lambda(r)>0$ and $\mathbf{x}(r)>\mathbf{0}$, with

$$\lambda(r)\mathbf{x}(r)=(1+r)\hat{\mathbf{A}}(r)\mathbf{x}(r)$$

and $\sum_{i=1}^{f} x_i(r) = 1$. By virtue of the Theorem 3,

$$\lambda(0) = \lambda(0) \sum_{i=1}^{f} x_i(0) = \sum_{i=1}^{f} \sum_{j=1}^{f} \hat{a}_i^j(0)\, x_j(0)$$
$$= \sum_{j=1}^{f} \sum_{i=1}^{f} \hat{a}_i^j(0) x_j(0) < \sum_{j=1}^{f} x_j(0) = 1$$

On the other hand, $\lambda(r)$ tends to infinity for $r \to \infty$. To prove this, consider

$$\lambda(r) = \lambda(r) \sum_{i=1}^{f} x_i(r) = \sum_{i=1}^{f} (1+r) \sum_{j=1}^{f} \hat{a}_i^j(r) x_j(r)$$

$$= (1+r) \sum_{j=1}^{f} \sum_{i=1}^{f} \frac{\sum_{t=1}^{T_i} (1+r)^{T_i - t} a_i^j(t)}{\sum_{t=1}^{T_i} (1+r)^{T_i - t} b_i^i(t)} x_j(r)$$

Clearly, the sum should diverge as required if $\sum_{i=1}^{f} a_i^j(1)$ were positive for all j. Unfortunately, all $a_i^j(1)$ may be zero for all i, given j, if commodity j has the character of a 'spare part', i.e. if j is a finished good that is used as an input only in conjunction with old machines. But we have assumed that $\mathbf{a}_i(1) \neq \mathbf{0}$ for all i. After suitable rearrangement the first s rows and columns of the (f,f) matrix $[a_i^j(1)]$ will form an indecomposable matrix. We change the normalisation of $\mathbf{x}(r)$ to $\sum_{i=1}^{s} x_i(r) = 1$ and get

$$\lambda(r) = \lambda(r) \sum_{i=1}^{s} x_i(r) = (1+r) \sum_{i=1}^{s} \sum_{j=1}^{f} \hat{a}_i^j(r) x_j(r)$$
$$\geq (1+r) \sum_{j=1}^{s} \sum_{i=1}^{s} \hat{a}_i^j(r) x_j(r)$$

Since each column of the matrix $[a_i^j(1)]$, $i,j = 1, 2, \ldots s$, has at least one positive element, there is for each j at least one i such that $(1+r)\hat{a}_i^j(r)$ is a rational function which tends to infinity as r rises. Hence one can conclude that $\lim_{r \to \infty} \lambda(r) = \infty$, while $\lambda(0) < 1$.

Since all elements of $\hat{\mathbf{A}}(r)$ are continuous functions of r and since the dominant root of an indecomposable semi-positive matrix is a continuous function of the elements of the matrix, there is a definite smallest positive R such that $\lambda(R) = 1$.

It follows that $\det[\hat{\mathbf{B}}(r) - (1+r)\hat{\mathbf{A}}(r)] \neq 0$ for $0 \leq r < R$.

(ii) R is the smallest value for which the dominant root of the indecomposable semipositive matrix $(1+r)\hat{\mathbf{A}}(r)$ equals one. Hence dom $[(1+r)\hat{\mathbf{A}}(r)] < 1$, $[\mathbf{I}-(1+r)\hat{\mathbf{A}}(r)]^{-1} > \mathbf{0}$, and $[\check{\mathbf{B}}(r)-(1+r)\check{\mathbf{A}}(r)]^{-1} = [\mathbf{I}-(1+r)\hat{\mathbf{A}}(r)]^{-1}[\check{\mathbf{B}}(r)]^{-1} > \mathbf{0}$, $0 \leq r < R$.

(iii) $1/(1+R)$ is the dominant root of the matrix $\hat{\mathbf{A}}(R)$. R is therefore a simple root of the equation det $[\mathbf{I}-(1+r)\hat{\mathbf{A}}(R)] = 0$ and also of the equation det$[\check{\mathbf{B}}(R)-(1+r)\check{\mathbf{A}}(R)] = 0$. Consequently, the row vector $\tilde{\mathbf{q}}$ solving

$$\tilde{\mathbf{q}}[\check{\mathbf{B}}(R)-(1+R)\check{\mathbf{A}}(R)] = \mathbf{0}$$

is unique. By arguments similar to those already used, $\check{\mathbf{A}}(R)[\check{\mathbf{B}}(R) - \check{\mathbf{A}}(R)]^{-1}$ exists and is positive. Hence $\tilde{\mathbf{q}} > \mathbf{0}$.

Spare parts are defined as finished goods which are used as inputs to secondary processes only. The proof of Lemma 1 indicates that they play a special role, the reason being that their production may not be necessary if the system as a whole remains productive when secondary processes using them are discontinued or 'truncated'.

We are now in a position to prove a first set of important results for fixed-capital systems (which have been assumed to be productive and indecomposable).

Theorem 4

(i) Finished goods are separately producible.
(ii) All primary processes (except possibly those producing spare parts) are indispensable.
(iii) Relative prices of finished goods are positive for all r, $0 \leq r \leq R$, where R is the 'maximum rate of profit'. R is positive.
(iv) There is a unique row vector $\mathbf{q} > \mathbf{0}$ such that

$$\mathbf{q}(\mathbf{B}-(1+R)\mathbf{A}) = \mathbf{0}$$

i.e. the fixed capital system has a positive 'standard commodity'. $\mathbf{q}(\mathbf{B}-\mathbf{A})$, the 'standard net product', is positive.

Proof

(i) Define the row vectors $\tilde{\mathbf{q}}_i = \mathbf{e}_i(\check{\mathbf{B}}(0)-\check{\mathbf{A}}(0))^{-1}$ and

$$\mathbf{q}_i = (\underbrace{\tilde{q}_i^{\,1}, \ldots \tilde{q}_i^{\,1}}_{T_1}, \underbrace{\tilde{q}_i^{\,2}, \ldots \tilde{q}_i^{\,2}}_{T_2}, \ldots \underbrace{\tilde{q}_i^{\,f}, \ldots \tilde{q}_i^{\,f}}_{T_f}), \qquad i = 1, 2, \ldots f$$

Clearly, $\mathbf{q}_i > \mathbf{0}$, where $\mathbf{q}_i$ is the vector of activity levels appropriate for the production of one unit of the ith finished good.

(ii) The tth of the T_i processes in group i cannot be activated without activating processes $1, 2, \ldots t-1$, too, if the net output of intermediate goods is not to contain negative elements. Therefore, if a positive output can be obtained while k primary processes are not activated, the corresponding k groups are not activated and the finished goods to be produced by them are not produced at all. But $\tilde{\mathbf{A}}(0)$ is indecomposable. Hence, every finished good is an input to some processes; and a primary process, if not activated, belongs to a group producing a spare part.

(iii) Follows from Lemma 1 and $\tilde{\mathbf{l}}(r) > \mathbf{0}$, $0 \leq r < R$; $r = R$ is obvious.

(iv) There is a unique $\tilde{\mathbf{q}} = (\tilde{q}^1, \ldots \tilde{q}^f) > \mathbf{0}$, with $\tilde{\mathbf{q}}[\tilde{\mathbf{B}}(R) - (1+R)\tilde{\mathbf{A}}(R)] = \mathbf{0}$. It is easily checked that $\mathbf{q}[\mathbf{B} - (1+R)\mathbf{A}] = \mathbf{0}$, where

$$\mathbf{q} = [\tilde{q}^1(1+R)^{T_1-1}, \tilde{q}^1(1+R)^{T_1-2}, \ldots \tilde{q}^1, \tilde{q}^2(1+R)^{T_2-1}, \ldots \tilde{q}^f]$$

To prove that $\mathbf{q}$ is unique, note that the rank of the matrix $\mathbf{B} - (1+R)\mathbf{A}$ is equal to that of the triangular matrix

$$\mathbf{F} = \underbrace{\left[\begin{array}{l|r}
\tilde{\mathbf{B}}(R) - (1+R)\tilde{\mathbf{A}}(R) & \mathbf{0} \\
\hline
\mathbf{b}_1(2) - (1+R)\mathbf{a}_1(2) & \mathbf{m}_1(2) - (1+R)\mathbf{m}_1(1) \\
\ldots & \ldots \\
\mathbf{b}_1(T_1) - (1+R)\mathbf{a}_1(T_1) & -(1+R)\mathbf{m}_1(T_1-1) \\
\ldots & \ldots \\
\mathbf{b}_f(2) - (1+R)\mathbf{a}_f(2) & \mathbf{m}_f(2) - (1+R)\mathbf{m}_f(1) \\
\ldots & \ldots \\
\mathbf{b}_f(T_f) - (1+R)\mathbf{a}_f(T_f) & -(1+R)\mathbf{m}_f(T_f-1)
\end{array}\right]}_{f \qquad\qquad\qquad n-f}
\begin{array}{l} \}\, f \\ \\ \\ \}\, n-f \\ \\ \\ \\ \end{array}$$

$$= \begin{bmatrix} \mathbf{F}_1{}^1 & \mathbf{0} \\ \mathbf{F}_2{}^1 & \mathbf{F}_2{}^2 \end{bmatrix}$$

The matrix $\mathbf{F}_1{}^1 = \tilde{\mathbf{B}}(R) - (1+R)\tilde{\mathbf{A}}(R)$ has rank $f-1$, since $\tilde{\mathbf{q}}$ in Lemma 1 was unique. It is easy to see that the rank of the matrix $\mathbf{F}_2^2$ is $n-f$, and hence that the rank of $\mathbf{F}$ is $n-1$.

It is quite puzzling that it has been possible to say so much about the fixed-capital system without taking prices of intermediate goods explicitly into account. Already at this point we can show that the 'rate of surplus value' in value terms is positive and uniform if the wage is a historically given subsistence wage. For it is then consistent to regard the labour force as homogeneous in its consumption pattern. Since the wage rate is uniform, the workers in every industry will buy a fraction of the total wage $\mathbf{d} = (d^1, d^2, \ldots d^n)$ proportional to their number or (what amounts to the same thing) proportional to the labour time necessary in that industry so that the matrix $\mathbf{D} = \mathbf{ld}$ represents the real wage consumed by the workers in each industry. (It depends on the existence of a uniform wage rate, but not of a uniform rate of profit! In this sense the rate of surplus value is 'prior' to the rate of profit.) $\mathbf{l}_w = \mathbf{Du}$, $\mathbf{u} = (\mathbf{B} - \mathbf{A})^{-1}\mathbf{l}$ is, then, the labour time the workers spend in each industry to earn their living. We assume that the wage consists of finished goods only. Since the labour values of finished goods are positive, and since clearly $\mathbf{d} \leq \mathbf{e}(\mathbf{B} - \mathbf{A})$, it follows from

$$\mathbf{l}_w = (\mathbf{ld})\mathbf{u} = \mathbf{l}(\mathbf{du}) = \alpha\mathbf{l}$$

$$\alpha = \mathbf{du} < \mathbf{e}(\mathbf{B} - \mathbf{A})(\mathbf{B} - \mathbf{A})^{-1}\mathbf{l} = \mathbf{el} = 1$$

that the labour time the workers have to work for themselves (the 'necessary labour time') is a positive fraction of the time they spend working for the capitalists. That is to say, Marx's 'rate of surplus value' $\varepsilon = (1 - \alpha)/\alpha$ is uniform and positive (irrespective of whether the rates of profit are uniform in different industries).

Conversely, if the rate of surplus value is positive, and if the rate of profit is known to exist and to be uniform, it must be positive too (cf. Morishima, 1973).

Sraffa's straight-line relationship between wages expressed in terms of the standard commodity $\mathbf{q}(\mathbf{B} - \mathbf{A})$ and a uniform rate of profit r can also be derived without prior knowledge about the behaviour of prices of intermediate goods. If prices are expressed in terms of the standard commodity, i.e. if $\mathbf{q}(\mathbf{B} - \mathbf{A})\mathbf{p} = 1$, $0 \leq r \leq R$, with $\mathbf{q}$ normalised so that $\mathbf{ql} = 1$, we have

$$1 = \mathbf{q}(\mathbf{B} - \mathbf{A})\mathbf{p} = r\mathbf{qAp} + w\mathbf{ql} = r\left[\frac{1}{R}\mathbf{q}(\mathbf{B} - \mathbf{A})\right]\mathbf{p} + w = \frac{r}{R} + w$$

Therefore, if the rate of profit is given, the 'value' of the wage in terms of the standard commodity equals $w = 1 - r/R$, whatever the goods of which the real wage consists.

The generality of these two results is not as great as may seem at first sight, however. Whether there is an unambiguous trade-off between profits and real wages depends on whether prices of wage goods rise monotonically in terms of the wage rate as the rate of profit rises. Conditions which will ensure that this fundamental relationship of the theory of distribution holds will be derived presently. They are based on an analysis of prices of intermediate goods.

5 Prices of intermediate goods (old machines)

To calculate relative prices of intermediate goods is easy, because the integrated system determines relative prices of finished goods. The T_i processes of group i,

$$(1+r)[\mathbf{a}_i(t)\mathbf{p}_1(r)+\mathbf{m}_i(t-1)\mathbf{p}_2(r)]+wl_i(t)$$
$$=\mathbf{b}_i(t)\mathbf{p}_1(r)+\mathbf{m}_i(t)\mathbf{p}_2(r), \qquad t=1,2,\ldots T_i$$

can be transformed into the recursive relation

$$p_{i,t-1}(r)=\frac{1}{1+r}[Y_{i,t}(r)+p_{i,t}(r)], \qquad t=1,2,\ldots T_i-1$$

$$p_{i,T_i-1}(r)=\frac{1}{1+r}Y_{i,T_i}(r)$$

where the following abbreviations have been used:

$$Y_{i,t}(r)=[\mathbf{b}_i(t)-(1+r)\mathbf{a}_i(t)]\mathbf{p}_1(r)-wl_i(t), \qquad t=2,\ldots T_i$$

$$p_{i,t}(r)=\mathbf{m}_i(t)\mathbf{p}_2(r), \qquad t=1,2,\ldots T_i-1$$

and where a special notation has to be introduced for $t=1$: $\mathbf{a}_i(1)$ denotes the inputs of finished goods to the first process of group i, including the new machine. Let $\dot{\mathbf{a}}_i(1)$ denote the same inputs without the new machine; define

$$Y_{i,1}(r)=[\mathbf{b}_i(1)-(1+r)\dot{\mathbf{a}}_i(1)]\mathbf{p}_1-wl_i(1)$$

and write $p_{i,0}$ for the price of the new machine (we assume in this chapter for the sake of simplicity that we can always point to one finished good entering the primary process as being the machine). $p_{i,t}(r)$ is the price of the machine employed by group i in process (or at age) t at rate of profit r. $Y_{i,t}(r)$ equals output produced by the machine employed by group t minus the value of the machine which leaves the process and minus 'costs' of wages, profits and circulating capital. It represents the *net return* generated by the machine at age $t-1$ and at rate of profit r. The recursive relation means therefore that the price of the $t-1$ years old machine is equal to that of its discounted output in the current year, including the price of the remaining t years old machine. Or, as one could also put it, $Y_{i,t}(r)$ equals the difference between the price (including profits) of the machine entering the process and that of the machine leaving it.

From the recursive formulas one obtains by induction the discounting formula

$$p_{i,t}(r)=\sum_{\tau=1}^{T_i-t}\frac{Y_{i,t+\tau}(r)}{(1+r)^{\tau}}, \qquad t=0,1,\ldots T_i-1$$

since the formula holds for $t = T_i - 1$; and, supposing that it holds for t, we get (omitting index i)

$$p_{t-1} = \frac{1}{1+r}(Y_t + p_t) = \frac{1}{1+r}\left(Y_t + \sum_{\tau=1}^{T_i-t} \frac{Y_{t+\tau}}{(1+r)^\tau}\right)$$

$$= \frac{Y_t}{1+r} + \sum_{\tau=1}^{T_i-t} \frac{Y_{t+\tau}}{(1+r)^{\tau+1}} = \sum_{\tau=0}^{T_i-t} \frac{Y_{t+\tau}}{(1+r)^{\tau+1}}$$

$$= \sum_{\tau=1}^{T_i-(t-1)} \frac{Y_{t-1+\tau}}{(1+r)^\tau}$$

The discounting formula for $p_{i,t}$ expresses again that the value of a machine is equal to its discounted future earnings; now, all of them are shown. In the case of the new machine we get

$$p_{i,0}(r) = \frac{Y_{i,1}}{1+r} + \frac{Y_{i,2}}{(1+r)^2} + \ldots + \frac{Y_{i,T_i}}{(1+r)^{T_i}}$$

The price of a new machine is that of a finished good. Both in the original joint-production system and in the derived integrated system this price appeared to be determined from the side of cost of production. Here it seems determined by the sum of discounted 'expected' returns. The equality between 'costs of production' of a machine and its 'expected future earnings' has thus been *deduced*. The equality is usually presented as a 'fundamental equilibrium condition' linking the 'past' with the 'future'. However, in a joint-production system in a self-replacing state, it appears not as an assumption but as a consequence of the calculation of prices on the basis of a uniform rate of profit on the prices of the produced means of production. The 'link between the past and the future' is automatically provided if the rate of profit is uniform for any one period. In a world where competition is so perfect that the prices of old machines are always known, competition will ensure a tendency for the rate of profit to equalise from period to period, as in the case of circulating capital. To assume a uniform rate of profit in fixed-capital systems does not, then, imply more foresight than is implied in circulating-capital systems.

The fact that the discounting formula has here been derived and not simply assumed is of great theoretical importance, because the same cannot be done in the neoclassical system. There is (except for flukes) no uniform rate of profit in a model with stocks of capital goods which are also produced and where production and distribution are exclusively governed by supply and demand. In the neoclassical system the rentals of existing capital goods have to be related to the cost of production of new capital goods by means of discounting, and, since the demand for consumption goods will in general require a structure of the capital stock which differs from the one in existence, either production of capital goods will be erratic and take place only in the sectors affected by a scarcity of existing capital goods or it has to be admitted that some industries are more profitable than others. (The argument would not hold only if capital were perfectly malleable.) In order to overcome the difficulty, i.e. in order to show why rates of profit may tend to equalise, *expectations* about future developments of markets have to be introduced. (Marshall was aware of this; see Marshall, 1920, appendix H.)

But, then, the supply of 'factors' and commodities is not governed by given patterns of demand (consumer preferences). Present production, i.e. the activity of the workers, cannot any more be considered as the supply of a factor directed towards the satisfaction of a known want and rewarded at its proper price: it is instead subjected to the plans of the capitalists who *speculate* on being able to sell the product later. The process of production is therefore not the supply of 'labour' and 'capital' for the production of a demanded commodity; it is the use ('exploitation') of the 'labour power' of the worker by the capitalist, who, in order to be able to sell a commodity at the end of the period of production, has to buy the means (including 'labour power') at the beginning. (If the wage is – as usual – not advanced by the capitalist, the worker advances his labour power.)

With the real wage considered as given, capitalists will enter those lines of production which they expect to be more profitable on the basis of their (uncertain) expectations. If they are not deceived, a uniform rate of profit will gradually come about. If the real wage cannot be considered as given, systematic differentials of rates of profits between industries may persist. Ignoring this complication of the real accumulation process, we only concern ourselves with the imaginary state of affairs where perfect equality has been achieved. From a mathematical point of view, the 'fundamental equilibrium condition' does then appear to be formally equivalent with uniformity of the rate of profit. But we should keep the processes in mind which tend to, and move away from, the 'equilibrium' level of the rate of profit as defined by technological conditions and, for example, a given real wage, for only then will it be understood that the uniformity of the rate of profit (the magnitude of which remains to be determined) has to be treated as the primary phenomenon: in the real world there has to be a movement of the rates of profit towards an average before that average can be used for discounting.

Although the formula for the equality of the price of a machine with its discounted future earnings should be considered as a consequence, rather than as a precondition, of the tendency of rates of profit to equalise – at least as long as prices of old machines are known – the formula provides a useful tool in our model, for it allows us to interpret the analysis of the prices of old machines with the known results about the prices of finished goods. First of all, we obviously have the following theorem.

Theorem 5

If net returns are positive at all ages of machine i (if $Y_{i,t}(r) > 0, 1 \leq t \leq T_i$) at rate of profit r, the machine has positive prices at all ages ($p_{i,t}(r) > 0$, $0 \leq t \leq T_i - 1$) at rate of profit r.

The result is trivial: if a machine generates a positive income at all ages, its price will be positive.

We shall now define that a machine i is of (initially) rising efficiency in price terms at rate of profit r from age zero up to age θ, if we have

$$Y_{i,1}(r) \leq Y_{i,2}(r) \leq \ldots \leq Y_{i,\theta+1}, \qquad 0 \leq \theta \leq T_i - 1$$

It is of (eventually) falling efficiency from age θ onwards, if

$$Y_{i,\theta+1} \geq Y_{i,\theta+2} \geq \ldots \geq Y_{i,T_i}, \qquad 0 \leq \theta \leq T_i - 1$$

Efficiency in price terms according to this notion depends on the rate of profit. A machine may be of rising efficiency in price terms throughout its lifetime at one rate of profit and of falling at another. But the notion does not depend on the chosen standard of prices.

Theorem 6

(i) If a machine i generates negative returns from age zero to age θ, i.e. if $Y_{i,1} < 0, \ldots Y_{i,\theta+1} < 0$, prices are positive and rising up to age θ.
(ii) If a machine i is of rising efficiency up to age $T_i - 1$, all prices are positive.

Proof

(i) By induction, using the recursive formula and the fact that

$p_{i,0} > 0$.

(ii) Use (i) up to the age where $Y_{i,t}$ turns positive, and the discounting formula for $p_{i,t}$ afterwards.

Theorem 7

(i) If machine i generates negative returns from age θ onwards up to age $T_i - 1$, prices turn negative no later than at age θ.
(ii) If a machine is of falling efficiency from age θ onwards, with net return in the last year still being positive ($Y_{i,T_i} > 0$), prices are falling from age θ onwards.

Proof

(i) Using the recursive formula and $p_{i,T_i-1} = \dfrac{Y_{i,T_i-1}}{1+r}$

(ii) By induction using the formula

$$p_{i,t} - p_{i,t-1} = \frac{Y_{i,t+1} - Y_{i,t}}{1+r} + \frac{Y_{i,t+2} - Y_{i,t+1}}{(1+r)^2} + \dots + \frac{Y_{i,T_i} - Y_{i,T_i-1}}{(1+r)^{T_i-t}} - \frac{Y_{i,T_i}}{(1+r)^{T_i-t+1}}$$

where all terms on the right-hand side are negative.

Why are the results about rising and falling efficiency so asymmetrical? Falling efficiency is easy to understand. Prices may turn negative (the machine may reach economic death before it is physically worn out) because the processes using old machines are in fact not indispensable and prices indicate that they have to be eliminated no later than the returns of the machine have turned negative, i.e. no later than the processes have turned unprofitable. A car, for instance, works only at the expense of excessive repairs after some years. (We shall return to this point later.) But machines of rising efficiency may have positive value in real life even before they produce a current positive return, if (as in the case of a machine under construction) there is sufficient confidence in their future productivity. In our model the price is then certain to be positive, because we have assumed that the system as a whole is both productive (i.e. capable of producing a surplus) and indecomposable, so that each group is indispensable in the system (excepting, perhaps, spare parts). What the theorem then says is that, as long as the processes have not yet begun to yield a return, the machine cannot have a negative price.

However, one should not read too much into these statements. Efficiency in price terms is dependent on, and sensitive to, changes in the rate of profit. One can easily construct examples which confirm that a machine may be of rising efficiency at one rate of profit and of falling at another. This should be borne in mind especially in discussions of the truncation theorem and of the economic lifetime of machines where these difficulties in the theory of capital get eliminated by heroic assumptions.

Before we turn to this, let us note in passing that efficiency can nevertheless be independent of the rate of profit in very special circumstances. Machine i may be said to be of rising physical efficiency if

$$\mathbf{b}_i(1) \le \mathbf{b}_i(2) \le \dots \le \mathbf{b}_i(T_i), \qquad \mathbf{a}_i(1) \ge \mathbf{a}_i(2) \ge \dots \ge \mathbf{a}_i(T_i)$$
$$l_i(1) \ge l_i(2) \ge \dots \ge l_i(T_i)$$

i.e. if physical output does not fall with age, while physical inputs do not rise. Conversely for falling efficiency; the meaning of constant physical efficiency is obvious.

Since prices of finished goods are positive, it immediately follows that rising physical efficiency entails rising efficiency in price terms for all rates of profit. But situations such that rising or falling physical efficiency is unambiguously defined are *a priori* hardly more likely to occur than are situations in circulating-capital systems such that the value of capital can be defined independently of the rate of profit. Attempts to separate 'inter-industry relations' from the 'time structure' of fixed capital are therefore apt to be misleading.

The separation of 'inter-industry relations' from the 'time structure' of fixed capital is reminiscent of old attempts to reconcile partial and general equilibrium by proving that what is true for individual firms is true for their aggregate as well. For example, the discounting formula is still often analysed under the assumption that the returns $Y_{i,t}$ are independent of variations of the rate of profit, as seems correct from the microeconomic point of view. But this approach leads to conclusions which are the opposite of what holds for the 'macro' system. If $Y_{i,t}$ were constant, the price of a new machine would *fall* with the rate of profit, and some neoclassical text books (for instance, Schneider) take this microeconomic phenomenon as sort of a proof for the negative interest elasticity of investment as a whole. But, if prices are measured in terms of the wage rate, the price of the new machine rises, as we shall see (after the appropriate truncation), because at least some of the $Y_{i,t}$ rise more strongly than $(1+r)^t$. That economists should conclude from the assumption of invariable returns in the recursive formula that the price of a new machine is the less the higher the rate of profit indicates that it is just as dangerous and misleading to teach price theory exclusively from the point of view of the firm as it is false to teach that since a firm may protect itself in the face of a crisis by cutting wages and investment the same must be true for society as a whole.

6 Reduction to dated quantities of labour, the 'centre' and switches of technique

We shall now try to establish a link between the analyses of inter-industry relations and of integrated processes. It is based on a generalisation of the reduction to dated quantities of labour.

In the case of single-product industries, the reduction to dated quantities of labour consists in resolving the price of a product into the series of the past inputs of direct and indirect labour which have gone into it. Each labour input is multiplied by the wage rate (measured in the standard chosen) and a power of the rate of profit indicating the number of periods which have elapsed between the expenditure of that amount of labour and its embodiment in the product. Take, for example, prices in terms of the wage rate in an indecomposable single-product system with input matrix **A** and labour vector **l**. The mathematical series for dated inputs can then be derived as follows:

$$\begin{aligned}\hat{\mathbf{p}}(r) = \frac{1}{w}\mathbf{p}(r) &= \mathbf{l} + (1+r)\mathbf{A}\hat{\mathbf{p}}(r)\\ &= \mathbf{l} + (1+r)\mathbf{A}\mathbf{l} + (1+r)^2\mathbf{A}^2\hat{\mathbf{p}}(r)\\ &= \mathbf{l} + (1+r)\mathbf{A}\mathbf{l} + \ldots + (1+r)^n\mathbf{A}^n\hat{\mathbf{p}}(r)\end{aligned}$$

hence

$$\hat{\mathbf{p}}(r) = \mathbf{l} + (1+r)\mathbf{A}\mathbf{l} + (1+r)^2\mathbf{A}^2\mathbf{l} + \ldots$$

for it is well known that this series converges for $0 \leq r < R$, if **A** is productive, i.e. if dom $\mathbf{A} = (1+R)^{-1} < 1$. The term $\mathbf{A}^n\mathbf{l}$ denotes the vector of labour inputs expended n periods ago which indirectly enter a vector of unit outputs today. Sraffa has shown (1960, Ch. 6) that the erratic character of the movements of relative prices in response to changes in the rate of profit is intuitively best understood by considering the irregular pattern of the distribution of direct and indirect labour inputs over the past.

Unfortunately, the same reduction in general does not converge in the case of joint production, for the series

$$\begin{aligned}\hat{\mathbf{p}} &= [\mathbf{B} - (1+r)\mathbf{A}]^{-1}\mathbf{l} = [\mathbf{I} - (1+r)\mathbf{B}^{-1}\mathbf{A}]^{-1}\mathbf{B}^{-1}\mathbf{l}\\ &= \mathbf{B}^{-1}\mathbf{l} + (1+r)\mathbf{B}^{-1}\mathbf{A}\mathbf{B}^{-1}\mathbf{l} + (1+r)^2(\mathbf{B}^{-1}\mathbf{A})^2\mathbf{B}^{-1}\mathbf{l} + \ldots\end{aligned}$$

which is the closest analogue to Sraffa's reduction, may not converge even for $r = 0$. The series

$$\begin{aligned}\hat{\mathbf{p}} &= [\mathbf{B} - (1+r)\mathbf{A}]^{-1}\mathbf{l} = \{(\mathbf{B}-\mathbf{A})[\mathbf{I} - r(\mathbf{B}-\mathbf{A})^{-1}\mathbf{A}]\}^{-1}\mathbf{l}\\ &= [\mathbf{I} - r(\mathbf{B}-\mathbf{A})^{-1}\mathbf{A}]^{-1}(\mathbf{B}-\mathbf{A})^{-1}\mathbf{l}\\ &= (\mathbf{B}-\mathbf{A})^{-1}\mathbf{l} + r(\mathbf{B}-\mathbf{A})^{-1}\mathbf{A}(\mathbf{B}-\mathbf{A})^{-1}\mathbf{l}\\ &\quad + r^2[(\mathbf{B}-\mathbf{A})^{-1}\mathbf{A}]^2(\mathbf{B}-\mathbf{A})^{-1}\mathbf{l} + \ldots\end{aligned}$$

does always converge for sufficiently small r, but not necessarily in the full range of r where prices are positive and well defined. Moreover, some of its terms will usually be negative, since $(\mathbf{B}-\mathbf{A})^{-1}$ is generally not positive for joint-production systems. It is true that the single terms of the series possess an economic meaning[8] but I suggest that yet another series provides a better understanding of the specific features of fixed capital systems.

To construct it, we revert to the concept of an integrated process. The

[8] $(\mathbf{B}-\mathbf{A})^{-1}\mathbf{l}$ is the total of direct and indirect labour expended on one unit of each good. The subsequent expressions can be explained in terms of integrated industries, as Pasinetti has shown (Ch. 2 above).

integrated process for the production of good i was written

$$(1+r)\tilde{\mathbf{a}}_i(r)\mathbf{p}_1 + w\tilde{l}_i(r) = \tilde{\mathbf{b}}_i(r)\mathbf{p}_1$$

where $\mathbf{p}_1$ is the vector of prices of finished goods in some standard, and where $\tilde{\mathbf{a}}_i(r)$, $\tilde{\mathbf{b}}_i(r)$, $\tilde{l}_i(r)$ denote vectors of dated commodity inputs, outputs and labour inputs to integrated process i. Since superimposed joint production was excluded, we can again divide by $\tilde{b}_i^i(r)$ and obtain

$$\hat{a}_i^j(r) = \frac{\tilde{a}_i^j(r)}{\tilde{b}_i^i(r)} = \frac{\sum_{t=1}^{T_i} (1+r)^{T_i-t} a_i^j(t)}{\sum_{t=1}^{T_i} (1+r)^{T_i-t} b_i^i(t)}$$

$$\hat{l}_i(r) = \frac{\tilde{l}_i(r)}{\tilde{b}_i^i(r)} = \frac{\sum_{t=1}^{T_i} (1+r)^{T_i-t} l_i(t)}{\sum_{t=1}^{T_i} (1+r)^{T_i-t} b_i^i(t)}$$

so that the equation of the integrated process becomes

$$(1+r)\hat{\mathbf{a}}_i(r)\mathbf{p}_1 + w\hat{\mathbf{l}}_i(r) = \mathbf{p}_1, \qquad \hat{\mathbf{a}}_i = (\hat{a}_i^1, \ldots \hat{a}_i^f)$$

or, in matrix form,

$$(1+r)\hat{\mathbf{A}}(r)\mathbf{p}_1 + w\hat{\mathbf{l}}(r) = \mathbf{p}_1$$

where

$$\hat{\mathbf{A}} = [\hat{a}_i^j(r)], \qquad \hat{\mathbf{l}}(r) = [\hat{l}_1(r), \ldots \hat{l}_f(r)]'$$
$$\hat{\mathbf{A}} = \tilde{\mathbf{B}}^{-1}\tilde{\mathbf{A}}, \qquad \hat{\mathbf{l}} = \tilde{\mathbf{B}}^{-1}\tilde{\mathbf{l}}$$

We have thus constructed a sort of a single-product system with variable coefficients. We call it the 'centre' and its coefficients the centre coefficients. $\hat{\mathbf{A}}(r)$ is an indecomposable matrix for each r and $(1+r)\hat{\mathbf{A}}(r)$ has a dominant root smaller than 1 for each r, $0 \leq r < R$. We can therefore form the mathematical series

$$\begin{aligned}\hat{\mathbf{p}}_1(r) &= [\mathbf{I} - (1+r)\hat{\mathbf{A}}(r)]^{-1}\hat{\mathbf{l}}(r) \\ &= \hat{\mathbf{l}}(\tilde{r}) + (1+r)\hat{\mathbf{A}}(r)\hat{\mathbf{l}}(r) + (1+r)^2[\hat{\mathbf{A}}(r)]^2\hat{\mathbf{l}}(r) + \ldots\end{aligned}$$

which converges for $0 \leq r < R$. It looks like a reduction to dated quantities of labour for finished goods, but what do the variable centre coefficients mean economically?

First of all, the reduction is identical with the familiar reduction to dated quantities of labour if the lifetimes of machines are all equal to one and the machines are thus indistinguishable from circulating capital.

Secondly, at $r = 0$ the reduction shows that values of finished goods are equal to the sum of 'dated' quantities of labour, whatever the lifetime of machines and their efficiency pattern. For

$$\hat{\mathbf{p}}_1(0) = [\mathbf{I} - \hat{\mathbf{A}}(0)]^{-1}\,\hat{\mathbf{l}} = \hat{\mathbf{l}}(0) + \hat{\mathbf{A}}(0)\hat{\mathbf{l}}(0) + \ldots$$

where $\hat{l}_i(0)$ denotes the amount of labour expended on the production of one unit of good i in group i, and $\hat{a}_i^j(0)$ the total amount of finished good j used up in group i (remember $b_i^i(1) + \ldots + b_i^i(T_i) = 1$). The coefficients of the series represent in a certain sense 'dated' inputs of labour, for, in order to allow the interpretation of the ith element of the column vector $[\hat{\mathbf{A}}(0)]^t\hat{\mathbf{l}}(0)$ as the amount of indirect labour 'now embodied in good i and expended 't periods ago', one has only to revert to the 'long period' considered above (end of section 3).

For $r > 0$, the reduction remains simple in the extreme case of physically constant efficiency. Each process in a group belonging to a machine of constant efficiency produces $1/T_i$ units of the total output of good i (which is itself normalised to one). The coefficients of inputs of circulating capital and of labour are all equal; hence

$$\hat{l}_i(r) = \frac{\sum_{t=1}^{T_i} (1+r)^{T_i - t}\, l_i(t)}{\sum_{t=1}^{T_i} (1+r)^{T_i - t}\, b_i^i(t)} = T_i l_i(1) = \ldots = T_i l_i(T_i)$$

Equally

$$\hat{a}_i^j(r) = \frac{\sum_{t=1}^{T_i} (1+r)^{T_i - t}\, a_i^j(t)}{\sum_{t=1}^{T_i} (1+r)^{T_i - t}\, b_i^i(t)} = T_i a_i^j(1) = \ldots = T_i a_i^j(T_i)$$

if j is not the machine engaged in the production of good i. If m denotes the index of the new machine entering the first process of group i, and if, for the sake of simplicity, $a_i^m(1) = 1$, we obtain

$$\hat{a}_i^m(r) = \frac{(1+r)^{T_i - 1}}{\sum_{t=1}^{T_i} (1+r)^{T_i - t}\, b_i^i(t)} = T_i \frac{r(1+r)^{T_i - 1}}{(1+r)^{T_i} - 1}$$

which is a textbook depreciation formula. If the rate of profit is zero, $\hat{a}_i^m(0) = 1$, i.e. the labour value of the machine is embodied in the product in a straightforward manner. As the rate of profit rises, $\hat{a}_i^m(r)$ rises monotonically and tends to T_i for $r \to \infty$. The initial rise of $\hat{a}_i^m(r)$ is the steeper the longer the lifetime of the machine. The centre coefficients which do not correspond to machines remain constant; only the depreciation quotas rise. If the maximum rate of profit of the system as a whole is sufficiently great, the depreciation quotas approach T_i at high rates of profit, i.e. the mere rise in the rate of profit increases them to such an extent that 'costs' rise as if a new machine had to be bought for every process in the group and not only for the first.

In the general case, when the efficiency of the machine varies, all centre coefficients may vary with the rate of profit. These variations are independent of the standard of prices chosen and they can cause movements of relative prices which are more complicated than those engendered by the distribution of the dated labour coefficients in the single-product case. It is tempting, though not quite correct, to say that the variations of the centre coefficients express the efficiency of the machines while the structure of the $\hat{\mathbf{A}}$ matrix expresses interindustry relations.

Such an interpretation of the reduction could be supported by repeating that relative prices of finished goods as determined by the full fixed-capital system are, at the given rate of profit r, equal to those determined by the centre considered as an imaginary single-product system, which may be written as

$$(1+r)\mathbf{G}\mathbf{p}_1 + w\mathbf{v} = \mathbf{p}_1$$

where $g_i^j = \hat{a}_i^j(r)$, $v_i = \hat{l}_i(r)$. The centre coefficients $\hat{a}_i^j$ for a raw material (or labour $\hat{l}_i$) are at $r = 0$ equal to the total input of the raw material (or labour) used up during the lifetime of a machine for the production of a unit of output of the finished good. That is to say, the centre coefficients $\hat{a}_i^j(0)$, $\hat{l}_i(0)$ (machines, raw materials and labour) at $r = 0$ are simply the total of each input j and labour used for a unit output in the ith integrated process. The centre coefficients $\hat{a}_i^j(r)$, $\hat{l}_i(r)$ deviate from $\hat{a}_i^j(0)$, $\hat{l}_i(0)$ only to the extent that the distribution of inputs is uneven over the integrated process, for, if the machine is of constant efficiency and lasts T_i years, the centre coefficients of a raw material and of labour are (independently of the rate of profit) equal to T_i times the inputs to the integrated process during any one year. (They are the same per unit of output.) The only centre coefficients that differ a great deal at $r > 0$ from at $r = 0$ are those that represent machines or spare parts, because the inputs of the machine itself and of the spare parts are naturally the most unevenly distributed: the input of a machine (and often also of a spare part) occurs only once during the integrated process.

The interpretation of the centre as an imaginary single-product system is of importance not only because it helps us to visualise the generalised reduction to dated quantities of labour. It is also interesting in itself, because it proves that (provided wear and tear are calculated correctly, i.e. provided, the centre coefficients are known) we can intuitively deal with a fixed-capital system as with a single-product system, if the rate of profit is given and fixed. Moreover, we find that the rate of profit is not only equal to net income minus wages over total capital: it is also equal to net income minus wages in the centre over capital employed in the centre; i.e. net profits over total capital, including the entire stock of machines, are equal to net profits over total raw materials used up during the integrated process (corrected with a factor dependent on r and expressing the unevenness of the inputs during the integrated process) *plus* annual wear and tear of the machine as expressed by the proper amortisation coefficient. In formulas, we get from the price equations

$$(1+r)\mathbf{A}\hat{\mathbf{p}}+\mathbf{l}=\mathbf{B}\hat{\mathbf{p}}$$

$$(1+r)\hat{\mathbf{A}}(r)\hat{\mathbf{p}}_1+\hat{\mathbf{l}}(r)=\hat{\mathbf{p}}_1$$

for any non-vanishing pair of activity levels two formulas for the rate of profits: either

$$r=\frac{\mathbf{q}\,(\mathbf{B}-\mathbf{A})\hat{\mathbf{p}}-\mathbf{q}\mathbf{l}}{\mathbf{q}\mathbf{A}\hat{\mathbf{p}}}$$

or

$$r=\frac{\mathbf{q}_1\,(\mathbf{I}-\hat{\mathbf{A}})\hat{\mathbf{p}}_1-\mathbf{q}_1\hat{\mathbf{l}}}{\mathbf{q}_1\,\hat{\mathbf{A}}\hat{\mathbf{p}}_1}$$

This means that Marx was not far off the mark when he treated constant capital as a flow. The two formulas show that net profit per period over the total stock of capital is equal to net profit per period over the circulating capital used up per period in the centre as an imaginary single-product system. (Activity levels in the centre system can be related to those in the original system in a meaningful way, but we shall not discuss this matter.)

We now consider the effect of the uneven distribution of inputs during the integrated process.

As an example, take the case where finished good i is produced by a machine (finished good no. 1) which lasts for two years, so that

$$\hat{a}_i^j(r)=\frac{(1+r)a_i^j(1)+a_i^j(2)}{(1+r)b_i^i(1)+b_i^i(2)},\qquad j=2,\ldots f$$

and

$$\hat{l}_i(r)=\frac{(1+r)l_i(1)+l_i(2)}{(1+r)b_i^i(1)+b_i^i(2)}$$

These functions will *fall* as r rises, if

$$\frac{a_i^j(1)}{a_i^j(2)}<\frac{b_i^i(1)}{b_i^i(2)},\qquad j=2,\ldots f$$

and

$$\frac{l_i(1)}{l_i(2)} < \frac{b_i^i(1)}{b_i^i(2)}$$

which is the case if the machine is of falling physical efficiency. If $\hat{a}_i^j(r)$, $j = 2, \ldots f$, and $\hat{l}_i(r)$ fall sufficiently fast,[9] the price may fall in those ranges of the rate of profit where the prices of the inputs rise only very moderately or fall with r. Examples in two- or three-sector models are easily constructed.

The possibility of a falling price in terms of the wage rate looks disturbing, since it could seem to imply that the trade-off between wages and profits does not always exist. If all machines were of rising efficiency in physical terms, it could not happen, as is obvious from the reduction, since all $\hat{a}_i^j(r)$, $\hat{l}_i(r)$ are then monotonically rising functions of r (proof by differentiation). The possibility of a falling price in terms of the wage rate therefore seems connected with falling efficiency. We also saw in the last section that prices of old machines may be negative if the efficiency of the machine is falling. Later it will be shown that, if those cases of inefficiencies

[9] If physical efficiency falls moderately with r, the functions $\hat{a}_i^j(r)$, $\hat{l}_i(r)$ will tend to fall slowly and may just about offset the rising tendency of $\hat{a}_i^1(r)$.

As a consequence, 'linear' depreciation as practised by most firms may be quite rational. The theorist must consider more complicated efficiency patterns not only because they are logically possible, but also because they arise frequently in the context of plants or machines which are not in operation but are under construction, or because they are old and have to undergo substantial repairs to be kept operating. Such qualitative changes in the use of the machine induce the practical entrepreneur to treat the machine as a different good in the three most typical stages mentioned above (construction, normal operation, operation with frequent repairs). The entrepreneur will be inclined to apply linear-depreciation rules only to the middle stage, where they are in fact quite suitable. Note also the following: if the net output of the machine is negative at first, then rises to a positive maximum and eventually falls off again, and if all prices of the machine are positive, they will also rise at first and fall later, but the maximum of the price of the machine will be reached before its net output reaches a maximum. If the latter maximum is 'flat', prices will be highest at a time such that p_{t-1} is approximately equal to p_t. Since the recursive formula can be written as

$$p_t - p_{t-1} = rp_{t-1} - Y_t$$

a maximum with $p_t = p_{t-1}$ will be characterised by

$$r = \frac{Y_t}{p_t}$$

The relationship shows that the machine's prices are stationary (here at their maximum) when the ratio of 'income' to price is equal to the rate of profit. If the rate of profit is zero, the machine has its maximum value at the point where the income generated by the machine turns positive. If the rate of profit rises, the maximum will *ceteris paribus* shift to older ages. Thus, a male slave in the American South was most expensive towards the age of thirty, not twenty, years (see Fogel and Engerman, 1974, p. 72).

are ruled out which lead to negative prices of old machines, prices in terms of the wage rate can be proved to rise with r.

As a further application of the reduction to dated quantities of labour, let us note a case of switching and reswitching which is connected with the variable efficiency of machines. Suppose, for instance, that a process producing good i by means of circulating capital $\mathbf{a}_i$ and labour l_i could be replaced by a group of two processes – $\mathbf{a}_i(1)$, $l_i(1)$ and $\mathbf{a}_i(2)$, $l_i(2)$ – using a machine which already exists in the system and is of falling efficiency. Suppose for simplicity that $a_i^j(1)$, $a_i^j(2)$ are positive if and only if a_i^j is positive, $j = 2, \ldots f$, and that $a_i^1 = 0$. The curves for $\hat{a}_i^j(r)$, $\hat{l}_i(r)$ could then be of the following type:

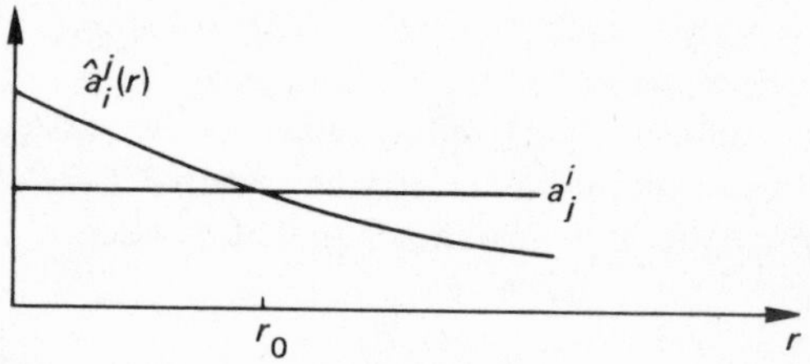

FIGURE 7.1

In the graph, the function $\hat{a}_i^j(r)$ expressing the new process cuts the constant a_i^j, which corresponds to the inputs used in the old process at $r = r_0$. If, by coincidence, this happened simultaneously for all inputs $a_i^j, j = 2, \ldots f$, and l_i, one should expect the system as a whole to have a switch in the neighbourhood of r_0 if $\hat{a}_i^1(r)$ does not exert too great an influence at low rates of profit. Since $\hat{a}_i^1(r)$ rises monotonically, it is conceivable that a reswitch occurs before the maximum rate of profit is reached. It goes without saying that the pattern of switches increases in complexity if the efficiency of the machine is rising in respect of some inputs and falling in respect of others.

7 Roundabout processes

The above considerations suggest that it would be at least as difficult to construct an aggregate of 'capital' in fixed-capital systems as in single-product systems. Even more than in the single-product case, one seems, then, to be bereft of any general results about capital theory which would allow the character to be determined of the 'substitutions' which are supposed to take place in response to changes in the rate of profit.

There are, however, some classes of alternative methods of production which are related to each other in a simpler fashion. Since they can be thought of as being developed in a historical sequence, they allow a classification of various forms of technical progress. We shall discuss them at the end of this essay. As a preliminary to that discussion, we now introduce 'roundabout processes'.

We speak of a roundabout process if raw materials and machines that are already being produced in the existing system are being used to construct a new machine which, in conjunction with raw materials, replaces an existing process.

Such roundabout processes are already contained in our analysis. To see this, suppose that process 1, which is a circulating-capital process $\mathbf{a}_1, l_1$, is to be replaced by a roundabout process; i.e. a new process 0 is introduced which employs raw materials $\mathbf{a}_0$ and labour l_0 to produce one unit of a machine, finished good 0 with price p_0, that is in turn used in an integrated process with lifetime T_1 to produce good 1. The new system is assumed to be productive and to satisfy all other assumptions of fixed-capital systems.

The point is now that the new processes can be taken together to form *one* roundabout process which looks like an integrated process where nothing is produced in the first year. For the T_1+1 processes

$$
\begin{aligned}
&(1+r)\mathbf{a}_0\mathbf{p}_1 + w\,l_0 = \mathbf{b}_0\mathbf{p}_1 = p_0\\
&(1+r)[p_0 + \mathbf{a}_1(1)\mathbf{p}_1] + w\,l_1(1) = \mathbf{b}_1(1)\mathbf{p}_1 + \mathbf{m}_1(1)\mathbf{p}_2\\
&(1+r)[\mathbf{a}_1(2)\mathbf{p}_1 + \mathbf{m}_1(1)\mathbf{p}_2] + w\,l_1(2) = \mathbf{b}_1(2)\mathbf{p}_1 + \mathbf{m}_1(2)\mathbf{p}_2\\
&\quad\vdots\\
&(1+r)[\mathbf{a}_1(T_1)\mathbf{p}_1 + \mathbf{m}_1(T_1-1)\mathbf{p}_2] + w\,l_1(T_1) = \mathbf{b}_1(T_1)\mathbf{p}_1
\end{aligned}
$$

can be combined into one integrated process where

$$\hat{\mathbf{a}}_1(r) = \sum_{t=0}^{T_1} (1+r)^{T_1-t}\mathbf{a}_1(t), \qquad \mathbf{a}_1(0) = \mathbf{a}_0, \text{ etc.}$$

Thus, a roundabout process is equivalent to the group of processes of a machine under construction, as in the case of a ship which takes a year to be built and then runs for several years. (The analysis is at once extended to the case of a construction period of more than one year.)

Nobody denies that technical progress entails the use of roundabout processes. The question is whether neoclassical economists were right in asserting that roundabout processes will be introduced in response to a falling rate of profit and a rise in wages, and that this introduction of roundabout processes corresponds to a rise in the capital–labour ratio.

On purely logical grounds, there is nothing to substantiate this claim if roundabout processes are defined in the abstract fashion suggested above. We have already indicated that the introduction of machines can produce a number of switches. Only if specific assumptions about the technological character of 'increasing roundaboutness' are made does it become possible to construct a hierarchy of techniques, based on 'technological development', that simultaneously corresponds to the hierarchy of capital–labour ratios. We shall argue this at the end of the essay. It will be seen, however, that the analysis has at best only limited historical applicability, and the approach vindicates Marx rather than the neoclassical economists.

Appendix

One might think that a roundabout process is more labour intensive than the process it replaces if the total sum of labour employed is greater and the total sum of each input of finished goods used is smaller for the former than for the latter. But the conjecture is wrong. It would be equally wrong to think the assumption sufficient to ensure that the maximum rate of profit rises.

Consider the familiar corn–corn economy (p_c is the price of corn in terms of the wage rate):

$$(1+r)ap_c + l_c = p_c$$

Suppose a machine with price p_0 is invented, produced by means of corn and labour, and used for two years to produce corn. The price of the one-year-old machine is p_1:

$$(1+r)a_0 p_c + l_0 = p_0$$

$$(1+r)(a_1 p_c + p_0) + l_1 = b_1 p_c + p_1$$

$$(1+r)(a_2 p_c + p_1) + l_2 = b_2 p_c$$

Of course, $a_0 + a_1 + a_2 < b_1 + b_2 = 1$.

If $a = 1/2, l = 1$ in the original corn–corn economy, the maximum rate of profit R_I equals one. Suppose a little labour is diverted to produce the machine, and suppose that the machine entails reduced use of corn ($a_0 + a_1 + a_2 < a$) while $l_0 + l_1 + l_2 > l$. If the particular values $l = 1$, $a = 1/2$, $b_1 = b_2 = 1/2$, and

$$a_0 = \frac{31}{504} \qquad l_0 = \frac{3}{140}$$

$$a_1 = \frac{1}{4} \qquad l_1 = 1$$

$$a_2 = \frac{2}{315} \qquad l_2 = \frac{1}{3}$$

are chosen, there is a new maximum rate of profit R_{II} such that p_1 is positive for $0 \leq r < R_{II}$. There are no fewer than *three* switchpoints, at $r = 1/4$, $r = 1/2$, and $r = 3/4$, where the price of corn in terms of labour commanded is the same in both systems. Contrary to what one might expect at first sight, the roundabout process is more profitable at $r = 0$ and $R_{II} < R_I$, although the total sum of raw materials used is diminished.

8 Truncation theorems

The concept of the 'centre' seems to allow us to deal with the question of switching at a given rate of profit in a very simple manner. By means of a slight extension of any of the conventional methods, one can prove the following theorem.

Theorem 8

If two (or several) alternative integrated processes are given for the production of one finished good, and if they are such that the centre of each resulting system is productive, indecomposable and has a maximum rate of profit greater than a given rate of profit r, one of these techniques will yield prices in terms of the wage rate at r that are lower than or equal to those of the other technique(s).

The theorem suggests that the choice of techniques in a fixed capital system is determined by relations between finished goods alone. But this can be true only if intermediate goods yielding negative prices can be eliminated from the systems. And the wage curves of each technique must be shown to be falling monotonically, for it could otherwise be possible to increase both the wage and the rate of profit without changing the technique.

Since the wage goods can reasonably be assumed to consist of finished goods only, the following theorem shows that a falling wage curve is ensured if negative prices can be ruled out.

Theorem 9[10]

All prices of finished goods in terms of the wage rate $\hat{\mathbf{p}}_1(r) = (1/w)\mathbf{p}_1$ rise monotonically with the rate of profit r in the neighbourhood of $r = r_0$, $0 \leq r_0 < R$, if all prices of intermediate goods are non-negative at r. More generally, $\hat{\mathbf{p}}_1(r_2) > \hat{\mathbf{p}}_1(r_1)$ for $r_2 > r_1$, if $\mathbf{p}_2(r_2) > \mathbf{0}$, $0 \leq r_1 < r_2 < R$.

Proof

By differentiation of

$$\mathbf{B}\hat{\mathbf{p}}(r) = (1 + r)\mathbf{A}\hat{\mathbf{p}}(r) + \mathbf{1}$$

[10] For historical references about truncation theorems, see Nuti (1973).

with respect to r, we get

$$[\mathbf{B}-(1+r)\mathbf{A}]\frac{d}{dr}\hat{\mathbf{p}}(r)=\mathbf{A}\hat{\mathbf{p}}(r)$$

The system obtained by multiplying each equation by $(1+r)^{T_i-t}$ and summing up for each group,

$$\sum_{t=1}^{T_i}(1+r)^{T_i-t}\{[\mathbf{b}_i(t)-(1+r)\mathbf{a}_i(t)]\frac{d}{dr}\hat{\mathbf{p}}_1$$

$$+[\mathbf{m}_i(t)-(1+r)\mathbf{m}_i(t-1)]\frac{d}{dr}\hat{\mathbf{p}}_2\}$$

$$=\sum_{t=1}^{T_i}(1+r)^{T_i-t}[\mathbf{a}_i(t)\hat{\mathbf{p}}_1+\mathbf{m}_i(t-1)\hat{\mathbf{p}}_2],\qquad i=1,2,\ldots f$$

is on the left-hand side equal to

$$[\tilde{\mathbf{B}}-(1+r)\tilde{\mathbf{A}}]\frac{d}{dr}\hat{\mathbf{p}}_1$$

since

$$\sum_{t=1}^{T_i}[\mathbf{m}_i(t)-(1+r)\mathbf{m}_i(t-1)](1+r)^{T_i-t}=\mathbf{0}$$

The right-hand side is positive if $\hat{\mathbf{p}}_2\geq\mathbf{0}$.

The first assertion then follows from $[\tilde{\mathbf{B}}-(1+r)\tilde{\mathbf{A}}]^{-1}>\mathbf{0}$, $0\leq r<R$. The generalisation follows by considering the first difference equation, $[\mathbf{B}-(1+r_1)\mathbf{A}][\hat{\mathbf{p}}(r_2)-\hat{\mathbf{p}}(r_1)]=(r_2-r_1)\mathbf{A}\hat{\mathbf{p}}(r_2)$, instead of the differential equation.

Next we prove the following theorem.

Theorem 10

In the stationary state, the ratio P/W of profits P divided by wages W, i.e. the rate of exploitation measured in price terms, rises monotonically with the rate of profit in those ranges of r where all prices are positive.

Proof

If the total labour is numerically equal to unity, the sum of wages is numerically equal to the wage rate and

$$\frac{P}{W}=\mathbf{e}(\mathbf{B}-\mathbf{A})\frac{1}{w}\mathbf{p}-1$$

where $\mathbf{e} = (1, 1, \ldots 1)$. Now $\mathbf{e}(\mathbf{B}^2 - \mathbf{A}^2) = \mathbf{0}$, since there is no net output of intermediate goods in the stationary state; therefore

$$\frac{P}{W} = \mathbf{e}(\mathbf{B}^1 - \mathbf{A}^1)\hat{\mathbf{p}}_1 - 1$$

where $\hat{\mathbf{p}}_1$ rises monotonically with r if $\mathbf{p} > \mathbf{0}$.

The main difficulty is now to show that the processes yielding negative prices can actually be eliminated from the system.

If some prices of intermediate goods are negative, some processes obviously have to be replaced or eliminated. It is a most remarkable result that the assumptions of indecomposability and productiveness of the system as a whole are in themselves sufficient to ensure that no new processes have to be brought in: it is possible to scrap or to 'truncate' some machines at any given rate of profit before they are worn out physically and to discontinue the corresponding intermediate processes in such a way that the remaining system is not only again a productive and indecomposable fixed-capital system, but in addition yields positive prices.

More specifically, an admissible truncation consists in deleting from the system some intermediate goods, together with the processes in which they are used, in such a way that (a) if a machine of age t in group i is scrapped, all machines of ages $t, t+1, \ldots T_i - 1$ and all processes $t+1, t+2, \ldots T_i$ in group i are eliminated from the system, and (b) the resulting system is productive.[11] The truncated system is therefore a fixed-capital system. For each admissible truncation and for the original system we now draw the wage curve $w(r)$ where $w(r)$ is the real wage measured in the number of baskets of *finished* goods that can be bought by one unit of labour at rate of profit r.[12] The number of admissible truncations may be as great as $T_1 T_2 \cdot \ldots \cdot (T_f - 1)$ or as small as zero, depending on the number of truncations yielding a productive system.

Regarding the original system with its admissible truncations as so many alternative fixed-capital systems, we may form the integrated system (it has the same wage curve) for each. If we abstract from intermediate goods, the outer envelope of all the wage curves indicates at each rate of profit the technique (truncation or original system) which is superior in that it entails

[11] Each process may have to be multiplied by some positive factor if the truncated system is to be productive at unit activity levels $\mathbf{e} = (1, 1, \ldots 1)$.

[12] One unit of labour times the wage rate, w, equals the number, λ, of baskets of wage goods, $\mathbf{d} = (d_1, d_2, \ldots d_f; 0, 0, \ldots 0)$, multiplied by the price vector, $\mathbf{p}$: $w = \lambda \mathbf{dp}$ or $\lambda = 1/\mathbf{d}\hat{\mathbf{p}}$. This is equivalent to expressing prices in terms of $\mathbf{d}$, i.e. to normalising $\mathbf{dp} = 1$, or $1 = \mathbf{d}\hat{\mathbf{p}} w_d$, where w_d is the wage rate in terms of standard $\mathbf{d}$. For simplicity we usually write w for the real wage per unit of labour. The second derivation shows better than the first that it is independent of the total labour employed, i.e. the activity levels.

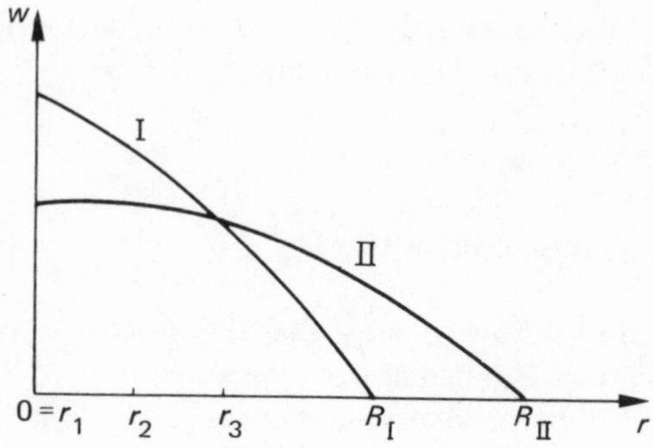

FIGURE 7.2 Wage curves for admissible truncations

the highest real wage, given the rate of profit, and the highest rate of profit, given the real wage. (For the dual interpretation in terms of maximum consumption per head in the steady state corresponding to a given rate of growth, see below.)

This seems again to suggest that intermediate goods do not matter for the choice of techniques. Indeed, the abstraction from intermediate goods implied in the notion of an integrated system is economically real if only finished goods are actually traded and have their prices determined in actual markets, while the prices of intermediate goods are not even taken into account as book values. It is possible for an entrepreneur to calculate the necessary cost price corresponding to a given rate of profit without calculating book values of machines, if he dates his inputs and sets up the equations for the integrated process as described above. This possibility of an abstraction from intermediate goods is even necessary, from the theoretical point of view, for the discussion of the wage curves, in so far as it would not be meaningful to talk of the real wage corresponding to a given rate of profit for each truncation if negative prices for intermediate goods meant that the system was in no way economically viable – for example, as would be the case if *traded* goods had negative prices. (Trade of intermediate goods *between* groups had to be excluded anyway.)

Book values may be relevant, however. (And our assumptions do not exclude trade of intermediate goods within groups.) To be consistent with both interpretations, our model therefore requires that the same truncation should emerge as superior irrespective of whether intermediate goods are explicitly shown to have positive prices or not. Hence, we have to be able to prove that the technique corresponding to a point on the envelope at any given rate of profit always yields positive prices, by virtue of the fact that it is superior to the other truncations.

An admissible truncation which yields positive prices at a rate of profit r (and whose maximum rate of profit is greater than r) is now called feasible at

r. Only feasible truncations must thus appear on the envelope, so that it will fall monotonically with r.

But this is not enough. If the superior technique is to be introduced through competition at a given rate of profit, two more results have to be shown. First, since finished goods are actually traded, their prices in terms of the wage rate have to be lowest for the superior technique. That, at least, is the reason usually put forward for why the superior of two alternative techniques in a circulating-capital system comes into use. It implies that the superiority of the superior technique does not depend on the standard of the real wage provided that it consists of finished goods. We shall also show that the adoption of the superior technique implies surplus profits for those capitalists who are the first to make the transition.

Secondly, since the superior technique does not necessarily entail lower prices in terms of the wage rate for intermediate goods, something else should indicate when truncation is advantageous in a competitive system where intermediate goods are traded to some extent. In fact, we shall prove that the real wage can be raised by truncation at some rate of profit in a fixed-capital system if and only if the prices of some intermediate goods are negative in the untruncated system. And *that* explains the economic function of the occurrence of negative prices in our model.

The following theorem summarises at some length our various assertions.

Theorem 11[13]

(i) If and only if some intermediate goods have negative prices at r, $0 \leq r \leq R$, there is a feasible truncation (i.e. with $\mathbf{p}(r) \geq \mathbf{0}$) yielding a higher rate of profit, r', at the same real wage per unit of labour.
(ii) If and only if some intermediate goods have negative prices at $\bar{r}$, $0 \leq \bar{r} \leq R$, there is a feasible truncation at $\bar{r}$ yielding a higher real wage per unit of labour.
(iii) The truncated system has lower prices of finished goods in terms of the wage rate at r, if some prices in the original system are negative. Conversely, if prices are not negative in both, prices of finished goods in terms of the wage rate are lower or equal in the original system.
(iv) The envelope of the wage curves corresponding to the fixed-capital system and its truncations falls monotonically between $r = 0$ and some greatest 'maximum' rate of profit, $\bar{R} \geq R$. The corresponding prices of finished goods in terms of the wage rate rise monotonically. The

[13] To each of these results about the rate of profit and the price system there corresponds a dual result about the rate of growth and the quantity system in a theory of steady growth under constant returns to scale.

technique (original fixed-capital system or truncation) appearing on the envelope at a rate of profit r, $0 \leq r \leq \bar{R}$, is feasible (is a productive fixed-capital system with non-negative prices at r and having a maximum rate of profit greater than r).

(v) Its vector of prices of finished goods in terms of the wage rate is smaller at r than is that of any other technique.

(vi) If $w(r_1) < w(r_2)$, $r_2 > r_1$, for a fixed-capital system, there exist truncations which are superior at least between $r = r_1$ and the first $r_3 > r_2$ for which $w(r_3) \leq w(r_1)$ (cf. Fig. 7.2 above, where I is a truncation of II).

Proof

(a) We start by proving (ii) for $0 \leq \bar{r} < R$. Let the n-row vector $\mathbf{d} = (d_1, d_2, \ldots d_f; 0, \ldots 0)$ denote the basket of finished goods of which the total real wage at $r = \bar{r}$ consists. Of course, $\mathbf{0} \leq \mathbf{d} \leq \mathbf{e}(\mathbf{B} - \mathbf{A})$. The system

$$\left(\mathbf{A} + \frac{1}{1+\bar{r}}\mathbf{l}\mathbf{d}, \mathbf{B}, \mathbf{l}\right)$$

fulfils the formal requirements for a fixed-capital system. It has a maximum rate of profit which must be equal to $\bar{r}$, since $\det[\mathbf{B} - (1+\bar{r})\mathbf{A} - \mathbf{l}\mathbf{d}] = 0$ and $\det[\mathbf{B} - (1+r)\mathbf{A} - \mathbf{l}\mathbf{d}] \neq 0$, $0 \leq r < \bar{r}$. Hence, there are unique vectors $\mathbf{q} > \mathbf{0}$ and $\mathbf{p} = \mathbf{p}(\bar{r})$ such that

$$\mathbf{q}[\mathbf{B} - (1+\bar{r})\mathbf{A}] = \mathbf{d}, \qquad \mathbf{q}\mathbf{l} = 1$$

$$[\mathbf{B} - (1+\bar{r})\mathbf{A}]\mathbf{p} = \mathbf{l}, \qquad \mathbf{d}\mathbf{p} = 1$$

In the linear programme

$$\max \mathbf{d}\mathbf{x}! \text{ s.t. } [\mathbf{B} - (1+\bar{r})\mathbf{A}]\mathbf{x} \leqq \mathbf{l}, \qquad \mathbf{x} \geq \mathbf{0}$$

$$\min \mathbf{y}\mathbf{l}! \text{ s.t. } \mathbf{y}[\mathbf{B} - (1+\bar{r})\mathbf{A}] \geqq \mathbf{d}, \qquad \mathbf{y} \geq \mathbf{0}$$

any sufficiently small positive vector is feasible in the primal, because $\mathbf{l} > \mathbf{0}$, while $\mathbf{q}$ is feasible in the dual. The programme therefore has semi-positive solutions $\bar{\mathbf{x}}$, $\bar{\mathbf{y}}$. If $\bar{\mathbf{y}} > \mathbf{0}$, there are equalities everywhere in the primal; hence $\bar{\mathbf{x}} = \mathbf{p}$, which is impossible, since $\mathbf{p} = \mathbf{p}(\bar{r})$ is by assumption not semi-positive. Hence $\bar{\mathbf{y}}$ is not positive. Delete all processes with activity levels which are not positive in $\bar{\mathbf{y}}$. If an activity, say the tth process in the ith group, is deleted, the intermediate product produced by it (the ith machine at age t) disappears from the system. Because $\bar{\mathbf{y}}[\mathbf{b}^j - (1+r)\mathbf{a}^j] \geq 0$, if j denotes an intermediate product, processes $t+1, t+2, \ldots T_i$ in group i disappear as well. On the other hand, $\bar{\mathbf{y}}(\mathbf{B} - \mathbf{A}) \geq \mathbf{0}$. Hence, no primary processes are deleted, primary processes being indispensable if no spare parts exist. (We assume this for brevity, as we did that **A**, **B** form an indecomposable system.)

If truncation occurs in group i, it involves deleting processes t, $t+1, \ldots T_i$ where $t \geq 2$, while the machine of age $t-1$ appears overproduced and fetches a zero price, by virtue of the balancing theorem. Deleting the unutilised processes together with the intermediate goods used and produced by them from matrices **A** and **B** thus leads to a truncated system $\bar{\mathbf{A}}, \bar{\mathbf{B}}$ where $\bar{\mathbf{A}}, \bar{\mathbf{B}}$ are square matrices. Deleting the corresponding elements in $\bar{\mathbf{y}}$, $\bar{\mathbf{x}}$, $\mathbf{l}$ leads to vectors $\bar{\mathbf{q}} > \mathbf{0}$, $\bar{\mathbf{p}} \geq \mathbf{0}, \bar{\mathbf{l}}$ where

$$\bar{\mathbf{p}} = [\bar{\mathbf{B}} - (1+\bar{r})\bar{\mathbf{A}}]^{-1}\bar{\mathbf{l}}$$

because $\bar{\mathbf{q}} > \mathbf{0}$. $\bar{\mathbf{A}}, \bar{\mathbf{B}}$ have the same structure as a fixed-capital system, and they are indecomposable because of the indispensability of the primary processes.

We now show that $\bar{\mathbf{A}}, \bar{\mathbf{B}}$ form a productive fixed-capital system with a maximum rate of profit greater than $\bar{r}$. Let $\mathbf{C}(r)$, $\mathbf{D}(r)$ denote the integrated system of $\bar{\mathbf{A}}$, $\bar{\mathbf{B}}$, and $\hat{\mathbf{C}}(r) = [\mathbf{D}(r)]^{-1}\mathbf{C}(r)$. Denote the row vector consisting of the first f components of **p** by $\bar{\mathbf{p}}_1$. Because $(1+r)\hat{\mathbf{C}}(r)\bar{\mathbf{p}}_1 \leq \bar{\mathbf{p}}_1$, $\bar{\mathbf{p}}_1 \geq \mathbf{0}$, the dominant root dom$[(1+\bar{r})\hat{\mathbf{C}}(\bar{r})]$ of the indecomposable semi-positive matrix $(1+\bar{r})\hat{\mathbf{C}}(\bar{r})$ is smaller than one. Suppose dom$[(1+r)\hat{\mathbf{C}}(r)] = 1$ for $r = \hat{r}$. We know from part (iii) of the proof of Lemma 1 and from (iv) of the proof of Theorem 4 that we should then have a row vector $\hat{\mathbf{q}} > \mathbf{0}$ such that

$$(1+\hat{r})\hat{\mathbf{q}}\bar{\mathbf{A}} = \hat{\mathbf{q}}\bar{\mathbf{B}}$$

But, since

$$(1+\bar{r})\bar{\mathbf{A}}\bar{\mathbf{p}} \leq \bar{\mathbf{B}}\bar{\mathbf{p}}$$

$$(1+\bar{r})\hat{\mathbf{q}}\bar{\mathbf{A}}\bar{\mathbf{p}} < \hat{\mathbf{q}}\bar{\mathbf{B}}\bar{\mathbf{p}} = (1+\hat{r})\bar{\mathbf{q}}\bar{\mathbf{A}}\bar{\mathbf{p}}$$

it follows that $\hat{r} > \bar{r}$. This establishes at the same time that the 'maximum' rate of profit of the system $\bar{\mathbf{A}}, \bar{\mathbf{B}}$ is greater than $\bar{r}$ and that it is a productive system, since dom$(1+r)\hat{\mathbf{C}}(r)$ is continuous, hence smaller than $1, 0 \leq r < \bar{r}$. Thus, $\bar{\mathbf{A}}$, $\bar{\mathbf{B}}$, $\bar{\mathbf{l}}$ are a feasible truncation. We have $(d_1, d_2, \ldots d_f)$ $(\bar{p}_1, \bar{p}_2, \ldots \bar{p}_f) = \bar{\mathbf{q}}\bar{\mathbf{l}} < \mathbf{ql} = \mathbf{dp}$, so that the real wage per unit of labour has risen. This proves the first part of (ii).

Conversely (using the same notation), if a truncation is possible which increases the real wage, we have $\bar{\mathbf{y}} \geq \mathbf{0}$, where $\bar{\mathbf{y}}$ is not positive, and

$$\bar{\mathbf{y}}[\mathbf{B} - (1+\bar{r})\mathbf{A}] \geq \mathbf{d}$$

Suppose $\mathbf{p} = [\mathbf{B} - (1+\bar{r})\mathbf{A}]^{-1}\mathbf{l} \geq \mathbf{0}$. We get

$$\bar{\mathbf{y}}[\mathbf{B} - (1+\bar{r})\mathbf{A}]\mathbf{p} \geq \mathbf{dp}$$

The left-hand side equals $\bar{\mathbf{y}}\mathbf{l}$, the right-hand side $\mathbf{ql}$; hence $\bar{\mathbf{y}}\mathbf{l} \geq \mathbf{ql}$, and $\bar{\mathbf{y}}$ is not optimal, which is a contradiction.

(b) Only techniques with non-negative prices appear on the envelope of the wage curves for all truncations, and given $\mathbf{d}$, because of (ii). This is clear for $0 \leq r < \bar{R}$, but it must also be true for $r = \bar{R}$; for, if the technique appearing at $\bar{R}$ had a negative price, this would also be the case, in contradiction to (ii), at $r = \bar{R} - \varepsilon$ for some $\varepsilon > 0$ sufficiently small for the technique on the envelope to be unchanged. This proves (iv) by virtue of the preceding theorem. (i) is then easily derived from (ii) and (iv); it could also be proved similarly to the way in which (ii) was proved under (a), using the extremality properties of the von Neumann system instead of linear programming.

(c) We shall now vary the composition of the real wage to prove (iii). Suppose that the wage curve for a feasible technique I was higher than that of an admissible technique II at $r = \bar{r}$, and I was a truncation of II. Since technique II must then have some negative prices for intermediate goods at $\bar{r}$, it has to remain inferior whatever finished goods enter the real wage. Prices do not depend on the composition of the wage. Hence, prices of finished goods in terms of the wage rate are lower for technique I, i.e. $\hat{\mathbf{p}}_1{}^{\mathrm{I}} < \hat{\mathbf{p}}_1{}^{\mathrm{II}}$. Conversely, if I is a feasible technique and is a truncation of a feasible technique II, the real wage of II must be at least as high as that of I, whatever its composition; hence $\hat{\mathbf{p}}_1{}^{\mathrm{I}} \geqq \hat{\mathbf{p}}_1{}^{\mathrm{II}}$.

(d) Now, suppose that there are two feasible techniques at $\bar{r}$ such that neither is superior to the other, i.e. such that neither $\hat{\mathbf{p}}_1{}^{\mathrm{I}} \leqq \hat{\mathbf{p}}_1{}^{\mathrm{II}}$ nor $\hat{\mathbf{p}}_1{}^{\mathrm{II}} \leqq \hat{\mathbf{p}}_1{}^{\mathrm{I}}$. We have to show that if no technique, III, with either $\hat{\mathbf{p}}_1{}^{\mathrm{III}} \leqq \hat{\mathbf{p}}_1{}^{\mathrm{I}}$ or $\hat{\mathbf{p}}_1{}^{\mathrm{III}} \leqq \hat{\mathbf{p}}_1{}^{\mathrm{II}}$, or both, exists, a contradiction follows.

Since $\hat{\mathbf{p}}_1{}^{\mathrm{I}} > \mathbf{0}$, $\hat{\mathbf{p}}_1{}^{\mathrm{II}} > \mathbf{0}$, and $f \geq 2$ ($f = 1$ is trivial), one can choose a $\mathbf{d} = (d_1, d_2, \ldots d_f; 0, 0, \ldots 0)$ such that $(d_1, d_2, \ldots d_f)\hat{\mathbf{p}}_1{}^{\mathrm{I}} = (d_1, d_2, \ldots d_f)\hat{\mathbf{p}}_1{}^{\mathrm{II}}$. Let $\hat{\mathbf{p}}_1$ be the price vector of finished goods of the original system, and $\delta = \mathbf{d}\hat{\mathbf{p}}_1$. The vector $(1/\delta)\mathbf{d}$ can then be taken as the real wage which appears in the linear programme in (a). Under the assumptions stated, both techniques I and II yield solutions to this programme. Vectors of activity levels $\mathbf{y}^{\mathrm{I}}$ and $\mathbf{y}^{\mathrm{II}}$ and of prices $\mathbf{x}^{\mathrm{I}}$ and $\mathbf{x}^{\mathrm{II}}$ correspond to these solutions. The vectors $(1/2)\mathbf{x}^{\mathrm{I}} + (1/2)\mathbf{x}^{\mathrm{II}}$, $(1/2)\mathbf{y}^{\mathrm{I}} + (1/2)\mathbf{y}^{\mathrm{II}}$ are, then, solutions too. They define a feasible technique, III, of which I and II are both truncations, since an activity level in III is positive if it is positive in either I or II. III is feasible at $\bar{r}$. But, then, $\hat{\mathbf{p}}_1^{\mathrm{III}} \leqq \hat{\mathbf{p}}_1^{\mathrm{I}}$, $\hat{\mathbf{p}}_1^{\mathrm{III}} \leqq \hat{\mathbf{p}}_1^{\mathrm{II}}$, by virtue of (iii), in contradiction to the assumption. (vi) follows from Theorems 9 and 11; (ii), for $\mathbf{p}_2(r)$, cannot be positive at any $r > r_1$ where $w(r) > w(r_1)$.

9 Remarks on the truncation theorems, the choice of techniques and duality

(1) The theorem now proved exhibits an asymmetry which seems puzzling at first sight. Whenever a truncation is advantageous at a given rate of profit, negative prices of machines will indicate it. But the converse is not true. If a truncated system is given, it may have positive prices, and positive prices then mean that it would be advantageous to *reverse* the truncation, provided that the untruncated system also has positive prices.

The apparent paradox is resolved if we think of the truncated system as of an independent fixed-capital system on its own. The processes which could be added to it ('grafted' onto it) appear to lie 'outside' from this point of view, so that the grafted system looks like an alternative technique. The advantage of grafting therefore is revealed only through the possibility of lowering the prices of finished goods in terms of the wage rate. On the other hand, processes which are candidates for truncation always lie within the system, so that the advantage of truncation is directly signalled by negative prices of intermediate goods, and is, in addition, but less directly, revealed through the possibility of lowering prices of finished goods in terms of the wage rate.

The pattern of feasible truncations may nevertheless be quite complicated even at one rate of profit; and it changes in an erratic manner if the rate of profit changes. The optimal lifetimes of machines fluctuate accordingly. In particular, the return of the same truncation at different intervals of the rate of profit is – contrary to what Nuti (1973, pp. 489, 494) emphatically asserts – possible and analogous to reswitching. In the following example, involving two finished goods and one intermediate good,

Corn (*k*)	*New machine* (M_0)	*Old machine* (M_1)	*Labour*	(K)	(M_0)	(M_1)
1/16	0	0	1/10	0	1	0
1/16	1	0	43/40	1	0	1
1/4	0	1	1	1	0	0

truncation is superior between $r = 1/3$ and $r = 1/2$, while the original system is superior between $0 \leq r < 1/3$ and $1/2 < r \leq R$ (where $3 < R < 4$). Accordingly, the price of M_1 is negative between $r = 1/3$ and $r = 1/2$ and positive for $0 \leq r < 1/3$ and $1/2 < r \leq R$. The return of the same truncation is thus possible.

Now it is true that a return of the same truncation cannot occur if a machine is engaged in the production of a finished good i (with price p_i)

without using any finished goods as inputs in the last process (which is to be truncated). For, if a return of the same truncation were possible in such a case, we should have two intervals, $r_1 \leq r \leq r_2$, $r_3 \leq r \leq r_4$, with $0 \leq r_1 < r_2 < r_3 < r_4 \leq R$ such that without loss of generality either the price p_{T-1} of the last machine is positive in the two intervals and negative in between (where it is truncated), or, conversely, p_{T-1} is positive in between and negative in the two intervals. In the former case the untruncated system returns; in the latter the truncated system.

At any rate, we should have $p_{T-1}(r_2) = p_{T-1}(r_3) = 0$ at the switchpoints r_2, r_3. Since the process T using the machine at age $T-1$ does not require any finished goods as inputs, the equation using the machine at age $T-1$ is

$$(1+r)p_{T-1} + wl(T) = b_i^{\prime i}(T)p_i$$

Since at the switchpoints $p_{T-1}(r) = 0$, we get $\hat{p}_i(r_3) = \hat{p}_i(r_2) = (b_i^{\prime i}(T))^{-1}l(T)$. But this is impossible, because the switchpoints are on the envelope. $\hat{p}_i(r)$ is therefore monotonically rising between r_3 and r_4. A return of truncation cannot occur.

This conclusion does not hold if process T uses some finished goods as inputs. The absence of the return of the same truncation is therefore most characteristic for one-machine systems where a new machine is produced by means of (in the primary process) itself and labour, or (in the secondary process) the old machines at various ages and labour alone. The absence of a return of the same truncation is thus analogous to the absence of reswitching in one-commodity circulating-capital systems.

The often-supposed inverse relationship between the rate of interest and the optimum lifetimes of machines need not exist in general. If wages rise, labour for repairing old machines becomes more expensive, but, if the cost of spare parts to be used falls at the same time, in terms of new machines, it may nevertheless be profitable to have the repair work done. Once it is recognised that the economic lifetime of a machine may rise as well as fall with a rise in wages, it becomes less of a surprise to see that truncations may return.

(2) The question naturally arises of what the changing truncations mean in economic terms. As we have presented the problem, the superior technique appears to be superior at any point by a criterion which is similar to that of Pareto optimality. The superior technique is superior in theory because it allows a higher real wage at a *given* rate of profit and a higher rate of profit at the given wage in the same way as general equilibrium is Pareto optimal only relative to a given distribution of initial resources. Hence, not distribution but the chosen technique appears to be justified, and the justification is based not on technical efficiency or productivity, but on the argument that the superior technique provides a distributional advantage

to both classes, given the initial distribution. However, that practical advantage may not be great for the capitalists: if the real wage and total employment are given, it can happen that the technique associated with a higher rate of profit employs so much less 'capital' that total profits are *reduced*, as we shall argue in greater detail below. And, if wages rise to the extent that the rate of profit after the transition is the same it was before, even if the value of capital does not change, the capitalists have no visible gain at all.

The driving force for the adoption of the new technique must therefore come from elsewhere. If the rate of profit stays the same, it arises from surplus profits which accrue to any capitalist who is able to employ the superior method of production in the old system while the old prices are still ruling. The existence of these surplus profits (though not their total amount) is independent of the standard of prices. We show this for an indecomposable singleproduct system $\mathbf{A}, \mathbf{l}$. (The same reasoning applies for the centre of a fixed-capital system.) For simplicity, we assume that $r = 0$. Prices are $\mathbf{p}^{\mathrm{I}}$, where $\mathbf{a}_i\mathbf{p}^{\mathrm{I}} + l_i = p_i^{\mathrm{I}}$; $i = 1, 2, \ldots n$, and where

$$\mathbf{A} = \begin{bmatrix} \mathbf{a}_1 \\ \vdots \\ \mathbf{a}_n \end{bmatrix}, \qquad \mathbf{l} = \begin{bmatrix} l_1 \\ \vdots \\ l_n \end{bmatrix}$$

We assume that the first process, $\mathbf{a}_1, l_1$, can be replaced by an alternative process $\mathbf{a}_0, l_0$ which is superior to $\mathbf{a}_1, l_1$; i.e. there are new prices $\mathbf{p}^{\mathrm{II}} < \mathbf{p}^{\mathrm{I}}$ such that $\mathbf{a}_i\mathbf{p}^{\mathrm{II}} + l_i = p_i^{\mathrm{II}}$, $i = 0, 2, 3, \ldots n$.

Suppose that $\mathbf{a}_0\mathbf{p}^{\mathrm{I}} + l_0 \geqq p_1^{\mathrm{I}}$. Therefore

$$\bar{\mathbf{l}} \geqq (\mathbf{I} - \bar{\mathbf{A}})\mathbf{p}^{\mathrm{I}}$$

where

$$\bar{\mathbf{l}} = \begin{bmatrix} l_0 \\ l_2 \\ \vdots \\ l_n \end{bmatrix}, \qquad \bar{\mathbf{A}} = \begin{bmatrix} \mathbf{a}_1 \\ \mathbf{a}_2 \\ \vdots \\ \mathbf{a}_n \end{bmatrix}$$

Since $(\mathbf{I} - \bar{\mathbf{A}})^{-1} > 0$, it follows that

$$\mathbf{p}^{\mathrm{II}} = (\mathbf{I} - \bar{\mathbf{A}})^{-1}\bar{\mathbf{l}} \geqq \mathbf{p}^{\mathrm{I}}$$

which is a contradiction. Hence,

$$\mathbf{a}_0\mathbf{p}^{\mathrm{I}} + l_0 < p_1^{\mathrm{I}}.$$

which means that a capitalist who employs method $\mathbf{a}_0$, l_0 while prices $\mathbf{p}^{\mathrm{I}}$ still rule obtains a surplus profit. The prices considered in this proof are measured in terms of the wage rate, but the argument clearly does not depend on this assumption. One can also show the converse: once the new prices $\mathbf{p}^{\mathrm{II}}$ rule, it is not possible to return to the former method, $\mathbf{a}_1$, l_1, without incurring a loss.

The technique which we have called superior at a given rate of profit will therefore be introduced through competition even if wages rise to the extent that the rate of profit is not increased. This applies to inventions as well as to the truncations of a given system. Of course, in reality real wages usually do not rise at once when productivity rises. When capitalists decide about the introduction of a new technique, they face a given level of the wage. The transition to the new technique will then raise the general rate of profit.

Our question is now whether any advantage other than the one regarding distribution is associated with the superior technique.

(3) In this context, the dual to the wage–profit relationship is usually invoked, i.e. the curve which relates consumption per head with the rate of balanced growth, g. We derive it as follows: if an (indecomposable) fixed-capital system $\mathbf{A}, \mathbf{B}, \mathbf{l}$ with maximum rate of profit R is given, there exists for each rate of growth g, $0 \leq g < R$, and each vector of finished goods $\mathbf{d} = (d_1, d_2, \ldots d_f; 0, \ldots 0)$ a positive vector $\mathbf{q}$ such that

$$\mathbf{q}[\mathbf{B} - (1+g)\mathbf{A}] = \lambda \mathbf{d}$$

where λ is a positive number. We have proved that $\mathbf{q} > \mathbf{0}$, i.e. that balanced growth is possible at any given g, $0 \leq g < R$. $\lambda \mathbf{d}$ may be interpreted as a vector of goods available for consumption at the rate of balanced growth g.

We define λ to be such that total employment $\mathbf{ql}$ is constant: $\mathbf{ql} = L$. From $\mathbf{q} = \lambda \mathbf{d}[\mathbf{B} - (1+g)\mathbf{A}]^{-1}$, we then get λ as a function of g:

$$\lambda(g) = \frac{\mathbf{ql}}{\mathbf{d}[\mathbf{B} - (1+g)\mathbf{A}]^{-1}\mathbf{l}} = \frac{L}{\mathbf{d}[\mathbf{B} - (1+g)\mathbf{A}]^{-1}\mathbf{l}}$$

National income at rate of growth g physically consists of a baskets of goods $\mathbf{q}(\mathbf{B} - \mathbf{A})$ which divides into investment goods and consumption goods:

$$\mathbf{q}(\mathbf{B} - \mathbf{A}) = g\mathbf{qA} + \lambda \mathbf{d}$$

These goods are valued at prices ruling at rate of profit r. Suppose that prices are normalised in such a way that $\mathbf{dp} = 1$, i.e. the basket of consumption goods is the standard of prices and $w(r) = 1/\mathbf{d\hat{p}}(r)$, hence $\lambda(g) = Lw(g)$. The national accounting identity is

$$\lambda \mathbf{dp} + g\mathbf{qAp} = \mathbf{q}(\mathbf{B} - \mathbf{A})\mathbf{p} = r\mathbf{qAp} + w\mathbf{ql}$$

or, in per capita terms,

$$c + gk = y = rk + w$$

where $c = \lambda \mathbf{dp}/L$ is consumption per head, $k = \mathbf{qAp}/L$ capital per head, $\mathbf{y} = \mathbf{q}(\mathbf{B} - \mathbf{A})\mathbf{p}/L$ national income per head, net of depreciation. Since $\mathbf{dp} = 1$, by definition of the price standard, we have

$$c = \frac{\lambda \mathbf{dp}}{L} = \frac{\lambda(g)}{L} = w(g)$$

Consumption per head, valued at prices ruling at rate of profit r, is therefore equal to what the wage-rate expressed in terms of **d** could be at rate of profit g. For given **d**, we construct c as a function of g.

It follows that $c(g) = w(r)$ for $g = r$; i.e. the curve indicating the level of consumption per head in function of the rate of balanced growth is geometrically the same as the wage curve.

The same well known result holds for every fixed-capital system; in particular, it also holds for all admissible truncations of a given fixed-capital system. Hence, if available consumption per head is to be maximised, that technique or truncation ought to be chosen at a *given* rate of growth, g, which yields the highest real wage at the rate of profit $r = g$. This is the famous golden rule for a fixed-capital system. It is independent of the particular composition of consumption and the real wage as long as both are measured in the same standard basket of finished goods. The rule shows that the technique which is optimal from the point of view of distribution is also optimal from a technical point of view *if* $r = g$.

The elegance of this argument has often been recognised. But it has also been noted that the rate of accumulation does not emerge from a democratic decision-making process in capitalist society, nor is there any mechanism to reduce the rate of profit to the rate of growth. If workers did not save, the capitalists would have to invest all their profits to establish the equality of r and g. The neoclassical authors ought to be the first to recognise that r cannot be expected to be equal to g, for they insist that capitalists invest in order to consume. Everybody agrees that the capitalist's right to consume part of the surplus is an essential feature of capitalism, and the capitalists use their right individually and collectively.

(4) We now want to consider the effects of not following the golden rule. To this end, we need a graphic representation of the duality relations. Following von Weizsäcker (1963, 1971) we draw consumption per head and the wage curve for a given technique in the same diagram. If $0 \leq g < r < R$, it follows from the national-income identity $c + gk = w + rk$

that

$$k = \frac{c - w}{r - g}$$

i.e. capital per head is equal to $tg\alpha$ in Figure 7.3. It follows from Theorem 11 that $k = tg\alpha$ is always positive, i.e. $c(g) > w(r)$, if the wage curve represents the superior truncation at r, although the wage curve may be rising (and inferior to some other truncation) in the neighbourhood of g.

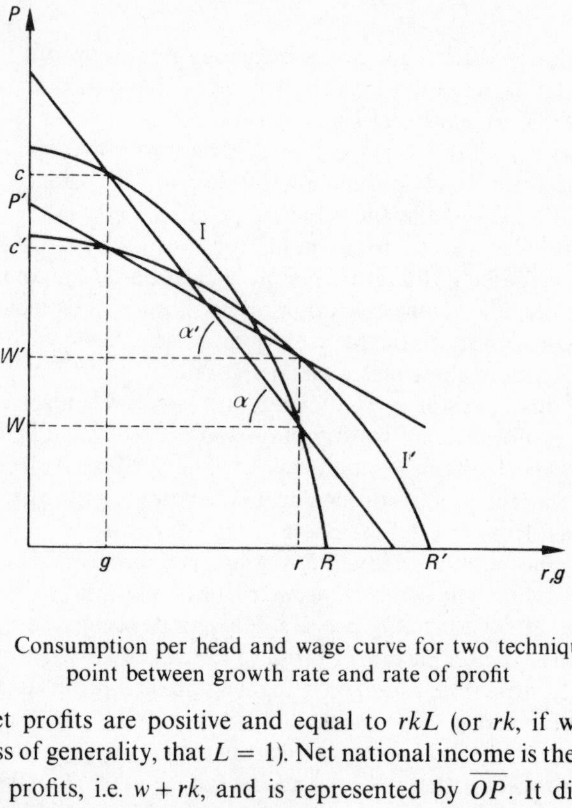

FIGURE 7.3 Consumption per head and wage curve for two techniques: switchpoint between growth rate and rate of profit

Total net profits are positive and equal to rkL (or rk, if we assume, without loss of generality, that $L = 1$). Net national income is then equal to wages and profits, i.e. $w + rk$, and is represented by $\overline{OP}$. It divides into consumption c and investment $y - c$.

If a new technique is introduced with employment ($L = 1$), rates of profit, r, and growth, g, all unchanged, it is possible that consumption per head at the given rate of growth falls, while the wage rate at the given rate of profit rises. This will happen if and only if the wage curves of the two techniques have an odd number of switchpoints in common – a situation which is quite likely to occur if we believe Sraffa (1960, section 95; see also Bharadwaj, 1970):

> We can now extend the supposition of an alternative method for producing one commodity and suppose that there are many such alternatives with at least as many distinct points of intersection; and not only for one of the products, but for each of them. So that as the rate of profit rises there will be a rapid succession of switches in the methods of production of one or the other of the commodities.

The introduction of the new technique is advantageous to the capitalists in that those earn surplus profits who first make the transition to the new technique, while all workers earn higher wages.

Yet, consumption per head falls. Why? Because the value of total capital has fallen to the extent that total profits fall (in Figure 7.3, national income falls to OP' while wages rise to w'). Hence, the pursuit of surplus profits on the part of some capitalists leads to a fall in profits for the class as a whole if employment stays constant.

From the point of view of economic theory, the fall in profit is perhaps more disturbing than the fall in consumption, for, if all saving is out of profits, it is capitalists' consumption which must necessarily suffer, since wages go up. It is true that traditional economic theory has mostly acknowledged that the working of competition may reduce the income of capitalists while it benefits others. But the situation is incompatible with neoclassical theory under the assumption of perfect foresight and a 'distant' time horizon. For, in neoclassical theory, the capitalists invest in the new technique in order to be able to consume later. If the attraction of temporary surplus profits lures them into adopting techniques that reduce their collective consumption, their foresight must be deficient. This is true, at any rate, for the capitalist class as a whole. The fall in his capital–labour ratio enables the *individual* capitalist to expand his business by investing the difference between the amortisation funds required for the old technique and those required for the new. But this will not be possible for all capitalists if employment is constant. A struggle for survival between the capitalists ensues. There will be an excess of funds. It may, together with the reduction of the capital–labour ratio, also stimulate investment and lead to increased employment. It will then be beneficial for the economy as a whole: the fall of profits per man employed is compensated by an increased mass of total profits. Conversely, if there is a transition to a technique with a higher capital–labour ratio, there is a need for more funds, or, more generally, a higher level of investment, if no unemployment is to arise. The crux is that changes of the capital–labour ratio imply changes of relative shares, if the rate of profit stays constant.

If the choice of technique leads to a fall in consumption per head, profits per man employed fall; but the converse is not always true. A fall in profits may result without a fall in consumption, for if r, g, L are given and all saving is out of profits, both total profits and profits for consumption fall with any fall in the capital–labour ratio. Total consumption is maintained if wages rise sufficiently. A fall in profits may thus occur even if the two techniques have no switchpoints in common, and the golden rule ($r = g$) makes no exception.

There is one case where the fall in profits per man employed is necessarily associated with a fall in consumption per head. That is when the rate of growth is zero and the wage is given. It is the case analysed by the classical economists. Their theory of accumulation starts from a stationary system with a given 'subsistence' wage. It is not necessary, however, to confine one's attention to this simplest case in order to explain the (at first sight paradoxical) situation where the capitalists who choose the technique with the aim of maximising profits end up by reducing them. It will be seen that it cannot be excluded *a priori* that new techniques which reduce output per head are introduced from time to time, when a lower capital–labour ratio makes their introduction profitable for the individual capitalist. But we shall try to argue why the main thrust of technical progress takes different forms.

(5) Next we consider a special consequence of the inequality of r and g. As soon as it is admitted that the rate of growth and the rate of profit will diverge, there is a new meaning to negative prices. If the rate of profit is 'normal' and the rate of growth is low, say near zero, the technique chosen at the ruling rate of profit may have positive prices and yet be compatible with negative labour values of old machines. As we have seen, the negative labour values indicate that the same net product could be produced with less labour if the old machines having negative values were scrapped. A truncation which is appropriate at the given rate of profit may thus imply a *waste of social labour*. This solves the 'paradox of negative labour values' referred to earlier and provides a satisfactory explanation for the inefficiency of old machines.

(6) Of course, one should always bear in mind that actual prices (market prices) deviate from the prices of production which we are considering. Even if the average rate of profit were equal to the average rate of growth, the deviation of individual market prices from prices of production might prevent the adoption of the 'correct' technique or truncation. It is often not sufficiently well realised that the assumption of a correct choice of technique implies a far-reaching assumption about the correct working of an economic mechanism. Thus, the problem of truncation is usually concealed under the heading of 'free disposal'. One eagerly discusses whether it is realistic to assume that all waste products can be eliminated free of charge or how commodities with miraculous rates of self-reproduction

(Koopman's rabbits) can be eliminated from the von Neumann system as overproduced goods. One does not see that the chief question is whether accounting practices are sufficiently sophisticated and market prices sufficiently close to prices of production to determine when old machines (the main 'waste products') ought to be scrapped, or, more generally, which joint products are economically useful.

In the real world the problem of truncation is even more complicated than in our most involved examples, because depreciation is influenced by expectations about technical progress. (If there is no uncertainty, obsolescent machines of an old type which are still being used, but not produced, can in principle be dealt with through a theory of quasi-rent [see Sraffa, 1960, p. 78]. We shall not try to generalise the model in this direction, however.)

(7) Having stated that the deviation of market prices from prices of production, and the deviation of the rate of growth from the rate of profit may easily lead to an inefficient choice of techniques and to a waste of social labour, we are left with a formidable problem. Nobody denies, least of all the Marxist school, that capitalism fosters technical progress – in particular, the productivity of labour. Orthodox growth theory is concerned with the following 'stylised facts': constant shares, constant rate of profit, constant capital–output ratio, with output per head and wage rate continuously rising with productivity.

This implies that the wage curve (assuming that it is more or less straight) shifts upwards at its left end by turning round a constant maximum rate of profit so that the capital–labour ratio rises continuously while labour values fall, expressing the fact that output per head goes up. Diagrammatically this may be expressed as in Figure 7.4.

So far we have not found any reason whatever which could lead us to expect that this particular constellation is more likely to be found in reality than is any other. How can technical progress then come about as a result of the capitalist drive for profit, if prices are as poor a guide for the choice of technique as we have made them to be? There has been much controversy about the importance of reswitching, but, if there is only one switch between the rate of growth and the rate of profit, the technique chosen will be suboptimal, and consumption per head will be reduced. It cannot be denied that this may really happen sometimes, if a new technique reduces total profits even when the wage does not rise, but surely it does not occur very frequently. Why not? This is a puzzle, and I can do no more than offer, at the end of this essay, a few preliminary ideas for its solution.

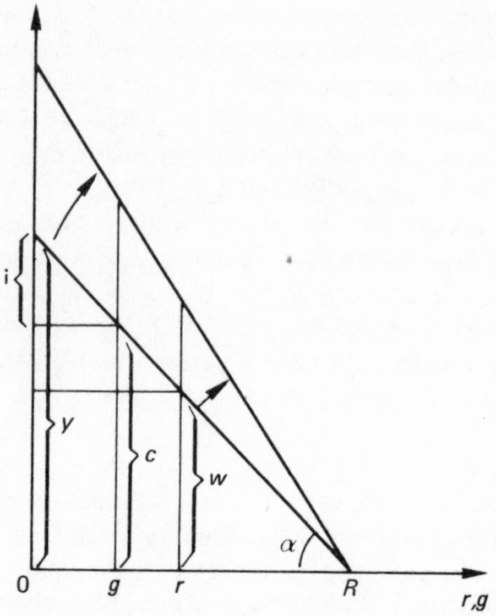

FIGURE 7.4 'Stylised facts': the wage curve is a straight line, and technical progress causes it to turn round the maximum rate of profit. y is output, i investment, c consumption, w wage, all in per capita terms. If workers do not save, $c - w$ is profits consumed, i profits invested (per man employed). The capital–labour ratio equals $tg\alpha$, and the capital–output ratio k/y is the reciprocal of OR and stays constant.

10 Reconsidering some assumptions

The notation in this essay has been chosen with a view to making it easy for the reader to check which results are modified if certain assumptions are relaxed. One verifies, for instance, that superimposed joint production does not alter the main conclusions as long as Lemma 1 remains true; i.e., essentially, as long as prices of finished goods are positive between $r = 0$ and a positive maximum rate of profit. However, superimposed joint production is in general not compatible with this condition, since not even labour values of finished goods are necessarily positive as soon as some primary processes are not indispensable. The problem of superimposed joint production can therefore only be dealt with in the context of a more general theory of joint production. Reasonably satisfactory conditions can be found to eliminate the possibility of negative prices of finished goods, but we shall not pursue the matter any further here. (cf. Schefold 1978c).

It is more interesting to inquire what happens when more than one machine is engaged in the production of a finished good.

Suppose, first, that trade of old machines between groups is still excluded. The set of machines used in the production of a finished good i consists, then, of, say, g_i machines with physical lifetimes $T_{i,1}, \ldots T_{i,g_i}$. The integrated process will start with g_i new machines. Whenever a machine reaches the end of its physical lifetime, it has to be replaced by a new one until, after a time equal to the minimum common multiple of $T_{i,1}, \ldots T_{i,g_i}$, all machines are worn out simultaneously. Of course, it will in general be profitable to scrap some machines earlier than that. By looking at all possible combinations, the optimum truncation can (at least in theory) be determined as above, since each possible combination of old machines can be considered as *one* commodity or composite machine at the appropriate age. This is permissible as long as trade between groups is ruled out, so that only the relative values of the different combinations of machines have to be determined; the relative prices of old machines need not be known separately. (Relative prices of new machines are given.) If, for example, two machines, a lorry M and a trailer N, which last two and three years respectively, are given, there will be six equations: symbolically,

$$\begin{aligned}
&M_0, N_0 \rightarrow M_1, N_1 \\
&M_1, N_1 \rightarrow N_2 \\
&M_0, N_2 \rightarrow M_1 \\
&M_1, N_0 \rightarrow N_1 \\
&M_0, N_1 \rightarrow M_1, N_2 \\
&M_1, N_2 \rightarrow \text{—}
\end{aligned}$$

The equations determine the prices of the five 'composite' old machines (M_1, N_1), (N_2), (M_1), (N_1), (M_1, N_2); the second, third and fourth are each to be used in conjunction with a new machine (finished goods M_0, N_0, M_0, respectively).

Difficulties arise only when we allow for trade between groups. It will then be possible that the relative price of two old machines used in the production of finished good 1 is determined in the production of finished good 2. Consider an example: there are two kinds of machines, blast furnaces M and lorries N, each lasting for two years (M_0, M_1, N_0, N_1), and together producing steel (G), by which they are also produced. Old and new lorries are then used to produce corn (X):

$$\begin{aligned}
&(1+r)G_1 p_g + w l_1 = M_0 p_{m0} \\
&(1+r)G_2 p_g + w l_2 = N_0 p_{n0} \\
&(1+r)(M_0 p_{m0} + N_0 p_{n0}) + w l_3 = G_3 p_g + M_1 p_{m1} + N_1 p_{n1} \\
&(1+r)(M_1 p_{m1} + N_1 p_{n1}) + w l_4 = G_4 p_g \\
&(1+r)(N_0 p_{n0} + X_1 p_x) + w l_5 = X_2 p_x + N_1 p_{n1} \\
&(1+r)(N_1 p_{n1} + X_3 p_x) + w l_6 = X_4 p_x
\end{aligned}$$

The system is basic, yet corn emerges as a non-basic in the integrated system:

$$(1+r)G_1 p_g + wl_1 = M_0 p_{m0}$$
$$(1+r)G_2 p_g + wl_2 = N_0 p_{n0}$$
$$(1+r)^2(M_0 p_{m0} + N_0 p_{n0}) + w[(1+r)l_3 + l_4] = [(1+r)G_3 + G_4]p_g$$
$$(1+r)^2 N_0 p_{n0} + [(1+r)^2 X_1 + (1+r)X_3]p_x + w[(1+r)l_5 + l_6] = [(1+r)X_2 + X_4]p_x$$

A non-basic integrated system is not a grave anomaly. Some adaptations of results have to be made, but, as long as the integrated system is not completely disconnected, the essential characteristics of the model do not have to be altered. (Note that M_1, N_1 have to be treated as a composite commodity in the standard system. The equations for the production of corn cannot enter it, despite the fact that corn is basic in Sraffa's sense.) The essential condition for our model to work unaltered even when trade of old machines exists between groups is that the groups do in fact have a separate existence, i.e. that the equations involving the same machine can be combined into an integrated process producing one and only one finished good. This condition is violated if an intermediate good is transferred from the production of one finished good to that of another. If, for example, a racehorse (M) is transferred from racing (G) to breeding (X),

$$(1+r)M_0 p_{m0} + wl_1 = G_1 p_g + M_1 p_{m1}$$
$$(1+r)M_1 p_{m1} + wl_2 = G_2 p_g + M_2 p_{m2}$$
$$(1+r)M_2 p_{m2} + wl_3 = X_3 p_x + M_3 p_{m3}$$
$$(1+r)M_3 p_{m3} + wl_4 = X_4 p_x$$

the corresponding integrated equation contains two joint products. Such transfers raise essentially the same problems as superimposed joint production (the same conclusion was also reached by Mirrlees, 1969) and cannot be discussed separately from a discussion of joint production in general.

Let us now try to apply the theory of prices of production to the analysis of technical progress.

PART III

11 Simple forms of technical progress: saving of labour, mechanisation and saving of raw material

The Clark-type production function, which is still hovering about in countless textbooks, resembles in this the Flying Dutchman, who has perished many times and cannot die. Most academic economists still share a stubborn belief that there must be some meaning to the ideas of substitution between 'capital' and 'labour'. They invoke the authority of natural laws to prove that if you want to produce the same amount of Y using L, you will have to sacrifice more K. If a trade-off exists for labour and land, why not for labour and capital?

The trouble with all theories based on the presumption that a measurable entity called 'capital' is sacrificed as a 'factor of production' is, as we know, twofold (take the case where capital is supposed to be substituted for labour because of a rise in the real wage and where the 'book of blueprints' is given). On the one hand (at the 'microlevel'), the capitalist who needs more money to buy additional or different capital goods gets the money from the banks without a discernible sacrifice on his own part. On the other (at the 'macrolevel'), the price of the capital goods used to substitute for too-expensive labour may be such that the overall capital–labour ratio falls. Not more, but less, capital was needed to 'substitute' for labour. The rate of profit has fallen, but the naïve, fetishistic idea that 'giving money away', 'investing', 'buying means of production', 'using more capital' are all one and the same thing, has not been born out; 'capital' is 'cheaper', although it is less 'plentiful'. Neither the dubious sacrifice involved in taking (mostly somebody else's) money to obtain more capital, nor the 'productivity of capital', nor both, can be used to explain the rate of profit.

Once this is recognised (the complete refutation takes more than the above, of course), we are left with the task of explaining how microeconomic investment decisions really interact with relations between macroeconomic quantities. The Walrasian theory is unsuited to such an analysis. The reasons for its failure do not concern us here. Suffice it to state that the neoclassical economists have never been able to show how their *piece de résistance*, general equilibrium analysis, could be used to discuss the interaction between the choice of techniques and technical progress, on the one hand, and distribution and investment, on the other. By contrast, the chief function of the theory of value of the classical economists, in particular Ricardo, is that of providing a rigorous 'microeconomic' basis for the theory of accumulation, technical progress, and the long-term trend of distribution. Marx went still further in this direction. He undertook vast studies of the history of technology and related it to the evolution of the productive relations. The chapters in *Das Kapital* on co-operation, on the division of labour and on modern industry are the best-known distillates of that research. What is less well understood is how these chapters link up with his theory of accumulation. Although they are interesting for other reasons too, the central chapters in the first volume of *Das Kapital* have the function of providing the main argument for the theory of the falling rate of profit, which is completed in the third volume, where Marx's theory of accumulation reaches its culmination.

The purpose of the present section is to throw some light on this particular aspect of the Marxian theory. We take up only two or three points, and, for simplicity, we identify the Sraffa prices we have been analysing with Marxian prices of production. The analysis must naturally concentrate on technical progress; the real process of accumulation will not be considered in detail.

The historically first and conceptually simplest form of technical progress is the division of labour. A capitalist assembles artisans with their tools in a workshop and is thereby able to raise the productivity of their labour without providing a machine, because he imposes working discipline and improves performance through enforced specialisation.[14] Since the amount of raw materials remains basically the same, this form of technical progress implies that in a single-product system some coefficients in the labour vector fall, while the input matrix remains the same. The wage curve is shifted upwards for all rates of profit smaller than the maximum. This type of progress can therefore be introduced at every point of the wage curve (except R). If the wage rate is fixed, the rate of profit rises, while, if income distribution, i.e. the ratio P/W of profits P to wages W, tends to remain constant, the rate of profit will tend to stay the same while wages rise.

To prove the latter point, note that

$$\frac{P}{W}=\frac{P}{K}\cdot\frac{K}{W}=r\cdot\omega$$

where $\omega = K/W$ is the ratio of total capital to wages or the 'organic composition of capital' in price terms.[15] It is a pure number and independent of the standard of prices for a given technique and a given composition of output (activity levels). As such, it is a superior concept to the capital–labour ratio, which is dimensionally hybrid. Moreover, it does not exhibit 'Wicksell price effects', for the organic composition of capital rises monotonically with the rate of profit for a given technique, since it is equal to total capital measured in terms of labour commanded, divided by total labour employed, and since prices in terms of labour commanded rise monotonically with the rate of profit. Symbolically;

$$\omega=\frac{K}{W}=\frac{\mathbf{qAp}}{w\mathbf{ql}}=\frac{\mathbf{qA\hat{p}}}{\mathbf{ql}}=\mathbf{qA\hat{p}}$$

if $\mathbf{ql} = 1$, where $\mathbf{q}$ represents fixed activity levels.

[14] The raising of efficiency is preceded by a prolonged period during which the capitalist does nothing but subordinate a heterogeneous workforce to his discipline. At first he reaps profits by stretching the working day to its physical limits, while the real wage remains unchanged. This is what Marx calls 'production of absolute surplus value'. The process is discussed with great insight by Marglin (1971), but we, by contrast, are only concerned with the 'production of relative surplus value'.

[15] I apologise for my not-quite-accurate translations of Marx's terms into those of Sraffa.

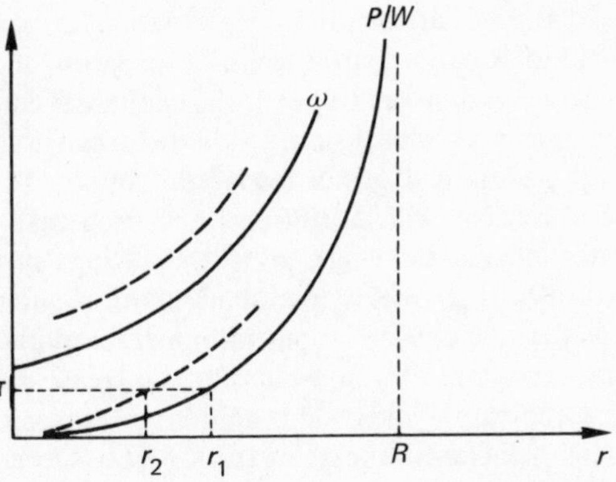

FIGURE 7.5 Showing that, if the curve for ω shifts upwards because of a technical change, the P/W curve also shifts upwards. As in Marx, the rate of profit then falls from r_1 to r_2 in consequence of the technical change, if P/W is given and equal to π.

Suppose now that the increasing division of labour in the above restricted sense proceeds in all industries at the same pace, so that the labour vector falls by some factor $\alpha < 1$. As a consequence, all prices at a given rate of profit will also fall by a factor α.

$$\hat{\mathbf{p}} = [\mathbf{I} - (1+r)\mathbf{A}]^{-1}\mathbf{l}$$

becomes

$$[\mathbf{I} - (1+r)\mathbf{A}]^{-1}\alpha\mathbf{l} = \alpha\hat{\mathbf{p}}, \qquad \alpha < 1$$

Consequently, the organic composition of capital stays constant and the distribution of income remains invariant with increasing technical progress, if the rate of profit remains constant while the wage rate increases in every standard. Conversely, if P/W remains constant, the rate of profit remains constant, since the organic composition does not change.

The result is neat and clear if all components of the labour vector fall evenly. If some sectors gain more in productivity than others, it will still be true that a fall in a component of the labour vector does not necessarily raise the organic composition of capital, since the fall in wages paid per unit of output will be compensated to some extent by the fall in prices of raw materials at the given rate of profit. Thus, the overall effect always tends to be 'neutral' for given r; the organic composition of capital tends to stay constant despite the fact that the physical 'ratio' of capital goods to labour has risen.

So far we have only been comparing different steady states, and the real process of accumulation has not been discussed. To discuss it, many other elements would have to be considered – in particular, thriftiness conditions.

Suffice it to say that, since an overall saving of labour is, paradoxically, the archetypical form of Harrod neutral technical progress, the economy will sustain a golden age, once it has begun, if the capitalists continue to invest and save at constant rates and if no outside disturbance takes place – for example, through abrupt changes in the labour supply. The rate of profit (supposed to be uniform) will be constant and such that the investment process generates adequate savings, given the savings propensity of the capitalists. The uniform gradual reduction in labour requirements per unit of output means that the capital–labour ratio measured in terms of labour commanded stays constant as well, while wages increase with productivity in a state of near-full employment. This golden age corresponds exactly to the 'stylised facts' mentioned above, in section 9(7). Other constellations than this golden age are conceivable, but they will not be discussed here.

We now consider a different form of technical progress: *mechanisation*. The capitalist buys a newly developed machine and employs some workers to produce a commodity which was previously produced by artisans. Mechanisation means, therefore, the introduction of a roundabout process as defined in section 9(7) above. We shall now add the assumption that mechanisation as such does not permit the saving of raw materials. (Saving of raw materials will be considered separately). We ignore the tools used by the artisan. In a more modern context it would be equivalent to assume that mechanisation means the replacement of an old machine by a new one, using the same raw materials, after the old machine has been written off.

It is then an admissible abstraction to assume that production by means of the machine requires in each year of its lifetime at least as much of each raw material (such as cotton) per unit of output (such as cloth) as is required by the artisans. We assume also, for simplicity's sake, that the process to be replaced uses circulating capital only and is the first in the system; as such, it is denoted by $\bar{\mathbf{a}}_1, \bar{l}_1$. Suppose, now, a new process $\mathbf{a}_0, l_0$ is introduced which produces the machine by means of (without loss of generality) circulating capital only. The T_1 new processes producing the first good by means of the machine (taken together with the process $\mathbf{a}_0, l_0$ producing the machine) give rise to the centre coefficients

$$\hat{a}_1{}^j(r) = \frac{\sum_{t=0}^{T_1} (1+r)^{T_1-t} a_1{}^j(t)}{\sum_{t=1}^{T_1} (1+r)^{T_1-t} b_1{}^1(t)}$$

$$\hat{l}_1(r) = \frac{\sum_{t=0}^{T_1} (1+r)^{T_1-t} l_1(t)}{\sum_{t=1}^{T_1} (1+r)^{T_1-t} b_1{}^1(t)}$$

where $a_1{}^j(0) = a_0{}^j$, $l_1(0) = l_0$, $j = 1, 2, \ldots f$.

Our assumption about the impossibility of saving raw materials by means of mechanisation (the importance of this assumption can be inferred from the example in the appendix to section 7 above) can now be expressed as

$$\mathbf{a}_1(t) \geqq \bar{\mathbf{a}}_1 b_1{}^1(t), \qquad t = 1, 2, \ldots T_1$$

This implies $\hat{\mathbf{a}}_1(r) \geqq \bar{\mathbf{a}}_1$ for $r \geq 0$. At any one rate of profit $\bar{r}$ where the roundabout process is superior, it must yield a lower price of production for good 1. We must therefore have

$$\hat{l}_1(\bar{r}) < \overline{l_1}$$

We now denote by $\hat{\mathbf{p}}_1^{\mathrm{I}}(r)$ the vector of prices of finished goods in terms of the wage rate corresponding to the old technique. We assume that at each rate of profit the best truncation is chosen in the old system. Each component of $\hat{\mathbf{p}}_1^{\mathrm{I}}(r)$ will then be a continuous and monotonically rising function of r between zero and a maximum rate of profit R_{I}. Equally, the real wage, measured in some basket of finished goods, will be denoted by w_{I}. w_{I} is a monotonically falling function of r. It may have corners which correspond to truncations. The old and the new method will be equally profitable if and only if

$$(1+r)\hat{\mathbf{a}}_1(r)\hat{\mathbf{p}}_1{}^{\mathrm{I}} + \hat{l}_1(r) = (1+r)\bar{\mathbf{a}}_1\,\hat{\mathbf{p}}_1{}^{\mathrm{I}}(r) + \overline{l_1}$$

i.e. if and only if

$$(1+r)[\hat{\mathbf{a}}_1(r) - \bar{\mathbf{a}}_1]\hat{\mathbf{p}}_1{}^{\mathrm{I}} = \overline{l_1} - \hat{l}_1(r)$$

We shall now assume that $\hat{\mathbf{a}}_1(r)$ and $\hat{l}_1(r)$ are monotonically increasing functions of the rate of profit. This is a crucial assumption; it will, however, easily be fulfilled. It does not exclude moderately falling physical efficiency of the machine, since the polynomials in the nominators of $\hat{\mathbf{a}}_1(r)$ and $\hat{l}_1(r)$ are of greater degree than those in the denominators and since all mechanical processes must satisfy $\mathbf{a}_1(t) \geqq \bar{\mathbf{a}}_1 b_1{}^1(t)$.

Under this second assumption about roundabout processes, expressing mechanisation, the left-hand side of the above equation is a monotonically rising function of r, the right-hand side is monotonically falling. There exists, therefore, at most one intersection, corresponding to a switchpoint between the techniques.

Next we note that the maximum rate of profit of the new system, R_{II}, is lower than R_{I}. For, since $\hat{\mathbf{a}}_1(R_{\mathrm{I}}) \geq \mathbf{a}_1$, the centre coefficients $\hat{\mathbf{A}}_{\mathrm{II}}(r)$ of the new system are not smaller and some are greater than those of the old system $\hat{\mathbf{A}}_{\mathrm{I}}(r)$ at $r = R_{\mathrm{I}}$, so that

$$\hat{\mathbf{A}}_{\mathrm{II}}(R_{\mathrm{I}}) \geq \hat{\mathbf{A}}_{\mathrm{I}}(R_{\mathrm{I}})$$

Hence

$$\text{dom}\,[(1+R_{\text{I}})\hat{\mathbf{A}}_{\text{II}}(R_{\text{I}})] > \text{dom}\,[(1+R_{\text{I}})\,\hat{\mathbf{A}}_{\text{I}}(R_{\text{I}})] = 1$$

which implies, by definition of the maximum rate of profit in a fixed-capital system,

$$R_{\text{II}} < R_{\text{I}}$$

It follows that the new technique will have at least one switchpoint with the old, since we assume that the more mechanical technique is profitable at least at one rate of profit. Taking both results together, we find that there is one and only one switchpoint: the curve of the real wage in the new system, $w_{\text{II}}(r)$, intersects $w_{\text{I}}(r)$ in one and only one point, and from above.

One minor correction remains to be made: we have taken account of truncation in the old system only, not in the new one. We must suppose that our assumptions about roundabout processes expressing mechanisation are fulfilled for each admissible truncation. Each of these wage curves will then cut w_{I} in exactly one point, and from above. Hence, the same is true for their envelope w_{II}. w_{I} and w_{II} are both monotonically falling.

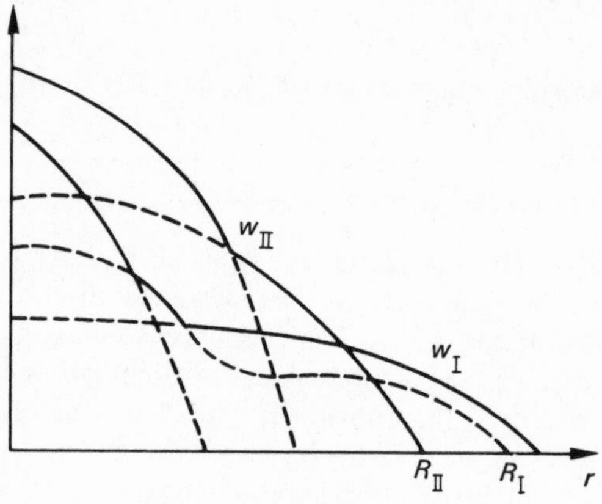

FIGURE 7.6

We may now imagine the successive introduction of a series of roundabout processes expressing increasing mechanisation. At each step the maximum rate of profit falls, while the amount of labour required per unit of gross output diminishes. The techniques can then be ordered hierarchically according to the maximum rate of profit; intermediate techniques may sometimes not appear on the envelope, but no technique appears on it twice. Figure 7.7 shows the two possible constellations for the intermediate technique (II) if three techniques are given.

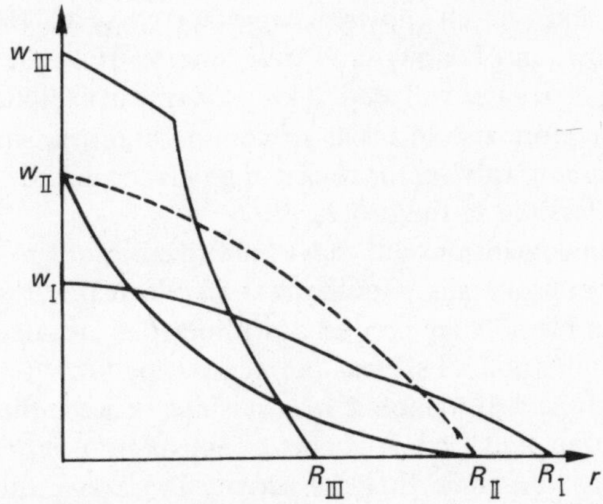

FIGURE 7.7

The diagram looks familiar. Is this perhaps the neoclassical parable? I do not think so. First of all, mechanisation is a special form of technical progress. It occurs at all times, but it may have been dominant only during the Industrial Revolution. The form of accumulation associated with it is far from the neoclassical equilibrium world, where the emphasis is on alternative *given* techniques. The considerable increase in the amount of raw materials used in the more mechanised techniques implies an increase in cost that can be offset only through an even more considerable displacement of labour, if the financial means of each enterprise are not increased and production is not expanded to absorb the redundant labour force. The social importance of this technological unemployment is made to disappear in neoclassical theory where one abstracts from autonomous investment and considers the techniques as alternatives for a stable equilibrium which adapts to savings and the labour supply.

But, even if we look at mechanisation from the neoclassical point of view and consider the various processes not as emerging from technical progress, but as a set of blueprints with the possibility of substitution between them, and if full employment is simply assumed, income distribution can still not be determined by the 'marginal product of capital' in combination with time preferences; the absence of reswitching is not a sufficient condition for the existence of a proper 'marginal product of capital' (see Garegnani, 1970).

The process of increasing mechanisation was analysed in a quite different manner by Ricardo and Marx. In Ricardo's account the capitalists manage to keep the rate of profit constant so that the rate of exploitation (P/W) rises. In Marx there is a complicated interplay between the rate of exploitation and the rate of profits. The basic story – or, rather, what Marx ought to have said – is well known: technical progress will tend to raise the organic composition of capital and thus tend to bring the rate of profit down, since class struggle will tend to keep the rate of exploitation in check. Wages will therefore rise in terms of commodities; the value of labour power, i.e. the labour value of the basket of goods consumed by the workers, may none the less *fall* in the process.[16]

The Marxian conclusions are easily confirmed in our model. Since the maximum rate of profit falls as mechanisation is increased, the actual rate of profit is susceptible of being pressed down somehow, whatever happens to the rate of exploitation. (This was pointed out by Okishio, 1961.)

To bring out the real economic relationships between the rate of profit and the rate of exploitation, it is convenient to start with an unrealistic assumption, i.e. to assume that the activity levels are equal to the von Neumann expansion vector – in other words, that the economy is in 'balanced proportions' irrespective of the fact that the rate of profit will be lower than its maximum (and the rate of growth in all probability will be much lower).

Under this assumption, we have

$$(1+R)\mathbf{qA} = \mathbf{qB}$$

hence

$$R\mathbf{qA}(\mathbf{B}-\mathbf{A})^{-1} = \mathbf{q}$$

$$\mathbf{q}[\mathbf{I} - r\mathbf{A}(\mathbf{B}-\mathbf{A})^{-1}] = \frac{R-r}{R}\mathbf{q}$$

[16] This may look surprising to some, since the real wage expressed in commodities is often confused with the value of labour power. In our model the real wage in terms of commodities is simply w, where $w = 1/\mathbf{d}\hat{\mathbf{p}}$ (total labour equals one). Suppose that workers consume a multiple λ of the basket of finished goods, $\mathbf{d} = (d_1, d_2, \ldots d_f; 0, 0, \ldots 0)$, which serves as our standard of measurement. Clearly, $\lambda = w$, since the price of the wage goods is equal to the wage: $(\lambda\mathbf{d})\mathbf{p} = w$. The value v of labour power becomes

$$v = (\lambda\mathbf{d})\hat{\mathbf{p}}(0) = \frac{w(r)}{w(0)} = \frac{\mathbf{d}\hat{\mathbf{p}}(0)}{\mathbf{d}\hat{\mathbf{p}}(r)}$$

The values, i.e. $\hat{\mathbf{p}}(0)$, may fall faster than $w(r)$, the real wage, rises; i.e. $\hat{\mathbf{p}}(0)$ may fall faster than $\hat{\mathbf{p}}(r)$. Hence it becomes a logical possibility that the value of labour power and the rate of profit fall simultaneously as the wage curve shifts upwards with technical progress.

Using this formula, we can calculate the organic composition of capital K/W as defined above.

$$\frac{K}{W}=\frac{\mathbf{qAp}}{w\mathbf{ql}}=\frac{\mathbf{qA\hat{p}}}{\mathbf{ql}}=\frac{1}{\mathbf{ql}}\mathbf{qA}[\mathbf{B}-(1+r)\mathbf{A}]^{-1}\mathbf{l}$$

$$=\frac{1}{\mathbf{ql}}\mathbf{qA}(\mathbf{B}-\mathbf{A})^{-1}[\mathbf{I}-r\mathbf{A}(\mathbf{B}-\mathbf{A})^{-1}]^{-1}\mathbf{l}=\frac{1}{\mathbf{ql}}\frac{1}{R}\frac{R}{R-r}\mathbf{ql}$$

$$=\frac{1}{R-r}$$

Thus, it immediately follows that the organic composition rises at a given rate of profit if the maximum rate of profit falls in consequence of the introduction of mechanisation and if the activity levels are in balanced proportions both in the old system and in the new.

On the other hand, the rate of exploitation P/W is equal to

$$\frac{P}{W}=\frac{P}{K}\cdot\frac{K}{W}=r\frac{K}{W}=\frac{r}{R-r}$$

It is a monotonically rising function for $0\leq r<R$. Therefore, if the workers are sufficiently organised to check the tendency of P/W to rise, they will force down the rate of profit as the organic composition increases.[17]

If the economy is not in standard proportions, we have to resort to a geometric argument. The organic composition $\omega=K/W$ equals k/w where k is the capital–labour ratio and w the real wage rate, both measured in terms of the basket of wage goods **d**. In the familiar wage–curve/consumption-per-head diagram (see Figure 7.8), ω is the reciprocal of $\overline{P_1P_2}$, since $k=tg\alpha$.

[17] If we add another bad assumption and suppose that the wage bundle **d** is equal to the standard net product $\mathbf{q}(\mathbf{B}-\mathbf{A})$, we get Sraffa's straight-line relationship for the real wage (see above, section 4). Since $w(0)=1$, and since we assume that $\mathbf{d}=\mathbf{q}(\mathbf{B}-\mathbf{A})$, the 'standard real wage' is equal to the value of labour power: $v=1-(r/R)$ (see note 16). By eliminating r, we can combine these with the equation for P/W and obtain $P/W=1/v-1$, independently of r and R. Hence, if mechanisation lowers R, and r falls only a little because P/W rises, v falls too. Those who maintain that Marx was wrong on logical grounds in claiming a simultaneous fall of the value of labour power and the rate of profit are thus mistaken. The contention is also factually incorrect. Marx's point in *Das Kapital* is neither that the average real wage of the employed workers falls in the process of accumulation at full capacity, nor that the value of labour power falls. He only envisages a fall in living standards for either a reserve army without public support or as a general condition during crises when capacity is idle. This has nothing to do with Lassalle's 'iron law of wages' which is still attributed to Marx in some modern textbooks. Lassalle's slogan was taken up by 'opportunist' German Social Democrats towards the end of the nineteenth century, although Marx had fought it vehemently.

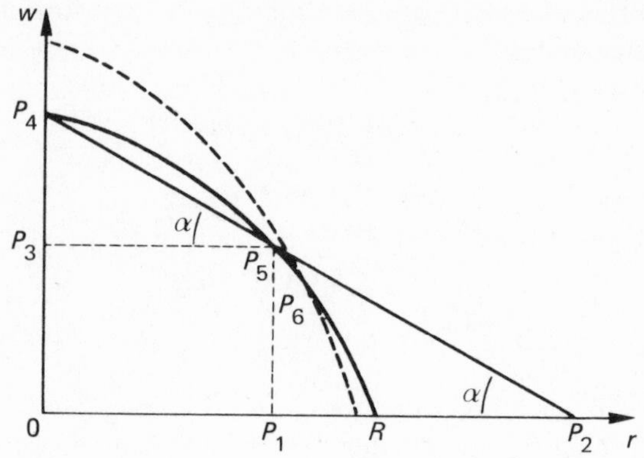

FIGURE 7.8 For simplicity, it is assumed that $g = 0$. For the same reason, a smooth curve has been drawn which implies that there are no truncations. $\overline{OP_1}$ is the actual rate of profit, $\overline{OP_3}$ is the wage, $\overline{P_3P_4}$ is total profits. Note that the organic composition will rise with the rate of profit for a given technique in most cases, even if the wage curve is concave. It always rises for single-product systems and/or if the wage curve is convex.

The introduction of a more mechanised technique (dotted line) implies the existence of one switchpoint (P_6) between P_1 and R such that the maximum rate of profit falls. Hence, it can be expected that P_4 will shift upwards more than P_5 for given P_1; the distance $\overline{P_1P_2}$ becomes shorter, while $\overline{P_3P_4}$ rises more than $\overline{OP_3}$. In other words, at a given rate of profit the organic composition falls, while the rate of exploitation goes up. We have proved (for $g = 0$) that P/W is a monotonically rising function of the rate of profit. Check on the former is bound to reduce the latter; the visible link is provided by the organic composition. Such a situation is what Joan Robinson called (1969, p. 171) 'a technocrat's nightmare': the capitalist's efforts to raise profits through the introduction of technical progress are frustrated by the nature of the form of technical progress that is known or feasible.

Of course, it is not possible to predict in detail what will happen during the process of accumulation, if mechanisation is the only form of technical progress available. So far, we have only been comparing steady states. Without further information it cannot be said whether accumulation will proceed more along Ricardian lines with a rising rate of exploitation and a constant rate of profit or along Marxian lines with a check on the rate of exploitation and a falling rate of profit. Further information is also needed to determine under which conditions technological unemployment will arise. We shall not try to elaborate various hypotheses about possible paths of accumulation with mechanisation as the dominant form of technical progress. The possibilities are too varied, and the concept of the rate of exploitation would require some prior clarification.

At present, we are only interested in a clarification of the concept of mechanisation. For this purpose, the above analysis may have been of some use, since mechanisation is usually either tautologically defined, in macroeconomic terms, as technical progress which raises the capital–output ratio, or it is defined in microeconomic terms as the introduction of a machine; but in the latter case it is never clear whether the introduction of the machine will actually lead to a rise in the capital–output ratio, measured in long-run prices. As a result, it is not possible to decide on the basis of conventional definitions whether 'waves of mechanisation' which are known to have happened in history are linked to reported rises in the capital–output ratio or whether the rise of the latter must have been owing to other causes.

According to the above analysis, the capital–output ratio is bound to rise in consequence of the introduction of machinery to replace labour, if no simultaneous saving of raw materials takes place. To prove this, let us calculate the capital–output ratio K/Y. Since $Y/K = P/K + W/K = r + (R - r)$, the capital–output ratio of an economy in balanced proportions is equal to

$$\frac{K}{Y} = \frac{1}{R}$$

and therefore rises as R falls. More generally, $K/Y = k/y = \overline{OP_2}$ in Figure 7.8. Hence, the capital–output ratio goes up for a given rate of profit if and only if the organic composition of capital does the same. Since it is fairly well agreed that the capital–output ratio was more or less steadily rising in the first three-quarters of the nineteenth century and only afterwards fell to its twentieth-century level (Dean and Cole, 1969, p. 306), and since verbal descriptions of mechanisation in Marx and elsewhere correspond to the picture of technical progress which we have formalised here, I venture to suggest that 'mechanisation' in the sense defined above was indeed the dominant form of technical progress in the first half of the nineteenth century and that the rise in the capital–output ratio and in part also the fall in the rate of profit have to be explained by a rise in the ratio of the total *physical* quantity of raw materials to labour per unit of output.

Of course, there are forms of technical progress other than the two so far considered. The direct counterpart to the pure saving of labour is saving of raw materials. It is remarkable in that it will almost always tend to lower the organic composition of capital in an indecomposable fixed-capital system with positive prices at a given rate of profit. For, if an element denoting an input of a finished good in the input matrix **A** is diminished while the output matrix and the labour vector remain unchanged, it is plain from the reduction that all prices of finished goods will fall. And, since it is likely that the prices of old machines will follow suit (it is certain if the machines are of constant efficiency), it follows that the organic composition will be reduced by more than the reduction in inputs. This result is in striking contrast to that obtained for the division of labour, where the saving of labour tended to leave the organic composition of capital unchanged at a given rate of profit. Both forms are similar, however, in that in neither case are there any switchpoints between the old and the new techniques (except at R, when all saving is of labour).

Saving of raw materials is very important, since such savings usually result from the opportunity to choose the optimum scale of a process. (This observation does not violate our assumption of constant returns for a given technique.) As Kaldor (1972) has noted, doubling the diameter of a pipeline means increasing the flow at least fourfold, while the requirements for steel will only a little more than double. Only big firms are able to exploit both the advantages of small-scale production (by means of decentralisation) and the advantages of big-scale production, by means of increasing the size of plants up to the technical limit (which is, however, seldom reached, because of limits to demand). Savings of raw materials are not always accompanied by a direct saving of labour; yet they necessarily lead to an indirect saving of labour.

12 Other forms of technical progress and Marx's temporary retreat to Ricardo

There are changes in production which can hardly be called 'technical progress' and which nevertheless affect profitability and the organic composition of capital: the introduction of night shifts is an example.

There are also forms of technical progress other than the three discussed in the last section. Marx discusses some of them (for instance, specific forms of technological development in agriculture, which are influenced by the law of rent). Saving of some raw materials at the expense of using more of others is at least conceivable (though probably not frequent) at a given rate of profit, and the introduction of new commodities creating and serving new needs is undoubtedly very important.

However, we shall confine ourselves to the discussion of only one other type of technical progress: 'inventions' of radically new methods of production to produce the same commodity. This comprises the replacement of one roundabout process by another, or of one type of machinery by another.

Again, we shall try to narrow down the definition by means of bold assumptions, in order to overcome the abstractions of the 'reswitching debate'.

There are two possibilities: *either* the invention represents a new method of production such that not just the same commodity, but actually the physically same good, is produced (the good consists, after the invention, of the same elementary raw materials as before); *or* some of the raw materials change. In the first case it is at least possible that the switch does not represent a new form of technical progress, but represents merely a combination of the forms already considered. If the raw materials that make up the product are still the same, and it is, for example, only the machine that has been replaced, and that in such a way that the new machine consists of essentially the same raw materials as the old, with some new components added to it, it means that we have a more mechanised method for producing the machine, therefore 'mechanisation in the second degree': the process of making the machine has been mechanised. Simple mechanisation is, for instance, the addition of small computers or robots to an otherwise unchanged assembly line, to facilitate or replace some manual operations in the production of a finished good. From the point of view of the finished good, we have mechanisation of the second degree if the production of robots is mechanised. Mathematically, such a process of iterated mechanisation is basically still a roundabout process with the characteristics of simple mechanisation, and it follows that only in the second case, (i.e. if some of the raw materials of which the final product is composed change) are we really certain to encounter a new form of technical progress which can in no way be reduced to any combination of labour saving, mechanisation and saving of raw materials.

For simplicity we shall assume that all 'inventions' are of this second type: i.e. they involve the replacement of at least some of the raw materials of which the final product consists. By implication we assume that all changes of technique which do not change the raw materials are either labour saving, saving of raw materials, or mechanisation as defined above. But, if the new product after the invention is not composed of the same raw materials as the old, it does not have exactly the same use value. Whether the old and the new good are the 'same' commodities must therefore depend on the reaction of the market; the entrepreneur can only guess what the assessment of the consumer will be. If the new good fails to be recognised as a substitute for the old, it may still command a market on its own, but that is even less certain.[18]

[18] Examples of successful inventions of this type are the replacement of the petroleum lamp by the electrical or of the coach by the car. Attempts to replace with plastic the metal in the body of a car have so far proved unsuccessful: it was found that the use value of the car suffered too much.

Thus, more uncertainty is generally associated with 'inventions' as we have now defined them than with the three specific forms of technical progress which we considered earlier. This rather obvious point will become important later on.

As a form of technical progress, inventions are at least as old as mechanisation, but they were not always as important. In the Industrial Revolution, machines were introduced to transform the same materials as before into the same products, but by means of less labour. Later, the processes were expanded on a greater scale (saving of raw materials per unit of output). It seems, therefore, that the potential diminishing influence of inventions could not make itself felt before the industrial system was developed and new materials were introduced.

Once inventions have become an important feature of technological development, the Marxian analysis of accumulation loses much of its force: *a priori*, the organic composition of capital can go either way and one can hardly do more than state the tautology: if the capitalists are unable to keep the organic composition of capital low, the workers must either see the rate of exploitation raised or the rate of profit is depressed. There is then neither an obvious link between the substitution of 'capital' for labour at the microlevel and what happens to the capital–output ratio at the macrolevel, nor any reason why technical progress should exhibit a secular tendency towards an increasing organic composition of capital.

Marx was very worried about this latter possibility. It would be unjust to say that he worried because he wished the organic composition to rise and to cause a sharpening of class conflict. After all, he had to explain a phenomenon that we now know was occurring at his time; and we have shown that the one aspect of his story which we have considered proved consistent when formalised.

But for Marx the question was not just one of cosistency. He felt insecure whether the observed increase in the mass of material means of production would really cause their *value* to rise in relation to the *value* of labour power *in spite* of various counteracting tendencies. After a long discussion of different forms of technical progress, he asks in the *Theorien über den Mehrwert* ('Theories of Surplus Value') whether the cheapening of raw materials (achieved by whatever form of technical progress in the raw-material sector) will not decisively counteract the tendency, which he sees as engendered by mechanisation, for the organic composition to rise. He argues, he swears, he doubts, and finally he asserts:[19]

[19] Marx (1862–3; 1971 edn, pp. 356–61), my translation; emphasis in part changed and expressions in brackets added. It should be borne in mind that the quoted material are excerpts from a first draft.

It is an indisputable fact that the part of capital invested in machinery and raw materials increases, while that invested in wages diminishes as capitalism develops. . . . The question is one not of the proportion of the [physical] quantities but of [their] values.

If one worker is able to spin as much cotton as one hundred, the raw material has to be multiplied by one hundred, and, in addition, the process is made possible only through the spinning machine where *one* directs one hundred spindles. . . .

Concerning the *machine*: it does not cost as much as the labour which it replaces, although the spinning machine costs much more than the spindle. The single capitalist who owns a spinning machine needs more capital than the single spinner who buys a spinning wheel. But the spinning machine is cheaper than the spinning wheel in proportion to the number of workers which it employs [rather: which it renders superfluous]. Otherwise it would not displace the latter. . . .

All circumstances which cause the application of machinery to cheapen the *price of commodities* can ultimately be reduced to the reduction of the quantum of labour absorbed in a single commodity, and, secondly, to the reduction of the *dechet* [wear and tear] whose value enters in the single commodity. The slower the *déchet* of the machine, the less work is required for the reproduction [of the latter]. [This] increases, therefore, the quantum and the value of the capital existing in [the form of] machinery relatively to that existing in [the form of] labour.[20]

There remains, therefore, only the question concerning the *raw material*. It is obvious that its quantity must increase in relation to the productivity of labour, therefore the mass of raw materials in relation to that of labour. . . .

[*However*], *as regards raw materials, one may ask: if, for example, the productive power of spinning is increased tenfold–therefore, if one worker spins as much as ten did previously–why should a 'nigger' not produce as much cotton as ten did previously; therefore, why should not the proportion*

[20] Marx here subdivides the effect of roundabout processes into (1) the reduction of the labour embodied in the product through direct labour and the consumption of raw materials, and (2) the reduction of wear and tear of the machine through its prolonged use. We have not discussed the second point separately, since lengthening the lifetime of a machine does not in itself always lead to the conclusions surmised by Marx. Take, for instance, the case of a machine, of constant physical efficiency, the lifetime of which is lengthened without a change in the amount of raw materials used per unit of output per period. The centre coefficients representing the raw materials used in conjunction with the machine will then remain unchanged, while the amortisation charge of the machine will fall. In consequence, the lengthening of the lifetime of the machine will be advantageous at all rates of profit; the maximum rate of profit rises so that the organic composition falls, if the economy is in standard proportions. The 'mass of the means of production in existence' has increased relative to the same net product of finished goods, but their 'total value' has fallen.

> *of values remain the same*? The spinner absorbs in the same period ten times more cotton, but the 'nigger' produces in the same period ten times more cotton. The quantity of cotton which is ten times greater is not more expensive than the previous quantity, which was a tenth the size. Thus, in spite of the increase in the quantity of the raw material, the proportion of its value to the variable capital would remain the same. In fact, it was only through the considerable cheapening of cotton that this industry could at all develop to such an extent. . . .
>
> To this one must reply quite simply that part of raw materials such as wool, silk, leather are produced by *organic* processes in animals; cotton, linen, and so on, by organic processes in plants; and that capitalist production has not so far and *will never* [emphasis added] be able to achieve the same command over these processes as over purely mechanical or anorganic-chemical processes. Raw material such as that derived from hides and other animal components in part becomes more expensive simply *because the insipid law of rent increases the value of these products as civilisation develops* [emphasis added]. Concerning coal and metals [wood]: they become much cheaper as production develops; however, this too, gets more difficult as the mines are exhausted. . . .

The reader is baffled. Did Marx not scorn Ricardo for his false technological determinism? Marx, who had studied the new science of agricultural chemistry in Liebig, knew that capitalism was capable of developing the fertility of the soil to the point socially necessary for the survival of the mode of production. He thought, however, that, since capitalism was based on the exploitation of labour for the purpose of creating ever more surplus value, technical progress or 'the production of relative surplus value' would have to make labour ever more productive by means of more sophisticated equipment. The equipment would tend to cost more and more, the organic composition of capital would rise, and the rate of profit would fall. Thus, the antagonistic nature of the relations of production would eventually lead the capitalists to develop the productive forces in a way detrimental to their own interest. Not technical progress (or the lack of it) *per se*, but technical progress as developed by capitalism, would create an ever greater obstacle to the continued working of the system. The fall in the rate of profit (observed and discussed by all major classical economists), repeated crises and the dominant form of technical progress all seemed to confirm the prediction.

At this point, Marx's position became ambiguous, however. He had an aprioristic theory of why technical progress would have to reflect the basic contradiction of capitalism 'somehow', but at the same time he knew that it does not tautologically follow from the theory of surplus value that all production of relative surplus value increases the ratio of constant to variable capital or of total capital to wages. Hence, he seems to have occasionally been tempted to buttress his theory by means of a reference to *invariable* links between technical conditions of production and the social relations of capitalism. *Das Kapital* reads in some places as if almost all changes of the conditions of production under capitalism had to lead not only to increased productivity in response to the pressure of wages, but also to an increased use of raw materials, such that the organic composition of capital rises. When he noted (in the *Theorien über den Mehrwert*) that the rise in the organic composition does not follow with *logical* necessity, he was compelled to admit that it may occur during some periods of capitalist development and not in others. In order to show that the rise would ultimately prevail over the opposing tendencies, he resorted to the Ricardian argument which looks so desperate.

The argument is clearly wrong if it is understood to mean that it can be known now with absolute certainty that capitalism is ultimately doomed because of its eternal inability to reach sufficient command over organic nature, and so on. But a new synthesis of Ricardian and Marxian ideas is suggested by this argument as well as by recent historical events: the rise in oil prices reflects at the same time natural scarcity and social contradictions; and it may well increase the latter directly as well as indirectly, through an increase in the organic composition of capital. I conclude that the fundamental message of the Marxian theory of the falling rate of profit is not that there is one particular reason why the rate of profit falls but that one has to inquire into the *historically changing* interaction between different forms of the accumulation of capital and the struggle about the distribution of income. The pressure of wages and competition will always tend to reduce the rate of profit. But the ability of the capitalists to reverse the trend is not always the same. It depends on which opportunities for technical improvements happen to be at hand. Thus, I have tried to show that Marx was probably right in asserting that the introduction of machinery raised the organic composition of capital in the early nineteenth century, because the machines came to replace labour, not obsolescent machines, and because the consequent increased use of raw materials per unit of output was not offset by a corresponding technical progress in the production of raw materials. A similar inquiry should be made concerning the wave of automatisation in the 1920s. In both cases the capitalists may have liked to save capital as well as labour, but they had no option.

The question of the tendency of the rate of profit should be discussed in a historical context, where the organic composition of capital may sometimes be seen to rise and sometimes to fall. Nevertheless, it makes some sense to stick to Marx's theory of the tendency of the rate of profit to fall, if one accepts that capitalists – although they do whatever is profitable – always have special reasons to reduce labour requirements, because of wage pressures, discipline, and so on. In so far as the possibilities for a pure saving of labour are limited, mechanisation is the main way to achieve this goal. Since mechanisation leads to a pressure on the rate of profit if wages continue to rise, other forms of technical progress – in particular, the saving of raw materials by means of taking advantage of increasing returns to scale – are then called for to reverse the rising trend of the organic composition of capital. From this point of view, even a series of technical changes which on balance turns out to be neutral could be regarded as compatible with the hypotheses of the theory of the tendency of the rate of profit to fall. (It would be accompanied by a process of concentration.) I do not want to insist on this point, however. It provides a justification for not abandoning the theory of the falling rate of profit in that one may continue to regard mechanisation as the primary tendency, and saving of raw materials, and so on, as a counter tendency. But Marx would never have attached so much importance to the hypothesis of a rising organic composition of capital if he had not believed himself to have proved that the 'main tendency' would ultimately prevail over the counter tendencies.

13 Profitability and technical progress

We are now at last in a position to solve the puzzle discussed in the section 9. It was observed there that the technique which is superior at a given rate of profit *r* may not yield the maximum attainable consumption per head at rate of growth $g < r$. Moreover, it was found that total profits fall for a given level of employment, if the superior technique has a lower capital–labour ratio and uses more labour per unit of composite output. (It was noted that the paradox does not exist from the point of view of the single capitalist. Those capitalists who are the first to introduce the new technique with a lower capital–labour ratio are thereby enabled to use the reduction in their amortisation funds for an expansion of their business so that the mass of their profits may actually rise. A consequent increase of investment could be beneficial if it increased employment.) The two effects (reduction of consumption and of profits per head) occur simultaneously if the two techniques have an odd number of switchpoints in common between the rate of profit and the rate of growth. Nothing could be said as to the likelihood of such switches from the abstract point of view where alternative techniques are totally unrelated. This seemed to be counter to economic intuition: economists of all schools agree in a belief that the pursuit of profits leads to gains in productivity, however defined.

The first and most important point to be made is simply this: any actual technique exists (as Joan Robinson would put it) in historical time. The decision to replace it by one which exists as yet only on paper (be it on an old page in the book of blueprints or on a new addition to it) will, in view of the uncertainties involved, be taken only if the expected reduction of costs looks sufficiently important. This condition rules out all but a few alternative techniques and explains why small changes in relative prices, such as those caused by a small change in the rate of profit, will not cause many substitutions, and why not any new technique will be adopted, even if it promises to allow a small reduction of costs. 'Mistakes' in the course of accumulation such that consumption per head (and/or output per head) falls because there is one switchpoint (or, more generally, an odd number of switchpoints) between the rate of growth and the rate of profit are possible, but the reduction of consumption per head will be at the expense of profits if the new technique is introduced at a given rate of profit, so that the wage rate rises. The real wage rate represents, therefore, the lowest bound to the fall in consumption per head, when the capital–labour ratio is lowered in the course of adopting a new technique at a given rate of profit while at the same time more labour is used per unit of (composite) consumable output. A reduction in profits in consequence of technical progress is much less paradoxical than a reduction of consumption per head as such. If real wages stood constant, it would theoretically be conceivable that consumption per head would stagnate or fall towards the level of the real wage with a progressive lowering of the capital–labour ratio, while profits would get wiped out. But, if real wages rise, for whatever reason, consumption per head must also rise, although the rise may, because of a fall in profits per man employed, owing to a fall in the capital–labour ratio, temporarily be slowed down or reversed.

The pressure of rising real wages hastens not only mechanisation but also technical progress in general. A detailed discussion of the interaction of the rise in real wages and technical progress lies beyond the scope of this essay, however. Instead, we shall focus on the remarkable fact that the 'odd' switchpoints are excluded if the alternative to a given technique results from any of the four forms of technical progress which we have defined.

To see this, consider the wage curve and its dual. If a superior technique is introduced at a given rate of profit (so that the wage rate rises), consumption per head c may go up or down at the rate of growth (also considered to be given). Output per head y may also go up or down, but a little reflection shows that

(i) a rise in the capital–labour ratio k implies a rise in c and y;
(ii) a fall in c implies a fall in y; and
(iii) a fall in y (not necessarily accompanied by a fall in c) implies a fall in k, which is in turn equivalent to a fall in profits per man employed.

All labour values of finished goods will be lower for the technique for which the wage rate at $r = 0$, i.e. $w(0)$, is higher. Formally, we can have eight possible constellations, which the reader is advised to draw for himself: y and c can go up, with k going up or down and $w(0)$ going up or down (four cases); c going up, y down, with $w(0)$ going up or down (two cases); c and y falling, with $w(0)$ going down or up (two cases; the last implies a double switch). Are all possibilities equally likely? If the wage curves have, as in the case of saving of labour, saving of raw materials and mechanisation, no switchpoint in common in the relevant range, c and $w(0)$ go up simultaneously, and output per head goes up as well, if k does not fall much and/or the rate of growth is small.

Therefore (and this is the result to be kept in mind), if switchpoints between zero and the actual rate of profit are excluded for technical reasons, consumption per head goes up if, and only if, labour values fall. That output per head will go up with consumption per head is certain if k rises and possible even if k falls; it is more likely the smaller the rate of growth is. In a stationary system ($g = 0$), c and y coincide and go up if, and only if, labour values fall. Saving of labour, saving of raw materials and mechanisation do not lead to switchpoints between zero and the actual rate of profit. The same can, as we shall see later, be expected in the case of 'inventions'.

Technical progress going on steadily in all sectors in a process of accumulation at a roughly constant rate of growth and a much greater rate of profit could thus raise profits, output and consumption per head more or less steadily on average, and lower labour values, if it consisted of a mix of the four forms of technical progress considered above. While there does not seem to exist an inbuilt mechanism which ensures that capitalist accumulation proceeds according to the 'stylised facts', a steady process of accumulation, with technical progress raising k, y and c at about the same rate and leaving k/y more or less constant appears, after a consideration of what seemed to be the four main forms of technical progress, at least less hopelessly unlikely than on the basis of abstract comparisons of the totally arbitrary and abstract wage curves of capital theory (cf., however, Schefold, 1976c).

It is in fact intuitively obvious that savings of labour, raw materials and mechanisation all increase consumption per head under the assumptions stated. Yet it is useful to note some differences.

'Technical progress' in its simplest form has always consisted in developing given techniques by better application. Such progress amounts to direct saving of labour and raw materials. Both types of saving simply push the wage curve upwards, but no elaborate price calculation is necessary to convince the capitalist that it pays to itensify the work process and to avoid waste of materials wherever possible. The main prerequisite for this type of technical progress is a docile and disciplined labour force which can be made to accept the goals of management. Since it is more gratifying to work well than to work fast, more can be gained from inducing the worker to speed up his production than from advising him to care about his working materials, which he is likely to do anyway. 'Improving' the application of a given method of production consists, therefore, chiefly in forcing the worker to intensify his efforts. The intensification of labour, if accepted by the workers, carries no economic risk for the capitalist.

Saving of raw materials and labour through increasing the scale of an operation (like building a bigger ship) is already a different matter, for it implies that the capitalist increases production; hence, he must generally be able to extend his share of the market, either within the nation or outside. The market does not increase by itself: it is necessary to lower the price or to intensify the sales effort in order to conquer a greater market. The expansion is risky; and the capitalist will be the more prone to undertake it the greater his potential advantage.

The same holds true for mechanisation, but with the additional difficulty that the capitalist will have to overcome the workers' resistance to displacement. Such resistance is inevitable, and it is the greater the harder it is for the worker to find alternative employment. Capitalists will therefore tend to postpone the introduction of more highly mechanised techniques and will introduce them no sooner than real pressure or extraordinary market opportunities appear. The pressures of an unruly labour force take usually the form of wage claims. Thus, mechanisation which is really a form of technical progress often appears under the neoclassical disguise of a 'substitution effect'.

All three forms have in common that they raise productivity if and only if they are profitable. They differ, however, in that the expected gains do not always seem equally secure. There can be no doubt that intensification of work increases productivity and profits as long as wages remain constant. Expansion of scale is, by contrast, risky, because there has to be a market for the expanded production and the transition is difficult. The same is true to an even greater degree for mechanisation. The transition will therefore not be undertaken unless the potential surplus profits are great.

If we now turn to 'inventions' in the restricted sense defined above, we find that the risks involved are even greater, for it is necessary not only to dismantle the plant and set up a new one, but also to convince the market that the new product, based on substitute materials, is as good as the old one. Not only has a new market to be won, but, in addition, the old market has to be held in the face of a qualitative change. The expected potential reduction in the price of production in terms of the wage rate at the given real wage has thus to be very considerable if the transition is to be attempted. Moreover, the expected gain has to be fairly secure, i.e. the new technique has to be profitable even if relative prices change a little. And the prices which are immediately observable, i.e. market prices, fluctuate all the time.

A price of production is only some rather ill defined average of market prices. The entrepreneur who tries to estimate the future course of prices must always reckon with the possibility of fairly large variations. Hence, he will not undertake an important investment unless it appears to be profitable not only at the given set of prices but also if all prices change within a certain range.

But, since wage curves are continuous, this means that the wage curve representing the invention will be 'far apart' from the wage curve representing the old technique at the given rate of profit, and the two curves will not intersect in a fairly broad neighbourhood of the rate of profit. Hence, it is likely that, simply for reasons of continuity, there are no switchpoints between zero and the rate of profit; the inefficiency does not occur. One might also say that, since labour values are not too far removed from prices of production, and since the profitability of an invention should not depend on small variations of relative prices, the majority of inventions may thus unwittingly be subjected to the test of profitability at prices equal to values.

Of course, there will be exceptions. But it is important to note that the more complicated forms of technical progress are in any case the ones which involve greater risk – not only because it is less certain whether the new technique will 'work', but also because of factors such as increased production requiring a greater market, displacement of labour, and change of product. The greater the risk, the more cautious the investor, and the greater the difference in the price of production at the same rate of profit between the old and the new technique.

From this point of view one might conclude that there are no switches between any two consecutive techniques which succeed each other in a process of accumulation; the simple changes of technique (saving of labour and raw materials) give rise to no switchpoints at all, because simple changes imply 'parallel' shifts of the wage curve, and the more complicated changes of technique imply no switchpoints at least between zero and the rate of profit, because sufficiently large variations in price will be taken into account before the new technique is adopted. Our analysis has shown, however, that it would be wrong to conclude that a superior technique is almost invariably advantageous at *all* rates of profit from zero to the maximum. It is the essence of mechanisation that a trade-off occurs, in the sense that the saving of labour is possible only at the expense of increased use of raw materials, hence that a switchpoint exists between the actual rate of profit and the maximum rate.

It may be asked, then, why the converse constellation should not be conceivable: a switchpoint between zero and the actual rate of profit. The answer is that such a situation cannot be excluded. The above analysis suggests only that it is less likely to occur in reality, since, as has been argued, the obviously simplest and most frequent forms of technical progress generate no such switch. It follows from the microeconomic definition of savings of labour, raw materials and mechanisation that there is no switchpoint between zero and the rate of profit. The same can be said in the case of inventions on the basis of a quite different hypothesis – namely, that inventions are introduced only if they allow a considerable reduction of the price of production, and this implies a reduction of the labour value of the commodity as well, since the rate of profit is small in relation to the maximum rate of profits, because the greater part of national income goes to wages.

The argument thus becomes less well founded and more 'empirical' as one approaches the complexities of real changes in methods of production. Exceptions therefore cannot be ruled out. It is conceivable, for instance, that raw materials are saved at the expense of using more labour, because work is being done with greater care so that a switchpoint between zero and the actual rate of profit arises. One feels that this case is of lesser economic importance than its counterpart, mechanisation. A capitalist who has read his Taylor (1911) will get his workers to save raw materials without allowing them a reduction of speed. But the lesser importance of an event does not mean that it can be ruled out. The point is then to have a theory of accumulation which can cope with the odd cases. Such a theory is the neo-Keynesian but not the neoclassical.

A last observation: it may be easier to realise that an invention is going to be profitable, whatever the relative prices within a certain range, than to apply the technique in the most efficient manner. If machines have a complicated efficiency pattern, switches owing to alternative truncations may occur quite easily. Indeed, it seems plausible to say (although it is only guesswork) that the social loss owing to a false truncation is small, but occurs frequently, while the social loss owing to an inefficient invention may be much greater, but occurs less often.

Our reasoning implies that many minor inventions which may or may not be efficient in terms of raising output per head are not introduced, because the expected gain of profitability does not warrant the risk of introducing them. This is another instance of a cause of social losses from the point of view of comparative statics, but the loss is less certain than in the case of a mistaken truncation. It may be a good idea not to change techniques whenever a new little invention comes up, because of the trouble involved in the process of transition. By contrast, it does not require any complicated transition to rectify a wrong truncation. The difference between prices and values is thus not without effect.

The main conclusion, however, seems to be that deviations of prices from values are unimportant. On the one hand, this may be because technical progress takes simple forms such as learning by doing. In these cases, the increase in output and consumption per head is basically equivalent to a fall in the labour value of the commodity produced and occurs if and only if prices at the ruling rate of profit are reduced, which entails that an analysis in terms of values automatically leads to the same result as one in terms of prices. On the other hand, the reason may be that technical progress is more complicated. But more complicated technical progress is, as we have tried to show in a limited number of cases, inherently more risky. Hence, it may be expected that the invention will be introduced if it is so obviously advantageous that it would be profitable even if prices were equal to values.

Thus we find, on the basis of admittedly restrictive assumptions, that the difference between prices and values does not much affect the influence on accumulation of those types of technical progress which have a chance of really being introduced. This conclusion confirms the profound economic intuition of the classical economists, but it does not warrant a dogmatic return to the classical theory of labour values and labour productivity.

We have found that the notion of productivity is ambiguous even within the restrictive theoretical framework (steady states) used in this paper. Technical progress was initially just a name for the introduction of a new technique at a given rate of profit (as opposed to substitution where the rate of profit changes and the technique to be introduced has been known before). The transition to the new technique is undertaken because it yields surplus profits (see above, section 9 (2)). In what sense does *productivity* rise with technical progress?

In *Das Kapital*, volume I, 'technical progress' is mainly 'production of relative surplus value', which is close to our 'raising profits per man employed' (the analogy would be better if wages were kept constant). Marx insisted that the correct classical notion of 'productive labour' was labour which produced 'surplus value', but Smith interpreted productive labour also as labour producing commodities for exchange as opposed to labour employed in the feudal sector. On the basis of the labour theory of value, the second notion must mean that productivity increases if labour values fall. Neoclassical theory would, under appropriate conditions, predict that a new technique is adopted if consumption per head rises, while the modern pragmatic approach prepared by Keynes focuses on the growth of income per head.

There exist, therefore, even in a simple steady-state model, at least four different notions of productivity, but the point is that on the whole the four forms of technical progress raise productivity according to all possible meanings. The classical interpretation does not take logical precedence, but the labour theory of value, which measures productivity in terms of output per unit of labour embodied, has here been vindicated as an approximation which permits an intuitively simple discussion of important aspects of technological development. The theory of prices of production is necessary precisely in order to assess the quality of the approximation.

The main purpose of this paper has been to develop the analytical properties of the price system in the case of fixed capital. The results should help towards a better understanding of pure theory and could be used for a criticism of neoclassicism. An application to the theory of accumulation has indicated that important results gained by assuming that market prices fluctuate around prices of production could also be gained simply by assuming that market prices fluctuate around labour values, but this insight in no way exhausts the meaning of the debates around the labour theory of value, since the latter has generated heat not because of its 'technocratic usefulness' but because Marx turned it against Ricardo and vulgar economics. Is there a need to revive it for positive economics today? As an extension of our argument one is tempted to say that values are a more convenient measure than prices in the theory of accumulation, in the same sense as minutes are a more convenient measure for railway timetables than are milliseconds. In this sense, the theory of value was, in the hands of the classical economists, an extremely fruitful tool for the analysis of real economic processes, while the modern theory of prices of production has mainly become a powerful instrument of criticism (cf. Schefold, 'Nachworte', in Sraffa, 1976, pp. 131–226). Today it remains to be seen in how far *either* theory will be relevant for the understanding of modern economic problems. Few empirical analyses do not compel one to leave the framework of the theories of both value and price of production, yet both remain indispensable for theoretical discussions.

References

Bharadwaj, K. R., 'On the Maximum Number of Switches Between Two Production Systems', *Schweizerische Zeitschrift für Volkswirtschaft und Statistik*, CVI (1970) 409–428.

Deane, P. and Cole, W. A., *British Economic Growth(1688–1959)*, 2nd ed (Cambridge: Cambridge University Press, 1969).

Dorfman, R., Samuelson, P. and Solow, R., *Linear Programming and Economic Analysis* (New York: McGraw-Hill, 1958).

Fogel, R. W. and Engermann, S. L., *Time on the Cross* (London: Wildwood House, 1974).

Garegnani, P., 'Heterogeneous Capital, the Production Function and the Theory of Distribution', *Review of Economic Studies*, XXXVII (1970) 407–36.

Hicks, J., 'A Neo-Austrian Growth Theory', *Economic Journal*, LXXX (1970) 257–81.

Hicks, J., *Capital and Time* (Oxford: Clarendon Press, 1973).

Kaldor, N., 'The Irrelevance of Equilibrium Economics', *Economic Journal*, LXXXII (1972) 1237–55.

Marglin, S. A., *What Do Bosses Do?– The Origins and Functions of Hierarchy in Capitalist Production*, Discussion Paper no. 222 of the Harvard Institute of Economic Research (Cambridge, Mass., 1971).

Marshall, A., *Principles of Economics* (London: Macmillan, 1966, repr. from 8th edn. 1920).

Marx, K., *Theorien über den Mehrwert* (written in 1862–3), vol. XXVI of the *Marx–Engels Werke*, 2nd reprint (Berlin: Dietz, 1971).

Marx, K., *Das Kapital*, 3 vols (first published in 1867, 1885, 1894), vols XXIII–XXV of the *Marx–Engels Werke*, 14th reprint, (Berlin: Dietz, 1969).

Mirrlees, J., 'The Dynamic Nonsubstitution Theorem', *Review of Economic Studies*, XXXVI (1969) 67–76.

Morishima, M., *Marx's Economics* (Cambridge: Cambridge University Press, 1973).

Nuti, D. M., 'Capitalism, Socialism and Steady Growth', *Economic Journal*, LXXX (1970) 32–57.

Nuti, D. M., 'On the Truncation of Production Flows', *Kyklos*, XXVI (1973) 485–94.

Okishio, N., 'Technical Changes and the Rate of Profit', *Kobe University Economic Review*, VII (1961) 85–99.

Pasinetti, L. L., 'Switchings of Techniques and the "Rate of Return" in Capital Theory', *Economic Journal*, LXXIX (1969) 508–31.

Robinson, J., *The Accumulation of Capital*, 3rd edn (London: Macmillan, 1969).

Schefold, B., *Theorie der Kuppelproduktion* (*Mr. Sraffa on Joint Production*) (Basel: privately printed, 1971: second edition in preparation).

Schefold, B., 'Different Forms of Technical Progress', *Economic Journal*, LXXXVI (1976[a]) 806–19.

Schefold, B., 'Reduction to Dated Quantities of Labour, Roundabout Processes, and Switches of Techniques in Fixed Capital Systems', *Metroeconomica*, XXVIII (1976[b]) 1–15.

Schefold, B., 'Relative Prices as a Function of the Rate of Profit', *Zeitschrift fur Nationalokonomie*, XXXVI (1976[c]) 21–48.

Schefold, B., 'Fixed Capital as a Joint Product', *Jahrbücher für Nationalökonomie und Statistik*, CXCII (1978 [a]) 415–39.

Schefold, B., 'Multiple Product Techniques with Properties of Single Product Systems', *Zeitschrift für Nationalökonomie*, XXXVIII (1978[b]) 29–53.

Schefold, B., 'On Counting Equations', *Zeitschrift für Nationalökonomie*, XXXVIII (1978 [c]) 253–85.

Schefold, B., 'Capital, Growth and Definitions of Technical Progress, *Festschrift für G. Bombach, Kyklos*, XXXII (1979) 236–250.

Sraffa, P., *Production of Commodities by Means of Commodities* (Cambridge: Cambridge University Press, 1960).

Sraffa, P. *Warenproduktion mittels Waren* (Frankfurt-am-Main: Suhrkamp 1976). (German translation of Sraffa, 1960, with *Nachworte* by Schefold, pp. 129–226.)

Taylor, F. W., *The Principles of Scientific Management* (first published in 1911) (New York, 1967).

Weizsäcker, C. C. von, 'Bemerkungen zu einem Symposium über Wachstumstheorie und Produktionsfunktionen', *Kyklos*, XVI (1963) 438–55.

Weizsäcker, C. C. von., *Steady State Capital Theory* (Berlin: Springer, 1971).

CHAPTER EIGHT

Rent, Income Distribution, and Orders of Efficiency and Rentability[1]

ALBERTO QUADRIO-CURZIO

1 The present essay

(1) This contribution is associated with one of the analytic trends, originating from the recent work by Piero Sraffa (1960), which go back to the classical economists. To be more exact, the present writer, as the reader will be able to see from what follows, has re-examined in modern terms a series of problems that are typical of the theory of David Ricardo.

The contributions of Sraffa and subsequent writers are of two types: one is critical of 'marginalist' and 'neoclassical' theory; the other is constructive, aiming at the creation of a new theory. This constructive aspect is less well known at present, but it is of great importance and research in this direction should be taken further. Indeed, it is only in this direction that the new theory can fully demonstrate if and where it is a complete alternative to the neoclassical theory.

(2) The present essay follows the constructive trend, with the particular aim of studying rent and 'non-produced means of production', which we shall henceforward refer to as 'NPMPs'. These subjects are connected with the distribution of income, production and the accumulation of capital in economic systems where NPMPs have a significant place alongside produced and reproduced commodities and means of production.

(3) The study of rent, NPMPs and 'land' has had its ups and downs in the history of economic analysis. We immediately remember Ricardo, and then realise that after him the subject was to a certain extent abandoned. There

[1] A paper very similar to this was presented by the author at three different seminars – in Barcelona, in Geneva and in Tokyo.

were two aspects to Ricardo's theory: 'scarcity', connected with rent, and 'productiveness', connected with wages and profits. These were two sides of the same coin for Ricardo; subsequent analysis, however, has separated them.

From Wicksteed onwards, the neoclassical economists transformed the theory of rent into a general theory of scarcity and scarce resources. There has been a consequent tendency, from those reacting against neoclassical theory, to overlook 'scarcity', as though it were essential to deal with productiveness alone in order to maintain the difference from the neoclassical economists. This is not the case with Sraffa, however, who takes both 'scarcity' and 'land' into consideration, and, though he does not treat the subject as one of his main points, he does dedicate a chapter (1960, ch. 11) to it.

(4) We can say, therefore, that most of the work on a modern interpretation of Ricardo's approach to 'scarcity' has yet to be done. The subject is very important for two specific reasons.

The first reason is to show that, even if we introduce NPMPs and 'scarcity' into the theory of the Sraffa type, it does not make the latter become neoclassical. There are in fact deeper differences between the two theories, i.e. the configuration of the productive process, the concept of the net product (or income), its distributive criteria, and the criteria for determining prices.

The second reason emerges from the economic history. One of the most important and obvious characteristics of the last few centuries is the antagonism–coexistence between scarcity and productiveness. However, economic analysis, impressed by technical progress and the rapid growth of industrialised economies, was for a long time unable to understand or represent this antagonism–coexistence. It is only recently, with regard to the problems of raw materials and natural resources, that the above dilemma has become more important.

The category of NPMP is greatly influenced by technical progress, which changes its quality, extension and number, but this does not mean that it disappears. Oil has replaced coal, but this does not mean that the scarcity of oil has disappeared. NPMPs influence prices and distribution, the relations between these two entities and production, the continuous but non-regular growth and dynamics of economic systems, and international trade.

(5) In the following pages we shall consider only a few initial aspects, concerning distribution and prices, of the problem we have described. These aspects have already been presented in a book by the present writer; any readers wanting a more extensive treatment are advised to refer to this work (see Quadrio-Curzio, 1967; chapters 3 and 6 are especially relevant to this essay).

2 The system of prices and the distribution of income

Let us consider the following system of equations, taken substantially from Sraffa (1960):

$$\mathbf{a}'_{i1}(b)\mathbf{P}(1+r)+l_1(b)w+t(b)\rho(b) = p_1; \qquad b = \text{I, II, } \ldots \text{K} \tag{8.1}$$

$$\mathbf{a}'_{ij}\mathbf{P}(1+r)+l_j w = p_j, \qquad j = 2, \ldots m+1 \tag{8.2}$$

$$p_1 = 1 \tag{8.3}$$

$$\prod_{b=\text{I}}^{K} \rho(b) = 0 \tag{8.4}$$

$$w = \bar{w} \geq 0 \qquad \text{or} \qquad r = \bar{r} \geq 0 \tag{8.5}$$

The data are $\mathbf{a}'_{i1}(b) = [a_{1,1}(b), \ldots a_{m+1,1}(b)]$, $\mathbf{a}'_{ij} = [a_{1j}, \ldots a_{m+1,j}]$, i.e. the technical coefficients (including Leontief coefficients) raised by 'coefficients of necessary consumption'. All these coefficients concern commodities needed to produce commodities, since they are all supposed to be of the basic type. In turn, $l_1(b)$ and l_j are the technical labour coefficients and $t(b)$ are those for the NPMPs.

The unknowns are $\mathbf{P}' = [p_1, \ldots p_{m+1}]$, the prices of the commodities; r, the rate of profit; w, the unitary wage; $\rho(b)$, the unitary rents.

Let us now consider the significance of the above equations.

Each (8.1) equation refers to a productive process that uses an NPMP of a given quality b that produces the commodity of type 1. Since 1 is a basic commodity, at least one process of type 1 must operate, otherwise the entire economy would not be able to function. Let us suppose that there are K processes available with NPMPs, for b = I, II, . . . K. The number of these actually operating has to be determined.

For the active processes, it must be that $\rho(b) \geq 0$, except for the least efficient b^*, where we must have $\rho(b^*) = 0$. This is owing to the differential nature of the rents under examination. Since rent is the measure of the greater efficiency (as we shall define it) of a process over the least efficient still active, the latter will have a zero rent.

The different efficiency of the various processes will also depend on the employments of labour and circulating capital given by the vectors $[\mathbf{a}_{i1}(b), l_1(b)]$, which we suppose cannot be ordered directly, but can be ordered only on the basis of prices.

Each (8.2) equation represents a process of production that generates a different commodity using labour and circulating capital.

(8.3) shows that the *numéraire* is commodity 1.

(8.4) is the condition that at least one rent must be zero.

(8.5) is the condition that r or w must be exogenously fixed. Remember that w is the 'surplus wage', since the 'subsistence wage' is included in the 'technical' coefficients by means of the necessary consumption.

We have, therefore, an open theory of the distribution of income: a distributive magnitude must be determined by elements that lie outside the scope of this theory. Of course, in order to connect the theory to a specific historical, economic and institutional situation (in particular, to a market economy or a planned economy for particular historical and institutional periods), it is necessary to choose the exogenous magnitude between r and w and to indicate the elements that determine it.

3 The price–wage–profit sub-system

The solutions to system (8.1)–(8.5) are easy to find. With r or w given, the solutions change with the $\rho(b^*)$ made equal to zero. Hence, there are K solutions. In order to find them we substitute for (8.4) the following:

$$\rho(b^*) = 0 \tag{8.6}$$

taking each b separately one after the other.

From equations (8.1) it is equation b^*, for which we have chosen condition (8.6), that becomes the 'resolving' equation, since it allows us to resolve the whole system (the term 'resolving' will also be applied to the process b^*). Indeed, taken together with (8.2), it gives rise to the following system of equations:

$$[1 + r(b^*)]\,\mathbf{A}'(b^*)\,\mathbf{P}(b^*) + \mathbf{L}(b^*)w(b^*) = \mathbf{P}(b^*) \tag{8.7}$$

where $\mathbf{A}(b^*)$ is a matrix of technical coefficients and $\mathbf{L}(b^*)$ is the vector of labour coefficients. All the entities have b^* as argument, because the only difference between one (8.7) and another is due to the process b^*, taken from (8.1) and then inserted into (8.2).

Equations (8.7), (8.3), (8.5) constitute a 'price–wage–profit sub-system', which we shall henceforward refer to as a 'PWΠ sub-system'. It is a sub-system with respect to equations (8.1)–(8.5). The term therefore has a different meaning from that given to it by Sraffa. Indeed, every PWΠ sub-system coincides with a Sraffa single-product system and gives economically significant solutions $\mathbf{P}(b^*) > 0$, $r(b^*) \geq 0$, $w(b^*) \geq 0$. $\mathbf{A}(b^*)$, in fact, is indecomposable, since all commodities are of a basic type, and its maximum eigenvalue falls in the interval

$$0 < \lambda(b^*) < 1 \tag{8.8}$$

This means that there exists an interval of values for the exogenous distributive magnitude for which the system is economic and viable.

4 The rents sub-system

We now have to consider the remaining K – 1 equations of (8.1). We shall call them a 'rents subsystem' (henceforward an 'R subsystem'), even if every equation contains only one unknown: rent. With $P(b^*), r(b^*), w(b^*)$ given, we can calculate

$$\rho(b, b^*) = \{p_1 - a'_{i1}(b)\mathbf{P}(b^*)[1 + r(b^*)] - l_1(b)w(b^*)\}[t(b)]^{-1} \tag{8.9}$$

b^* being given, and $b = \text{I}, \text{II}, \ldots \text{K}$, with $b \neq b^*$.

A PWΠ sub-system with its associated R sub-system constitutes a complete 'price-distribution system', or 'PD system'.

Let us consider for a moment the nature of rents.

First of all we talked of differential rent. It may be said that it would be better to talk of extensive rent, since the presented case is known as typical of limited 'lands' of different qualities. However, this seems unnecessarily precise. In fact, even intensive rent may be treated as differential rent. In the intensive case, two processes operate on a 'land', of equal quality in both cases. The first process has a cost per unit of product which is lower than that of the second, which is activated only because it has a greater output per 'acre' (cf. Sraffa, 1960, section 87).

It is sufficient for the determination of the prices of production that the price of 'grain' cover the cost of production of the less efficient process, i.e. the second. This is the only objective condition of efficiency to be applied, and from it follows a positive rent for the first process. We find ourselves, therefore, with a simplified case of differential rent. The result would be very different (as would be the difference between extensive and intensive rent) if the case were referred to an economic and institutional context of competition. In this case, rent should be uniform per acre, and therefore the price of 'grain' would be higher than in the case of differential rent just considered.

Secondly, if the reader really wishes to consider extensive rent, then let him at least bear in mind that not considering intensive rent does not mean leaving aside 'intensive' cultivation. In fact, the effects of intensive 'cultivation' remain, even when intensive rent has disappeared: they show themselves in the diversity of productive processes applied to the various 'lands' and they influence the extensive differential rent.

Thirdly, we are more interested in differential rent than in the means of production that generate it. In this essay we give first consideration to the land. It is well known, however (cf. Ricardo, 1817, chs 2 and 3; Sraffa, 1960, ch. 11), that the rent dealt with here may be extended to other natural resources, such as mineral deposits, and even to machines of an obsolete type, no longer currently produced, though still employed in production. In order to keep these possible extensions in mind, though we shall not discuss them below, we shall continue to talk here of NPMPs.

5 Four problems

The NPMPs are therefore fundamental for the determination of prices and distribution. According to which b^* process has a zero rent, there will be different values for $\mathbf{P}$, r, w, $\rho(b)$. Two elements determine process b^*.

The first of these is the order of efficiency, henceforth referred to as the OE, of the K processes with NPMPs. This is the order to follow when activating the K processes.

The second is the economy's level of activity. In fact, every NPMP is available in a given 'extension': $T(b)$. Hence, the maximum quantity of commodity 1 producible is given by

$$T(b)[t(b)]^{-1} = \max q_1(b) \tag{8.10}$$

In addition, since commodity 1 is a basic commodity, growth in production of the economy is possible only if K processes with NPMPs are activated one after the other. In what follows, we shall make some hypotheses about the level of activity, but we shall not consider a system with quantities symmetrical to that of the PD system, even if we know that it is not less important than those we shall consider here.

Studying the PD system, we shall consider four problems, all owing to NPMPs.

The first problem is how to find the OE. This is not given by the production per unit of $T(b)$, which is not significant by itself, since processes $[\mathbf{a}_{i1}(b); l_1(b)]$ cannot be arranged in order. We shall also see that the OE is not given either by the order of the $\rho(b)$ associated with any $\rho(b^*) = 0$. In fact, changing the $\rho(b^*)$ fixed at zero may change the order of the other $\rho(b)$ as a result of the change in prices and in the endogenous distributive variable. With r or w given exogenously, we therefore must find an order for the K processes that does not change with the $\rho(b^*)$ fixed at zero. If we do not do this, we shall find ourselves faced with a circularity. The number of activated processes depends on the OE and on the constraints (8.10) only if the OE does not change with the number of activated processes.

With the first problem solved, the second is posed by the study of how the order of $\rho(b)$ changes when, following the OE, the number of activated processes increases and consequently the $\rho(b^*)$ fixed at zero changes. This is the problem of changes in the 'order of rentability' (OR) for every given OE.

The third problem, which is related to the second, concerns the changes in income distribution caused by changes in the level of activity.

The fourth problem is posed by the study of how the independent changes of r or w influence the remaining distributive entities, the OE and the OR. This may possibly occur through changes in the active processes with NPMPs.

6 The order of efficiency

The OE depends on the choice of the exogenous distributive entity. Let us consider all the possible cases.

(1) We shall begin with the case of

$$w = 0 \tag{8.11}$$

for which (8.7) becomes

$$\{[1 + \max r(b^*)]\mathbf{A}'(b^*) - \mathbf{I}\}\mathbf{P}(b^*) = \mathbf{0} \tag{8.12}$$

or

$$[\mathbf{A}'(b^*) - \lambda(b^*)\mathbf{I}]\mathbf{P}(b^*) = \mathbf{0}$$

since $\lambda(b^*) = [1 + \max r(b^*)]^{-1}$.

From the properties of $\mathbf{A}(b^*)$ and from the theorems of Perron–Frobenius (for the theorems of linear algebra, see Gantmacher, 1959), we know that there is only one maximum eigenvalue $\lambda(b^*)$, which gives the maximum rate of profit $\max r(b^*)$ and which is associated with an eigenvector $\mathbf{P}(b^*) > \mathbf{0}$.

On the basis of the calculated values of $\max r(b^*)$ and $\mathbf{P}(b^*)$ we can order the K sub-systems PWΠ, i.e. the K processes with NPMPs, as follows:

$$\begin{aligned} &\max r(\mathrm{I}) > \max r(\mathrm{II}) > \ldots > \max r(\mathrm{K}) \\ &\mathbf{P}(\mathrm{I}) \geq \mathbf{P}(\mathrm{II}) \geq \ldots \geq \mathbf{P}(\mathrm{K}) \end{aligned} \tag{8.13}$$

after permuting the indices b^*, up to now arranged in chance order, and taking into account that the only element of equality among the $\mathbf{P}(b)$ is $p_1 = 1$.

Obviously, the orders of r and $\mathbf{P}$ are the same. In fact, the diversity among the $\mathbf{P}(b^*)$ is caused by the process b^* included in the PW Π sub-system. As we move along the order of r given in (8.13), the production cost of commodity 1 increases. Consequently, the price of every other commodity falls in terms of commodity 1 (the *numéraire*). For a formal demonstration of this, see part (6) of this section.

Let us now consider sub-system R. When $b^* = \mathrm{I}$, i.e. when $\rho(\mathrm{I}) = 0$, the prices and the rate of profit of the economy are $\mathbf{P}(\mathrm{I})$ and $\max r(\mathrm{I})$. These then become the data in (8.9) and allow us to determine $\rho(b; \mathrm{I})$ for $b = \mathrm{II}, \ldots \mathrm{K}$. Such rents are necessarily negative, since $\mathbf{P}(\mathrm{I})$ and $\max r(\mathrm{I})$ are greater than those values that would make them equal to zero. In general,

$$\rho(b; b^*) > 0 \text{ for } b < b^*; \qquad \rho(b; b^*) < 0 \text{ for } b > b^* \tag{8.14}$$

The order given by (8.13) is therefore the OE. As we move along it, i.e. as we pass from one to K active processes with NPMPs, it can never happen that an already active process becomes uneconomical, i.e. with a negative rent.

(2) The order (8.13) also allows us to identify the 'absolute maximum', max r(I), and the 'relative maximum', $\dot{\text{m}}$ax r(K), of the rate of profit. When r is exogenously fixed, these maxima assume significance, and also the meaning of the terms becomes clear. If $0 \leq r = \bar{r} \leq \max r(\mathrm{K})$, all the existing processes with NPMPs can operate, if this is required by the economy's level of activity. If $\max r(\mathrm{K}) < r = \bar{r} \leq \max r(\mathrm{I})$, one or more processes with NPMPs become uneconomical at that level of r and cannot be activated. Finally, if $r = \bar{r} > \max r(\mathrm{I})$ no process with NPMPs can operate and neither can the economy as a whole.

(3) Let us now consider the choice of the exogenous magnitude which is the opposite of (8.11), i.e.

$$r = 0 \tag{8.15}$$

Equations (8.7) then become

$$[\mathbf{I} - \mathbf{A}'(b^*)]\mathbf{P}(b^*) = \mathbf{L}(b^*)\max w(b^*) \tag{8.16}$$

or $$[\mathbf{I} - \mathbf{A}'(b^*)]^{-1}\mathbf{L}(b^*) \max w(b^*) = \mathbf{P}(b^*)$$

Since $\mathbf{L}(b^*)$ and $[\mathbf{I} - \mathbf{A}'(b^*)]^{-1}$ are positive (the latter as a consequence of well known theorems of linear algebra), it follows that $\mathbf{P}(b^*) > \mathbf{0}$.

We now have the following OE:

$$\max w(\mathrm{I}) > \max w(\mathrm{II}) > \ldots > \max w(\mathrm{K})$$

$$\mathbf{P}(\mathrm{I}) \geq \mathbf{P}(\mathrm{II}) \geq \ldots \geq \mathbf{P}(\mathrm{K}) \tag{8.17}$$

with the equals sign introduced for the reason given in (8.13).

Such an OE may be different from (8.13), since, as a result of the various proportions among means of production and labour, it may change in response to changes of r or w. Hence, process b^*, or the PWΠ sub-system of type b^*, may be different in (8.13) from what they are in (8.17).

(4) The above analysis also gives us the 'absolute maximum' wage rate, max w(I), and the 'relative maximum' wage rate max w(K). The significance of these can be understood from what has been said in part (2) of this section.

(5) Let us now consider the OE when

$$r = \bar{r} > 0 \qquad 0 < \bar{r} \leq \max r(b^*) < \max r(\mathrm{I}) \tag{8.18}$$

Equations (8.7) become

$$[\mathbf{I}-(1+\bar{r})\mathbf{A}'(b^*)]^{-1}\mathbf{L}(b^*)w(b^*) = \mathbf{P}(b^*) \tag{8.19}$$

which gives $\mathbf{P}(b^*) > \mathbf{0}$. The inverse matrix is positive (as we know from theorem of linear algebra), since matrix $(1+\bar{r})\mathbf{A}(b^*)$ is non-negative, indecomposable and with a maximum eigenvalue less than one.

As usual we find the OE:

$$w(\mathrm{I}) > w(\mathrm{II}) > \ldots > w(\mathrm{K})$$

$$\mathbf{P}(\mathrm{I}) \geq \mathbf{P}(\mathrm{II}) \geq \ldots \geq \mathbf{P}(\mathrm{K}) \tag{8.20}$$

Since the number of processes is greater than two, OE (8.20) may differ from both (8.13) and (8.17), even though there may be partial coincidences.

The conclusions just reached may be extended to the case which the exogenous magnitude is w such that $0 < w = \bar{w} \leq \max w(b^*) < \max w(\mathrm{I})$. In fact, there is a unique inverse relation between $w(b)$ and $r(b)$ for every PWΠ sub-system.

(6) Before leaving the subject to the OE, we shall demonstrate analytically that the order of the $w(b^*)$s is associated with an equal order of the $\mathbf{P}(b^*)$s.

Let us consider only the processes relative to commodities $j = 2, \ldots m + 1$ in every PWΠ sub-system (8.7). The system of equations for these commodities is:

$$[1+r(b^*)]\mathbf{a}_{1j}+[1+r(b^*)]\mathbf{A}'_{jj}\mathbf{P}_j(b^*)+\mathbf{L}_j w(b^*) = \mathbf{P}_j(b^*) \tag{8.21}$$

where $\mathbf{a}'_{1j} = [a_{1,2}, \ldots a_{1,m+1}]$and $\mathbf{A}_{jj}$ is the sub-matrix obtained from $\mathbf{A}$ by removing the first row and the first column. It does not, therefore, depend on the NPMPs. In turn, vectors $\mathbf{L}_j$ and $\mathbf{P}_j$ are obtained respectively from $\mathbf{L}$ and $\mathbf{P}$ by removing the first element.

Equations (8.21) may be rewritten as

$$\{\mathbf{I}-[1+r(b^*)]\mathbf{A}'_{jj}\}^{-1}\{[1+r(b^*)]a_{1j}+\mathbf{L}_j w(b^*)\} = \mathbf{P}_j(b^*) \tag{8.22}$$

Let us consider the cases in which the exogenous magnitude is w:

$$0 \leq w = \bar{w} \leq \max w(b^*) \leq \max w(\mathrm{I}) \tag{8.23}$$

and let us compare two PWΠ sub-systems, for example I and II.

Since $r(\mathrm{I}) > r(\mathrm{II})$ the second factor within braces in (8.22) falls with r. But the first factor also falls. This can be stated as a consequence of well known theorems of linear algebra if $[1+r(\mathrm{I})]\mathbf{A}_{jj} > [1+r(\mathrm{II})]\mathbf{A}_{jj}$ and if the maximum eigenvalue of each of these matrices is less than one. Both these conditions exist. Remember, for the second condition, that the two matrices are sub-matrices of $[1+r(b)]\mathbf{A}(b)$, for $b = \mathrm{I}, \mathrm{II}$, and that the eigenvalues of these latter matrices are never greater than one.

Let us now consider cases in which r is exogenous:

$$0 \leq r = \bar{r} \leq \max r(b^*) \leq \max r(\mathrm{I}) \tag{8.24}$$

From (8.22) it immediately follows that prices fall with $w(b^*)$ as successive PWII sub-systems are passed through.

(7) The above analysis gives us the OE of the NPMPs or the K sub-systems for every given exogenous r or w. We therefore have K different 'technologies' with one, two . . . kappa active processes, involving NPMPs. For the time being, these K technologies and the associated PD systems are by their very nature 'theoretical'. The choice of one of these technologies and the move to an 'effective' technology will, in practice, depend on the different level of activity of the economy.

7 The order of rentability

(1) Let us consider what happens to rents and to their order when the number of processes with NPMPs, following the OE, rises with the economy's level of activity. To simplify the analysis, let us take r as exogenously given.

We already know the effect on wages of the activation of an additional process with NPMPs. We shall come back to this later on.

The effects on rents are a little more complicated. We shall study two properties: the first is that the OR may change when the number of activated processes with NPMPs increases, i.e. when b^* increases; the second is that one or more ORs may not coincide with the OE. Clearly, the first property implies the second.

From (8.9) we see how every rent grows when w and p_i fall. But the growth of rents may occur in different measures and may therefore change the order of the rents themselves. If we indicate $\mathbf{a}'_{j1} = [a_{2,1} \ldots a_{m+1,1}]$, we can rewrite (8.9) as follows:

$$\rho(b, b^*) = \frac{l_1(b)}{t(b)} \left\{ \left[\frac{1 - a_{11}(b)(1+\bar{r})}{l_1(b)} - \frac{(1+\bar{r})}{l_1(b)} \mathbf{a}'_{j1}(b)\mathbf{P}_j(b^*) \right] - w(b^*) \right\}$$

$$.\rho(b, b^*) = \frac{l_1(b)}{t(b)} [w(b, b^*) - w(b^*)] \tag{8.25}$$

from which also follows the definition of $w(b, b^*)$. We can see from this relation that, while the sign of every ρ depends on the coefficients of circulating capital and labour, the order of the ρs of the same sign also depends on the coefficients $t(b)$. We can also see that the decrease of p_i and w has a different influence on the costs of production of the different processes with NPMPs.

For these reasons, the OR may change. Since equations (8.25) are linear, it is only possible to have one change of OR in every pair of processes with NPMPs. The maximum number of changes, when the number of processes with NPMPs increases from one to K, is therefore given by the combination $\binom{K}{2}$, K here indicating the maximum number of processes with NPMPs.

(2) Let us examine the properties we have identified for a simplified case, in which the PD system is given by

$$\rho(b, b^*) = \frac{l_1(b)}{t(b)} \left\{ \left[\frac{1 - a_{11}(b)(1+\bar{r})}{l_1(b)} - \frac{a_{21}(b)(1+\bar{r})}{l_1(b)} p_2(b^*) \right] - w(b^*) \right\} \tag{8.26}$$

with $b = \text{I, II, III, IV}$; and by

$$p_2(b^*) = \frac{a_{12}(1+\bar{r})}{1 - a_{22}(1+\bar{r})} + \frac{l_2}{1 - a_{22}(1+\bar{r})} w(b^*) \tag{8.27}$$

Only two commodities are produced, therefore.

For every $\rho(b^*) = 0$ we therefore have PWΠ sub-system, given by (8.27) and by

$$w(b^*) = \frac{1 - a_{11}(b^*)(1+\bar{r})}{l_1(b^*)} - \frac{a_{21}(b^*)(1+\bar{r})}{l_1(b^*)} p_2(b^*) \tag{8.28}$$

which is obtained from (8.26) for $b = b^*$.

The solutions of (8.27)–(8.28) inserted in (8.26) give $\rho(b, b^*)$ for $b \neq b^*$. In this way, we obtain four PD systems, each of which becomes effective according to the level of activity, i.e. to the number of processes with NPMPs operating.

Let us consider a graphic representation of the solutions of the four PD systems (see Figure 8.1). Equation (8.27) is a rising straight line, while equations (8.28) are falling straight lines, which we write in the form $p_2(b^*) = f(b^*)w(b^*)$. The particular position of the straight lines in the figure depends on the hypotheses about coefficients.

Points $S(\text{I})$, $S(\text{II})$, $S(\text{III})$, $S(\text{IV})$ give, respectively, the solutions of the PWΠ sub-systems I, II, III, IV. The OE is thus I, II, III, IV, being $w(\text{I}) > w(\text{II}) > w(\text{III}) > w(\text{IV})$.

Let us now consider the sign of the rents. Let us first examine the term in square brackets in (8.26). If we compare it with (8.28), we see that it represents a 'hypothetical' wage rate, i.e. that wage rate which process b would give on the basis of price $p_2(b^*)$. We have already indicated this hypothetical wage as $w(b, b^*)$.

The sign of the rent b will thus be given by $w(b, b^*) - w(b^*)$. From Figure 8.1 we see how: at $S(\text{I})$, $\rho(\text{I}) = 0$ and $\rho(b, \text{I}) < 0$; at $S(\text{II})$, $\rho(\text{I, II}) > 0$, $\rho(\text{II}) = 0$, $\rho(\text{III, II}) < 0$, $\rho(\text{IV, II}) < 0$; at $S(\text{III})$, $\rho(\text{I, III}) > 0$, $\rho(\text{II, III}) > 0$, $\rho(\text{III}) = 0$, $\rho(\text{IV, III}) < 0$; at $S(\text{IV})$, $\rho(b, \text{IV}) > 0$, $\rho(\text{IV}) = 0$.

Let us now consider the OR. This may change more than once: at every intersection of two falling straight lines. The maximum number of changes is $\binom{4}{2} = 6$. But the changes with economic significance are only those that occur within the interval of economically significant solutions, i.e. in the area below the rising straight line and delimited by two horizontal straight lines for $S(\text{I})$ and $S(IV)$. Economically significant changes are therefore at points I, L, M. From Figures 8.1 and 8.2, we see that at $S(\text{II})$ we have $\rho(\text{I, II}) > \rho(\text{II, II})$. At $S(\text{III})$, on the other hand, we have $\rho(\text{II, III}) > \rho(\text{I, III})$, supposing that the coefficients $l_1(b)/t(b)$ do not change the order given by $w(\text{II, III}) - w(\text{III})$ and by $w(\text{I, III}) - w(\text{III})$. Finally, according to the same hypothesis, at $S(\text{IV})$ we have $\rho(\text{III, IV}) > \rho(\text{II, IV}) > \rho(\text{I, IV})$. And this OR is exactly the opposite of the OE. (Note that Figures 8.1 and 8.2 are of different scale and that the lines connecting the points do not show a continuous change of ρ.)

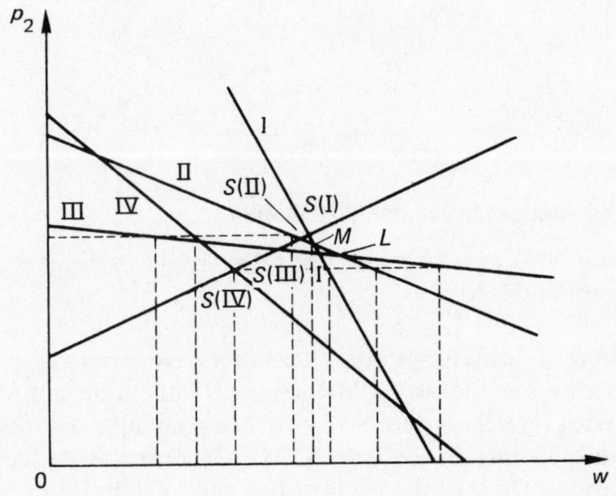

FIGURE 8.1

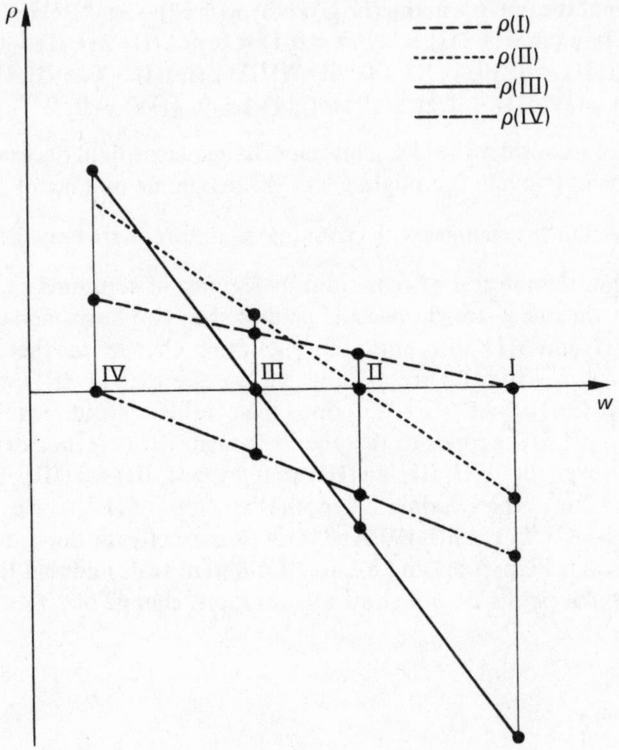

FIGURE 8.2

8 Induced changes in income distribution

We shall now look at some more effects that change in the level of activity has on distribution.

(1) If the level of activity, for causes that do not concern us here, increases with an extension of the last NPMP activated, without the introduction of new processes, then the effects on distribution are simple. The rents do not vary, because it is only the use of the NPMP of the process in which ρ is zero which increases. On the other hand, wages and total profits do grow, as a result of the increase in the employment of labour and in the means of production, although **P**, w and r remain unchanged.

(2) If the number of operating processes with NPMP increases along with the level of activity, the consequences are more complex.

We have already seen, in section 7, the consequences for unitary rents. Total rents will also increase, in the case both of r given and of w given.

For the effects on the other distributive entities we should isolate a few cases.

(3) With w given.

For $w = 0$, the total surplus wages do not change. Total profits may grow, remain unchanged or diminish, according to whether the reduction of r is or is not compensated by the associated increase in the entity of means of production. When r becomes zero, total profits will also be zero, but, before this extreme case, the three cases indicated may be found.

For $w = \bar{w} > 0$, total surplus wages grow with employment. The purchasing power of the surplus wage rate (and of the total surplus wage) also increases. In fact, since w is fixed in terms of commodity 1 ('grain'), its purchasing power increases with respect to all the other m commodities, the prices of which fall with respect to commodity 1. As a result, both employed workers and workers previously unemployed benefit from the rise in production.

This conclusion may change if the *numéraire* changes. We should remember, in fact, that commodity 1 is the only one the productive process of which becomes less efficient with the activation of a further NPMP. Hence, the price of the other commodities will vary according to the direct or indirect amount of commodity 1 that they contain. By permuting the indices of the commodities, we can call commodity 2 the *numéraire* in relation to which p_1 increases and all the other prices decrease. Commodity $m+1$ will be the *numéraire* in relation to which all prices increase. Commodity $m+1$ is therefore the commodity which depends least on the first productive process in correspondence to the given level of w.

Hence, if the *numéraire* chosen were commodity $m+1$, employed workers would suffer a reduction in their purchasing power; those who stop being unemployed, on the other hand, would enjoy an increase. The result would be antagonism between these two categories of workers and a coincidence of interests between formerly unemployed workers and those who receive rents.

Finally, if the *numéraire* chosen were a commodity j, with $1 < j < m+1$ we should have to consider the composition of the wage in order to establish whether its purchasing power increases or decreases, and whether, therefore, antagonism between workers will arise.

As far as the behaviour of profits is concerned, we may repeat what was said in the case of zero w.

(4) With r given.

In this case the wage rate, even in real terms, falls with respect to any one of the $m+1$ commodities. Let us take as *numeraire* the nominal wage, which we shall call w^*. The activation of increasingly less efficient processes with NPMPs raises the production cost of all commodities and therefore also prices. In fact, $w(b) = w^*(b)/p_i(b) = 1/[p_i(b)/w^*(b)]$. Since for $p_1 = 1$ we have $w(b) > w(b+1)$, and therefore $[p_i(b)/w^*(b)] < [p_i(b+1)/w^*(b+1)]$ for $w^*(b) = 1$, we have $p_i(b) < p_i(b+1)$ with $i = 1, 2, \ldots m+1$, and therefore a falling wage.

As a result, the real wages of the workers already employed decrease and an antagonism arises between the formerly unemployed, who now receive a wage, even if w^* equals zero, since a subsistence wage is always paid to those employed. There is therefore a coincidence of the interests of formerly unoccupied workers and receivers of rents.

The behaviour of profits will depend on two contrasting movements: the increase in the means of production, on one hand; and the fall in prices, on the other.

The above conclusions do not change with the *numéraire*.

(5) The conclusion to be drawn, therefore, is that the presence of NPMPs has a remarkable influence on prices and distribution as the level of activity changes in association with a change in the number of operating NPMPs.

9 Autonomous changes in income distribution

(1) Let us now consider the effects of variations in the exogenous distributive magnitude, and the differences, owing to the NPMPs, with respect to single-product models.

We shall concentrate in particular on five stylised cases, going from one very close to the single-product case and ending with cases very different from this. In the course of this examination, we shall see the effects of change in the OE on the level of activity, on the relationship between r and w, and on the OR.

(2) Before beginning this analysis, it would be useful to recall certain well known aspects of the single-product problem.

In a single-product system (in our case, in every PWΠ sub-system) using the standard commodity as *numéraire*, it is possible to establish the following linear relation between r and w:

$$r(b^*) = \max r(b^*)[1 - L(b^*)w(b^*)] \tag{8.29}$$

where $L(b^*)$ is the labour of the PWΠ sub-system b^*.

If, on the other hand, we use commodity 1 as the *numéraire*, we obtain the following equation from (8.19):

$$\mathbf{e}'_1[\mathbf{I} - (1 + r(b^*))\mathbf{A}'(b^*)]^{-1}\mathbf{L}(b^*)w(b^*) = 1 \tag{8.30}$$

with $\mathbf{e}'_1 = [1, 0, \ldots 0]$. This is a polynomial of degree $m+1$ (this being the order of the matrix) in r. We are therefore able to study the relation between r and w, which, in explicit form, becomes

$$w(b^*) = \frac{\det[\mathbf{I} - (1+r)\mathbf{A}'(b^*)]}{\mathbf{L}'(b^*)\mathbf{C}_{1i}(b^*)} \quad \text{for } r = r(b^*) \tag{8.31}$$

since $\mathbf{C}_{1i}(b^*)$ is the vector of the algebraic complements of the first row of the matrix $[\mathbf{I} - (1+r)\mathbf{A}(b^*)]$. Each of these algebraic complements is an equation of degree m in the exogenous variable r. (8.31) therefore has a polynomial of degree $m+1$ as numerator, and a polynomial of degree m as denominator, since r is the variable. In this case all we can say about the relation between $w(b^*)$ and r is that it is a relation which is inverse and monotonic.

The great simplification allowed by the standard commodity does not mean, however, that there is anything simple in the study of the relations between r and prices. Changes of r influence prices in an unpredictable way, which depends on the proportions between the means of production of commodities with respect to the *numeraire* and on the interrelation between the sectors of the economy. And, since these factors are in turn dependent on prices, their influence may vary with r.

With commodity 1 as the *numéraire*, prices are given by

$$p_j(b^*) = \frac{\mathbf{L}'(b^*)\mathbf{C}_{ji}(b^*)}{\mathbf{L}'(b^*)\mathbf{C}_{1i}(b^*)}, \qquad j = 2, \ldots m+1 \tag{8.32}$$

i.e. by the ratio of two polynomials of degree m, with $\mathbf{C}_{ji}$ the vector of the algebraic complements of the jth row of matrix $[\mathbf{I} - (1+r)\mathbf{A}(b^*)]$.

It results from this that the relative efficiency of processes b and b^* may change with r. The most well known case goes under the name of switching of techniques (Sraffa, 1960, ch. 12; cf. Pasinetti *et al.*, 1966) and involves many changes in the OE of techniques. This can be seen by comparing the wage–profit frontiers of the PWΠ sub-systems of types I and II in Figure 8.3.

(3) The unpredictable movement of prices as r varies has analogous consequences on the change in rents. Deriving (8.25) we obtain

$$\frac{d\rho(b, b^*)}{dr} = \frac{l_1(b)}{t(b)}\left[\frac{dw(b, b^*)}{dr} - \frac{dw(b^*)}{dr}\right]$$

$$= \frac{l_1(b)}{t(b)}\left\{\left[\frac{a_{11}(b^*) + \mathbf{a}'_{j1}(b^*)\mathbf{P}_j(b^*)}{l_1(b^*)} - \frac{a_{11}(b) + \mathbf{a}'_{j1}(b)\mathbf{P}(b^*)}{l_1(b)}\right]\right.$$

$$\left. + (1+r)\left[\frac{1}{l_1(b^*)}\mathbf{a}'_{j1}(b^*)\frac{d}{dr}\mathbf{P}_j(b^*) - \frac{1}{l_1(b)}\mathbf{a}'_{j1}(b)\frac{d}{dr}\mathbf{P}_j(b^*)\right]\right\} \tag{8.33}$$

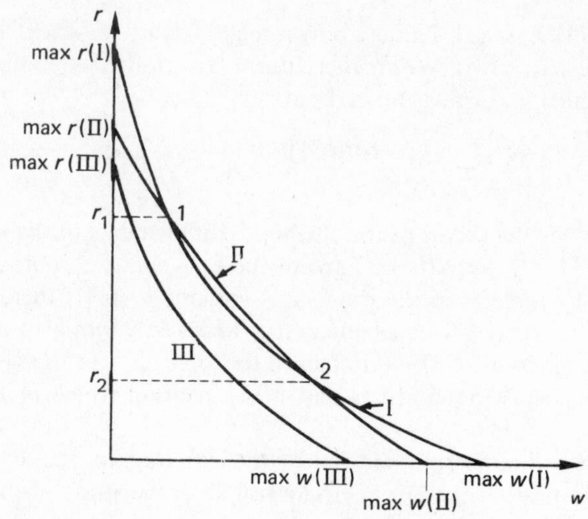

FIGURE 8.3

We cannot generally determine the sign of the above. The first addend, which expresses the effect of the capital–labour composition, may be positive or negative and may vary with r. Remarks that may be made about the signs in the case of $l_1(b) > l_1(b^*)$ do not help us to give a general answer. Nothing can be said about the sign of the second addend.

Consequently, as r increases, there may follow either an increase or a decrease of $\rho(b, b^*)$. And these behaviours may alternate one with another.

(4) Let us now consider a first case. Suppose that the movements of r in the interval $0 \leq r \leq \max r(b^*)$ do not change the active processes, including the least efficient of these b^*. Hence, we cannot exclude changes in the OE of the first $b^* - 1$ processes, but we suppose that they do not interfere with the process b^* or with the remaining $K - b^*$ processes with NPMPs.

The relations between r and w may therefore be studied in a single PWΠ sub-system: sub-system b^*. And the standard commodity does not change with r.

Changes can therefore only occur in the R sub-system. Let us examine them.

We should first of all note that the changes in the OE and OR of the first $b^* - 1$ processes with NPMPs may occur for different levels of r. Consider Figure 8.3, which is based on a very simple case: three processes with NPMPs and one process generating commodity 2. Subsequent figures also refer to this example with two commodities.

The changes in the OE, occurring at points 1 and 2 in Figure 8.3, do not imply corresponding changes in the OR. Let us consider (8.25) and suppose that $[l_1(\mathrm{I})/t(\mathrm{I})] = [l_1(\mathrm{II})/t(\mathrm{II})]$. In this case $\rho(\mathrm{I, III})$ may be equal to $\rho(\mathrm{II, III})$ only if $w(\mathrm{I, III}) = w(\mathrm{II, III})$. This condition cannot be fulfilled, however, for prices $\mathbf{P}(\mathrm{III})$, which are those currently in force in the economy. It would be fulfilled only for prices $\mathbf{P}(\mathrm{I}, r_1) = \mathbf{P}(\mathrm{II}, r_1)$ or for prices $\mathbf{P}(\mathrm{I}, r_2) = \mathbf{P}(\mathrm{II}, r_2)$ which, however are not currently in force in the economy.

An equal labour–land intensity, therefore, excludes changes in the OR at the switching points of techniques, but does not necessarily exclude them for other levels of r.

A second aspect to consider concerns the number of changes in the OR. This cannot be superior to that of the changes in OE. In fact, if we consider (8.9) and substitute $\mathbf{P}(b^*)$ and $w(b^*)$ with (8.31) and (8.32), the result is

$$\rho(b, b^*) = \left\{1 - a_{11}(b) - \sum_{j=2}^{m+1} a_{j1}(b)\frac{\mathbf{L}'(b^*)\mathbf{C}_{ji}(b^*)}{\mathbf{L}'(b^*)\mathbf{C}_{1i}(b^*)}\cdot[1 + r(b^*)] - l_1(b)\frac{\det[\mathbf{I} - (1 + r(b^*))\mathbf{A}'(b^*)]}{\mathbf{L}'(b^*)\mathbf{C}_{1i}(b^*)}\right\}[t(b)]^{-1} \tag{8.34}$$

which is a polynomial with numerator of degree $m+1$ and denominator of degree m, with r as the variable, i.e. the polynomial is of the same degree as (8.31).

Changes occur in the OR for values of r that make two rents equal. The points of switching therefore are given by

$$\rho(b, b^*) = \rho(^+b, b^*) \tag{8.35}$$

from which we obtain the polynomial of degree $m+1$, with r being the variable:

$$\begin{aligned}&\mathbf{L}'(b^*)\mathbf{C}_{1i}(b^*)\{t(^+b)[1 - a_{11}(b)] - t(b)[1 - a_{11}(^+b)]\}\\ &- t(^+b)\sum_{j=2}^{m+1} a_{j1}(b)\mathbf{L}'(b^*)\mathbf{C}_{ji}(b^*)[1 + r(b^*)]\\ &+ t(b)\sum_{j=2}^{m+1} a_{j1}(^+b)\mathbf{L}'(b^*)\mathbf{C}_{ji}(b^*)[1 + r(b^*)]\\ &+ \det\{\mathbf{I} - [1 + r(b^*)]\mathbf{A}'(b^*)\}[t(b)l_1(^+b) - t(^+b)l_1(b)] = 0\end{aligned} \tag{8.36}$$

for which the maximum number of real roots in the unknown r is $m+1$.

(5) A second case concerns changes in the active processes with NPMPs without any change in the resolving process b^* or, therefore, in the standard commodity either. This is a case of a switch in technology without a change in the relation between r and w.

Let us consider one of the many possible cases, as shown in Figure 8.4.

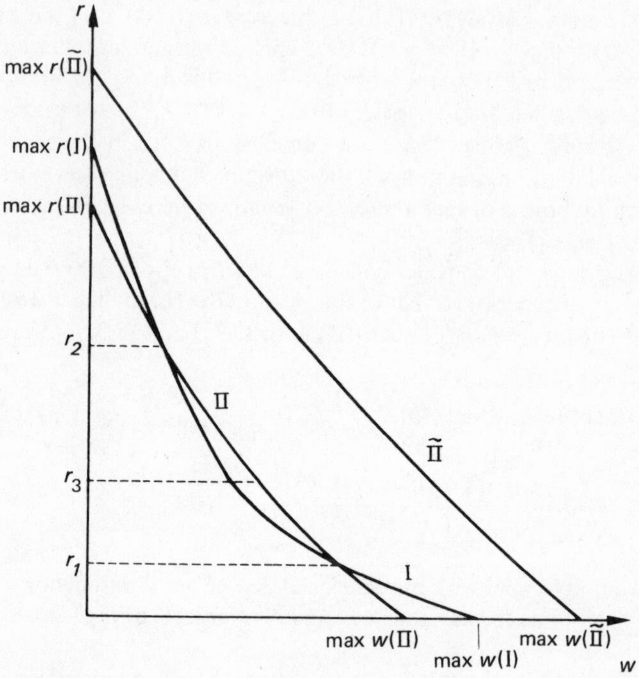

FIGURE 8.4

Leaving aside process $\tilde{\text{II}}$, we shall concentrate on processes I and II. Let us suppose that only process I operates in the interval $r_1 > r \geq 0$, since this is enough to satisfy the economy's objectives of production. Rent is therefore zero. Process II becomes more efficient than process I within the interval $r_1 > r > r_2$. If the constraint (8.10) of the NPMP of type II is such that it does not allow the achievement of the economy's production objectives, previously satisfied by process I, then both processes I and II must operate. The resolving process remains process I, and II will have a rent that may behave like the continuous line II in Figure 8.5.

In the interval max r(II) $> r > r_2$ we return to the situation of the interval $r_1 > r \geq 0$. Finally, for $r = r_1$ or r_2, either process I or II may operate, or processes I and II jointly. In both these cases, however, there is no rent.

In conclusion, in the interval max r(II) $\geq r \geq 0$ the relation between r and w depends solely on the PWΠ sub-system I, and the standard commodity does not change. Rent is present only for certain values of r, and, with respect to r, it first rises then falls, in a way that differs from the relation between w and r, which is always inverse. The same conclusions, qualitatively, are achieved for the opposite case, i.e. when process I cannot

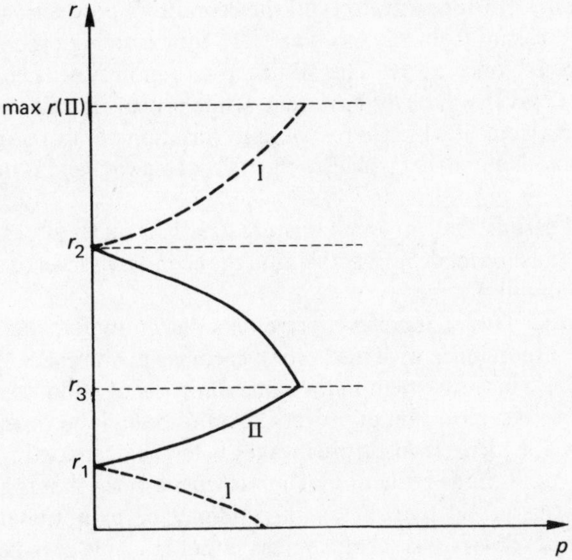

FIGURE 8.5

operate without II, while the reverse is possible. In this case, the relation between w and r is given by the PWΠ sub-system II. Only process I will have a rent, as shown by the broken lines in Figure 8.5.

(6) A third case is such that variations in the OE do not change the active processes but do change the resolving process b^*. Consequently, the production technique is not changed, although the relation between r and w is modified: this would be impossible in a single-product model.

Processes I and II always operate jointly, in order to fulfil the economy's production objectives. Consider the changes in the OE of processes I and II as shown in Figure 8.4.

The rent will remain positive, except for $r = r_1 = r_2$. It will pass from process I to process II and return then to I for $0 \leq r \leq \max r(\text{II})$. This is shown in Figure 8.5. The PWΠ sub-system which determines the relation between w and r will change twice. As a result, the standard commodity will change, but the active processes will not.

(7) The fourth case concerns changes in the OE that modify the active processes and the process that enters into the resolving PWΠ sub-system, without the rent's disappearing as a result.

We refer to the case in Figure 8.4. The process $\breve{\text{II}}$ is always activated, either with process I or process II, to fulfil the economy's production objectives.

For r increasing from zero to max r(II), the resolving process will be I, then II, then I once more. The standard commodity will change twice. Processes I and II will never have rent, while process $\tilde{\text{II}}$ will always have a rent the behaviour of which in response to variation of r can be represented by a continuous curve that will lie to the right of curves I and II in Figure 8.5.

(8) A final case is that in which r is greater than max $r(b^*)$. In this case, process b^* must be made non-active, and the economy's level of activity and employment will decline.

The frontier $f(w, r)$, therefore, presents a discontinuity, and w, which is zero in correspondence with max $r(b^*)$, becomes positive. See the example in Figure 8.4. This movement in the same direction of r and w is owing to a transfer to wages of the rent of process I. At this point it becomes of interest to compare the increase in surplus wages with the decrease in subsistence wages as a result of the reduction of employment. If the first is greater than or equal to the second, then, in certain economic or institutional situations, it would be possible to use surplus wages, either in whole or in part, to assist the unemployed. In other social situations, on the other hand, a coalition of profits and surplus wages might form against rents and employment.

These properties can also be seen in the opposite case, when, with $r >$ max $r(b^*)$, it is necessary to activate a new process.

However, in all these cases, relations are established between the exogenous variable r and the economy's level of activity employment.

10 Concluding remarks

It is hoped that two basic ideas have emerged from the preceding pages.

The first is that rent greatly complicates the relations between wages and profits. The order of efficiency, the order of rentability, and the influence on these of non-produced means of production create new situations that are not to be found in models with production of commodities by means of commodities alone. The above analysis has, it is hoped, clarified certain passages in Sraffa, such as (1960, section 87) 'the order of fertility . . . is not defined independently of the rents; that order, as well as the magnitude of the rents themselves, may vary with the variation of r and w'. It seems rather difficult to distinguish between order of efficiency and order of rentability in such passages, although to the present writer it seems that such a distinction is of no small importance. We ought to say, however, that Sraffa's work has the merit of an interesting treatment of rent, even if it does not seem that he has drawn all the possible consequences. For example, autonomous variations in income distribution are greatly complicated by the interference of rent on the relations betwen wages and profits. In addition, these relations cause variations in the level of activity. The analysis of this problem shows us that there are no univocal relations between wages, profits and rents, nor are there such relations between employed workers and unemployed workers.

The second basic idea concerns the study of the relations between level of activity and growth of the economy, distribution of income and prices. In our treatment, these relations are owing to the non-produced means of production and are an objective property of the economic system, independent of the economic–institutional context. Such relations are expressed in terms that are different from the relations that occur between the same entities in usual models of supply and demand. In the above pages we have considered the effects of a variation in the level of activity on income distribution. We should, in addition, explain how we determine the level of activity and the effects on this of a variation in the distribution of income. These problems are connected and are not less important than the problems considered in this essay. The author has, however, already considered them, in both a single-period context (Quadrio-Curzio, 1967, chs 4 and 5) and a dynamic context (Quadrio-Curzio, 1975).

The conviction behind this line of research is that reality lies between the pessimism of Ricardo's theoretic contribution, with its land-based stationariness, and the optimism of an eminent father of contemporary dynamic analysis, John von Neumann, who completely leaves aside non-produced means of production. This tells us that non-produced means of production, in their coexistence with produced and reproduced means of production, influence the distribution of income and have effects that range from a non-regular dynamic of economic systems, which continue to grow, to special international economic relations. By following this path of constructive research it will also be possible to utilise part of the theories of production of Leontief, with its formidable empirical content, and of von Neumann.

References

Gantmacher, F. R., *Theory of Matrices* (New York: Chelsea, 1959).

Leontief, W. W., *The Structure of American Economy 1919–1929* (Cambridge, Mass: Harvard University Press, 1941); *The Structure of American Economy 1919–1939* (New York: Oxford University Press, 1951).

Pasinetti, L. L., *et al.*, 'Paradoxes in Capital Theory: A Symposium', *Quarterly Journal of Economics*, Nov 1966.

Quadrio-Curzio, A., *Rendita e distribuzione in un modello economico plurisettoriale* (Milan: Giuffré, 1967).

Quadrio-Curzio, A., *Accumulazione del capitale e rendita* (Bologna: Il Mulino, 1975).

Ricardo, D., *On the Principles of Political Economy and Taxation* (London: John Murray, 1817).

Sraffa, P., *Production of Commodities by Means of Commodities* (Cambridge: Cambridge University Press, 1960).

Index